Topics in the Economics of Aging

A National Bureau
of Economic Research
Project Report

Topics in the Economics of Aging

Edited by David A. Wise

The University of Chicago Press
Chicago and London

DAVID A. WISE is the John F. Stambaugh Professor of Political Economy at the John F. Kennedy School of Government, Harvard University, and the area director for health and retirement programs at the National Bureau of Economic Research.

The University of Chicago Press, Chicago 60637
The University of Chicago Press, Ltd., London

Printed in the United States of America

01 00 99 98 97 96 95 94 93 92 1 2 3 4 5 6

ISBN (cloth): 0-226-90298-6

Library of Congress Cataloging-in-Publication Data

Topics in the economics of aging / edited by David A. Wise.
p. cm.—(A National Bureau of Economic Research project report)
"Papers presented at the National Bureau of Economic Research conference on the economics of aging, in Carefree, Arizona in April 1990"—Introd.
Includes indexes.
1. Aged—United States—Economic conditions—Congresses. 2. Aged—Economic conditions—Congresses. 3. Old age—Economic aspects—United States—Congresses. 4. Old age—Economic aspects—Congresses. 5. Retirement—Economic aspects—United States—Congresses. 6. Retirement—Economic aspects—Congresses.
I. Wise, David A. II. National Bureau of Economic Research.
III. Series
HQ1064.U5T59 1992
305.2′6′0973—dc20 91-40594
CIP

♾ The paper used in this publication meets the minimum requirements of the American National Standard for Information Sciences—Permanence of Paper for Printed Library Materials, ANSI Z39.48-1984.

Relation of the Directors to the Work and Publications of the National Bureau of Economic Research

1. The object of the National Bureau of Economic Research is to ascertain and to present to the public important economic facts and their interpretation in a scientific and impartial manner. The Board of Directors is charged with the responsibility of ensuring that the work of the National Bureau is carried on in strict conformity with this object.

2. The President of the National Bureau shall submit to the Board of Directors, or to its Executive Committee, for their formal adoption all specific proposals for research to be instituted.

3. No research report shall be published by the National Bureau until the President has sent each member of the Board a notice that a manuscript is recommended for publication and that in the President's opinion it is suitable for publication in accordance with the principles of the National Bureau. Such notification will include an abstract or summary of the manuscript's content and a response form for use by those Directors who desire a copy of the manuscript for review. Each manuscript shall contain a summary drawing attention to the nature and treatment of the problem studied, the character of the data and their utilization in the report, and the main conclusions reached.

4. For each manuscript so submitted, a special committee of the Directors (including Directors Emeriti) shall be appointed by majority agreement of the President and Vice Presidents (or by the Executive Committee in case of inability to decide on the part of the President and Vice Presidents), consisting of three Directors selected as nearly as may be one from each general division of the Board. The names of the special manuscript committee shall be stated to each Director when notice of the proposed publication is submitted to him. It shall be the duty of each member of the special manuscript committee to read the manuscript. If each member of the manuscript committee signifies his approval within thirty days of the transmittal of the manuscript, the report may be published. If at the end of that period any member of the manuscript committee withholds his approval, the President shall then notify each member of the Board, requesting approval or disapproval of publication, and thirty days additional shall be granted for this purpose. The manuscript shall then not be published unless at least a majority of the entire Board who shall have voted on the proposal within the time fixed for the receipt of votes shall have approved.

5. No manuscript may be published, though approved by each member of the special manuscript committee, until forty-five days have elapsed from the transmittal of the report in manuscript form. The interval is allowed for the receipt of any memorandum of dissent or reservation, together with a brief statement of his reasons, that any member may wish to express; and such memorandum of dissent or reservation shall be published with the manuscript if he so desires. Publication does not, however, imply that each member of the Board has read the manuscript, or that either members of the Board in general or the special committee have passed on its validity in every detail.

6. Publications of the National Bureau issued for informational purposes concerning the work of the Bureau and its staff, or issued to inform the public of activities of Bureau staff, and volumes issued as a result of various conferences involving the National Bureau shall contain a specific disclaimer noting that such publication has not passed through the normal review procedures required in this resolution. The Executive Committee of the Board is charged with review of all such publications from time to time to ensure that they do not take on the character of formal research reports of the National Bureau, requiring formal Board approval.

7. Unless otherwise determined by the Board or exempted by the terms of paragraph 6, a copy of this resolution shall be printed in each National Bureau publication.

(Resolution adopted October 25, 1926, as revised through September 30, 1974)

Contents

Acknowledgments

This volume consists of papers presented at a conference held at the Boulders Resort in Carefree, Arizona, 5–7 April 1990. It is part of the National Bureau of Economic Research's ongoing project on the economics of aging. The majority of the work reported here was sponsored by the U.S. Department of Health and Human Services, through National Institute on Aging grants P01-AG05842, R37-AG08146, and T32-AG00186 and National Center for Research Resources grant S07-RR05995.

Any opinions expressed in this volume are those of the respective authors and do not necessarily reflect the views of the National Bureau of Economic Research or any of the sponsoring organizations.

Introduction

David A. Wise

This volume contains papers presented at the National Bureau of Economic Research conference on the economics of aging in Carefree, Arizona, in April 1990. It is the third in a series of conference volumes associated with the NBER's ongoing project on the economics of aging. The first volume was *The Economics of Aging* (1989); the second was *Issues in the Economics of Aging* (1990). (Both were published by the University of Chicago Press.) The goal of the Economics of Aging Project is to further our understanding of the consequences for older people and for the population at large of an aging population. This volume pursued analysis of several of the issues addressed in the previous volumes and considers several new topics as well. This introduction summarizes the motivation for the papers and their principal findings. Much of the text is abstracted from the papers themselves.

Retirement

A great deal of effort has been devoted in recent years to the development of models of retirement that emphasize the need to compare present with future circumstances in deciding whether to retire. Some versions of these models are numerically complex, while others are much simpler. In "Three Models of Retirement: Computational Complexity versus Predictive Validity," Robin L. Lumsdaine, James H. Stock, and David A. Wise consider whether more complex models predict the actual retirement behavior of individuals better than less complex models. They conclude that retirement from the firm that they consider is poorly predicted by the simplest model but that the most complex model does no better than one that is numerically much simpler to implement. They also show that estimates of the effects on retirement of changes in Social Security provisions are very inaccurate if firm pension plan provisions are not also accounted for—as has been the case in previous analyses of Social Security.

Empirical analysis often raises questions of approximation to underlying individual behavior. Closer approximation may require more complex statistical specifications. On the other hand, more complex specifications may presume computational facility that is beyond the grasp of most real people and therefore less consistent with the actual rules that govern their behavior, even though economic theory may lead analysts to increasingly complex specifications. Thus, the issue is not only whether more complex models are worth the effort but also whether they are better. The answer must necessarily depend on the behavior that the analysis is intended to predict. In their paper, Lumsdaine, Stock, and Wise consider the relation between computational complexity and the predictive validity of three models of retirement behavior.

Retirement has been the subject of a large number of studies over the past decade. Most have emphasized the effect of Social Security provisions on retirement age, but a wide range of methods has been employed. The earlier studies in this time period were based on regression or multinomial logit analysis. Subsequent analysis relied on nonlinear budget constraint formulations of the retirement decision and on proportional hazard model formulations. More recently, several authors have developed models that focus on forward-looking comparison of the advantages of retirement at alternative ages in the future and on the updating of information as persons age. Although the spirit of these latter models is basically the same, they vary widely in computational complexity. The potential advantages in predictive validity of the computationally more complex versions of these models are the primary motivation for this study, although to broaden the scope of the comparison the authors consider a much simpler model as well.

They compare the predictive validity of three models of retirement. The first is a simple probit model. The second is the "option value" model developed in earlier papers by Stock and Wise. The third is a stochastic dynamic programming model.

The analysis is guided by several key ideas. First, all the models are theoretical abstractions; none of them can be reasonably thought of as "true." The important consideration is which decision rule is the best approximation to the calculations that govern actual individual behavior. In this paper, judgments on which rule is best are based on empirical evidence on the relation between model specification and predictive validity.

Second, the models vary substantially in the computational complexity of the decision rules that they attribute to individual decision makers. The option value and the dynamic programming rules are both intended to capture the same underlying idea, but implementation of dynamic programming rules typically implies considerably more computational complexity than implementation of the option value rule. The option value model makes a simplifying assumption that substantially reduces complexity. The probit model is much simpler than either of these.

Third, although the mathematically correct implementation of some decision rules requires dynamic programming, there is no single dynamic programming rule. The implied computational complexity depends in important ways on specific assumptions, in particular the disturbance term correlation structure. It is easier to incorporate more flexible correlation assumptions in the option value than in the dynamic programming formulations. Thus, for example, the option value specification may be a suboptimal solution to a dynamic programming rule that implies computational complexity difficult to implement even with a computer.

A question of practical importance is therefore whether different decision rules yield significantly different results.

The comparisons in this paper are made by estimating the models on the same data. The data, which pertain to the retirement decisions in a large *Fortune* 500 firm, have two important advantages. First, the retirement decisions can be related to the provisions of the firm's pension plan, and it is therefore possible to simulate the effect of changes in the pension plan provisions. Second, the firm offered an unanticipated "window" plan in one of the years covered by the data.

The principal measure of the predictive validity of the models is how well they predict the effects of the window plan. Like the typical defined benefit pension plan, this firm's plan provides substantial incentives to retire early. In addition, the window plan provided further incentive to retire early. Window plans, which have been offered by many firms in recent years, provide special bonuses to workers in a specific group—often defined by age, occupational group, or even a division within the firm—if the worker retires within a specified period of time, typically a year or less. The window plan allows a unique external test of the predictive validity of the models; it is possible to compare model predictions with actual retirement rates under the window plan.

The authors begin by obtaining model parameter estimates based on retirement decisions in a year (1980) prior to the window plan. They then use these estimates to predict retirement in a later year (1982) under the window plan. The estimates and predictions are based on male nonmanagerial employees.

Lumsdaine, Stock, and Wise find that the option value and dynamic programming models are considerably more successful than the less complex probit model in approximating the rules that individuals use to make retirement decisions but that the more complex dynamic programming rule approximates behavior no better than the simpler option value rule. The authors caution that definitive conclusions will have to await accumulated evidence based on additional comparisons using different data sets and with respect to different pension plan provisions.

The authors also use their analysis to show that predictions of the retirement effects of changes in Social Security provisions are likely to be grossly inaccurate if the analysis does not consider both Social Security and firm pension plan provisions. Firm plan provisions have been unavailable to researchers analyzing the effects of changes in the Social Security system.

Saving for Retirement

In "Stocks, Bonds, and Pension Wealth," Thomas E. MaCurdy and John B. Shoven consider past returns to stocks versus bonds. They present strong evidence that systematic contributions proportional to earnings over a career have always led to more wealth at the time of retirement if the investment is in stocks rather than bonds.

For many people, the present value of their future pension annuity is their largest financial asset. The retirement income may come from a variety of pension accumulations, including defined contribution plans, defined benefit plans, individual retirement accounts, Keogh plans, and tax-deferred annuity plans. With many of these accumulation vehicles, the individual participant bears the responsibility of determining the assets in which the funds are invested and bears any uncertainty about the rate of return that will be realized on those assets. In choosing between stocks and bonds for their pension accumulation vehicle, most people probably know that bonds have a lower average return and a lower variance in return; bonds offer additional "safety" at the expense of a lower expected outcome. While this risk-return trade-off is both correct and well understood for short-term investment horizons, the extent to which it applies for long holding periods is not clear. For many workers, the time between the current contribution to the retirement account and the purchase of an annuity is thirty years or more. What is the relative risk and return on stocks versus bonds for such a long horizon? The pension participant typically not only has a long horizon but also makes many contributions throughout his or her career. For example, faculty at Stanford University make payments to their retirement accounts twice each month over their term of employment. How does such a pattern of purchase affect the relative desirability of stocks versus bonds as pension accumulation assets? Finally, most individual retirement accounts, Keogh plans, and defined contribution plans allow the participant not only to choose which assets are purchased with new contributions but also to move existing accumulations between asset categories. This raises the question of the desirability of gradually moving stock accumulations into bonds late in one's career. Such an option offers the potential advantage that one's retirement annuity would depend on the value of the stock portfolio at several selling dates rather than just its value on the date of purchase of the annuity.

MaCurdy and Shoven examine how some naive investment strategies for pension accumulations would have performed for employment careers of varying length between 1926 and 1989. Given a strategy, they calculate the implied value for the pension account at the time of retirement for all possible completed careers of a specified horizon within the sixty-four-year period. They consider only strategies in which investors allocate their pension contributions either entirely into stocks (with all dividends and other returns reinvested in stocks) or entirely into bonds (with interest reinvested in bonds). These strategies are not optimal in any sense since they ignore any market timing issues as well as standard portfolio theory. They then consider some strategies for converting from stocks to bonds as a worker approaches retirement, but they do not attempt to determine the optimal portfolio composition as a function of years until retirement. Despite these limitations, they find that an "all stocks" strategy dominates all other investment policies considered for all career lengths of twenty-five years or longer. By "domination," they mean that an all stocks allocation would have generated a larger pension accumulation for every career that ended in retirement over the period 1926–89.

MaCurdy and Shoven's findings have important implications for pension investment policies, and they suggest that the vast majority of people choose the wrong accumulation strategies. Not only are their results applicable to defined contribution plans, but they are also relevant for defined benefit pension programs and for other long-horizon saving targets.

All the material presented in the paper is from the point of view of a participant in a defined contribution pension system. However, it is applicable to a wider class of problems, including the funding of defined benefit retirement plans by corporations. The findings simply say that systematic contributions proportional to earnings over a career have always led to more wealth at the time of retirement if the investments are in stocks rather than bonds. This information seems completely relevant to an employer who has promised retirement benefits based on final salary and years of service. The defined benefits can be funded with smaller cash contributions owing to the higher rates of return earned on stocks over long horizons.

Not only has an all stocks strategy always bested an all bonds one for all careers exceeding twenty-five years, but it has also always yielded more than the popular fifty-fifty allocation or any other constant mix of stock and bond purchases. While it is impossible to predict the likelihood that this dominance will continue, the evidence favoring stocks for long horizons is overwhelming.

Living Arrangements and Family Support

1. In "Health, Children, and Elderly Living Arrangements: A Multiperiod-Multinomial Probit Model with Unobserved Heterogeneity and Autocorrelated Errors," Axel Börsch-Supan, Vassilis Hajivassiliou, Laurence J. Kotlikoff, and John N. Morris develop a model of living arrangements that should have wide applications in future research in this area. The model overcomes major technical problems that have prevented implementation of the most re-

alistic models in past research. The paper also confirms that living arrangements are predominantly governed by functional ability and to a lesser degree by age. A surprising result is that changes in marital status have little effect on the choice of living arrangement, after controlling for other family characteristics.

Decisions by the elderly regarding their living arrangements (e.g., living alone, living with children, or living in a nursing home) seem best modeled as a discrete choice problem in which the elderly view certain choices as closer substitutes than others. For example, living with children may more closely substitute for living independently than living in an institution does. Unobserved determinants of living arrangements at a point in time are, therefore, quite likely to be correlated. In the parlance of discrete choice models, this means that the assumption of the independence of irrelevant alternatives (IIA) will be violated. Indeed, a number of recent studies of living arrangements of the elderly document the violation of this assumption.

In addition to relaxing the independence assumption of no intratemporal correlation between unobserved determnants of competing living arrangements, the authors also relax the assumption of no intertemporal correlation of such determinants. The assumption of no intertemporal correlation underlies most studies of living arrangements, particularly those estimated with cross-sectional data. While cross-sectional variation in household characteristics can provide important insights into the determinants of living arrangements, the living arrangement decision is clearly an intertemporal one. Because of moving and associated transactions costs, elderly households may stay longer in inappropriate living arrangements than they would in the absence of such costs. In turn, households may prospectively move into an institution "before it is too late to cope with this change." That is, households may be substantially out of long-run equilibrium if a cross-sectional survey interviews them shortly before or after a move. Moreover, persons may acquire a taste for certain types of living arrangements. Such habit formation introduces state dependence. Ideally, therefore, living arrangement choices should be estimated with panel data, with an appropriate econometric specification of intertemporal linkages.

These intertemporal linkages include two components. The first component is the linkage through unobserved person-specific attributes, that is, unobserved heterogeneity through time-invariant error components. An important example is health status, information on which is often missing or unsatisfactory in household surveys. Health status varies over time but has an important person-specific, time-invariant component that influences housing and living arrangement choices of the elderly.

However, not all intertemporal correlation patterns in unobservables can be captured by time-invariant error components. A second error component should, therefore, be included to control for time-varying disturbances, for example, an autoregressive error structure. Examples of the source of error components that taper off over time are the cases of prospective moves and habit formation mentioned above. Similar effects on the error structure arise when, owing to unmeasured transactions costs, an elderly person stays longer in a dwelling than he or she would in the absence of such costs.

While researchers have recognized the need to estimate choice models with unobserved determinants that are correlated across alternatives and over time, they have been daunted by the high dimensional integration of the associated likelihood functions. This paper uses a new simulation method developed by Börsch-Supan and Hajivassiliou to estimate the likelihood functions of living arrangement choice models that range, in their error structure, from the very simple to the highly complex.

The simulated likelihood method works well and requires a very small number of replications. It easily accommodates highly complex error structures and can handle different error structures without major programming effort

Two main conclusions follow from the estimation results. First, a careful specification of the temporal error process dramatically improves the model fit. It also appears that ignoring intertemporal linkages biases some parameter estimates, although the different specifications produce qualitatively similar coefficients on the substantive parameters.

Second, living arrangement choices are governed predominantly by functional ability and to a lesser degree by age. The analysis confirms that institutions are an inferior living arrangement as measured by a the willingness to spend more in order to avoid entering one. A somewhat surprising result is that changes in marital status do not appear to matter a great deal.

2. In "The Provision of Time to the Elderly by Their Children," Axel Börsch-Supan, Jagadeesh Gokhale, Laurence J. Kotlikoff, and John N. Morris consider the time that children spend with their parents. They conclude that time spent with parents is determined primarily by demographic factors, such as the age of the parent, but that economic factors such as income and wealth play an insignificant role.

There is substantial evidence that support of parents by children has declined in the postwar period. Over 60 percent of the elderly (those over 60) now live alone, compared with only 25 percent in the 1940s. For the old old (those over 85), the fraction living alone has increased from 13 to 57 percent. At the same time, there has been more than a tripling of the rate of institutionalization; today almost one-quarter of the old old live in institutions, compared with only 7 percent in the 1940s. In addition to not living with the elderly, the children of the elderly rarely provide financial transfers to the elderly, and when they do, the amounts are typically quite meager.

One defense of the children's behavior is demographic; the current number of children per elderly parent totals about half the number observed in the

1940s. Since the elderly of today had fewer children than did their parents and have, in some cases, succeeded in outliving their children, the current situation may be of their own making. A second defense is that the relative income position of the elderly has improved, permitting them to live alone and obviating the need for financial transfers from their children. A variety of studies have demonstrated that current poverty rates of the elderly are close to, if not below, those of the nonelderly. Much of the improvement in the relative incomes of the elderly is due to increases in real Social Security benefits legislated in the 1970s. A third point to consider in assessing child support of the elderly involves payment for nursing home care. A good fraction of the elderly in nursing homes are private pay patients. Some of these payments are being made directly by children. It seems plausible that such payments per child measured at constant dollars have increased over time.

The authors emphasize that, while the elderly may need and appear to be receiving less financial help from their children, their needs for companionship and physical assistance may well have increased in the postwar period; the increased longevity of the elderly often means living for years in poor states of health. In addition, those elderly who continue to live will lose a large fraction of their old friends and even some of their children along the way. Most studies of the increasingly separate living arrangements of the elderly conclude that these arrangements reflect the preferences and improved financial means of the elderly. In contrast, Kotlikoff and Morris suggested in prior research that about half the elderly would prefer to live with their children but continue to live apart because of their children's preferences coupled with their children's financial abilities to live apart from their parents.

One reason the jury remains out on family support of the aged involves the issue of time spent by children with their elderly parents. Children's provision of time to their elderly parents is an important, if not the most important, form of economic transfer to the elderly by their children. This papers studies the provision of time by children to their elderly parents. The authors use the 1986 Hebrew Rehabilitation Center for the Aged (HRCA) follow-up survey of Massachusetts elderly and the 1986 HRC-NBER survey of the children of these Massachusetts elderly.

They use these data to answer a number of questions about the provision of time by children to their parents. These questions include, How does the health status of the elderly influence the amount of time given by children? How does the health status of the children influence their provision of time to their parents? Do parents with more income and wealth receive more time from their children? How do the employment status and wage rates of children affect their provision of time? Do children free ride on their siblings' provision of time? Are home care corporations used by children as a substitute for their own time? Do the institutionalized elderly receive more or less time? Are daughters more or less likely to provide time?

The data reveal some clear patterns of time transfers from children to their elderly parents. Children appear to use institutions and home care as a substitute for their own provision of time. Parents who reside in nursing homes or are enrolled in home care programs receive, ceteris paribus, less than half the amount of time received by those in the community. The provision of time is strongly correlated with the age of the elderly parent; other things being equal, the old old receive over twice the time of the young old.

The sex, age, and health status of children are additional important determinants of time provided to the elderly. Male children and younger children spend relatively little time with their parents. Children with poor health spend almost no time with their parents. If the spouse of a child is in poor health, the child also gives very little time, at least according to the model results.

Other things being equal, those elderly who report their health to be "poor" receive over twice the amount of time received by elderly with better self-reports of health. Surprisingly, the degree of elderly disability does not appear to affect the amount of time provided to those elderly not living with their children, although it is a significant determinant in the larger sample that includes elderly living with their children.

The results for the entire sample of children, including those living with their elderly parents, indicate that more time is provided by single children and more time is received by single elderly, at least those who are widowed. There is strong evidence that widowed children spend substantially more time with their elderly parents.

The estimates indicate a small effect associated with higher children's wage rates; children with higher wage rates provide somewhat less time to their elderly parents than other children. In contrast to the modest effect of higher wage rates, the effect of larger values of children's wealth is quite sizable. Wealthier children and children with higher incomes appear to provide less time than poorer children, but the effects are not precisely measured.

To summarize, the results indicate that the main determinants of the amount of time given to parents are demographic. Economic variables, such as wage rate and income levels, appear to play an insignificant role in the provision of time.

On The Life-Cycle Model

In "Wealth Depletion and Life-Cycle Consumption by the Elderly," Michael D. Hurd considers evidence in the Retirement History Survey (RHS) with respect to life-cycle theory. He argues that the data are consistent with life-cycle theory but that they offer no support for a bequest motive as an important determinant of the consumption and saving behavior of the elderly.

Although the life-cycle hypothesis (LCH) of consumption has been the most important theory for the study of saving behavior, interest in the bequest motive for saving has grown considerably. This has been stimulated by three kinds of empirical results. (1) In simulations of lifetime earnings and consumption trajectories, "reasonable" utility function parameter values lead to savings that are considerably smaller than observed household wealth. This implies that a good deal of household wealth has been inherited. Although, when the date of death is unknown, large inheritances are not necessarily inconsistent with the life-cycle hypothesis, many people believe they indicate that at least part of the bequests are intentional. (2) From estimated earnings and consumption paths it is found that as much as 80 percent of household wealth is inherited. (3) The elderly do not seem to dissave as they age. Because this contradicts a prediction of the life-cycle hypothesis, it has been taken to be particularly damaging to the hypothesis.

In this paper, Hurd first reviews some evidence on how wealth changes as the elderly age. He argues that the best evidence is that the elderly do dissave as required by the life-cycle hypothesis. He then presents findings based on consumption data in the RHS. Hurd concludes that, as measured in the RHS, consumption declines as households age, which is in accordance with the life-cycle hypothesis. If a bequest motive for saving is an important determinant of consumption, the consumption paths of parents and nonparents should differ, but no systematic difference between their consumption paths is found. Hurd's overall conclusion is that the wealth and consumption data in the RHS are consistent with the life-cycle hypothesis; they do not support a role for a bequest motive as a determinant of consumption behavior. Hurd also concludes that in the RHS, observations on both consumption and wealth are consistent with the life-cycle hypothesis of consumption in that both are observed to decline after retirement.

While the findings that consumption and wealth decline with age are consistent with the LCH, they are not inconsistent with a bequest motive for saving: the bequest motive will change the shape and level of the consumption and wealth paths, but they will not necessarily rise. A test for the importance of the bequest motive is based on the assumption that the marginal utility of bequests of a parent is greater than the marginal utility of bequests of a nonparent. This assumption implies that, ceteris paribus, the wealth and consumption paths of a parent should decline more slowly than the wealth and consumption paths of a nonparent. In the RHS, the wealth paths decline at the same rate.

In short, Hurd concludes that the RHS data on wealth and consumption are consistent with the life-cycle hypothesis of consumption but that they offer no support for a bequest motive for saving as an important determinant of consumption behavior. Hurd also gives considerable attention to the substantial measurement problems that plague analysis based on consumption data.

Aging Issues in Developing Countries

In "Patterns of Aging in Thailand and Côte d'Ivoire," Angus Deaton and Christina H. Paxson consider aging issues in less developed countries (LDCs). They emphasize the important differences between developed and less developed countries and the implications of these differences for understanding aging issues and for appropriate directions for research. They draw attention to several issues and questions, emphasizing in particular that the life-cycle model of saving and capital accumulation cannot be applied without modification to economies where the functions of households are very different from those in developed countries.

The authors present and discuss facts about older people in two contrasting developing countries, Côte d'Ivoire and Thailand. They are concerned with standard questions in the aging literature, namely, demographic structure, living arrangements, urbanization, illness, labor force behavior, and economic status. In this paper, they do not attempt to go beyond the presentation of data from a series of household surveys from the two countries. Although recent years have seen increased attention in the demographic and sociological literatures to questions of aging in LDCs, data are still relatively scarce, particularly for Africa, and the authors see their current task as providing stylized facts to help focus further discussion.

There are two research issues that provide the structure for their discussion: household saving behavior and, more broadly, the economics of aging in countries with low living standards but with rapidly expanding shares of old people in the population.

Research on saving behavior in the United States, Japan, and Western Europe has been dominated by permanent income and life-cycle models since their introduction in the 1950s. There has been a good deal less work done on household saving behavior in LDCs, and much of the work that has been done has simply transferred the analytic framework from the more to the less developed context. It is not clear that this is the best way of proceeding. While it makes sense to work with the same basic ideas—that saving can smooth consumption over time and that assets provide a measure of insurance against an uncertain future—there are important differences in environment and in mechanisms, and the same aims may therefore be achieved in very different ways. A much larger share of the population in developing countries is engaged in agriculture, where incomes are very variable, and there are many poor people living close to the subsistence level, so consumption insurance may be of the greatest importance.

The authors find that their exploration of the data allows them to summarize some of what is known and what might usefully be learned:

1. Questions regarding the economic status of the old in LDCs cannot be answered and must be rethought. In more developed countries, where perhaps

nine-tenths of the elderly live by themselves or with elderly spouses, household surveys can tell us a great deal about their living standards. In LDCs, to a greater or lesser degree, older people do not live by themselves, and until a method can be found for measuring intrahousehold allocations, we have no method of assigning welfare levels to them or indeed to other members of the households in which they live.

2. More work needs to be done on the question of whether the source of income (i.e., who earns it) affects what individual members of the household receive. This cannot be done directly, but if the earnings of the elderly are spent differently than other household income, one should be able to detect that fact from consumption data. Data such as those from Thailand show considerable variation in source of income with age, although the patterns are quite different from those in the United States or Western Europe.

3. In the United States and other developed countries, where many elderly people live alone, there has been concern about the possible abandonment of the old. However, such cases seem to be rare; most old people live alone because they want to, and frequency of contract with children is generally high. In Côte d'Ivoire, under current living conditions, abandonment does not seem common because very few old people live alone. There are perhaps more grounds for concern in Thailand, but the population at risk is still small and is probably overstated by the survey results quoted in this paper. However, there is evidence from elsewhere that suggests that these results should not be generalized to all poor countries. In many areas of India, living arrangements for newlyweds are strictly patrilocal, with the result that, after marriage, women are effectively cut off from their parents' family. In turn, they will be looked after in old age by their sons, their daughters having themselves moved to their husbands' families. In consequence, women who fail to produce sons, or fail to produce surviving sons, are likely to fall into destitution as widows.

4. The living arrangements of the elderly will vary from place to place according to marriage arrangements, agroclimatic conditions, and the availability of labor and land. In Côte d'Ivoire, living patterns have been changing in response to the increasing scarcity of land since sons, who were previously guaranteed land nearby, are now often required to set up households at considerable distances. The shortage of land itself reflects a great deal of immigration to the cocoa and coffee areas, an immigration that responded originally to *labor* shortage and that contributed to the destruction of the original lineage system of cocoa and coffee production. One may also wonder whether the pattern of inheritance in northern Thailand—whereby, as a result of the residual stem family system, the youngest daughter typically inherits the land—will continue unmodified into an era where land is increasingly scarce.

5. Individual participation and earnings patterns show the standard life-cycle hump shapes in Côte d'Ivoire and Thailand and presumably do so more widely. However, households act so as to make average living standards

within households much less variable over the life cycle than are the individual patterns. The degree to which this happens in the data is different between the two counties and depends on how household size is measured. Even so, sharing resources between household members is presumably one of the main economic functions of the household. What needs a great deal more research is the extent to which household size and composition adapt to facilitate sharing and to guarantee the best possible living standards to household members. In both Thailand and Côte d'Ivoire, there is a great deal of migration, both seasonal and nonseasonal. In Thailand, the process of household formation is explicitly tied to the pressure on resources within the compound; the departure of a previously married child on the marriage of a younger sibling is therefore as much a matter of economics as of immutable custom. In the panel households in Côte d'Ivoire, there are major differences in membership between 1985 and 1986. The authors emphasize that there is scope for more modeling here, particularly for a simple unifying theory that explains how potential household members decide how to form household groups given the economic opportunities available to them.

6. There are a number of interactions between urbanization and age distributions. Migration tends to lead to young cities and an older countryside, as is the case in Côte d'Ivoire, but much urban growth in LDCs comes from reproductive behavior as well as from migration. The fall in fertility in the demographic transition often begins in the cities, with the result that cities are likely to age more rapidly than more rural areas. The balances between these forces will produce different age distributions in different countries, for example, young cities in Africa and older cities in Asia, and these have a number of repercussions for policy, for example, in the provision of services as well as in the likely effectiveness of older people as a political force.

7. Many LDCs are in a state of transition, not only demographic, but also educational. In both countries examined here, there are very large differences between the educational attainments of the different generations. The *consequences* of these differences are much less clear, and the authors do not wish to subscribe to the view that they always and everywhere undermine the status of the old. But Deaton and Paxson emphasize that models that provide a theoretical framework for the role of the elderly would do well to bear these facts in mind.

8. The life-cycle model of saving and capital accumulation, which has brought so many insights in developed countries, cannot be applied without modification to economies where the functions of households are different. Asset accumulation for old age, with a large share of the capital stock being accounted for (or not accounted for) by life-cycle saving, is not likely to be a very useful model for savings in LDCs. Households can and do provide old-age insurance without an obvious need to accumulate and decumulate assets. The authors' data do not suggest any run down of assets with the age of the household head. Of course, as in more developed economies, heads

have a range of other motives for keeping control of assets for as long as possible.

9. As in developed countries, there is a pronounced household life cycle, with a hump-shaped income, peaking much earlier in Côte d'Ivoire than in Thailand. However, the authors doubt that there is much long-term consumption smoothing associated with these humps, and they tend to attach more importance to saving as a means of smoothing consumption over short-term fluctuations in income that are typically associated with agricultural activities. Indeed, the authors say, it is possible that variations in household structure contribute more to long-term smoothing than do variations in assets.

Social Security Reform

In "Changing the Japanese Social Security System from Pay as You Go to Actuarially Fair," Tatsuo Hatta and Noriyoshi Oguchi consider the implications of changing from the current pay-as-you-go system to one that is actuarially fair. The authors note that, while the merits of a fully funded system are well known to economists, there is a reluctance to move from a pay-as-you-go to a fully funded system because the transition creates instability in benefit distribution and in the macro budget. The authors argue, however, that it is not necessary to accumulate a budget surplus to eliminate the distributional and efficiency problems associated with a pay-as-you-go system. They show that switching to an actuarially fair but unfunded system attains this objective.

The current Japanese public pension system is essentially pay as you go; hence, its rate of return is not actuarially fair for each participant. This is the root of the three problems that the Japanese public pension system faces.

First, the system transfers income intergenerationally. In particular, the generation following the baby boomers is expected to make a large transfer to the baby boomer generation. By the year 2025, the average Japanese worker will have to support three times as many retirees as in 1990. This period, which is characterized by a higher percentage of retirees, is referred as the high-average-age period (HAAP). The arrival of the HAAP will increase the required social security contributions to maintain the promised benefits, resulting in significant income redistributions among different generations. It may even make the very existence of the public pension system uncertain, the authors say.

Second, the system also transfers income within each generation in a way that is difficult to justify. For example, the nonworking wife of a corporate president typically gets a much higher rate of return on her pension benefits than a woman of that company who never marries.

Third, since the social security contribution is not directly linked to the future benefit payments, the current system distorts labor supply.

Had the system been actuarially fair from the beginning, these problems would not have arisen. Once a pay-as-you-go system is in place, however, making it actuarially fair may create new problems. The principal aim of the paper is to evaluate the economic effects of various reform plans that would eventually make the system actuarially fair.

Specifically, Hatta and Oguchi examine the following three plans:

1. *Switch to the Fully Funded System.* This quickly increases the government budget surplus to the level of social security wealth before the arrival of the HAAP.
2. *Switch to the Actuarially Fair System.* This switches the system over to an actuarially fair one before the HAAP. People in the baby boom and subsequent generations will contribute the amount that exactly matches benefits received. The budget surplus never reaches the level of social security wealth; the system never becomes fully funded.
3. *Gradual Shift to the Fully Funded System.* After an actuarially fair system is established as in plan 2, several generations pay taxes at levels greater than the actuarially fair amount until the system is eventually made fully funded. The burdens of building up the fund are shared by several generations.

The authors emphasize first that the Japanese social security system places a heavy burden on the post–baby boom generation by transferring income from it to the baby boom generation. Switching the system to a fully funded one in one generation shifts the heavy burden to the baby boom generation. It also creates national saving in the switching period larger than what would be attained if the system were fully funded from the beginning. Switching to an actuarially fair but unfunded system eliminates the microeconomic problems of the Japanese social security system without causing instability in the transition phase, the authors show.

If accumulation of a budget surplus is necessary to make the system fully funded, it can be done by first changing the system into an actuarially fair but unfunded one and then gradually building up the fund by taxing several generations. Economic effects of such a gradual shift are analyzed.

Nursing Home Stays

1. In "Payment Source and Episodes of Institutionalization," Alan M. Garber and Thomas E. MaCurdy explore the relation between the duration of nursing home stays and the source of payment for nursing home care. The authors conclude that the incentive effects of the subsidies of nursing home care—associated with types of payers—may play an important role in nursing home utilization.

This subject has assumed critical importance as a growing number of private insurers begin to offer long-term care insurance, millions of middle-aged and elderly Americans plan for future long-term care needs, and policymakers debate the role that government should play in financing, delivering, and regulating long-term care.

Both private and public initiatives for financing long-term care need accurate projections of utilization, but few studies have examined the effects of insurance on utilization. The size of the insurance subsidy effect on utilization, or moral hazard, is not readily inferred from observed price variation. It is notoriously difficult to gauge the price of nursing home care faced by consumers of this service, in part because price variation reflects differences in the characteristics of nursing homes (e.g., the quality of nursing services, meals, and housing amenities). In the absence of comprehensive, reliable price data or of direct measures of the effects of alternate financing mechanisms on long-term care utilization, studies of the relation between payment source and utilization provide important clues to the likely consequences of changing long-term care insurance benefits.

The measure of utilization that Garber and MaCurdy examine is the length of each nursing home stay. While information about the duration of spells is a key component, additional information is needed to complete any comprehensive picture of nursing home utilization. Comprehensive measures of utilization (or cumulative duration) also require information about both the likelihood that a spell will occur at all and the frequency of readmission. The length of an individual spell has an entirely different interpretation if it is only one of a series of admissions rather than a unique occurrence.

Nursing home utilization also depends on the mode of exit, which in most duration analyses is of little concern. In other medical contexts, the nature of exit may have minimal significance because there is only one way a spell (of an illness, e.g.) may terminate (in death); in economic contexts, even if there is more than one way to end a spell (of unemployment, e.g.), the nature of the exit may be of secondary interest. The type of exit from nursing homes, in contrast, has substantive economic and welfare implications. Nursing home admissions terminate in return to the community, transfer to a hospital, or death. Although the type of discharge clearly matters to the patient, it also affects future long-term care utilization and overall health expenditures. Transfer to a hospital, for example, is often a costly interruption in a lengthy nursing home stay, while discharge to the community may signal resumption of independent living. The length of a nursing home spell, if it terminates in hospital admission, may be short in relation to overall utilization. To accommodate these phenomena, the authors complement the analysis of duration distributions with an investigation of the association between the probabilities of alternate modes of exit and several other factors, including personal characteristics, payment source, and length of the nursing home admission.

Garber and MaCurdy investigate these issues by analyzing data on a sample of frail, disabled, and otherwise vulnerable elderly men and women who were believed to be likely to enter a nursing home. They were enrolled in the National Long-Term Care (Channeling) Demonstration, a randomized controlled trial of case management as a deterrent to institutionalization. While this sample is not representative of elderly Americans generally, it represents a group of particular interest: persons who are expected to consume a disproportionate share of long-term care and who are likely to be excluded from the purchase of private long-term care insurance. If associations between payment source and duration patterns are significant in this sample, the relation in the general population might be stronger, particularly if the demand for nursing home are among Channeling participants is inelastic.

As planning for and financing long-term care have achieved new prominence in policy circles, there is an urgent need for reliable estimates of the effect of insurance on long-term care utilization. The authors attempt to take a step toward understanding the effect of insurance by measuring the association between payer type and utilization within a high-risk population of older Americans. One might argue that the absence of an association between type of coverage and utilization suggests that the demand for nursing home care is inelastic, an assumption implicit in much of the policy discussion regarding long-term care insurance. Many advocates of broader long-term care insurance coverage believe that widespread adoption of long-term care insurance would not increase the utilization of nursing homes.

Garber and MaCurdy's analysis finds that the distribution of the length of nursing home stays differs substantially among payer types, in ways that may not simply reflect selection. These differences are apparent even in a population of frail elderly individuals who lack social supports and are felt to have "unmet needs." The differences also persist despite the control of the additional covariates incorporated into their model. Although their study was not designed to assess whether the differences in nursing home duration by payer are causal relations, the persistence of strong relations between payer type and duration of nursing home admission despite the selection of the population and the control for additional covariates suggests that the incentive effects of the subsidy of nursing home care may play an important role in nursing home utilization.

The results of the duration analyses reported here suggest that the payment source is strongly associated with the length of nursing home admissions. The covariates have a weak independent association with duration, at least within this population and in the time period studied, but some of them, such as the presence of a severe ADL impairment, are associated with the type of exit. Medicare-financed admissions are much shorter than admissions funded by either Medicaid or some other payment source, and there is a striking early peak in the hazard rate for Medicare admissions.

The type of exit from the nursing home is also highly associated with the payment source. Exit probabilities reflect the "success" of a nursing home admission, and they also give clues to future utilization of long-term care. Nursing home spells financed by "other," primarily private, payers last nearly as long as Medicaid admissions but are much more likely to end with return to the community. The length of admission and payment source interact, at least for Medicare spells; the longer a Medicare patient is in a nursing home, the more likely is discharge to home. Even long Medicare admissions seem short in comparison to Medicaid admissions and are much more likely to end in return to the community. For the Medicaid admissions, the high rate of discharge to hospitals and the high rate of death are discouraging signs for return to independent living.

The authors emphasize that their results to date should be viewed as suggestive findings, not as definitive answers about insurance effects. But the results make it clear that a complete understanding of nursing home utilization must be based on an adequate characterization of paths leading to and from nursing homes and that it must account for multiple admissions.

2. In "Incentive Regulation of Nursing Homes: Specification Tests of the Markov Model," Edward C. Norton considers whether Markov models can be appropriately used to model transitions in and out of nursing homes. The analysis rests on data from an experiment that tested the effects of performance-based reimbursement on the quality and cost of nursing home care. In prior work, Norton showed that the reimbursement system had a positive effect on both quality and cost. This paper, more narrowly focused on the use of the Markov model, concludes that, while the model may provide a reasonable tool for analysis of these data, it is an imperfect representation of transitions in nursing homes.

The analysis in Norton's previous work used a simple Markov model to estimate transition probabilities between states of health in the nursing home. A comparison of the probabilities for the control group (no incentives) and the experimental group (positive incentives) found them to be different. People in the experimental group stayed for a shorter time and had better outcomes.

The simple Markov model, however, maintains several strong assumptions. For example, it assumes that the transition probabilities are constant over time, independent of past states, and the same for all people. If any of these assumptions are false, the conclusions of the previous paper may be ill founded. This paper extends the analysis to more general models and in doing so subjects the simple Markov model to a series of specification tests. Most of the tests are done on data from the control group nursing homes only so that the effects of the experiment are not mixed with those of the assumptions. The paper tests the following series of assumptions. (1) The probability of being in state j next period depends only on the current state, not on past states. (2) The probabilities are independent of personal characteristics, such as age, sex, race, and marital status. (3) The probabilities are constant over time. (4) The probabilities are independent of how long a person has been in the nursing home. (5) Nursing homes in the experimental group instantly switched to optimize under the new reimbursement system with no learning period. (6) $P(T) = P(1)^T$ (the basic Markov assumption). (7) Reporting errors by nurses have no effect on the estimated transition probabilities.

This paper contains a summary of the experiment done by the National Center for Health Services Research and the data used in the analysis, followed by a brief review of Norton's earlier results. The remainder of the paper is an extension of the previous analysis.

Norton finds that the Markov model should be viewed as a reasonable but imperfect model of transitions in nursing homes. He concludes that research in this area could benefit from trying other kinds of duration models, such as competing hazard and semiparametric models. These models may have advantages in speed of computation, a more flexible form, and an emphasis on duration and outcome that are important for public policy.

1 Three Models of Retirement
Computational Complexity versus Predictive Validity

Robin L. Lumsdaine, James H. Stock, and David A. Wise

Empirical analysis often raises questions of approximation to underlying individual behavior. Closer approximation may require more complex statistical specifications. On the other hand, more complex specifications may presume computational facility that is beyond the grasp of most real people and therefore less consistent with the actual rules that govern their behavior, even though economic theory may lead analysts to increasingly complex specifications. Thus, the issue is not only whether more complex models are worth the effort but also whether they are better. The answer must necessarily depend on the behavior that the analysis is intended to predict. In this paper, we consider the relation between computational complexity and the predictive validity of three models of retirement behavior.

Retirement has been the subject of a large number of studies over the past decade. Most have emphasized the effect of Social Security provisions on retirement age, but a wide range of methods has been employed. The earlier studies in this time period were based on regression or multinomial logit analysis (see, e.g., Hurd and Boskin 1981). Subsequent analysis relied on nonlinear budget constraint formulations of the retirement decision (see, e.g., Burtless 1986; and Gustman and Steinmeier 1986) and on proportional hazard model formulations (see, e.g., Hausman and Wise 1985). More recently, sev-

Robin L. Lumsdaine is assistant professor of economics at Princeton University. James H. Stock is professor of political economy at the Kennedy School of Government, Harvard University, and a research associate of the National Bureau of Economic Research. David A. Wise is John F. Stambaugh Professor of Political Economy at the John F. Kennedy School of Government, Harvard University, and the area director for health and retirement programs at the National Bureau of Economic Research.

Financial support was provided by the National Institute on Aging (grants R37 AGO8146 and T32 AGO0186), the Hoover Institution, the National Science Foundation, and the Sloan Foundation. This chapter was written while Lumsdaine was a Ph.D. candidate in the Department of Economics, Harvard University.

eral authors have developed models that focus on forward-looking comparison of the advantages of retirement at alternative ages in the future and on the updating of information as persons age. Although the spirit of these latter models is basically the same, they vary widely in computational complexity. The potential advantages in predictive validity of the computationally more complex versions of these models are the primary motivation for this study, although to broaden the scope of the comparison we consider a much simpler model as well.

We compare the predictive validity of three models of retirement. The first is a simple probit model. The second is the "option value" model developed in Stock and Wise (1990a, 1990b). The third is a stochastic dynamic programming model. We experiment with two versions of this model: one is an adaptation of the extreme value distribution formulation proposed by Berkovec and Stern (1991), and the other is the normal distribution formulation proposed by Daula and Moffitt (1991). A related but still more complex model has been developed by Rust (1989), but we have not attempted to implement his formulation in the analysis in this paper.

The analysis is guided by several key ideas. First, all the models are theoretical abstractions; none of them can be reasonably thought of as "true." The important consideration is which decision rule is the best approximation to the calculations that govern actual individual behavior. In this paper, judgments on which rule is best are based on empirical evidence on the relation between model specification and predictive validity.

Second, the models vary substantially in the computational complexity of the decision rules that they attribute to individual decision makers. The option value and the dynamic programming rules are both intended to capture the same underlying idea, but implementation of dynamic programming rules typically implies considerably more computational complexity than implementation of the option value rule. The option value model makes a simplifying assumption that substantially reduces complexity. The probit model is much simpler than either of these.

Third, although the mathematically correct implementation of some decision rules requires dynamic programming, there is no single dynamic programming rule. The implied computational complexity depends in important ways on specific assumptions, in particular the disturbance term correlation structure. It is easier to incorporate more flexible correlation assumptions in the option value than in the dynamic programming formulations. Thus, for example, the option value specification may be a suboptimal solution to a dynamic programming rule that implies computational complexity difficult to implement even with a computer.

A question of practical importance is therefore whether different decision rules yield significantly different results.

The comparisons in this paper are made by estimating the models on the same data. The data, which pertain to the retirement decisions in a large *For-*

tune 500 firm, have two important advantages for our purposes. First, the retirement decisions can be related to the provisions of the firm's pension plan, and it is therefore possible to simulate the effect of changes in the pension plan provisions. Second, the firm offered an unanticipated "window" plan in one of the years covered by the data.

The principal measure of the predictive validity of the models is how well they predict the effects of the window plan. Like the typical defined benefit pension plan, this firm's plan provides substantial incentives to retire early. In addition, the window plan provided further incentive to retire early. Window plans, which have been offered by many firms in recent years, provide special bonuses to workers in a specific group—often defined by age, occupational group, or even a division within the firm—if the worker retires within a specified period of time, typically a year or less. The window plan allows a unique external test of the predictive validity of the models; it is possible to compare model predictions against actual retirement rates under the window plan.

We begin by obtaining model parameter estimates based on retirement decisions in a year (1980) prior to the window plan. We then use these estimates to predict retirement in a later year (1982) under the window plan. The estimates and predictions are based on male nonmanagerial employees.

A brief description of the firm plan, the special window plan, and the data is presented in section 1.1. A more detailed description, borrowed in large part from Lumsdaine, Stock, and Wise (1991), is provided in appendix A. The models that are compared are explained in section 1.2. The parameter estimates and window plan predictions are presented in section 1.3. Section 1.4 presents simulations of the effects of eliminating the Social Security early retirement option. Conclusions are presented in section 1.5.

1.1 The Data, the Firm Pension Plan, and the Temporary Window

The analysis is based on a random sample of 993 male nonmanagerial office employees at a *Fortune* 500 firm. They were employed at the firm and were at least 50 years old on 1 January 1980, and they had been employed by the firm for at least three years prior to 1980. (The criterion that they be employed three years facilitates the forecasting of future wage earnings on an individual basis.)[1]

The data, obtained from firm records, include the earnings history of each employee from his year of employment, or from 1969 if he was employed before then, to retirement, or to 1983 if he had not retired by then. The data allow determination of whether the employee continued to work at the firm in successive years from 1980 through 1984. The data do not include the employment status of workers who left the firm; some employees probably took another job after departure from this firm. Thus, strictly speaking, the data

1. Employees who died between 1980 and 1982 before retiring were not included in the sample.

pertain to departure from the firm rather than retirement, but because we have no information on postretirement employment, we treat departure as retirement.

The firm's employees are covered by a defined benefit pension plan. The plan provides a substantial incentive for the typical employee to remain in the firm until age 55 and then an additional incentive to leave the firm before age 65. The plan is described in detail in appendix A. It has four key features:

1. The "normal" retirement age is 65.
2. Workers are vested after ten years of service.
3. The early retirement age is 55: a worker who departs before age 55 receives benefits that are reduced actuarially (approximately 7 percent per year) from the normal retirement age benefits, but the benefits of an employee who retires at 55 or later are reduced only about 3 percent per year, thus creating an incentive to stay until 55 and then an incentive to leave the firm.
4. The benefit formula incorporates a Social Security offset—a reduction of firm benefits based on Social Security benefits—but the offset is waived until age 65 for persons who retire at 55 or later, thus creating an additional incentive for workers to retire between 55 and 65.

In addition, an employee accrues a benefit entitlement from Social Security, with early retirement at age 62 and normal retirement at 65.

Particularly important for this study is the firm's 1982 window plan. Under the window plan, the firm offered nonmanagerial office employees a temporary retirement incentive. The window plan applied to employees between 55 and 65 who were vested in the firm's pension plan and to all employees over 65. Employees who retired in 1982 were offered a bonus equivalent to 3–12 months' salary. Although the exact bonus varied by years of service, it was typically largest for employees who were between 58 and 62 years old and smallest for those 55 and 65.[2] Of the 993 employees in our sample, 800 remained in the firm until 1982. The actual 1982 departure rates of these 800 employees are used to assess the out-of-sample predictive validity of the three retirement models.

1.2 The Models

Three retirement models are described, beginning with the "option value" model. The simple probit model is explained next and then the dynamic programming specification.

2. For a detailed description of this window plan and a discussion of the design of efficient window plans, see Lumsdaine, Stock, and Wise (1990).

1.2.1 The Option Value Model

The conceptual model is discussed in some detail in Stock and Wise (1990b). It is described only briefly here. At any given age, it is assumed, on the basis of information available at that age, that an employee compares the expected present value of retiring at that age with the value of retiring at each age in the future through age 70, the mandatory retirement age in this firm. The maximum of the expected present values of retiring at each future age minus the expected present value of immediate retirement is called the option value of postponing retirement. A person who does not retire this year maintains the option of retiring at a more advantageous age later on. If the option value is positive, the person continues to work; otherwise, he retires. With reference to appendix figure 1A.1, for example, at age 50 the employee would compare the value of the retirement benefits that he would receive were he to retire then—approximately \$28,000—with the value of wage earnings and retirement benefits in each future year. The expected present value of retiring at 60 (discounted to age 50), for example, is about \$184,000. This calculation is repeated as the worker ages, using updated predictions of future wage earnings and related pension and Social Security benefits. Future earnings forecasts are based on the individual's past earnings as well as on the earnings of other persons in the firm.[3] The precise model specification follows.

A person at age t who continues to work will earn Y_s in subsequent years s. If the person retires at age r, subsequent retirement benefits will be $B_s(r)$. These benefits will depend on the person's age and years of service at retirement and on his earnings history; thus, they are a function of the retirement age. We suppose that, in deciding whether to retire, the person weighs the indirect utility that will be received from future income. Discounted to age t at the rate β, the value of this future stream of income if retirement is at age r is given by

$$(1) \qquad V_t(r) = \sum_{s=t}^{r-1} \beta^{s-t} U_w(Y_s) + \sum_{s=r}^{S} \beta^{s-t} U_r[B_s(r)],$$

where $U_w(Y_s)$ is the indirect utility of future wage income and $U_r[B_s(r)]$ is the indirect utility of future retirement benefits. It is assumed that the employee will not live past age S.

The gain, evaluated at age t, from postponing retirement until age r is given by

$$(2) \qquad G_t(r) = E_t V_t(r) - E_t V_t(t).$$

Letting r^* be the age that gives the maximum gain, the person will postpone retirement if the option value, $G_t(r^*)$, is positive,

$$(3) \qquad G_t(r^*) = E_t V_t(r^*) - E_t V_t(t) > 0.$$

3. For a description of the earnings forecasts, see Stock and Wise (1990b).

The utilities of future wage and retirement income are parameterized as

(4a) $$U_w(Y_s) = Y_s^\gamma + \omega_s,$$

(4b) $$U_r(B_s) = [kB_s(r)]^\gamma + \xi_s,$$

where ω_s and ξ_s are individual-specific random effects, assumed to follow a Markovian (first-order autoregressive) process

(5a) $$\omega_s = \rho\omega_{s-1} + \varepsilon_{\omega s}, \quad E_{s-1}(\varepsilon_{\omega s}) = 0,$$

(5b) $$\xi_s = \rho\xi_{s-1} + \varepsilon_{\xi s}, \quad E_{s-1}(\varepsilon_{\xi s}) = 0.$$

The parameter k is to recognize that, in considering whether to retire, the utility *associated* with a dollar of income while retired may be different from the utility associated with a dollar of income accompanied by work. Abstracting from the random terms, at any given age s, the ratio of the utility of retirement to the utility of employment is $[k(B_s/Y_s)]^\gamma$.

Given this specification, the function $G_t(r)$ can be decomposed into two components:

(6) $$G_t(r) = g_t(r) + \phi_t(r),$$

where $g_t(r)$ and $\phi_t(r)$ distinguish the terms in $G_t(r)$ containing the random effects, ω and ξ, from the other terms. If whether the person is alive in future years is statistically independent of his earnings stream and the individual effects ω_s and ξ_s, $g_t(r)$ and $\phi_t(r)$ are given by

(7a) $$g_t(r) = \sum_{s=t}^{r-1}\beta^{s-t}\pi(s|t)E_t(Y_s^\gamma) + \sum_{s=r}^{S}\beta^{s-t}\pi(s|t)\{E_t[kB_s(r)]^\gamma\} - \sum_{s=t}^{S}\beta^{s-t}\pi(s|t)\{E_t[kB_s(t)]^\gamma\},$$

(7b) $$\phi_t(r) = \sum_{s=t}^{r-1}\beta^{s-t}\pi(s|t)E_t(\omega_s - \xi_s),$$

where $\pi(s|t)$ denotes the probability that the person will be alive in year s, given that he is alive in year t. Given the random Markov assumption, $\phi_t(r)$ can be written as

(8) $$\phi_t(r) = \sum_{s=t}^{r-1}\beta^{s-t}\pi(s|t)\rho^{s-t}(\omega_t - \xi_t) = K_t(r)\nu_t,$$

where $K_t(r) = \Sigma_{s=t}^{r-1}(\beta\rho)^{s-t}\pi(s|t)$ and $\nu_t = \omega_t - \xi_t$. The simplification results from the fact that at time t the expected value of $\nu_s = \omega_s - \xi_s$ is $\rho^{s-t}\nu_t$, for all future years s. (The term $K_t[r]$ cumulates the deflators that yield the present value in year t of the future expected values of the random components of utility. The further r is in the future, the larger is $K_t[r]$. That is, the more distant the potential retirement age, the greater the uncertainty about it, yielding a heteroskedastic disturbance term.) $G_t(r)$ may thus be written simply as

(9) $$G_t(r) = g_t(r) + K_t(r)\nu_t.$$

If the employee is to retire in year t, $G_t(r)$ must be less than zero for every potential retirement age r in the future. If $r_t^\dagger$ is the r that yields the maximum value of $g_t(r)/K_t(r)$, the probability of retirement becomes

$$\text{(10)} \qquad \Pr[\text{retire in year } t] = \Pr[g_t(r_t^\dagger)/K_t(r_t^\dagger) < -\nu_t].$$

If retirement in only one year is considered, this expression is all that is needed.

More generally, retirement decisions may be considered over two or more consecutive years. In this case, the retirement probabilities are simply an extension of equation (10). The probability that a person who is employed at age t will retire at age $\tau > t$ is given by

$$\text{(11)} \qquad \begin{aligned} \Pr[\text{retire in year } \tau] = \Pr[& g_t(r_t^\dagger)/K_t(r_t^\dagger) > -\nu_t, \ldots, \\ & g_{\tau-1}(r_{\tau-1}^\dagger)/K_{\tau-1}(r_{\tau-1}^\dagger) > -\nu_{\tau-1}, \\ & g_\tau(r_\tau^\dagger)/K_\tau(r_\tau^\dagger) < -\nu_\tau]. \end{aligned}$$

The probability that the person does not retire during the period covered by the data is given by

$$\text{(12)} \qquad \begin{aligned} \Pr[\text{do not retire by year } T] = \Pr[& g_t(r_t^\dagger)/K_t(r_t^\dagger) > -\nu_t, \ldots, \\ & g_{T-1}(r_{T-1}^\dagger)/K_{T-1}(r_{T-1}^\dagger) > -\nu_{T-1}, \\ & g_T(r_T^\dagger)/K_T(r_T^\dagger) > -\nu_T], \end{aligned}$$

where T is the final period in the data set. This is a multinomial discrete choice probability with dependent error terms ν_s.

Finally, we assume that ν_s follows a Gaussian Markov process, with

$$\text{(13)} \qquad \nu_s = \rho\nu_{s-1} + \varepsilon_s, \quad \varepsilon_s \ i.i.d. \ N(0, \sigma_\varepsilon^2),$$

where the initial value, ν_t, is $i.i.d.$ $N(0, \sigma^2)$ and is independent of ε_s. The covariance between ν_τ and $\nu_{\tau+1}$ is $\rho\text{var}(\nu_\tau)$, and the variance of ν_τ for $\tau > t$ is $[\rho^{2(\tau-t)}]\sigma^2 + (\Sigma_{j=0}^{\tau-t-1}\rho^{2j})\sigma_\varepsilon^2$.

The estimates in this paper are based on retirement decisions in only one year, and the random terms in equation (5) are assumed to follow a random walk, with $\rho = 1$. In this case, the covariance between ν_τ and $\nu_{\tau+1}$ is $\text{var}(\nu_\tau)$, and the variance of ν_τ for $\tau \geq t$ is $\sigma^2 + (\tau - t)\sigma_\varepsilon^2$. Prior estimates show that one- and multiple-year estimates are very similar.[4]

1.2.2 The Probit Model

The option value model proposes that a person will continue to work if the option value of postponing retirement—given by $G_t(r^*) = E_tV_t(r^*) - E_tV_t(t)$ in equation (3)—is greater than zero. In that model, the option value is determined by estimation. That is, the observed retirement decisions are described in terms of $\Pr[G_t(r^*) > 0]$, which in turn is described by a particular parame-

4. Estimates based on several consecutive years and with ρ estimated are shown in Stock and Wise (1990b). These generalizations have little effect on the estimates.

terization of $V_t(r)$. The maximum likelihood estimation procedure determines these parameters—γ, k, β, and σ (and σ_ε if two or more consecutive years are used in estimation). Thus, one can think of this procedure as estimating the option value on the basis of how employees value future income and leisure.

An alternative approach is to specify retirement in terms of the gain from continuing to work but to calculate the gain on the basis of an assumed valuation of income (determined by γ and k) and an assumed discount rate (β) instead of estimating them. Assuming that retirement depends on this *calculated* option value as well as other unobserved determinants of retirement, a standard specification of retirement is

$$\text{(14)} \qquad \Pr[\text{retire in year } t] = \Pr[\delta_0 + \delta_1 \hat{G}_t(r^*) + \varepsilon > 0],$$

where $\hat{G}_t(r^*)$ is the option value calculated under the presumed parameter values, and assuming the random components of $G_t(r)$ ($\phi_t[r]$ in [6] and [7b]) are all zero. This is a probit formulation, assuming that ε has a normal distribution.

In this case, the effect of the assumed gain from retirement is estimated by the parameter δ_1. This formulation is the closest probit counterpart to the option value model. In addition to this specification, several others are also estimated. The alternative specifications predict retirement on the basis of Social Security (SS) benefits, pension benefits, the present value of SS benefits (SS wealth), the present value of pension benefits (pension wealth), the change in the present value of SS benefits from working another year (SS accrual), the change in the present value of pension benefits from working another year (pension accrual), predicted earnings in the next year, and age.

1.2.3 The Stochastic Dynamic Programming Model

The key simplifying assumption in the Stock-Wise option value model is that the retirement decision is based on the maximum of the expected present values of future utilities if retirement occurs now versus each of the potential future ages. The stochastic dynamic programming rule considers instead the expected value of the maximum of current versus future options. The expected value of the maximum of a series of random variables will be greater than the maximum of the expected values. Thus, to the extent that this difference is large, the Stock-Wise option value rule underestimates the value of postponing retirement. And to the extent that the dynamic programming rule is more consistent with individual decisions than the option value rule, the Stock-Wise rule may undervalue individual assessment of future retirement options. Thus, we consider a model that rests on the dynamic programming rule.

As emphasized above, it is important to understand that there is no single dynamic programming model. Because the dynamic programming decision rule evaluates the maximum of future disturbance terms, its implementation depends in important ways on the error structure that is assumed. Like other users of this model, we assume an error structure—and thus a behavioral rule—that simplifies the dynamic programming calculation. In particular, although the option value model allows correlated disturbances, the random disturbances in the dynamic programming model are assumed to be uncorrelated, except for a random individual effect that is used in some specifications. Thus, the two models are not exactly comparable. Whether one rule is a better approximation to reality than the other may depend not only on the basic idea but also on its precise implementation.

In fact, we implement two versions of the dynamic programming model. In the first model, disturbance terms are assumed to follow an extreme value distribution. This model is adopted from Berkovec and Stern (1991), with two modifications. First, Berkovec and Stern consider three outcomes (full-time work, part-time work, and retirement), whereas we consider only two (full-time work and retirement, the only states for which we have data). Second, the way that we account for individual-specific effects differs from Berkovec and Stern's formulation.

In the second dynamic programming model, the disturbances are assumed to be normally distributed. This formulation is adopted from Daula and Moffitt's (1991) dynamic programming model of retention in the military. Our model generalizes their specification by allowing for additive individual-specific disturbances and by specifying retirement in terms of a parameterized utility function. With the additional assumption that the unobserved individual-specific effects are normally distributed across employees, the error structure in this dynamic programming specification is similar to the structure in the option value model. In both cases, future errors are normally distributed with nonzero covariances. In the option value model, the covariance structure derives from the random walk assumption; in the dynamic programming model, the covariances derive from a components-of-variance structure, with an individual-specific effect.

A more general dynamic programming model of retirement has been developed by Rust (1989). Unfortunately, comparison with his model is beyond the scope of this study. He assumes that an employee optimizes jointly over both age of retirement and future consumption. By admitting continuous and discrete choice variables, his model poses substantially greater numerical complexity than the ones we implement.

In most respects, our dynamic programming model is analogous to the option value model. As in that model, at age t an individual is assumed to derive utility $U_w(Y_t) + \varepsilon_{1t}$ from earned income or $U_r[B_t(s)] + \varepsilon_{2t}$ from retirement benefits, where s is the retirement age. The disturbances ε_{1t} and ε_{2t} are random perturbations to these age-specific utilities. Unlike the additive disturbances in the option value model, these additive disturbances in the dynamic programming model are assumed to be independent. Future income and retirement benefits are assumed to be nonrandom; there are no errors in forecasting future wage earnings or retirement benefits.

Individuals will presumably have different preferences for employment versus retirement. Variation in preferences is allowed for in the extreme value distribution version of our model by including individual-specific effects in $U_r(\cdot)$ and $U_w(\cdot)$. They are assumed to be fixed for each person, but they vary randomly from person to person. Berkovec and Stern modeled these individual-specific effects as additional additive errors. In the extreme value distribution version of our model, they enter multiplicatively. In the normal distribution version of our model, the random effects enter additively, as explained below.

The Model

The dynamic programming model is based on the recursive representation of the value function. At the beginning of year t, the individual has two choices: retire now and derive utility from future retirement benefits, or work for the year and derive utility from income while working during the year and retaining the option to choose the best of retirement or work in the next year. Thus, the value function W_t at time t is defined as

$$W_t = \max\left[E_t[U_w(Y_t) + \varepsilon_{1t} + \beta W_{t+1}], \; E_t\left(\sum_{\tau=t}^{S} \beta^{\tau-t}\{U_r[B_\tau(t)] + \varepsilon_{2\tau}\}\right)\right], \tag{15}$$

with

$$W_{t+1} = \max\left[E_{t+1}[U_w(Y_{t+1}) + \varepsilon_{1t+1} + \beta W_{t+2}], \; E_{t+1}\left(\sum_{\tau=t+1}^{S} \beta^{\tau-t-1}\{U_r[B_\tau(t+1)] + \varepsilon_{2\tau}\}\right)\right],$$

where β is the discount factor and, as in the option value model, S is the year beyond which the person will not live.

Because the errors ε_{it} are assumed to be i.i.d., $E_t\varepsilon_{it+\tau} = 0$ for $\tau > 0$. In addition, in computing expected values, each future utility must be discounted by the probability of realizing it, that is, by the probability of surviving to year τ given that the worker is alive in year t, $\pi(\tau|t)$. With these considerations, the expression (15) can be written as

$$\begin{aligned} W_t &= \max(\bar{W}_{1t} + \varepsilon_{1t}, \bar{W}_{2t} + \varepsilon_{2t}), \text{ where} \\ \bar{W}_{1t} &= U_w(Y_t) + \beta\pi(t+1|t)E_tW_{t+1}, \\ \bar{W}_{2t} &= \sum_{\tau=t}^{S} \beta^{\tau-t}\pi(\tau|t)U_r[B_\tau(t)]. \end{aligned} \tag{16}$$

The worker chooses to retire in year t if $\bar{W}_{1t} + \varepsilon_{1t} < \bar{W}_{2t} + \varepsilon_{2t}$; otherwise, he continues working. The probability that the individual retires is $\Pr(\bar{W}_{1t} + \varepsilon_{1t} < \bar{W}_{2t} + \varepsilon_{2t})$. If a person works until the mandatory retirement age (70), he retires and receives expected utility $\bar{W}_{2t_{70}}$.

Recursions and Computation

With a suitable assumption on the distribution of the errors ε_{it}, the expression (16) provides the basis for a computable recursion for the nonstochastic terms $\bar{W}_{it}$ in the value function. The extreme value and normal distribution versions of the model are considered in turn.

Extreme Value Errors. Following Berkovec and Stern (1991), the ε_{it} are assumed to be i.i.d. draws from an extreme value distribution with scale parameter σ. Then, for the years preceding mandatory retirement, these assumptions together with equation (16) imply that

$$
\begin{aligned}
& E_t W_{t+1}/\sigma \equiv \mu_{t+1} \\
(17) \qquad & = \gamma_e + \ln[\exp(\bar{W}_{1t+1}/\sigma) + \exp(\bar{W}_{2t+1}/\sigma)] \\
& = \gamma_e + \ln\{\exp[U_w(Y_{t+1})/\sigma]\exp[\beta\pi(t+2|t+1)\mu_{t+2}] \\
& \quad + \exp(\bar{W}_{2t+1}/\sigma)\},
\end{aligned}
$$

where γ_e is Euler's constant. Thus, (17) can be solved by backward recursion, with the terminal value coming from the terminal condition that $\mu_{t_{70}} = \bar{W}_{2t_{70}}$.

The extreme value distributional assumption provides a closed form expression for the probability of retirement in year t:

$$
\begin{aligned}
(18) \qquad \Pr[\text{retire in year } t] & = \Pr[\bar{W}_{1t} + \varepsilon_{1t} < \bar{W}_{2t} + \varepsilon_{2t}] \\
& = \exp(\bar{W}_{2t}/\sigma)/[\exp(\bar{W}_{1t}/\sigma) + \exp(\bar{W}_{2t}/\sigma)].
\end{aligned}
$$

Gaussian Errors. Following Daula and Moffitt (1991), the ε_{it} are assumed to be independent draws from an $N(0, \sigma^2)$ distribution. The Gaussian assumption provides a simple expression for the probability of retiring:

$$
\begin{aligned}
(19) \qquad \Pr[\text{retire in year } t] & = \Pr[(\varepsilon_{1t} - \varepsilon_{2t})/\sqrt{2}\sigma \\
& < (\bar{W}_{2t} - \bar{W}_{1t})/\sqrt{2}\sigma] = \Phi(a_t),
\end{aligned}
$$

where $a_t = (\bar{W}_{2t} - \bar{W}_{1t})/\sqrt{2}\sigma$. Then the recursion (16) becomes:

$$
\begin{aligned}
(20) \qquad E_t W_{t+1}/\sigma \equiv \mu_{t+1} & = (\bar{W}_{1t+1}/\sigma)[1 - \Phi(a_{t+1})] \\
& + (\bar{W}_{2t+1}/\sigma)\Phi(a_{t+1}) + \sqrt{2}\phi(a_{t+1}),
\end{aligned}
$$

where $\phi(\cdot)$ denotes the standard normal density and $\Phi(\cdot)$ denotes the cumulative normal distribution function. As in (19), $\Phi(a_t)$ is the probability that the person retires in year t and receives utility $\bar{W}_{2t}$ plus utility from $E(\varepsilon_{2t} \mid \varepsilon_{1t} - \varepsilon_{2t} < \bar{W}_{2t} - \bar{W}_{1t})$. The latter term, plus a comparable term when the person continues to work, yields the last term in equation (20).

Individual-Specific Effects

Individual-specific terms are modeled as random effects but are assumed to be fixed over time for a given individual. They enter the two versions of the dynamic programming models in different ways. Each is discussed in turn.

Extreme Value Errors. Single year utilities are

$$U_w(Y_t) = Y_t^\gamma, \tag{21a}$$

$$U_r[B_t(s)] = [\eta k B_t(s)]^\gamma, \tag{21b}$$

where ηk is constant over time for the same person but random across individuals. Specifically, it is assumed that η is a lognormal random variable with mean one and scale parameter λ: $\eta = \exp(\lambda z + \frac{1}{2}\lambda^2)$, where z is i.i.d. $N(0, 1)$. A larger λ implies greater variability among employee tastes for retirement versus work; when $\lambda = 0$, there is no variation, and all employees have the same taste.

Normal Errors. In this case, the unobserved individual components are assumed to enter additively, with

$$U_w(Y_t) = Y_t^\gamma + \zeta, \tag{22a}$$

$$U_r[B_t(s)] = [kB_t(s)]^\gamma, \tag{22b}$$

where γ and k are nonrandom parameters, as above, but ζ is a random additive taste for work, assumed to be distributed $N(0, \lambda^2)$. When $\lambda = 0$, there is no taste variation.

To summarize, the dynamic programming models are given by the general recursion equation (15). It is implemented as shown in equation (17) under the assumption that the ε_{it} are i.i.d. extreme value and as shown in equation (20) under the assumption that ε_{it} are i.i.d. normal. The retirement probabilities are computed according to equations (18) and (19), respectively. The fixed effects specifications are given by equations (21) and (22). The unknown parameters to be estimated are (γ, k, β, σ, λ). Because of the different distributional assumptions, the scale parameter σ is *not* comparable across option value or dynamic programming models, and λ is *not* comparable across the two dynamic programming models.

1.3 Results

The option value and the dynamic programming specifications yield quite similar results, and both provide rather good predictions of retirement behavior under the window plan. The probit specifications yield very poor predictions of retirement under the window plan, although some specifications fit the sample data well. The parameter estimates are discussed first, together with standard measures of fit. We then graphically describe the correspondence between predicted versus actual retirement behavior, with emphasis on out-of-sample predictions of retirement under the 1982 window plan.

1.3.1 Parameter Estimates

The Probit Model

The parameter estimates for several probit specifications are shown in table 1.1. The variables are defined as follows:

Option value: $G_t(r^*)$ calculated as described in section 1.2.1 with $\gamma \equiv 1$, $k \equiv 1$, and $\beta \equiv .95$.
Age: Age in years.
Income: The predicted wage earnings in the following year if the person continues to work.
SS pv (present value): The predicted present value of entitlement to future SS benefits, were the person to retire at the beginning of the year, SS wealth.
Pension pv (present value): The predicted present value of entitlement to future firm pension benefits, were the person to retire at the beginning of the year, pension wealth.
SS accrual: The predicted change in the present value of entitlement to future SS benefits, were the person to continue to work for another year.
Pension acc (accrual): The predicted change in the present value of entitlement to future firm pension benefits, were the person to continue to work for another year.

The parameter estimates are with respect to the probability that a person will *retire*. Thus, the negative option value coefficient in specification 1 indicates that, the greater the option value of continuing to work, the less likely the person is to retire. To interpret this specification, recall that the principal difference between this probit specification and the option value model is the use of assumed parameter values to calculate the option value variable used in the probit model. If this probit specification were estimated using the optimized option value model parameters discussed below (see table 1.2), and if the intercept were forced to be zero, then the probit model would essentially reproduce the option value model, except for the heteroskedastic disturbance term incorporated in the option value model.

The addition of age (specification 2) substantially improves the model fit, but, as is shown in the graphic comparison below, this specification has little behavioral relevance.

Specifications 3–9 are intended to parallel the specification used by Hausman and Wise (1985) in their proportional hazard model of retirement. The probit model is a one-period counterpart to the Hausman and Wise analysis that followed older workers for ten years, covering five two-year periods. Their analysis relied solely on SS wealth and SS accrual (plus other personal attributes), however; they had no firm pension data. Specification 8 shows that

Table 1.1 Probit Parameter Estimates

Variable	Specification (1)	(2)	(3)	(4)	(5)	(6)	(7)	(8)	(9)	(10)
Constant	−.38	−7.18	−1.00	−.82	−1.10	−.61	−.76	−.93	−.71	−1.83
	(.11)	(1.09)	(.10)	(.09)	(.10)	(.11)	(.10)	(.48)	(.12)	(.24)
Option value	−.68	−.30								
	(.09)	(.09)								
Age		.11								
		(.02)								
Income			−.70	−5.11	−5.07	−1.71	−1.81	−2.66	−3.21	−.94
			(.28)	(.70)	(.70)	(.34)	(.33)	(.79)	(.76)	(.31)
SS pv				.69				.90		2.79
				(.08)				(1.09)		(.71)
Pension pv				1.39				.32	.53	
				(.18)				(.26)	(.24)	
SS + Pen pv					1.36					
					(.17)					
SS accrual						−26.47		−21.43		−27.54
						(2.44)		(8.64)		(5.68)
Pension acc						−10.65		−8.86	−7.59	
						(1.18)		(1.73)	(1.58)	
SS + Pen acc							−10.69			
							(1.11)			
Summary statistics:										
$-\ln \mathcal{L}$	299.22	277.75	339.69	298.52	298.38	282.62	284.22	281.38	284.85	329.98
χ^2 sample	59.1	35.5	179.5	68.6	65.3	29.1	31.1	28.2	38.2	145.9
χ^2 window	180.3	108.2	512.2[a]	191.2	164.9	76.4	75.8	67.5	57.3	229.7[a]

Note: Estimation is by maximum likelihood. All monetary values are in \$100,000 (1980 dollars). The χ^2 sample statistic is the chi-square statistic relative to the predicted vs. the actual number of retirements by age in the estimation sample; the χ^2 window statistic is the corresponding statistic for predicted vs. actual retirement under the window plan. Standard errors are in parentheses.

[a]The window plan bonus is treated as a one-time addition to income.

Table 1.2 Parameter Estimates for the Option Value and the Dynamic Programming Models

Parameter	Option Value Models		Dynamic Programming Models: Extreme Value			Dynamic Programming Models: Normal		
	(1)	(2)	(1)	(2)	(3)	(4)	(5)	(6)
γ	1.00[a]	.612	1.00[a]	1.018	1.187	1.00[a]	1.187	1.109
		(.072)		(.045)	(.215)		(.110)	(.275)
k	1.902	1.477	1.864	1.881	1.411	2.592	2.975	2.974
	(.192)	(.445)	(.144)	(.185)	(.307)	(.100)	(.039)	(.374)
β	.855	.895	.618	.620	.583	.899	.916	.920
	(.046)	(.083)	(.048)	(.063)	(.105)	(.017)	(.013)	(.023)
σ	.168	.109	.306	.302	.392	.224	.202	.168
	(.016)	(.046)	(.037)	(.036)	(.090)	(.021)	(.022)	(.023)
λ			.00[a]	.00[a]	.407	.00[a]	.00[a]	.183
					(.138)			(.243)
Summary statistics:								
$-\ln \mathcal{L}$	294.59	280.32	279.60	279.57	277.25	277.24	276.49	276.17
χ^2 sample	36.5	53.5	38.9	38.2	36.2	45.0	40.7	41.5
χ^2 window	43.9	37.5	32.4	33.5	33.4	29.9	25.0	24.3

Note: Estimation is by maximum likelihood. The option value model is described in sec. 1.2.1, and the stochastic dynamic programming model is described in sec. 1.2.3. All monetary values are in $100,000 (1980 dollars). See the note to table 1.1.

[a]Parameter value imposed.

both SS and pension *accrual* are associated with continued employment, but the estimated coefficients would suggest substantial difference in the magnitude of the effects; the SS accrual coefficient is two and a half times as large as the pension coefficient (−21.43 vs. −8.64). (When the SS and the pension wealth and accrual variables are combined [specifications 5 and 7], however, the estimated effects are much closer to the pension than the SS effects.) Neither the SS nor the pension wealth coefficient is significantly different from zero, although both are positive.

The exclusion of the SS variables has little effect on the estimated effects of pension wealth and accrual (specification 9 vs. 8), but the exclusion of the pension variables has a substantial effect on the estimated SS effects (specification 10 vs. 8). This suggests that other estimates of the effects of SS on retirement, such as those in Hausman and Wise, may be biased because they do not control for firm pension benefits. Hausman and Wise, for example, find a strong estimated effect of both SS present value and SS accrual, but they do not have data on the corresponding pension values. In addition, the χ^2 sample statistics show that the specifications with the pension variables fit the sample data much better than the specification with only SS variables (specifications 8 and 9 vs. 10). And with only SS variables the effect of the window plan cannot be predicted, except by assuming that the effect of pension accrual or wealth is the same as the corresponding SS effect. Specification 8 shows that this is far from accurate in this case.

Higher expected wage earnings prolong labor force participation, according to these results.

Likelihood values and two χ^2 statistics are shown at the bottom of table 1.2. Aside from the specification that explicitly includes age, the highest likelihood value is obtained using expected wage earnings for the coming year and SS and pension wealth and accruals (specification 8). The sample χ^2 statistic compares predicted versus actual departure rates by age on the basis of the 1980 data used in the estimation. The window χ^2 statistic compares predicted versus actual departure rates by age under the 1982 window plan.

The Option Value Model

Parameter estimates from the option value model are shown in the first two columns of table 1.2. The income parameter γ (the risk aversion parameter in $U_w[Y_s] = Y_s^\gamma + \omega_s$) is 0.612, suggesting essentially risk neutral preferences. The estimated value of k in $U_r(B_s) = [kB_s(r)]^\gamma + \xi_s$ is 1.477, implying that a dollar without working is worth more than a dollar with work, although the estimate is not significantly different from one. The estimated value of β, 0.895, suggests that future expected or promised income is rather highly discounted relative to income now.

Dynamic Programming Model

The estimated parameters based on the dynamic programming decision rule are shown in the remaining columns of table 1.2. In general, the estimates are similar to those based on the option value rule. The estimated value of γ in the extreme value version (specification 2) is close to, and not significantly different from, one, implying that individuals are risk neutral (that utility is linear in income). The normal version (specification 5) also yields an estimated γ that is not significantly different from one but is substantially larger than the option value estimate (1.19 vs. 0.61). Like the option value results, the dynamic programming results suggest that the value of income together with retirement is substantially greater than the value of income together with work, although the dynamic programming models yield larger estimated values of k. And, like the option value estimates, the dynamic programming estimates indicate that future income is substantially discounted relative to current income in the determination of retirement. The normal specifications yield discount factors close to the option value estimates; the extreme value specification implies larger discount rates.

Estimates of the models including random individual components are reported as specifications 3 and 6. In neither case does inclusion of random individual effects significantly affect other parameter estimates. In the normal version, the variance of the individual effect is not significantly different from zero, implying no variation in taste for retirement versus work among these employees. The extreme value version suggests variation that is significantly different from zero, and the specification fits the data somewhat better than the specifications without the individual component. In neither case does the individual component noticeably improve the prediction of the window plan effects.

Based on the likelihood values, the more forward-looking models fit the data better than the probit specifications, with the exception of the probit with age. Overall, there is little difference in the likelihood values of the option value and the dynamic programming specifications.

The most informative χ^2 statistics pertain to the prediction of departure rates under the 1982 window plan. In this case, the forward-looking models predict actual departure rates substantially better than the probit specifications.

1.3.2 Graphic Comparisons

The Option Value versus Dynamic Programming Results

The easiest way to compare the models is by graphing their implied departure rates. The option value results (model 2 in table 1.2) are used as a base for comparison, and the relevant results are shown in figures 1.1a and 1.1b. Figure 1.1a shows the within-sample fit. Departure (hazard) rates by age are shown in the top panel. The cumulative departures implied by the departures by age are shown in the bottom panel. For example, according to the observed departure rates, 72.0 percent of persons employed at age 50 would have left the firm by age 62; based on the predicted departure rates, the cumulative percentage is 77.7. In general, the predicted departure rates correspond

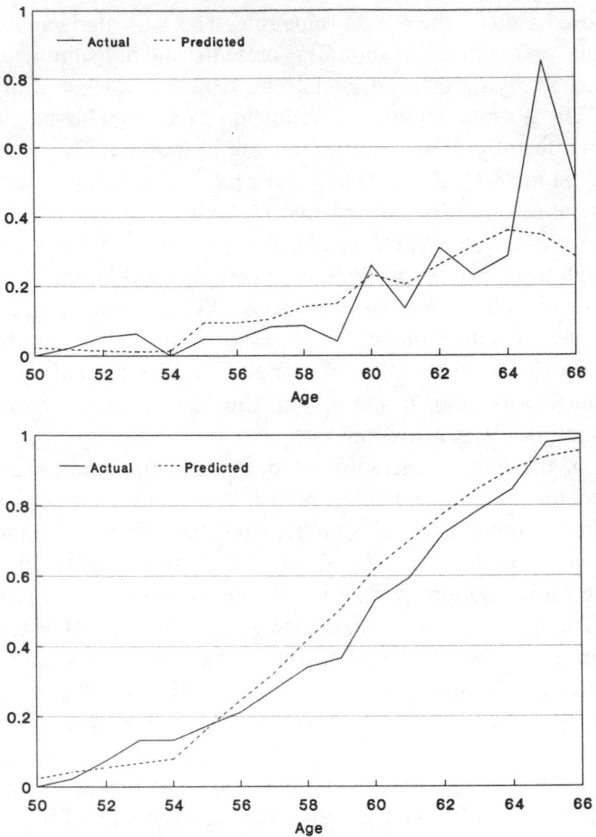

Fig. 1.1a Predicted vs. actual 1980 departure rates and implicit cumulative departures, by age: option value model 2

closely to the actual rates. For example, like the actual rates, the predicted rates show substantial jumps at 55, 60, and 62, all of which correspond to specific pension plan and SS provisions as described in appendix A. A noticeable exception occurs at age 65; among the small proportion of employees still in the firm at that age, a much larger proportion leaves the firm than the model predicts. This finding is common to all employee groups and to all versions of the option value model that we have estimated to date. It is apparently due to an "age-65-retirement effect" that is unrelated to earnings or retirement benefits.

As a test of the predictive validity of the model, the estimates based on 1980 departure rates have been used to predict departure rates under the 1982 window plan. The departure rates of persons offered the window plan bonus were typically about twice as high as they were without this special incentive. Predicted versus actual rates under the window plan are shown in figure 1.1b,

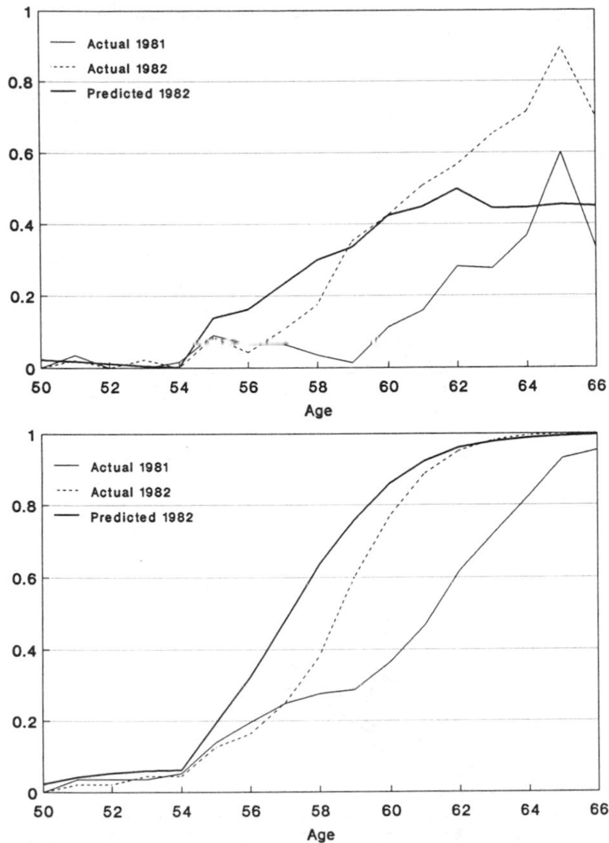

Fig. 1.1b Predicted vs. actual departure rates and implicit cumulative departures under the 1982 window plan, based on 1980 parameter estimates, and 1981 actual rates: option value model 2

together with 1981 actual rates. Like the actual rates, the predicted rates under the window plan are much higher than the 1981 rates. Thus, in general, the model predicts an effect that is comparable in order of magnitude to the actual effect. The option value model, however, tends to overpredict departure rates for persons between 55 and 58 and to underpredict rates for those between 63 and 65. Because departures between 55 and 58 are overpredicted, the predicted cumulative departures are higher than the actual cumulative rates through age 62, as shown in the bottom panel of the figure. (The actual and predicted departure rates used in figs. 1.1a and 1.1b are shown in appendix tables 1B.1a and 1B.1b.)

For comparison, the same graphs are reproduced in figures 1.2a and 1.2b, but with the extreme value dynamic programming (specification 2) predictions added. The two models yield very similar results. Although the likelihood

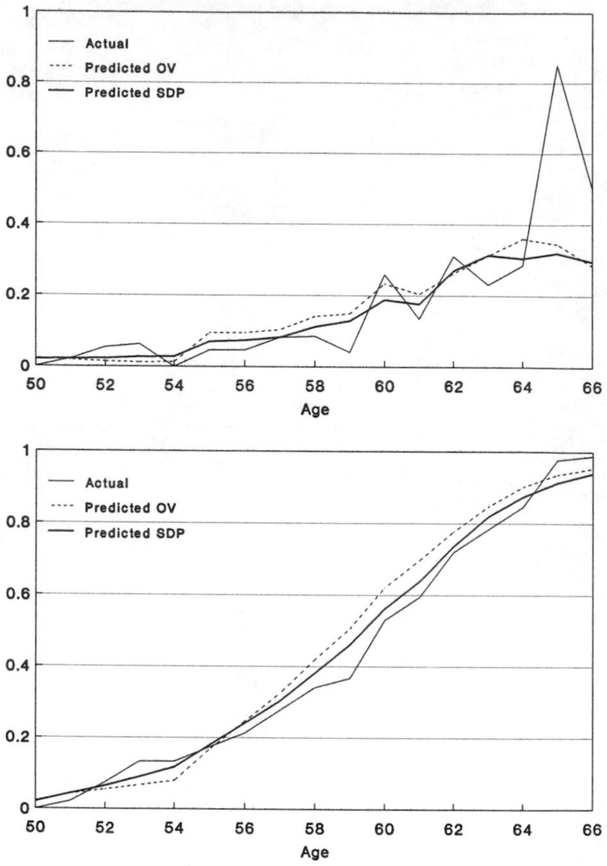

Fig. 1.2a Predicted vs. actual 1980 departure rates and implicit cumulative departures, by age: option value model 2 and stochastic dynamic programming model 2

values from the two models are about the same, the dynamic programming within-sample χ^2 measure of fit is better than the option value measure (as shown in table 1.2), and this is reflected in figure 1.2a. In particular, the dynamic programming model fits departure rates between 55 and 59 somewhat better than the option value model does. Thus, the implied cumulative rates from the dynamic programming model track the actual rates better than the option value model predictions do.

On the other hand, departure rates under the window plan (fig. 1.2b) are predicted better by the option value than by the dynamic programming model, although the differences are not large. The dynamic programming overprediction of departure rates between 55 and 59 is greater than the option value overprediction at these ages. In addition, the dynamic programming model

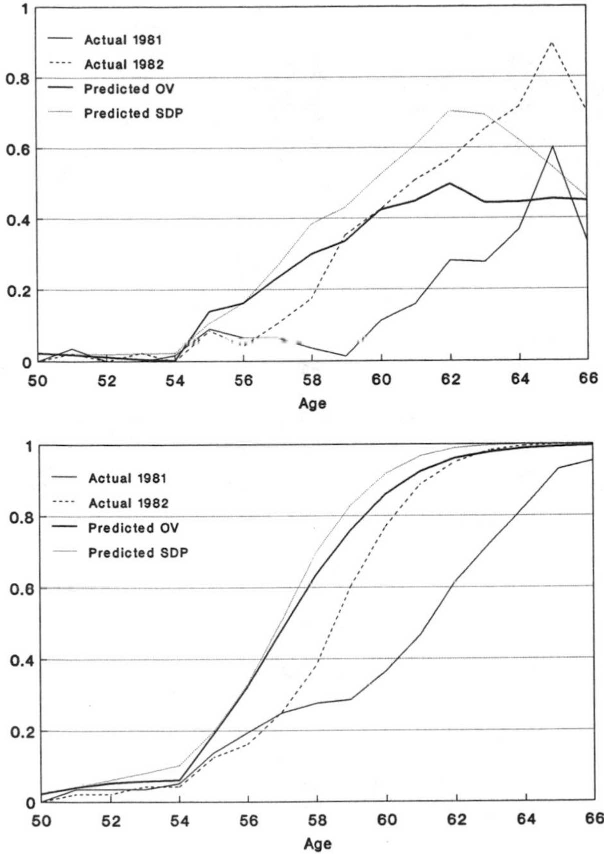

Fig. 1.2b Predicted vs. actual departure rates and implicit cumulative departures under the 1982 window plan, based on 1980 parameter estimates, and 1981 actual rates: option value model 2 and stochastic dynamic programming model 2

overpredicts departure rates through age 63 as well, while the option value model underpredicts departure rates beginning at age 61. (The actual and predicted departure rates used in figs. 1.2a and 1.2b are shown in appendix tables 1B.2a and 1B.2b.)

The extreme value and the normal versions of the dynamic programming model are compared in figures 1.3a and 1.3b. As the figures show, there is little difference between the predictions from the two specifications, although the normal version fits actual departure rates under the window plan somewhat better than the extreme value version. The normal model χ^2 sample statistic is slightly larger than the extreme value statistic, but the normal χ^2 window statistic is lower than the corresponding extreme value statistic, as shown in table 1.2.

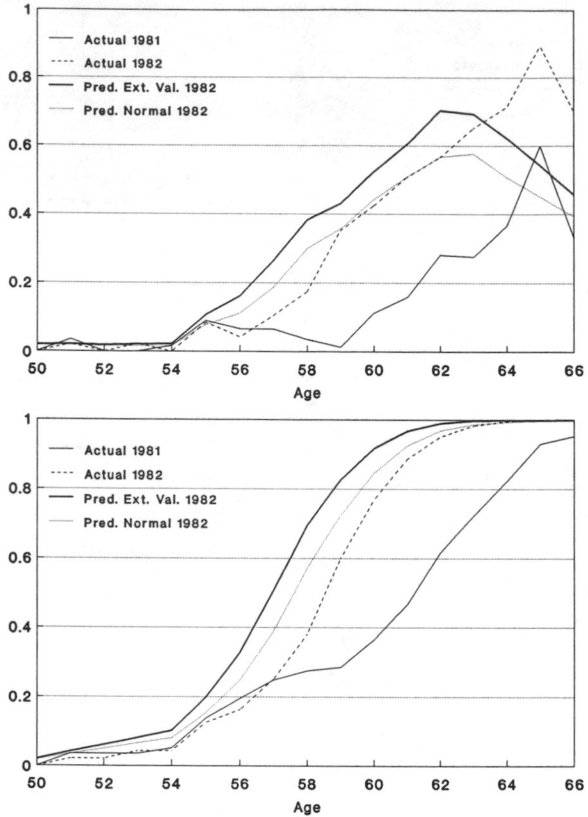

Fig. 1.3a Predicted vs. actual 1980 departure rates and implicit cumulative departures, dynamic programming model, by age: extreme value distribution (model 2) and normal distribution (model 5)

The three models are compared in figure 1.4. The figure shows the difference between the 1982 and the 1980 predicted departure rates based on the three models versus the difference between the actual 1982 and 1980 rates. As the previous figures suggest, the three models yield very similar results, although the option value model tends to underestimate the effects of the window plan whereas the dynamic programming models tend to overestimate the effects.

To summarize, in accordance with the actual effect of the window plan, both the option value and the dynamic programming models predict a large increase in departure rates under the window plan. This comparison does not suggest to us that one model is noticeably better or worse than the other.

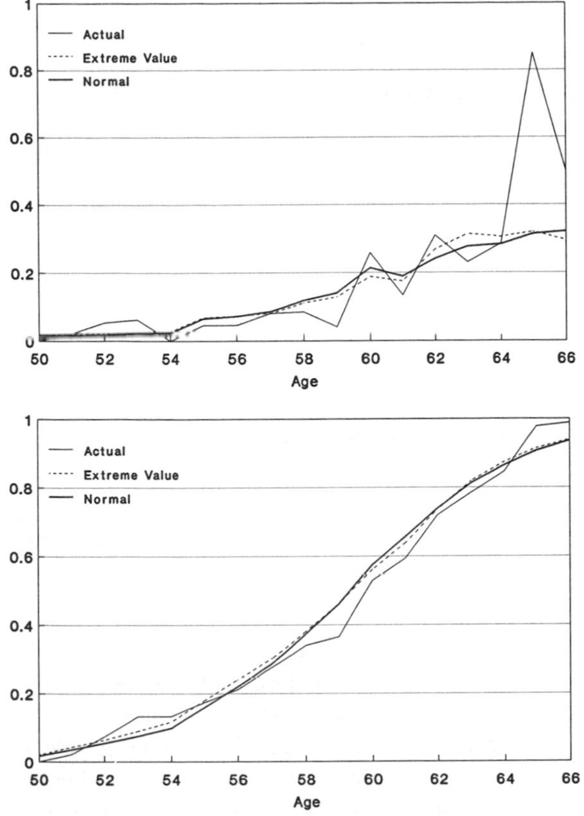

Fig. 1.3b Predicted vs. actual departure rates and implicit cumulative departures under the 1982 window plan, based on 1980 parameter estimates, and 1981 actual rates: dynamic programming model 2 (extreme value distribution) and model 5 (normal distribution)

Selected Probit Model Results

The graphs confirm that the probit models are typically inferior to the more behavioral forward-looking models. But probit specifications that include forward-looking variables capture some of the important features of the option value and the dynamic programming rules. The results of the probit model using the calculated option value variable (computed with $\gamma = 1$, $k = 1$, and $\beta = .95$) are graphed in figures 1.5a and 1.5b. This specification shows very little variation in retirement rates with age, as shown in the top panel of figure 1.5a, and the implied cumulative rates yield a poor approximation to the actual rates. The model predicts very little response to the window plan.

By using both the calculated option value variable and age, it is possible to

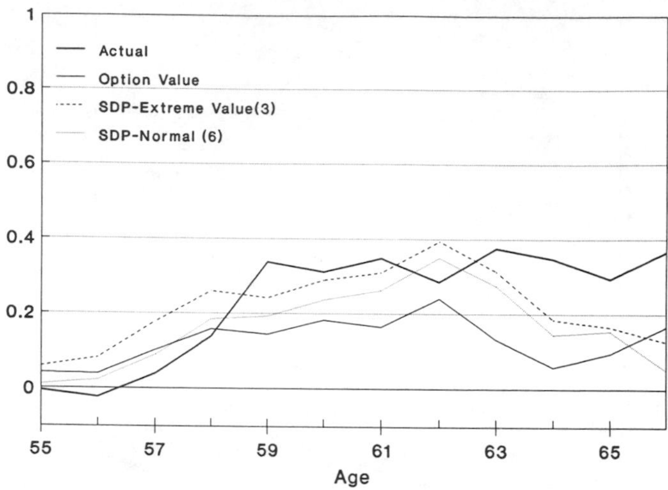

Fig. 1.4 Actual and predicted increases in retirement rates under the 1982 window plan: option value model, stochastic dynamic programming–extreme value model 3, and stochastic dynamic programming–normal model 6

fit the observed departure rates well, as shown in figure 1.6a. But this specification has essentially no behavioral implications: as revealed in figure 1.6b, there is almost no predicted response to the window plan.

The probit specification with the best fit (excluding the specification with age) is based on the current present value of SS and pension benefit entitlements (accumulated SS and pension wealth), the accrual in SS and pension wealth if the person works another year, and expected wage income if the person works another year (specification 8 in table 1.1). This is shown in figure 1.8a. This model fits the sample data about as well as the forward-looking models; indeed, it yields a lower within-sample χ^2 statistic than these more behavioral models. Essentially the same results are obtained when the SS and pension wealth variables are excluded (specification 6 in table 1.1), as shown in figure 1.7a.

But both these probit specifications greatly overpredict retirement rates under the window plan, as shown in figures 1.7b and 1.8b. The window χ^2 statistics also show that the forward-looking models predict the window plan departure rates much better than the probit models do. Aside from the details of functional form, the basic difference between the models is that the probit specification assumes that retirement decisions are based on a rule that involves looking ahead only one period whereas the option value and the dynamic programming rules consider all future potential retirement dates. In this instance at least, a rule that incorporates evaluation of events in the foreseeable future is more consistent with individual behavior than one that limits consideration to events in the next year only.

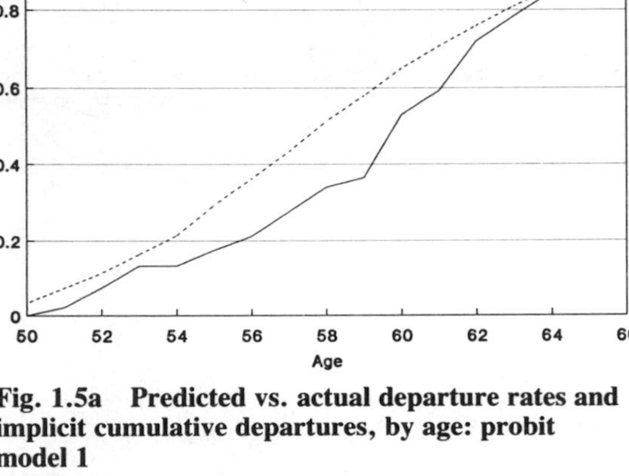

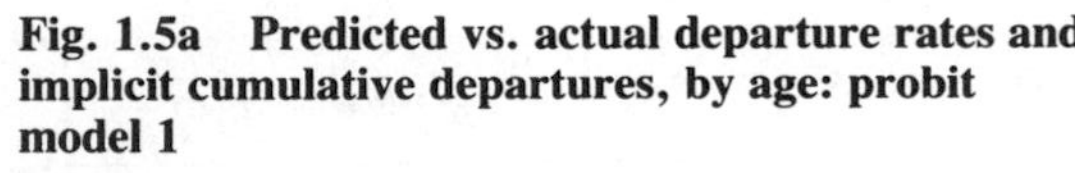

Fig. 1.5a Predicted vs. actual departure rates and implicit cumulative departures, by age: probit model 1

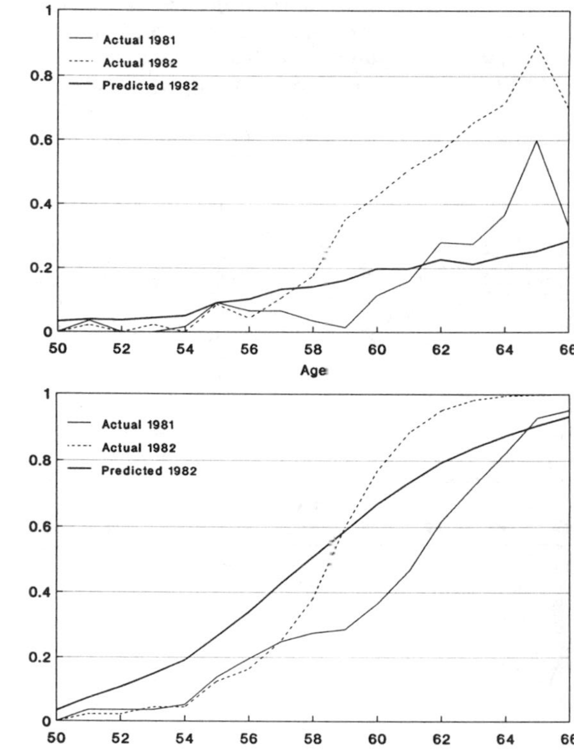

Fig. 1.5b Predicted vs. actual departure rates and implicit cumulative departures under the 1982 window plan, based on 1980 parameter estimates, and 1981 actual rates: probit model 1

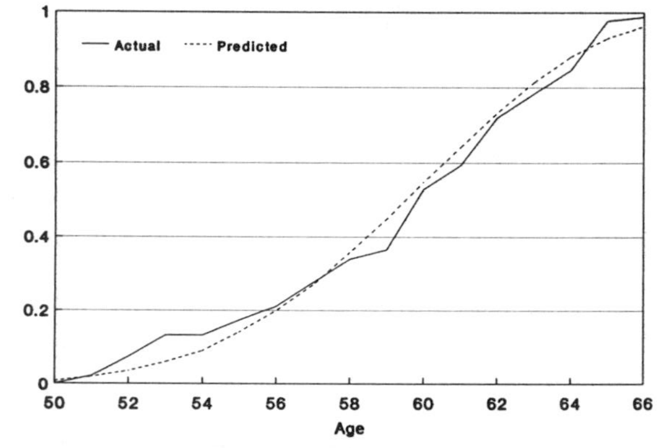

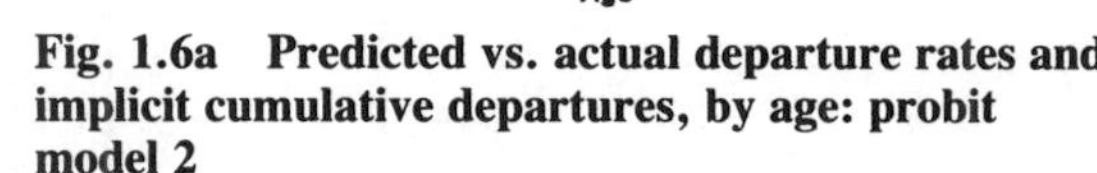

Fig. 1.6a Predicted vs. actual departure rates and implicit cumulative departures, by age: probit model 2

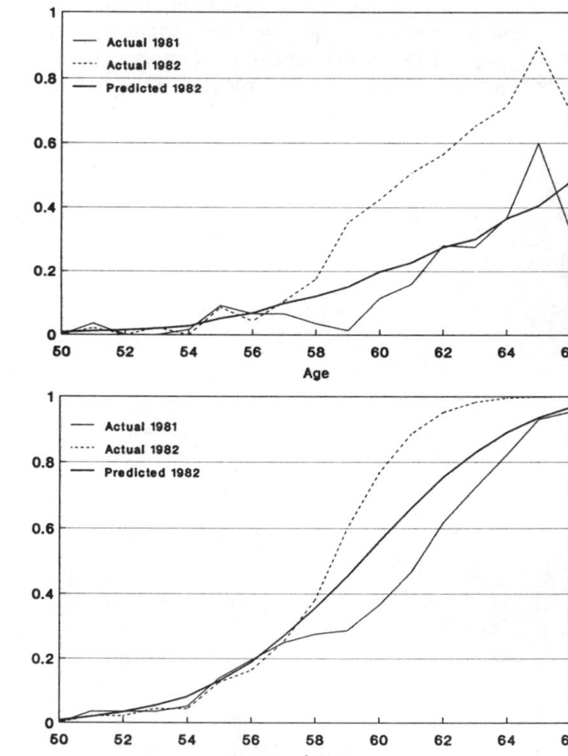

Fig. 1.6b Predicted vs. actual departure rates and implicit cumulative departures under the 1982 window plan, based on 1980 parameter estimates, and 1981 actual rates: probit model 2

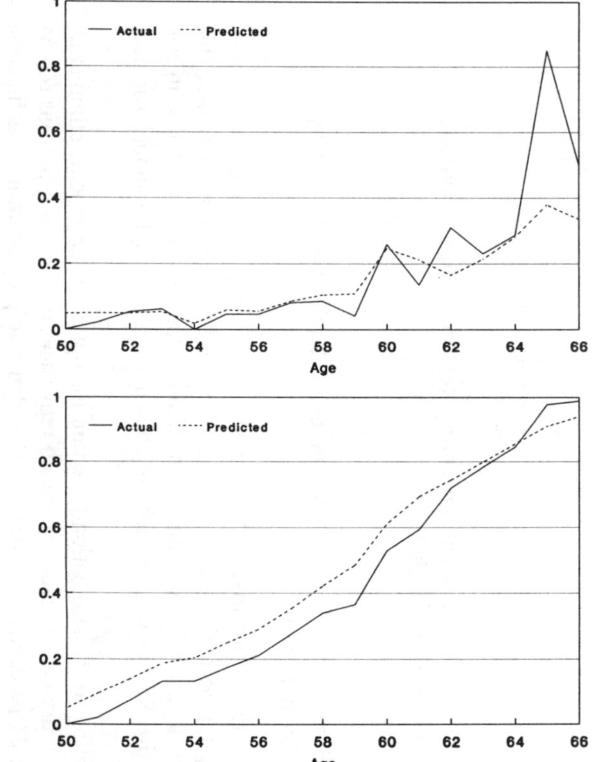

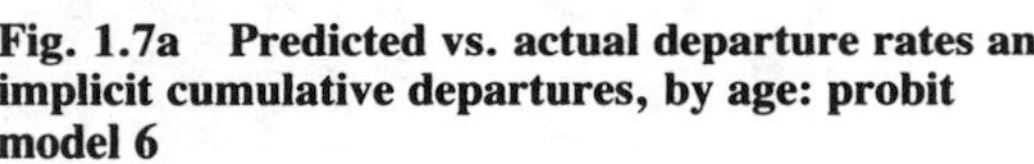

Fig. 1.7a Predicted vs. actual departure rates and implicit cumulative departures, by age: probit model 6

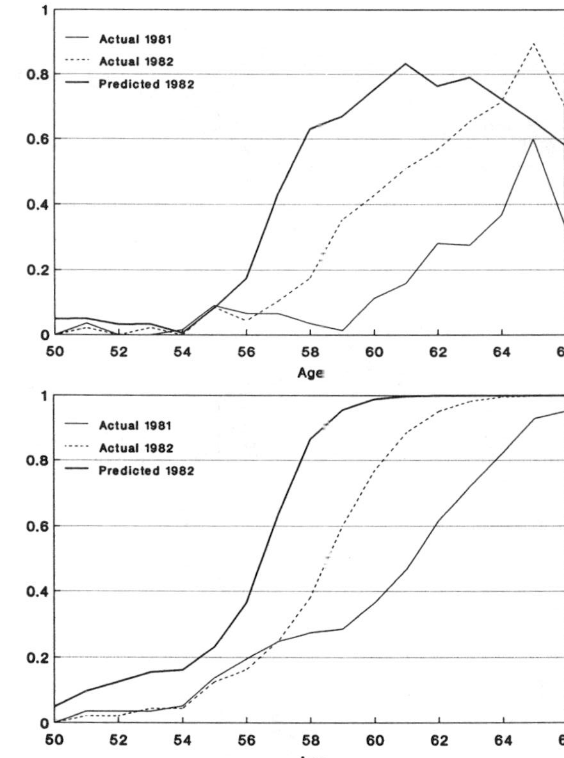

Fig. 1.7b Predicted vs. actual departure rates and implicit cumulative departures under the 1982 window plan, based on 1980 parameter estimates, and 1981 actual rates: probit model 6

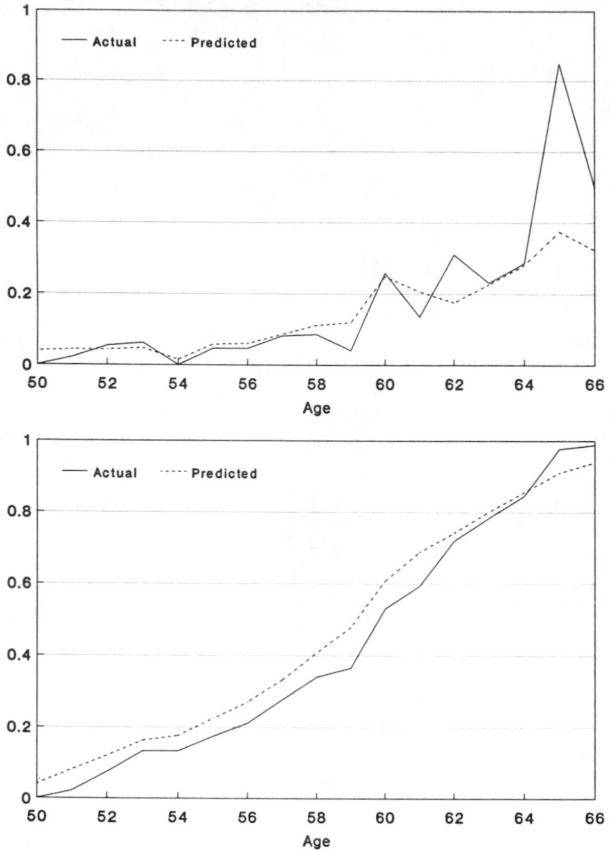

Fig. 1.8a Predicted vs. actual departure rates and implicit cumulative departures, by age: probit model 8

1.4 A Simulation: The Elimination of the Social Security Early Retirement Option

As a further comparison of the models, we have simulated the effect of removing the SS early retirement option so that SS benefits are only available beginning at age 65. A comparison of predicted retirement rates with and without the SS early retirement is shown in table 1.3 by model for ages 60–65.

According to the simulation based on the option value model, eliminating SS early retirement reduces predicted retirement rates among persons 62–64 by about 23 percent. The extreme value dynamic programming specification shows noticeably larger effects, but the effects based on the normal dynamic programming specification are smaller than the option value estimated effects.

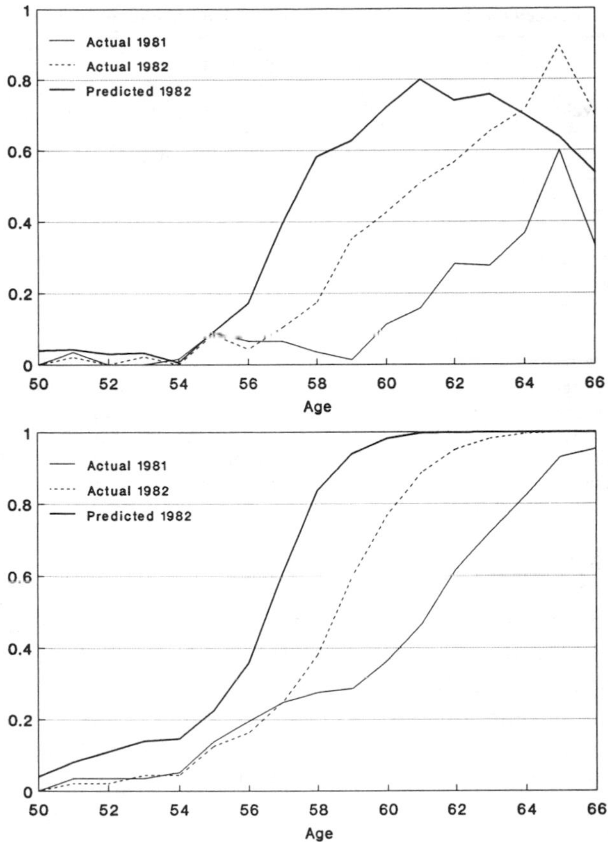

Fig. 1.8b Predicted vs. actual departure rates and implicit cumulative departures under the 1982 window plan, based on 1980 parameter estimates, and 1981 actual rates: probit model 8

Because a large proportion of employees in this firm have already left the firm before 62, the reduction applies to only the small proportion of employees who are still working, and thus the effect on the overall retirement is small. To the extent that these reductions generalize to workers not covered by defined benefit plans with incentives for early retirement, these estimates suggest that an increase in the SS early retirement age would have a very substantial effect on labor force participation. A large proportion of retired persons relies almost exclusively on SS benefits for retirement income. According to these estimates, substantially fewer of these employees would leave the labor force if they could not collect SS benefits.

Because of data limitations, it has been common to use parameter estimates from models that exclude firm pension plan data to simulate the effect of changes in SS provisions. To demonstrate the potential effect of the exclusion

Table 1.3 Retirement Rates in 1980 with and without Social Security Early Retirement

			Dynamic Programming					
	Option Value		Extreme Value		Normal		Probit	
Age	With	Without	With	Without	With	Without	With	Without
60	.233	.229	.188	.172	.214	.199	.249	.242
61	.204	.197	.176	.142	.190	.170	.206	.201
62	.262	.218	.269	.177	.241	.205	.175	.136
63	.313	.258	.314	.214	.277	.240	.227	.155
64	.360	.294	.305	.230	.284	.258	.281	.175
65	.346	.346	.320	.320	.314	.314	.375	.375

Note: The entries are the predicted retirement rates from maximum likelihood estimates of option value model 2, dynamic programming model 2, dynamic programming model 5, and probit specification 8. See the notes to tables 1.1 and 1.2. "With" refers to the base (current) specification. "Without" estimates are from a simulation that eliminates the possibility of SS receipt as early as age 62. Under the simulation, SS benefit receipt begins at age 65. Details are provided in the text.

of firm plans, we have estimated the dynamic programming normal model (specification 5) using only SS benefits—instead of SS and the firm pension benefits—and these estimates have been used to simulate the effect of the elimination of SS early retirement. The results are shown in table 1.4, where they are compared to the dynamic programming normal estimates. The estimated effect of the elimination of SS early retirement is much greater when the firm pension is not accounted for. For example, the retirement rate at 62 is reduced from .291 to .081; the base model yields a reduction from .241 to .205.

1.5 Summary

We have compared the in-sample and out-of-sample predictive performance of three models of retirement. The goal was to determine which of the retirement rules most closely matched observed retirement behavior in a large firm. The primary measure of predictive validity was the correspondence between the model predictions of retirement behavior and actual retirement under the firm window plan. Model parameter estimates were obtained on the basis of retirement in 1980. These estimates were then used to predict retirement in 1982 when the window plan was in effect. Retirement rates of persons eligible for the window plan bonus typically doubled in 1982 compared to earlier (and later) years.

The option value and the dynamic programming models fit the sample data equally well, with a slight advantage to the normal dynamic programming model. Both models correctly predicted a very large increase in retirement under the window plan, with some advantage in fit to the option value model.

Table 1.4 **Retirement Rates in 1980 with and without Social Security Early Retirement, Comparison with Estimates Based on Social Security Only, Using Dynamic Programming Normal Specification**

	Dynamic Programming: Normal			
	Base (SS & pension data)		SS Data Only	
Age	With	Without	With	Without
60	.214	.199	.114	.057
61	.190	.170	.167	.067
62	.241	.205	.291	.081
63	.277	.240	.310	.118
64	.284	.258	.334	.191
65	.314	.314	.356	.356

In short, this evidence suggests that the option value and dynamic programming models are considerably more successful than the less complex probit model in approximating the rules individuals use to make retirement decisions but that the more complex dynamic programming rule approximates behavior no better than the simpler option value rule. More definitive conclusions will have to await accumulated evidence based on additional comparisons using different data sets and with respect to different pension plan provisions.

Appendix A
The Firm Retirement Plan

To understand the effect of the pension plan provisions, figure 1A.1 shows the expected future compensation of a person from our sample who is 50 years old and has been employed by the firm for twenty years. For convenience, figure 1A.1 assumes a 5 percent real discount rate and zero inflation. In the estimated model reported in section 1.3, the discount rate is estimated, and the inflation rate is assumed to be 5 percent. Total compensation from the firm can be viewed as the sum of wage earnings, the accrual of pension benefits, and the accrual of Social Security benefits. (This omits medical and other unobserved benefits that should be included as compensation but on which we do not have data.) As compensation for working another year, the employee receives salary earnings. He also receives compensation in the form of future pension benefits. The annual compensation in this form is the change in the present value of the future pension benefits entitlement due to working an additional year. This accrual is comparable to wage earnings. The accrual of

Social Security benefits may also be calculated in a similar manner and is also comparable to wage earnings. Figure 1A.1 shows the present value at age 50 of expected future compensation in all three forms. The line labeled "wage earnings" represents cumulated earnings by age of retirement (more precisely, by age of departure from the firm, since some workers might well continue to work in another job). For example, if the person were to retire at age 62, his cumulated earnings between age 50 and age 62, discounted to age-50 dollars, would be about $144,000. The slope of the earnings line represents annual earnings discounted to age-50 dollars.

The solid line shows the accrual of firm pension plus Social Security benefits, again discounted to age-50 dollars. The shape of this profile is determined primarily by the pension plan provisions. The plan's normal retirement age is 65, and the early retirement age is 55. Cliff vesting occurs at ten years of service. Normal retirement benefits at age 65 are determined by age times years of service, multiplied by some constant factor. The most important additional provisions—those that determine the shape of the profile in figure 1A.1—are described here; full details of the plan provisions are presented in Kotlikoff and Wise (1987). The present value of retirement benefits increases between 50 and 54 because years of service, and possibly earnings, increase. An employee could leave the firm at age 53, for example. If he were to do that, and if he were vested in the firm's pension plan, he would be entitled to normal retirement pension benefits at age 65, based on his years of service and *current* dollar earnings at age 53. He could start to receive benefits as early as age 55, the pension early retirement age, but the benefit amount would be reduced actuarially. Thus, in present value terms, the stream of benefits received beginning at 55 would be equal to the stream of benefits beginning at 65; the annual benefit amount would be reduced just enough to offset the receipt of benefits for ten more years. If he started to receive benefits at age 55, they would be only 36 percent of the dollar amount he would receive at age 65. If, however, he were to remain in the firm until the early retirement age, the situation would be quite different. He would be entitled to normal retirement benefits based on his years of service and salary at age 55. But if he were to start to receive them at age 55, the benefits would be reduced less than actuarially, about 3 percent for each year that retirement precedes age 65, instead of 6 or 7 percent.

In addition, the plan has a Social Security offset provision. Pension benefits are offset by a specified amount, depending on the firm estimate of Social Security benefits. But if the person takes early retirement, between 55 and 65, the Social Security offset is not applied to benefits received before age 65. These two provisions create the large discontinuous jump in retirement benefits at age 55—from about $33,000 to $56,000. This increase is equivalent to more than 130 percent of his annual wage earnings at 55. Thus, there is an enormous bonus for remaining with the firm until that age. After age 55, however, the person who does not retire forgoes the opportunity of taking pension

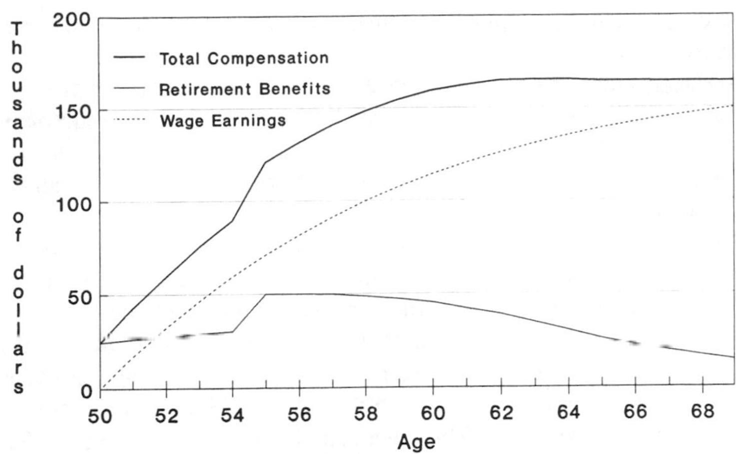

Fig. 1A.1 Present discounted values of future earnings and retirement benefits, as a function of date of retirement

benefits on very advantageous terms—thus the minimal change in the discounted value of benefits between 55 and 60.

If a person has thirty years of service at age 60, he is entitled to full normal retirement benefits. No early retirement reduction is applied to benefits if they are taken then. That is, by continuing to work, he will no longer gain from fewer years of early retirement reduction, as he did before age 60—thus the kink in the profile and the decline thereafter.

The top line shows total compensation. For example, if the employee were to leave the firm at age 60, his wage earnings between 50 and 60 would be $126,000, shown by the wage earnings line. Thereafter, he would receive firm pension plan and Social Security retirement benefits with a present value—at age 50—of about $58,000. The sum of the two is about $184,000, shown by the top line. The large jump at 55 reflects the early retirement provisions of the pension plan. Total compensation declines modestly each year through age 60 and very rapidly thereafter. After age 62 or 63, annual total compensation is close to zero.

Appendix B
Tabulations of Predicted and Actual Retirement Rates

This appendix presents tabulations of the values presented graphically in figures 1.1–1.2. These figures are the predicted and actual retirement rates, or hazard rates, for the employees in the data set and the associated cumulative retirement rates.

The actual retirement rates for each age group are the fraction of workers of that age who retire during the indicated year. The predicted retirement rates are the aggregate rates predicted by the indicated model; that is, the predicted retirement rate is the average predicted probability of retiring for all workers of the indicated age.

The cumulative retirement rates are computed from the single-year retirement rates by following a cohort of one hundred 50-year-olds at the firm for the next twenty years, assuming that the annual retirement rates for this cohort are the same as the annual retirement rates for the indicated year, predicted or actual, as the case may be. For example, in 1980, the actual retirement rates (in our sample of 993 workers) of 50-, 51-, and 52-year-olds were, respectively, .00, .022, and .054. Thus, the cumulative retirement rate for 52-year-olds is $1 - (1 - .00)(1 - .022)(1 - .054) = .075$.

The numbering of the tables in this appendix corresponds to the numbering of the figures in the text: the values plotted in figure 1.1a appear in table 1B.1a, etc.

Table 1B.1a **Data for Figure 1.1a**

Age	No. of Observations	Cumulative Retirement Rates		Annual Retirement Rates	
		Actual	Predicted	Actual	Predicted
50	83	.000	.023	.000	.023
51	89	.022	.042	.022	.019
52	74	.075	.055	.054	.014
53	64	.133	.067	.063	.012
54	77	.133	.079	.000	.013
55	64	.174	.167	.047	.095
56	64	.212	.246	.047	.095
57	61	.277	.324	.082	.104
58	81	.340	.419	.086	.141
59	74	.366	.506	.041	.149
60	85	.530	.621	.259	.233
61	37	.594	.698	.135	.204
62	42	.720	.777	.310	.262
63	39	.784	.847	.231	.313
64	35	.846	.902	.286	.360
65	20	.977	.936	.850	.346
66	4	.988	.954	.500	.283

Note: The actual retirement rates were computed for the 1,000 persons in the sample. The predicted retirement rates are based on option value model 2.

Table 1B.1b **Data for Figure 1.1b**

	Cumulative Retirement Rates			Annual Retirement Rates		
Age	Actual 1981	Actual 1982	Predicted 1982	Actual 1981	Actual 1982	Predicted 1982
50	.000	.000	.023	.000	.000	.023
51	.036	.022	.042	.036	.022	.019
52	.036	.022	.053	.000	.000	.012
53	.036	.044	.059	.000	.023	.006
54	.052	.044	.062	.017	.000	.003
55	.139	.126	.192	.091	.085	.139
56	.195	.163	.323	.066	.043	.162
57	.249	.251	.480	.066	.105	.232
58	.276	.382	.635	.036	.175	.299
59	.286	.600	.758	.014	.352	.335
60	.366	.770	.860	.113	.425	.424
61	.467	.887	.923	.159	.508	.448
62	.617	.951	.961	.281	.566	.498
63	.723	.983	.978	.276	.652	.444
64	.824	.995	.988	.367	.714	.445
65	.930	.999	.993	.600	.895	.454
66	.953	1.000	.996	.333	.700	.449

Note: Based on 1980 option value model 2 parameter estimates, reported in table 1.2. The simulation is described in the text.

Table 1B.2a **Data for Figure 1.2a**

		Cumulative Retirement Rates			Annual Retirement Rates		
Age	No. of Observations	Actual	Option Value	Dynamic Programming	Actual	Option Value	Dynamic Programming
50	83	.000	.023	.021	.000	.023	.021
51	89	.022	.042	.043	.022	.019	.022
52	74	.075	.055	.065	.054	.014	.023
53	64	.133	.067	.090	.063	.012	.027
54	77	.133	.079	.117	.000	.013	.029
55	64	.174	.167	.179	.047	.095	.070
56	64	.212	.246	.240	.047	.095	.074
57	61	.277	.324	.303	.082	.104	.082
58	81	.340	.419	.381	.086	.141	.112
59	74	.366	.506	.461	.041	.149	.129
60	85	.530	.621	.562	.259	.233	.188
61	37	.594	.698	.639	.135	.204	.176
62	42	.720	.777	.736	.310	.262	.269
63	39	.784	.847	.819	.231	.313	.314
64	35	.846	.902	.874	.286	.360	.305
65	20	.977	.936	.914	.850	.346	.320
66	4	.988	.954	.940	.500	.283	.295

Table 1B.2b **Data for Figure 1.2b**

	Cumulative Retirement Rates				Annual Retirement Rates			
Age	Actual 1981	Actual 1982	Predicted Option Value 1982	Predicted Dynamic Programming 1982	Actual 1981	Actual 1982	Predicted Option Value 1982	Predicted Dynamic Programming 1982
50	.000	.000	.023	.021	.000	.000	.023	.021
51	.036	.022	.042	.043	.036	.022	.019	.022
52	.036	.022	.053	.062	.000	.000	.012	.020
53	.036	.044	.059	.082	.000	.023	.006	.022
54	.052	.044	.062	.103	.017	.000	.003	.023
55	.139	.126	.192	.199	.091	.085	.139	.107
56	.195	.163	.323	.329	.066	.043	.162	.162
57	.249	.251	.480	.506	.066	.105	.232	.264
58	.276	.382	.635	.696	.036	.175	.299	.384
59	.286	.600	.758	.827	.014	.352	.335	.430
60	.366	.770	.860	.917	.113	.425	.424	.524
61	.467	.887	.923	.967	.159	.508	.448	.604
62	.617	.951	.961	.990	.281	.566	.498	.703
63	.723	.983	.978	.997	.276	.652	.444	.693
64	.824	.995	.988	.999	.367	.714	.445	.622
65	.930	.999	.993	.999	.600	.895	.454	.543
66	.953	1.000	.996	1.000	.333	.700	.449	.457

References

Berkovec, James, and Steven Stern. 1991. Job Exit Behavior of Older Men. *Econometrica* 59 (1):189–210.

Burtless, Gary. 1986. Social Security, Unanticipated Benefit Increases, and the Timing of Retirement. *Review of Economic Studies* 53 (October):781–805.

Daula, Thomas V., and Robert A. Moffitt. 1991. Estimating a Dynamic Programming Model of Army Reenlistment Behavior. In *Military Compensation and Personnel Retention: Models and Evidence,* ed. C. L. Gilroy, D. K. Horne, and D. Alton Smith. Alexandria, Va.: U.S. Army Research Institute for the Behavioral and Social Sciences.

Gustman, Alan, and Thomas Steinmeier. 1986. A Structural Retirement Model. *Econometrica* 54:555–84.

Hausman, Jerry A., and David A. Wise. 1985. Social Security, Health Status, and Retirement. In *Pensions, Labor, and Individual Choice,* ed. David A. Wise, 159–91. Chicago: University of Chicago Press.

Hurd, Michael, and Michael Boskin. 1981. The Effect of Social Security on Retirement in the Early 1970s. *Quarterly Journal of Economics* 46 (November):767–90.

Kotlikoff, Laurence J., and David A. Wise. 1987. The Incentive Effects of Private Pension Plans. In *Issues in Pension Economics,* ed. Z. Bodie, J. Shoven, and D. Wise, 283–339. Chicago: University of Chicago Press.

Lumsdaine, Robin L., James H. Stock, and David A. Wise. 1990. Efficient Windows and Labor Force Reduction. *Journal of Public Economics* 43:131–59.

———. 1991. Fenêtres et retraites (Windows and retirement). *Annales d'Économie et de Statistique* 20/21:220–42.

Rust, John P. 1989. A Dynamic Programming Model of Retirement Behavior. In *The Economics of Aging*, ed. David A. Wise, 359–98. Chicago: University of Chicago Press.

Stock, James H., and David A. Wise. 1990a. The Pension Inducement to Retire: An Option Value Analysis. In *Issues in the Economics of Aging*, ed. David A. Wise, 205–24. Chicago: University of Chicago Press.

———. 1990b. Pensions, the Option Value of Work, and Retirement. *Econometrica* 58 (5):1151–80.

Comment Sylvester J. Schieber

In their paper, Robin L. Lumsdaine, James H. Stock, and David A. Wise evaluate the complexity of models versus their validity in predicting the retirement rates of older male workers in a large firm. The firm, coincidentally, offered an early retirement window that allowed them to test the alternative models being considered by comparing predicted retirement rates at various ages with actual rates.

The paper is extremely interesting and is headed down an important track. Understanding the responses to retirement incentives that employers offer their employees is of interest to both the public policy and the employer communities. It is important to policymakers in the development of macro policy as shown by the authors' analysis of the effect of the early retirement option under Social Security. It is important to employers in the development of micro policies that are aimed at controlling their work forces through the structuring of incentives encouraging the continued work or retirement of older workers. Employers are particularly interested in anticipating the responses to special incentive programs that they introduce to encourage some of their workers to leave their current jobs. The introduction of an early retirement window by the firm on which the authors had data offered an ideal opportunity to test these models' relative predictive capabilities. While I found the paper interesting and to be moving in the right direction, I will voice a number of criticisms toward the end of my comments.

The authors test three different models in the course of their analysis. Their basic model, or at least the first one evaluated in the paper, is an "option value" model, described in Stock and Wise's earlier work.[1] In the option value model, an employee compares the value of retiring today with the maximum

Sylvester J. Schieber is a vice president of the Wyatt Company and director of its Consulting Support Services in Washington, D.C.

1. James H. Stock and David A. Wise, "Pensions, the Option Value of Work, and Retirement," *Econometrica* 58, no. 5 (September 1990): 1151–80.

of the value of retiring at discrete times in the future. If the difference is greater than zero, then the individual continues to work.

I find the option value model appealing because it corresponds with what I believe employers implicitly assume in designing their retirement programs. Employers today are in a position that they cannot systematically terminate older workers because of the Age Discrimination in Employment Act (ADEA). Yet they have concluded that the relative productivity of workers begins to decline at some age between 55 and 65.[2] Given the ADEA restrictions, the only way employers can get rid of workers with declining productivity is to bid them out of the firm. Using the option value model, a person will continue to work if the option value of postponing retirement is greater than zero. The employer typically structures the retirement plan in such a way that the option value of continuing to work is less than zero for most workers attaining some age. They do this by providing early retirement incentives in their pension plans. They can selectively override these early retirement incentives (i.e., manipulate the option value of continuing to work or retiring) by increasing current pay for those older workers they want to keep.

The parameters in the option value model are developed by estimation. The second model the authors consider, their probit model, is a variant of the option value model, except that the gains from added work life are based on assumed values and discount rates. The third model, a stochastic dynamic programming model, considers the expected value of maximum current options versus future options. Under this model, at the beginning of each year the worker decides to take up the utility of the retirement benefits or to work another year, deriving the utility of the related earnings and retaining the option to make another choice next year.

In terms of computational complexity, the models would be ranked from the easiest (the probit model) to the most complex (the stochastic dynamic programming model). The probit model does not generate nearly as good predictions of retirement under the window plan as the other two models, which are roughly equivalent.

One criticism of the paper is that the authors are looking at quit rates rather than retirement. There is likely to be a considerable amount of second career activity going on for individuals who are eligible to partake of many early retirement incentive programs, especially early retirement window plans. Certainly, workers looking at other job opportunities would be facing significantly different option values for quitting a firm under the circumstances described here than the option values of retirement they would face.

Another aspect of the value of continued work as it relates to quit or retirement decisions overlooked in the analysis is the availability of pre-65 retiree

2. There is no explicit information available documenting employers' conclusion that productivity begins to decline at a specific age. But the incentive effects in pension plans encouraging retirement at specific ages are strong implicit evidence that employers have concluded that they want certain workers to leave the firm.

health benefits and the health care needs of workers and their dependents. In some cases, the value of early retirement health benefits may actually exceed the value of lifetime pension benefits. In a similar vein, the availability of a defined contribution plan that would supplement the basic defined benefit plan should be considered in modeling retirement behavior.

The application of the three models to only one firm might render the consideration of early retirement benefits and defined contribution plan accumulations irrelevant if the firm did not have either type of plan. But that in itself is a problem. The models should be tested further over a range of firms with varying incentives in their basic pension benefits, but also with varying availability and generosity of these other supplemental plans.

In evaluating the relevance of being able to predict retirement under situations where explicit incentives are being offered, it is important to be able to predict how many workers will retire. The option value and stochastic dynamic programming models do a relatively good job in that regard. It is equally important, however, for employers to be able to predict which workers will quit under the plan. So the models should be evaluated on their ability to predict the quitters quitting and the stayers staying.

When employers offer early retirement windows, they never expect all eligible workers to take advantage of the incentives. They are typically looking to get rid of the less productive workers among the whole group to whom they offer the incentive. The window is considered to be only partly successful if the wrong people retire. The models were not tested in this regard. One problem with applying such a test would be in identifying which people the company wanted to keep and which they did not. One possible way of discriminating between the two groups is to look at wage increases over the prior two or three years. Presumably, a substantial wage increase above the norm for other workers in the company would be the company's way of indicating the employee's relative productivity. A worker who received a relatively low wage increase would presumably be perceived as relatively marginal.

The conventional wisdom on window plans is that they often, if not almost always, encourage the wrong people to quit the firms offering them. This suggests, at the applied level, that the options value model is not working, or at least that it does not appear to be working within the context that Lumsdaine, Stock, and Wise are testing it. If the firm is acting rationally and giving the workers they desire to keep good raises, it would suggest that the workers' option value for continuing to work should be positive. The converse is true for the workers the firm desires to have quit. Yet the keepers seem to leave, and the dregs seem to stay under window plans. If this is the case, it would be an interesting phenomenon to evaluate with the models being tested here. To do so would require added information on the quitters' subsequent work behavior. I suspect that there is a rational explanation for what generally seems to happen under these window plans that could be tested.

Through the process of annual reviews, raises, bonuses, etc., most employers tell their good workers that they are good. When they communicate a window plan, they tell their workers that things are not going well at the firm. The workers who are good and know that they are good, because they have been told, find the option value of quitting the firm greater than zero but the option value of retiring less than zero. They conclude, "I'm good, but my situation is bad, and my employer is offering me a bonus to tide me over during a transition." They take the money and run.

The poor performers, on the other hand, have been getting the message that they are not very productive people. The window communicates to them that the economic situation in the marketplace is not good. They perceive that their option value of continuing to work is greater than zero and that the value of continuing in their current job exceeds that of the alternatives they face. They conclude, "I may not get any more pay raises if I stay here, but at least I will get paid. Also, I do not have a good record to take to a bad market." Therefore, they stay put.

Finally, in closing, I would like to propose an alternative model to the ones tested by the authors. It is a simplified options value model, which I would characterize as a goals attainment model. Most workers do not calculate the present value of alternative income streams from working or retiring to decide when the combined value of a retirement income stream plus their added leisure more than offsets the value of their income stream if they continue to work.

Most workers want to maintain some preconceived standard of living in retirement. Employers gear much of the employee communications material to explaining the level of benefits their retirement plans provide and the target levels workers have to attain to reach their retirement income goals. Employees use this material to help define their goals, but they calculate their options values by looking around. They know people they have worked with over the years who have retired under their employer's plans or similar plans provided by other employers. They can tell which of those former workers are able to maintain a standard of living to which they themselves aspire and which are not. Through a process of elimination, they determine which of those former employees have the characteristics that they have to roughly match in order for their retirement goals to be met. Once they match the characteristics that they believe correlate with their retirement income goals, they retire.

2 Stocks, Bonds, and Pension Wealth

Thomas E. MaCurdy and John B. Shoven

For many people, the present value of their future pension annuity is their largest financial asset. The retirement income may come from a variety of pension accumulations, including defined contribution plans, defined benefit plans, individual retirement accounts, Keogh plans, and tax deferred annuity plans. With many of these accumulation vehicles, the individual participant bears the responsibility of determining the assets in which the funds are invested and bears any uncertainty about the rate of return that will be realized on those assets. In choosing between stocks and bonds for their pension accumulation vehicle, most people probably know that bonds have a lower average return and a lower variance in return; bonds offer additional "safety" at the expense of a lower expected outcome. While this risk-return trade-off is both correct and well understood for short-term investment horizons, the extent to which it applies for long holding periods is not clear. For many workers, the time between the current contribution to the retirement account and the purchase of an annuity is thirty years or more. What is the relative risk and return on stocks versus bonds for such a long horizon? The pension participant typically not only has a long horizon but also makes many contributions throughout his or her career. For example, faculty at Stanford University make payments to their retirement accounts twice each month over their term of employment. How does such a pattern of purchase affect the relative desirability of stocks versus bonds as pension accumulation assets? Finally, most

Thomas E. MaCurdy is professor of economics, Department of Economics, and senior fellow, Hoover Institution, Stanford University, and a research associate of the National Bureau of Economic Research. John B. Shoven is professor of economics, Department of Economics, and director of the Center for Economic Policy Research, Stanford University, and a research associate of the National Bureau of Economic Research.

This research was supported by the Center for Economic Policy Research at Stanford University. The authors would like to thank Steven N. Weisbart of TIAA-CREF for both advice and valuable data. They also would like to acknowledge the excellent research assistance of Stanford graduate students Bart Hamilton and Hilary Hoynes.

individual retirement accounts, Keogh plans, and defined contribution plans allow the participant not only to choose which assets are purchased with new contributions but also to move existing accumulations between asset categories. This raises the question of the desirability of gradually moving stock accumulations into bonds late in one's career. Such an option offers the potential advantage that one's retirement annuity would depend on the value of the stock portfolio at several selling dates rather than just its value on the date of purchase of the annuity.

Several papers investigate the effect of the length of investment horizon on optimal portfolio composition (e.g., Fischer 1983; and Merton and Samuelson 1974). Typically, these papers attempt to estimate the stochastic processes generating the returns on different assets, within some assumed class of models, and then determine optimal portfolios based on the maximization of expected lifetime utility, with the form of the utility function somewhat arbitrarily chosen. In general, these studies do not find that the length of the horizon unambiguously changes the optimal portfolio mix between stocks and bonds.

Our approach is quite different from the existing literature, and our results are more striking. We examine how some naive investment strategies for pension accumulations would have performed for employment careers of varying length between 1926 and 1989. Given a strategy, we calculate the implied value for the pension account at the time of retirement for all possible completed careers of a specified horizon within the sixty-four-year period. We consider only strategies in which investors allocate their pension contributions either entirely into stocks (with all dividends and other returns reinvested in stocks) or entirely into bonds (with interest reinvested in bonds). These strategies are not optimal in any sense since they ignore any market timing issues as well as standard portfolio theory. We then consider some strategies for converting from stocks to bonds as a worker approaches retirement, but we do not attempt to determine the optimal portfolio composition as a function of years until retirement. Despite these limitations, we find that an "all stocks" strategy dominates all other investment policies considered for all career lengths of twenty-five years or longer. By "domination," we mean that an all stocks allocation would have generated a larger pension accumulation for every career that ended in retirement over the period 1926–89.

Our findings have important implications for pension investment policies, and they suggest that the vast majority of people choose the wrong accumulation strategies. Not only are our results applicable to defined contribution plans, but they are also relevant for defined benefit pension programs and for other long-horizon saving targets.

2.1 Stock and Bond Returns

For calculating pension accumulations, our primary data source is the monthly-total-return statistics for stocks and bonds assembled by Ibbotson

Associates and published in their *Stocks, Bonds, Bills and Inflation: 1990 Yearbook*. For stock accumulations we use their monthly figures for the Standard and Poor's 500 Stock Composite Index (S&P 500), and for bond portfolio accumulations we use their monthly long-term corporate bond series, which is based on an index compiled by Salomon Brothers for long-term, high-grade corporate bonds. Both the series are available from December 1925 to December 1989.

The statistics of the annual inflation-adjusted returns for the S&P 500, for long-term corporate bonds, and for T-bills are shown below for 1926–88:

Asset	*Arithmetic Mean (%)*	*Standard Deviation (%)*
S&P 500	8.8	21.1
Long-term corporates	2.4	10.0
U.S. Treasury bills	.5	.5

Note that equities have an average yield premium of 6.4 percent over long-term corporate bonds. These mean real rates of return imply that $1.00 invested in December 1925 in the S&P 500 would have grown with dividends reinvested to roughly $76.00 in real terms by the end of 1989. One dollar invested in long-term corporate bonds would have grown to only $3.62 in constant dollar terms, whereas $1.00 invested in T-bills (and rolled over for the sixty-four years) would have grown to a real $1.37.

In another paper (MaCurdy and Shoven 1990), we document that stock investments generated higher returns for all holding periods twenty years and longer over the period 1926–89. Any one-time investment held for more than twenty years (with returns reinvested) would show a higher return if the asset was the S&P 500 than if it was a diversified portfolio of bonds, regardless of the date of purchase and the date of sale. The size of the equity premium is a fairly well-known puzzle since it seems to indicate an implausible degree of risk aversion. Our results in this other study suggest that holding a diversified portfolio including bonds rather than a pure stock portfolio for a period of more than twenty years would require an almost infinite degree of risk aversion since there has never been a span of time for which this strategy would be profitable.

We recognize that pension participants did not have the precise investment vehicles that we use to represent the returns on stock and bond funding strategies. Index funds, which nearly exactly reproduce the Ibbotson series, have been available only for the past few years. However, the S&P 500 index is a standard benchmark against which other diversified stock portfolios are compared.

In our pension accumulation calculations presented below, we attempt to capture the situation faced by college professors in making choices between CREF (a broadly diversified common stock portfolio) and TIAA (a bond portfolio). To compare the rate of return on the S&P 500 with the return on CREF, figure 2.1 plots the two annual rate-of-return series. The correspondence between the two series is so strong that one can barely identify the presence of

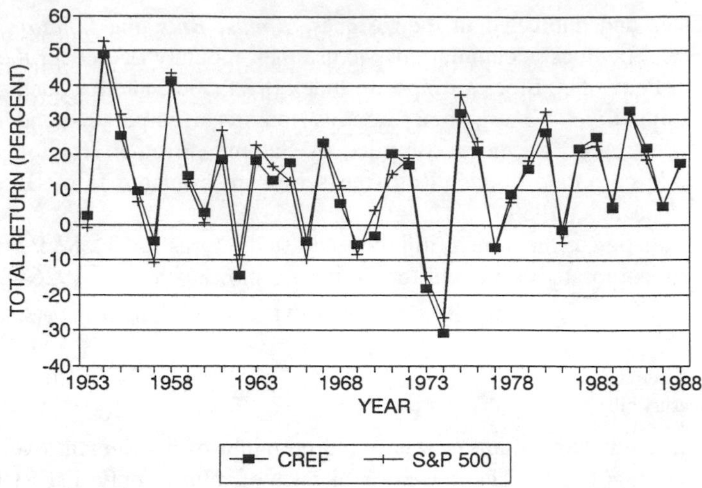

Fig. 2.1 Annual total rate of return on CREF and the S&P 500

two plots. We interpret this finding to indicate that the Ibbotson series for stocks is a reliable proxy for CREF's rate of return.

The bonds making up TIAA are higher yield and lower quality than those in the Ibbotson index. The Salomon Brothers long-term corporate bond index is a measure of the return earned by portfolios of high-grade corporate bonds. Funds that concentrate on private placements, "high-yield" bonds, and debt contracts with equity "kickers," such as TIAA, may perform differently than the Salomon Brothers index. Therefore, we feel that, while the Ibbotson bond index is completely satisfactory as a measure of the return on high-grade corporate bonds, it is a somewhat less satisfactory proxy for TIAAs returns.

2.2 Pension Accumulations

To characterize the implications of alternative investment strategies in pensions, we require a specification for the life-cycle profiles describing the earnings of cohorts over time, combined with an assumption about the fraction of earnings invested in pensions at each age. We formulate profiles designed to measure the earnings of academics over the period 1926–89. We further assume that each person contributes a fixed fraction of his current earnings to his pension fund each month throughout his working career. While we consider the case of college professors in carrying out this exercise, we believe that our findings are broadly applicable to any pension system where contributions are made periodically and are proportional to earnings.

2.2.1 Construction of Earnings Profiles

To describe our formulation of earnings profiles, let $\omega(c, \alpha)$ denote the annual nominal earnings of individuals who started jobs as assistant professors in September of the calendar year c when these persons reach α years of academic experience. The variable c indexes the cohort to which an individual belongs; it signals the academic year in which the group enters the profession. Assuming that all individuals making up an entry cohort are the same age in year c, the variable α equals the age of the cohort in the current year minus the cohort's age at the time of entry. With the variable t introduced to represent the relevant calendar year, the quantity $\omega(c, t - c)$ gives the annual earnings of cohort c in academic year t.

To construct the earnings quantities $\omega(c, \alpha)$, we combine data on academic salaries from several sources. From the *Campus Report* published by Stanford University on 22 March 1989, we acquired information on "cross-sectional" wage profiles for the academic year 1988–89. This publication reports graphs of the median of the annual salaries of assistant, associate, and full professors as functions of their seniority, which corresponds to a plot of the function $\omega(t - \alpha, \alpha)$ against α. Using data from the *Campus Report* to construct linear salary schedules for the year $t = 1988$ for assistant, associate, and full professors, we developed the following cross-sectional profile:

$$(1)\quad \omega(1988 - \alpha, \alpha) \equiv g(\alpha) = \begin{cases} 34{,}039 + 640\,\alpha & \text{for } \alpha = 0, 1, \ldots, 5; \\ 43{,}357 + 1{,}725(\alpha - 6) & \text{for } \alpha = 6, 7, \ldots, 10; \\ 64{,}012 + 622(\alpha - 11) & \text{for } \alpha \geq 11. \end{cases}$$

This formulation presumes that an individual spends six years as an assistant professor, five years as an associate professor, and the remainder of his or her career as a full professor.

Combining this cross-sectional profile with data on the growth of faculty salaries over the period 1926–89 provides sufficient information to calculate values for the annual earnings of all cohorts over this period. Define $r(t)$ as the annual nominal growth in faculty salaries. Assuming that wage growth in each year exerts a common influence on the earnings of all cohorts in that year yields the result:

$$(2)\qquad \omega(c, t - c) = \frac{g(\alpha)}{\prod_{k=t+1}^{1989} [1 + r(k)]}$$

where the spline function $g(\alpha)$ is given by (1). We impute values for the growth rates $r(t)$ for the years $t = 1926, \ldots, 1989$ from three distinct sources. Over the period 1929–65, we compute growth rates as $r(t) = [\text{Ave}(t) - \text{Ave}(t - 1)]/\text{Ave}(t - 1)$ where Ave(t) represents the average annual salary in year t of full professors in the University of California system reported in *The Centennial Record of the University of California* (1967). Over the period 1966–67, we calculate $r(t)$ with Ave(t) designating the average annual salary of full-time faculty at Stanford University reported in the *AAUP Bulletin,* published in the summers of 1966 and 1967 by the American Association of University Professors. Finally, over the period 1968–89, we construct $r(t)$ using the average annual salary of full professors at Stanford University as the measure of Ave(t), which comes from unpublished data supplied by the Provost's Office of Stanford.

2.2.2 Pension Values with Constant Allocation Policies

To calculate the accumulation of pensions, we assume that an individual of cohort c invests a fixed fraction of $\omega(c, t - c)$ in each year t over his or her entire working career. We consider careers of twenty-five, thirty, thirty-five, and forty years for those cohorts who entered and retired during the period 1926–89. A pure stock pension strategy refers to a policy whereby individuals allocate all their contributions to stocks. A pure bond strategy corresponds to all contributions invested in bonds. To compare the performance of these two pension policies, we calculate the ratio of what a person would have accumulated at the time of retirement by adopting a pure stock strategy to the accumulation associated with a pure bond approach. This ratio is independent of the absolute level of salaries and the fraction of salary applied to retirement accumulations (as long as that fraction is constant).

Figures 2.2–2.5 present plots of these ratios evaluated at the year of retirement for careers of twenty-five, thirty, thirty-five, and forty years, respectively. The numbers associated with these plots are reported in table 2.1 under the columns entitled "Stock(1)." The term "Stock(1)" signifies that an individual following a pure stock strategy makes only one transfer out of stocks at the very end of his or her career; there are no transfers from stocks to bonds just prior to retirement in an attempt to reduce risk.

Figure 2.2 shows the results for a twenty-five year career. We feel that this is an improbably short career for retirement accumulation (particularly for professors whose plan is almost completely portable from one employer to another). The ratio ranges from 1.17 to 5.06 with an average value of 2.64. That is, even for careers this short, accumulation in stocks has always led to more wealth (and a proportionately larger annuity). On average, a 100 percent stock strategy would have resulted in more than two and a half times as much retirement wealth as a 100 percent long-term corporate bond strategy. For retirements in the 1980s, the ratio ranges from 1.28 to 1.78, averaging 1.48. While these ratios are small relative to those in the three to five range for the mid-1950s to mid-1960s, they still indicate that the stock accumulator always did better than the bond accumulator, and by a very significant amount.

Figure 2.4 shows our calculations of the same ratio for the more realistic career length of thirty-five years. With this horizon, the ratio ranges from 1.56 to 6.25, averaging 3.58. Thus, the person who systematically accumulated stocks over a thirty-five-year career always ended up with at least 56 percent more pension wealth than someone who made the same pattern of contributions to a portfolio consisting of only long-term corporate bonds. On average,

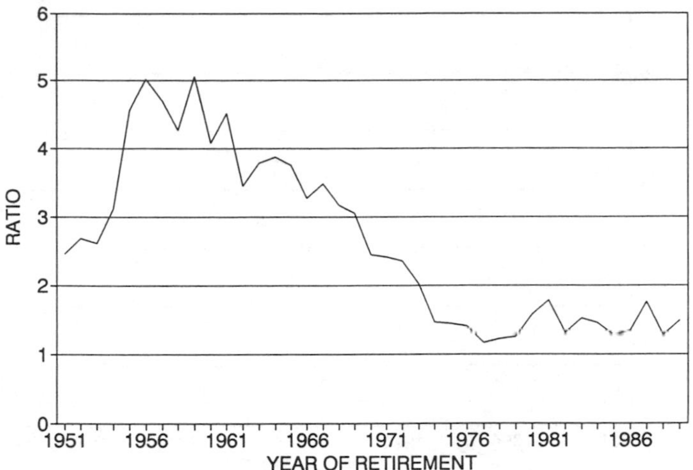

Fig. 2.2 Ratio of stock to bond accumulation for a twenty-five-year career

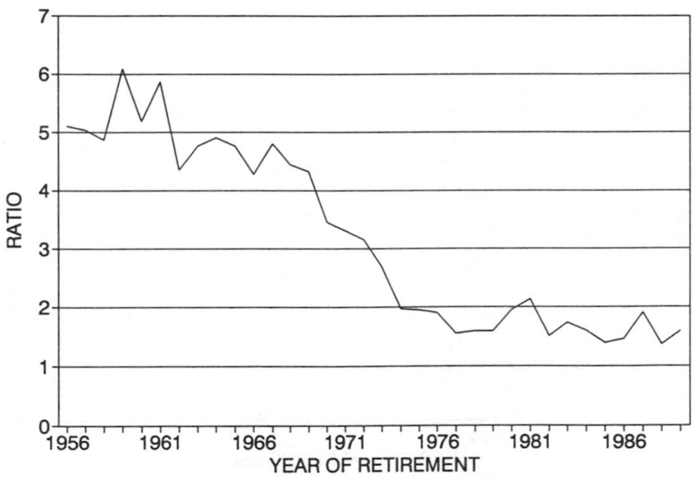

Fig. 2.3 Ratio of stock to bond accumulation for a thirty-year career

the stock strategy would have produced a monthly annuity in retirement that was over 3.5 times as large. The ratios for a forty-year career are even more dramatic, as seen in figure 2.5, with the minimum ratio of 1.95. Thus, the worst experience for a stock accumulator occurring in our data over a forty-year career was to end up with only 95 percent more pension wealth than someone investing in bonds.

It almost certainly is true that the variance in wealth at retirement is lower if one accumulates bonds rather than stocks. However, to say that bonds are a

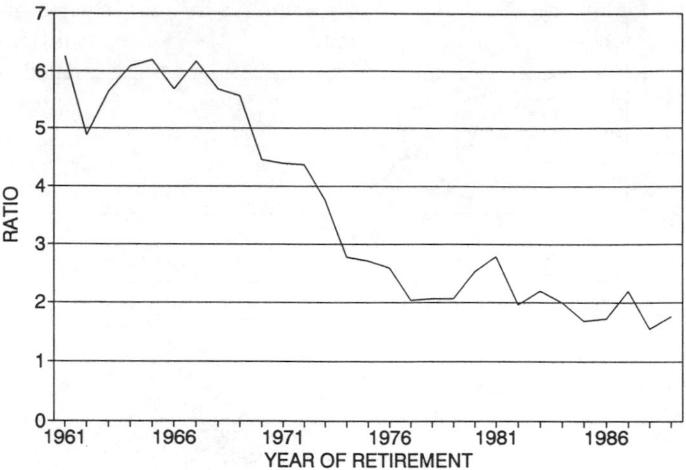

Fig. 2.4 Ratio of stock to bond accumulation for a thirty-five-year career

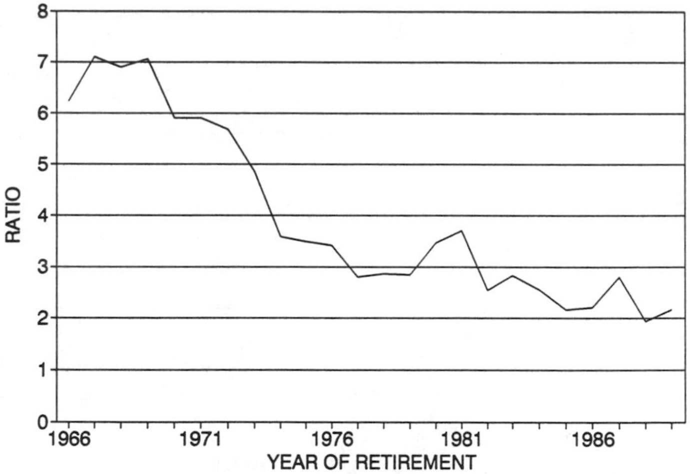

Fig. 2.5 Ratio of stock to bond accumulation for a forty-year career

safer investment vehicle seems fundamentally incorrect. The final wealth distribution with stock accumulation, even with its higher standard deviation, covers a range that is everywhere higher than the range associated with the bond distribution.

2.2.3 End of Career Strategies

The results shown in figures 2.2–2.5 assume that the stock accumulator does not deviate from a pure stock allocation strategy right up until retirement.

At the time of retirement, the wealth accumulation is evaluated and a life annuity purchased. A natural question to ask is whether one can significantly reduce the variance in the outcome by converting the accumulated stocks to bonds at multiple dates near the end of one's career. The idea, of course, is to reduce the importance of the level of the stock market on a particular day. The pension accumulator automatically does a lot of averaging by buying stock on many different dates. We now briefly examine the effect of some averaging on the sale dates.

We explore two simple end-of-career strategies designed to mitigate the risk of cashing out a 100 percent stock pension on a single day. The first involves making four transfers out of stocks, with one-quarter of the total accumulation sold at four distinct dates. We designate this investment policy as "Stock(4)." Nine months prior to retirement, an individual following a Stock(4) policy allocates all remaining pension contributions to bonds and converts one-quarter of his or her accumulated stock shares to bonds at quarterly intervals of nine, six, and three months before the retirement date. In the month of retirement, the resulting value of the diversified portfolio determines the pension accumulation associated with the Stock(4) policy. The second investment strategy examined the Stock(8) policy, eight transfers out of stocks. Following this strategy, an individual allocates all pension contributions to bonds starting twenty-one months prior to retirement. At quarterly intervals of twenty-one, eighteen, fifteen, twelve, nine, six, and three months preceding retirement, the person converts one-eighth of the stock accumulated at the twenty-one-month point into bonds. Thus, the pension value corresponding to a Stock(8) policy involves selling stocks at eight distinct dates distributed over a two-year period preceding retirement.

Table 2.1 reports the stock/bond ratios for the Stock(4) and the Stock(8) pension policies for careers of twenty-five, thirty, thirty-five, and forty years. Figures 2.6 and 2.7 plot the results comparing these two policies with the Stock(1) strategy considered above for the twenty-five- and thirty-five-year careers, respectively.

Naturally, such short-run sales strategies do not change the general shape of the gross return ratio curves. They do, however, effectively reduce the vulnerability to short-term movements in stock prices at the end of one's career. This is perhaps most clearly shown in 1961 and 1962 in table 2.1. Consider the case of a thirty-five-year career. Between 1961 and 1962, the ratio of the sell-all-stocks-at-the-end strategy to bonds falls from 6.25 to 4.88, whereas both the one- and the two-year averaging strategies do not suffer such sudden changes. The period 1986–88 offers another example. Recall that our participants begin their careers in September and retire twenty-five, thirty, thirty-five, or forty years later at the end of August. As many of us can remember, the stock market rose sharply in the first nine months of 1987, only to crash in October. For thirty-five-year careers, the sell-all-stocks-at-retirement strategy results in multiples relative to the wealth of bond accumulations of 1.72, 2.19,

Table 2.1 **Pension Savings: Ratio of Stock Plan to Bond Plan**

Retirement	25-Year Horizon			30-Year Horizon			35-Year Horizon			40-Year Horizon		
Year	Stock(1)	Stock(4)	Stock(8)	Stock(1)	Stock(4)	Stock(8)	Stock(1)	Stock(4)	Stock(8)	Stock(1)	Stock(4)	Stock(8)
1951	2.463	2.235	1.962									
1952	2.681	2.533	2.342									
1953	2.613	2.709	2.582									
1954	3.121	2.877	2.758									
1955	4.562	3.948	3.357									
1956	5.031	4.654	4.184	5.098	4.716	4.241						
1957	4.699	4.487	4.323	5.036	4.809	4.633						
1958	4.273	3.800	3.911	4.868	4.331	4.457						
1959	5.063	4.693	4.062	6.088	5.643	4.886						
1960	4.078	4.218	4.222	5.175	5.352	5.357						
1961	4.514	4.164	4.008	5.865	5.411	5.208	6.250	5.767	5.550			
1962	3.454	3.849	3.847	4.355	4.854	4.852	4.884	5.443	5.441			
1963	3.788	3.524	3.503	4.758	4.427	4.400	5.639	5.248	5.216			
1964	3.879	3.726	3.461	4.906	4.712	4.378	6.091	5.850	5.437			
1965	3.749	3.720	3.546	4.765	4.728	4.507	6.198	6.151	5.863			
1966	3.270	3.496	3.408	4.280	4.576	4.460	5.675	6.068	5.914	6.233	6.664	6.495
1967	3.483	3.172	3.121	4.799	4.371	4.300	6.168	5.617	5.525	7.107	6.473	6.367
1968	3.169	3.193	3.001	4.443	4.477	4.208	5.677	5.721	5.377	6.897	6.950	6.533
1969	3.054	3.169	3.011	4.330	4.492	4.269	5.561	5.770	5.484	7.056	7.322	6.959
1970	2.451	2.618	2.740	3.463	3.700	3.872	4.463	4.767	4.990	5.909	6.313	6.608
1971	2.417	2.428	2.420	3.323	3.339	3.327	4.391	4.412	4.397	5.905	5.935	5.914

1972	2.359	2.256	2.233	3.161	3.023	2.993	4.369	4.180	4.138	5.684	5.438	5.384
1973	2.022	2.071	2.058	2.690	2.756	2.738	3.765	3.857	3.832	4.854	4.973	4.941
1974	1.474	1.610	1.745	1.970	2.150	2.331	2.771	3.024	3.278	3.578	3.903	4.231
1975	1.450	1.369	1.426	1.944	1.836	1.913	2.710	2.560	2.666	3.496	3.303	3.439
1976	1.418	1.417	1.343	1.915	1.913	1.815	2.592	2.591	2.458	3.413	3.411	3.237
1977	1.165	1.215	1.274	1.553	1.620	1.698	2.044	2.131	2.234	2.796	2.914	3.056
1978	1.224	1.134	1.143	1.595	1.478	1.489	2.072	1.920	1.935	2.852	2.644	2.663
1979	1.254	1.157	1.115	1.593	1.470	1.417	2.068	1.909	1.840	2.850	2.630	2.536
1980	1.583	1.457	1.278	1.946	1.792	1.572	2.533	2.333	2.048	3.459	3.187	2.798
1981	1.781	1.772	1.573	2.128	2.117	1.880	2.788	2.774	2.466	3.706	3.689	3.280
1982	1.307	1.408	1.550	1.520	1.637	1.802	1.969	2.119	2.334	2.548	2.741	3.021
1983	1.522	1.379	1.367	1.736	1.573	1.558	2.205	1.999	1.979	2.822	2.559	2.532
1984	1.453	1.426	1.380	1.613	1.583	1.532	2.006	1.969	1.905	2.566	2.518	2.437
1985	1.276	1.307	1.347	1.399	1.432	1.476	1.692	1.731	1.785	2.166	2.217	2.286
1986	1.343	1.308	1.292	1.462	1.425	1.406	1.721	1.677	1.655	2.214	2.157	2.129
1987	1.763	1.487	1.379	1.907	1.609	1.493	2.194	1.852	1.719	2.795	2.359	2.190
1988	1.283	1.267	1.357	1.378	1.360	1.457	1.558	1.538	1.643	1.950	1.925	2.063
1989	1.487	1.372	1.304	1.595	1.472	1.399	1.763	1.626	1.545	2.163	1.996	1.896
Summary statistics for entire period:												
Minimum	1.165	1.134	1.115	1.378	1.360	1.399	1.558	1.538	1.546	1.950	1.925	1.896
Maximum	5.063	4.693	4.323	6.088	5.643	5.357	6.250	6.151	5.914	7.107	7.322	6.959
Average	2.640	2.555	2.460	3.196	3.123	3.039	3.580	3.538	3.47[illegible]	3.959	3.926	3.875
Std dev	1.230	1.155	1.070	1.551	1.500	1.416	1.682	1.686	1.618	1.702	1.766	1.721
Summary statistics for 1980s:												
Average	1.480	1.418	1.383	1.668	1.600	1.558	2.043	1.962	1.909	2.639	2.535	2.463
Std dev	.177	.135	.096	.241	.210	.153	.373	.355	.288	.547	.523	.424

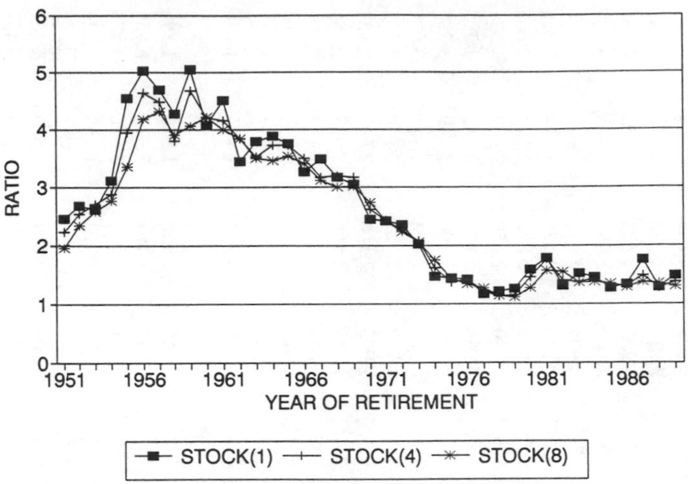

Fig. 2.6 Ratio of stock to bond accumulation for a twenty-five-year career

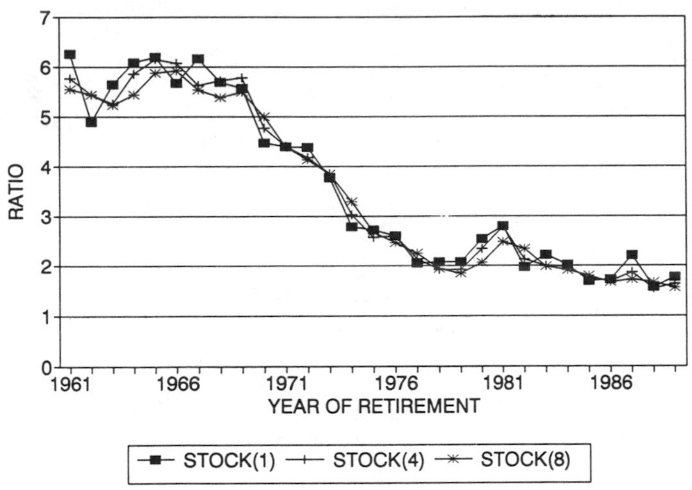

Fig. 2.7 Ratio of stock to bond accumulation for a thirty-five-year career

and 1.56 for retirements in 1986, 1987, and 1988, respectively. The stock accumulator who gradually converts to bonds over the final two years of his or her career realizes the much more stable set of ratios of 1.66, 1.72, and 1.65.

2.3 Allocation Policies of TIAA-CREF Participants

Despite the fact that stocks have outperformed bonds over long holding periods, many people saving for retirement use bonds or saving accounts as accumulation vehicles. The same is true for many other investors with presumably long horizons such as universities and foundations. For the purposes of this paper, we are most interested in the accumulation choices of professors for their retirement annuities.

TIAA-CREF generously shared some information about the allocation choices of its participants. The percentage of participants with various allocational choices are shown in figure 2.8 for the period 1969–87. These figures are for the basic TIAA-CREF retirement annuities accumulation plans and not for supplemental retirement annuities. It should be noted that CREF was not instituted until July 1952. Between the time of its inception and 31 December 1966, every contribution to CREF had to be accompanied by a contribution of at least as much to TIAA. Beginning in 1967, the premium allocation rules were changed to permit the payment of up to 75 percent of total retirement plan contributions to CREF. The rules were further changed on 1 July 1971 to provide complete flexibility, permitting the allocation of premiums between TIAA and CREF in any proportion, including 100 percent to either company.

Figure 2.8 shows that almost half of TIAA-CREF participants allocate their premiums on a fifty-fifty basis. This has been true throughout the period 1969–87. Surprisingly, at least to us, the 100 percent to TIAA option has become increasingly popular through time (being chosen by 22–24 percent in the 1980s), as has the 75 percent TIAA–25 percent CREF option (being chosen by 13–14 percent in the 1980s). The 100 percent CREF choice has been made by only about 3 percent of participants ever since this first became an option in 1971.

We have been able to obtain only a little information on the allocational choices by participants of different ages. In figure 2.9, we show the alloca-

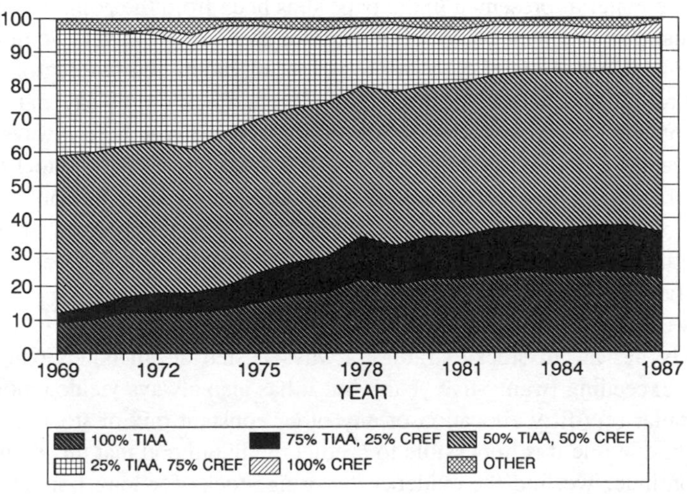

Fig. 2.8 Percentages of TIAA-CREF participants with indicated portfolio allocations

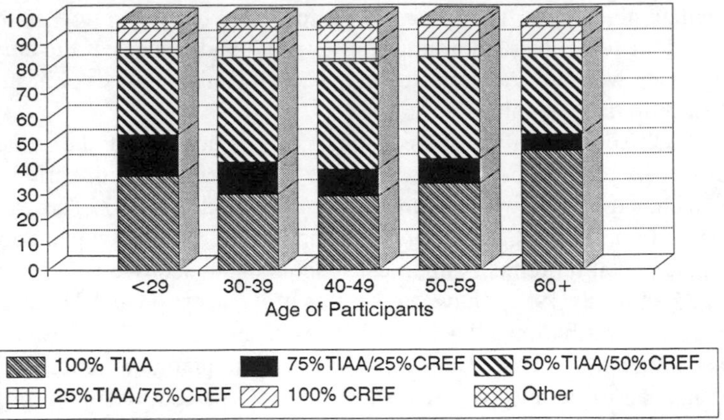

Fig. 2.9 Distribution of new supplemental retirement annuity participants by allocation choice and age

tional choices by age of new supplemental retirement annuity participants in 1984. Roughly 80 percent of the people who signed up for supplemental retirement annuity accounts choose to allocate 50 percent or less to stocks at all ages. One hundred percent stocks is not a common choice at any age. While it is true that more of the over 60 age group allocate all their funds to TIAA, our general conclusion from figure 2.9 is that there are no great differences in allocation by age.

2.4 Concluding Remarks

All the material presented in the paper has been from the point of view of a participant in a defined contribution pension system. However, we think that it is applicable to a wider class of problems, including the funding of defined benefit retirement plans by corporations. The findings simply say that systematic contributions proportional to earnings over a career have always led to more wealth at the time of retirement if the investments are in stocks rather than bonds. This information seems completely relevant to an employer who has promised retirement benefits based on final salary and years of service. The defined benefits can be funded with smaller cash contributions owing to the higher rates of return earned on stocks over long horizons.

As we have already stated, we find the results of this paper to be striking. Not only has an all stocks strategy always bested an all bonds one for all careers exceeding twenty-five years, but it has also always yielded more than the popular fifty-fifty allocation or any other constant mix of stock and bond purchases. While it is impossible to predict the likelihood that this dominance will continue, we find the evidence favoring stocks for long horizons overwhelming.

To answer the first question usually asked of us, Yes, we are allocating 100 percent of our pension contributions to stocks.

References

Fischer, Stanley, 1983. Investing for the Short and the Long Term. In *Financial Aspects of the United States Pension System,* ed. Zvi Bodie and John B. Shoven. Chicago: University of Chicago Press.

Ibbotson Associates, Inc. 1990. *Stocks, Bonds, Bills and Inflation: 1990 Yearbook.* Chicago.

MaCurdy, Thomas E., and John B. Shoven. 1990. Stock and Bond Returns: The Long and the Short of It. Stanford University. Manuscript.

Merton, Robert, and Paul A. Samuelson. 1974. Fallacy of the Log-Normal Approximation to Optimal Portfolio Decision-Making over Many Periods. *Journal of Financial Economics* 1:67–94.

Comment Jonathan S. Skinner

One finds many significant regression coefficients in empirical studies, but few empirical facts. By "empirical facts" I mean results unaffected by model specification or estimation technique—in short, findings about which all economists agree. In their paper, Thomas E. MaCurdy and John B. Shoven present a particularly interesting fact; in every twenty-five year period since 1926, the stock market has outperformed bonds. As they show, accumulated wealth from an all stock pension was as much as four times the accumulated wealth from an all bond pension.

If their finding holds true generally, it has far-reaching implications. First, as they note, the theoretical debate over the "equity premium" puzzle becomes irrelevant since there is no degree of risk aversion that would lead one to hold bonds if stocks outperform bonds in every state of the world. Second, the result implies a massive, and highly costly, degree of ignorance and irrationality on the part of investors. Their result using data on TIAA-CREF pension holdings is particularly strong since one cannot blame a short-sighted portfolio manager for choosing bonds over stocks; each individual employee is free to choose his or her own portfolio allocation of stocks and bonds. The authors' finding therefore casts doubt on investor rationality—the bedrock assumption of the theory of finance.

One could of course appeal to a portfolio explanation for why TIAA-CREF enrollees hold bonds. For example, suppose an enrollee finances 90 percent

Jonathan S. Skinner is associate professor of economics at the University of Virginia and a research associate of the National Bureau of Economic Research.

of his or her house with a fixed-rate mortgage. Given the substantial year-to-year variation in housing prices,[1] the homeowner can reduce his or her overall risk exposure by matching the long-term mortgage liabilities with long-term bonds. In this view, holding bonds in a pension fund may not make sense in isolation, but it does make sense in combination with the other household assets.

There are two problems with this explanation for holding bonds. The first is that the price of (long-term) bonds is negatively correlated with the nominal interest rate. If high nominal rates also depress housing prices, then buying long-term bonds could potentially increase overall risk. The second is that, if stocks dominate bonds in every state of the world, there is *no* combination of risk aversion or risk correlation that would imply that bonds should be held.[2] No matter what happens in the housing market, the risk-averse homeowner is still better off holding stocks over bonds.

The key question is whether the sixty-three years of data from 1926 to 1989 can allow one to conclude that stocks will dominate bonds in "all states of the world." The problem with calculating long-term yields of stocks versus bonds is that there are not really sixty-three independent observations since the return between, say, 1926 and 1951 obviously will be highly correlated with the return between 1927 and 1952. There are less than three twenty-five-year periods in the authors' data set, so we may reasonably conclude that the relevant degrees of freedom for making their inference are between three and sixty-three. Hence, standard errors on past stock and bond returns as applied to future returns may be quite generous given the long investment horizons involved.

One strategy to test the strength of their result is to extend the period of analysis. Stock and bond data exist from 1872, allowing one to roughly double the size of the sample. Using data on real stock yields calculated by Robert Shiller of Yale University and railroad bond yields from the 1949 *Historical Statistical Abstract,* I calculated the relative return on stocks and railroad bonds since 1900, assuming that the individual placed $1.00 each year in the "pension" fund. I calculated that, for every twenty-five-year period since 1900, the "pension" in stocks outperformed the same investment in bonds, even had the investor cashed out the stock portfolio at the depth of the Great Depression. If the investor had held off until 1935, the twenty-five-year stock investment would have beaten the bond investment by nearly three to one. So, in this respect, MaCurdy and Shoven's argument is even stronger—there is no twenty-five-year period since 1900 during which stocks did not outperform bonds.

The story is different between 1872 and 1899. As Snowden has carefully

1. See James Berkovec and Don Fullerton, "A General Equilibrium Model of Housing, Taxes, and Portfolio Choice," NBER Working Paper no. 3505 (Cambridge, Mass.: National Bureau of Economic Research, November 1990).

2. I am grateful to Tom MaCurdy for pointing this out to me.

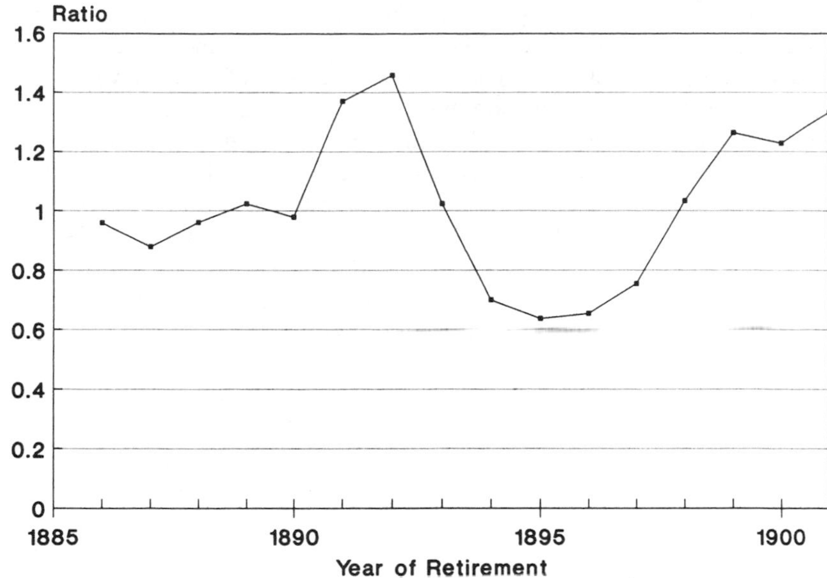

Fig. 2C.1 Ratio of stock to bond accumulation for fifteen-year holding period, 1872–1901

Source: Kenneth Snowden, "Historical Returns and Security Market Developmcnts, 1872–1925," Working Paper no. ECO 891001 (Greensboro: University of North Carolina, October 1989).

documented, bonds generally outperformed stocks during this period.[3] The real geometric mean return on stocks from 1872 to 1899 was 7.25, while the corresponding return on high-grade rail bonds was 8.20.[4] In part, the higher return was a consequence of unexpected deflation during the period and the (unrealized) possibility that the bonds would be repayed under an inflated silver standard. Furthermore, both the bond and the stock market were dominated by railroad company issues.

A similar exercise to that performed by MaCurdy and Shoven is shown for the period 1872–1901 in figure 2C.1. Because the period of analysis is so short, I focused on fifteen-year periods in which the investor contributes $1.00 per year along with the accumulated proceeds from previous years. As in MaCurdy and Shoven's paper, the ratio calculated is the accumulated stock wealth divided by accumulated bond wealth. During half the retirement dates between 1886 and 1901, the bond portfolio outperformed the stock portfolio.

3. Kenneth Snowden, "Historical Returns and Security Market Development, 1872–1925," Working Paper no. ECO 891001 (Greensboro: University of North Carolina, October 1989).

4. While railroad bonds dominated the bond market during this period, the geometric mean returns on government bonds (5.61) and commercial paper (6.65) were lower than the return on stocks (see ibid.).

And, as noted above, bonds outperformed stocks during the entire period 1872–99. This historical excursion therefore leads to a modification of the authors' statement that "there has never been a span of time for which this strategy [of holding a portfolio with bonds] would be profitable." The amended version is that, in the 117 years since 1872, there was one twenty-eight-year period (and many overlapping fifteen-year periods) during which railroad bonds outperformed stocks. This reversal does not deflect the main thrust of MaCurdy and Shoven's result since, even when bonds did outperform stocks, it was not by a large amount. But if there is any positive probability that bonds will yield a higher return than stocks, then investors can be rational, if astonishingly risk averse, to hold bonds.

3 Health, Children, and Elderly Living Arrangements
A Multiperiod-Multinomial Probit Model with Unobserved Heterogeneity and Autocorrelated Errors

Axel Börsch-Supan, Vassilis Hajivassiliou, Laurence J. Kotlikoff, and John N. Morris

Decisions by the elderly regarding their living arrangements (e.g., living alone, living with children, or living in a nursing home) seem best modeled as a discrete choice problem in which the elderly view certain choices as closer substitutes than others. For example, living with children may more closely substitute for living independently than living in an institution does. Unobserved determinants of living arrangements at a point in time are, therefore, quite likely to be correlated. In the parlance of discrete choice models, this means that the assumption of the independence of irrelevant alternatives (IIA) will be violated. Indeed, a number of recent studies of living arrangements of the elderly document the violation of IIA.[1]

In addition to relaxing the IIA assumption of no intratemporal correlation between unobserved determinants of competing living arrangements, one should also relax the assumption of no intertemporal correlation of such determinants. The assumption of no intertemporal correlation underlies most studies of living arrangements, particularly those estimated with cross-sectional data. While cross-sectional variation in household characteristics can provide important insights into the determinants of living arrangements, the living arrangement decision is clearly an intertemporal choice and a potentially complicated one at that. Because of moving and associated transactions costs,

Axel Börsch-Supan is professor of economics at the University of Mannheim and a research associate of the National Bureau of Economic Research. Vassilis Hajivassiliou is an associate professor of economics in the Department of Economics and a member of the Cowles Foundation for Economic Research, Yale University. Laurence J. Kotlikoff is professor of economics at Boston University and a research associate of the National Bureau of Economic Research. John N. Morris is associate director of research of the Hebrew Rehabilitation Center for the Aged.

This research was supported by the National Institute on Aging, grant 3 PO1 AG05842. Dan Nash and Gerald Schehl provided valuable research assistance. The authors also thank Dan McFadden, Steven Venti, and David Wise for their helpful comments.

1. Examples are quoted in Börsch-Supan (1986).

elderly households may stay longer in inappropriate living arrangements than they would in the absence of such costs. In turn, households may prospectively move into an institution "before it is too late to cope with this change." That is, households may be substantially out of long-run equilibrium if a cross-sectional survey interviews them shortly before or after a move. Moreover, persons may acquire a taste for certain types of living arrangements. Such habit formation introduces state dependence. Ideally, therefore, living arrangement choices should be estimated with panel data, with an appropriate econometric specification of intertemporal linkages.

These intertemporal linkages include two components. The first component is the linkage through unobserved person-specific attributes, that is, unobserved heterogeneity through time-invariant error components. An important example is health status, information on which is often missing or unsatisfactory in household surveys. Health status varies over time but has an important person-specific, time-invariant component that influences housing and living arrangement choices of the elderly. Panel data discrete choice models that capture unobserved heterogeneity include Chamberlain's (1984) conditional fixed effects estimator and one-factor random effects models, such as those proposed by McFadden (1984, 1434).

However, not all intertemporal correlation patterns in unobservables can be captured by time-invariant error components. A second error component should, therefore, be included to control for time-varying disturbances, for example, an autoregressive error structure. Examples of the source of error components that taper off over time are the cases of prospective moves and habit formation mentioned above. Similar effects on the error structure arise when, owing to unmeasured transactions costs, an elderly person stays longer in a dwelling than he or she would in the absence of such costs.

Ellwood and Kane (1990) and Börsch-Supan (1990) apply simple models to capture dynamic features of the observed data. Ellwood and Kane (1990) employ an exponential hazard model, while Börsch-Supan (1990) uses a variety of simple Markov transition models. Neither approach captures both unobserved heterogeneity and autoregressive errors. In addition, living arrangement choices are multinomial by nature, ruling out univariate hazard models. Börsch-Supan, Kotlikoff, and Morris (1989) also fail to deal fully with heterogeneous and autoregressive unobservables. Their study attempts to finesse these concerns by describing the multinomial-multiperiod choice process as one large discrete choice among all possible outcomes. By invoking the IIA assumption, a small subset of choices is sufficient to identify the relevant parameters. This approach, which converts the problem of repeated intertemporal choices to the static problem of choosing, ex ante, the time path of living arrangements, is easily criticized both because of the IIA assumption and because of the presumption that individuals decide their future living arrangements in advance.

While researchers have recognized the need to estimate choice models with unobserved determinants that are correlated across alternatives and over time, they have been daunted by the high dimensional integration of the associated likelihood functions. This paper uses a new simulation method developed in Börsch-Supan and Hajivassiliou (1990) to estimate the likelihood functions of living arrangement choice models that range, in their error structure, from the very simple to the highly complex. Compared with previous simulation estimators derived by McFadden (1989) and Pakes and Pollard (1989), the new method is capable of dealing with complex error structures with substantially less computation. Börsch-Supan and Hajivassiliou's method builds on recent progress in Monte Carlo integration techniques by Geweke (189) and Hajivassiliou and McFadden (1990). It represents a revival of the Lerman and Manski (1981) procedure of approximating the likelihood function by simulated choice probabilities overcoming its computational disadvantages.

Section 3.1 develops the general structure of the choice probability integrals and spells out alternative correlation structures. Section 3.2 presents the estimation procedure, termed "simulated maximum likelihood" (SML). Section 3.3 describes our data, and section 3.4 reports results. Section 3.5 concludes with a summary of major findings.

3.1 Econometric Specifications of Alternative Error Processes

Let I be the number of discrete choices in each time period and T be the number of waves in the panel data. The space of possible outcomes is the set of I^T different choice sequences $\{i_t\}$, $t = 1, \ldots, T$. To structure this discrete choice problem, we assume that in each period choices are made according to the random utility maximization hypothesis; that is,[2]

(1) i_t is chosen $<=> u_{it}$ is maximal element in $\{u_{jt} \mid j = 1, \ldots, t\}$,

where the utility of choice i in period t is the sum of a deterministic utility component $v_{it} = v(X_{it}, \beta)$, which depends on the vector of observable variables X_{it} and a parameter vector β to be estimated and on a random utility component ε_{it}:

(2) $$u_{it} = v(X_{it}, \beta) + \varepsilon_{it}.$$

We model the deterministic utility component, $v(X_{it}, \beta)$, as simply the linear combination $X_{it}\beta$.[3]

Since the optimal choice delivers maximum utility, the differences in utility levels between the best choice and any other choice, not the utility level of maximal choices, are relevant for the elderly's decision. The probability of a choice sequence $\{i_t\}$ can, therefore, be expressed as integrals over the differ-

2. Including some rule to break ties.
3. X_{it} is a row vector, and β is a column vector.

ences of the unobserved utility components relative to the chosen alternative. Define

$$w_{jt} = \varepsilon_{jt} - \varepsilon_{it} \quad \text{for } i = i_t, j \neq i_t. \tag{3}$$

These $D = (I - 1) \times T$ error differences are stacked in the vector w and have a joint cumulative distribution function F.

For alternative i to be chosen, the error differences can be at most as large as the differences in the deterministic utility components. The areas of integration are therefore

$$A_j(i) = \{w_{jt} \mid -\infty \leq w_{jt} \leq X_{it}\beta - X_{jt}\beta\} \quad \text{for } j \neq i, \tag{4}$$

and the probability of choice sequence $\{i_t\}$ is

$$P(\{i_t\} \mid \{X_{it}\}; \beta, F) = \tag{5}$$

$$\int_{\{w_{j1} \in A_j(i_1) | j=1, \ldots, I, j \neq i_1\}} \times \ldots \times \int_{\{w_{jT} \in A_j(i_T) | j=1, \ldots, I, j \neq i_T\}} dF(w).$$

Unless the joint cumulative distribution function F and the area of integration $A_j = A_j(i_1) \times \ldots \times A_j(i_T)$ are particularly benign, the integral in (5) will not have a closed form. Closed-form solutions exist if F is a member of the family of generalized extreme-value (GEV) distributions, for example, the cross-sectional multinomial logit (MNL) or nested multinomial logit (NMNL) models, contributing to the popularity of these specifications. Closed-form solutions also exist if these models are combined with a one-factor random effect that is again extreme-value distributed (e.g., McFadden 1984).

GEV-type models have the disadvantage of relatively rigid correlation structures. They cannot embed the more general intertemporal correlation patterns expounded in the introductory material. Concentrating on the first two moments, we assume a multivariate normal distribution of the w_{jt} in (3), characterized by a covariance matrix M that has $(D + 1) \times D/2 - 1$ significant elements: the correlations among the w_{jt} and the variances except one in order to scale the parameter vector β in the deterministic utility components $v(X, \beta)$. This count represents many more covariance parameters than GEV-type models can handle. Moreover, our specification of M is not constrained by hierarchical structures, as is the case in the class of NMNL models.

We estimate this multiperiod-multinomial probit model with different specifications of the covariance matrix M:

A. The simplest specification $M = I$ yields a pooled cross-sectional probit model that is subject to the independence of irrelevant alternatives (IIA) restriction and ignores all intertemporal linkages. The $D = (I - 1) \times T$ dimensional integral of the choice probabilities factors into D one-dimensional integrals.

There are several ways to introduce intertemporal linkages:

B. A random-effects structure is imposed by specifying

$$\varepsilon_{i,t} = \alpha_i + \nu_{i,t}, \quad \nu_{i,t} \text{ i.i.d.}, i = 1, \ldots, I - 1.$$

This yields a block-diagonal equicorrelation structure of M with $(I - 1)$ parameters $\sigma(\alpha)$ in M that need to be estimated. This structure allows for a factorization of the integral in (5) in $(I - 1)$ T-dimensional blocks, which in turn can be reduced to one dimension because of the one-factor structure.

C. An autoregressive error structure can be incorporated by specifying

$$\varepsilon_{i,t} = \rho_i \cdot \varepsilon_{i,t-1} + \nu_{i,t}, \quad \nu_{i,t} \text{ i.i.d.}, i = 1, \ldots, I - 1.$$

Again, this yields a block-diagonal structure of M where each block has the familiar structure of an AR(1) process. $(I - 1)$ parameters ρ_i in M have to be estimated.

D. The last two error structures can also be combined by specifying

$$\varepsilon_{i,t} = \alpha_i + \eta_{i,t}, \quad \eta_{i,t} = \rho_i \cdot \eta_{i,t-1} + \nu_{i,t}, \nu_{i,t} \text{ i.i.d.}, i = 1, \ldots, I - 1.$$

This amounts to overlaying the equicorrelation structure with the AR(1) structure. It should be noted that $\sigma(\alpha_i)$ and ρ_i are separately identified only if $\rho_i < 1$.

We now drop the IIA assumption. There are several distinct possibilities, depending on the intertemporal error specification:

E. Starting again with specification A and ignoring any intertemporal structure, the simplest possibility is to assume that the $\varepsilon_{i,t}$ are uncorrelated across t but have correlations across i that are constant over time. With the proper reordering of the elements in the stacked vector w, a simple block-diagonal structure of M emerges with $T \times (I - 1)$–dimensional blocks. In this case, $(I - 2)$ variances and $(I - 1) \times (I - 2)/2$ covariances can be identified.

F. This specification can be overlayed with the random effects specification. This destroys the block-diagonality, although the one-factor structure allows a reduction of the dimensionality of the integral in (5). $(I - 1)$ variances of the random effects $\sigma(\alpha_i)$ can be identified in addition to the parameters in specification E. Rather than allowing interalternative correlation in the $\nu_{i,t}$ (specification F1), it is also possible to make the random effects α_i correlated (specification F2).

G. Alternatively, specification E can be overlayed with an autoregressive error structure by specifying

$$\varepsilon_{i,t} = \rho_i \cdot \varepsilon_{i,t-1} + \nu_{i,t}, \quad \text{corr}(\nu_{i,t}, \nu_{j,s}) = \omega_{ij} \text{ if } s = t, \text{ else } 0.$$

The $\nu_{i,t}$ are correlated across alternatives but uncorrelated across periods. The familiar structure of an AR(1) process is additively overlayed with the block-diagonal structure of specification E. $(I - 1)$ additional parameters ρ_i in M have to be estimated.

H. Finally, all three features—interalternative correlation, random effects, and autoregressive errors—can be combined. The resulting error process is

$$\varepsilon_{i,t} = \alpha_i + \eta_{i,t}, \quad \eta_{i,t} = \rho_i \cdot \eta_{i,t-1} + \nu_{i,t}, \quad i = 1, \ldots, I - 1,$$

with

$$\text{corr}(\nu_{i,t}, \nu_{j,s}) = \begin{cases} 0 & \text{if t} \neq s \\ \omega_{ij} & \text{if } t = s \end{cases}$$

and

$$\text{cov}\,(\alpha_i, \alpha_j) = \sigma_{ij},$$

which implies

$$\text{cov}(\varepsilon_{i,t}, \varepsilon_{j,s}) = \sigma_{ij} + \rho_i^{(t-s)} \frac{\sqrt{(1 - \rho_i^2)} \cdot \sqrt{(1 - \rho_j^2}}{1 - \rho_i\rho_j} \omega_{ij}.$$

This model encompasses all preceding specifications as special cases. Again, all parameters are identified if $\rho_i < 1$, $i = 1, \ldots, I - 1$, although, in practice, the identification of this general specification may become shaky when there are only a small number of sufficiently long spells in different choices.

3.2 Estimation Procedure: Simulated Maximum Likelihood

The likelihood function corresponding to the general multiperiod-multinomial choice problem is the product of the choice probabilities (5):

$$\mathcal{L}(\beta, M) = \prod_{n=1}^{N} P(\{i_{t,n}\}|\{X_{it,n}\}; \beta, M), \tag{6}$$

where the index n denotes an observation in a sample of N individuals and the cumulative distribution function F in (5) is assumed to be multivariate normal and characterized by the covariance matrix M. Estimating the parameters in (6) is a formidable task because it requires, in the most general case, an evaluation of the $D = (I - 1) \times T$ dimensional integral in (5) for each observation and each iteration in the maximization process.

One may be tempted to accept the efficiency losses due to an incorrect specification of the error structure and simply ignore the correlations that make the integral in (5) so hard to solve. However, unlike the linear model, an incorrect specification of the covariance matrix of the errors M biases not only the standard errors of the estimated coefficients but also the structural coefficients β themselves. The linear case is very special in isolating specification errors away from β.

Numerical integration of the integral in (5) is not computationally feasible since the number of operations increases with the power of D, the dimension of M. Approximation methods, such as the Clark approximation (Daganzo 1981) or its variant proposed by Langdon (1984), are tractable—their number of operations increases quadratically with D—but they remain unsatisfactory since their relatively large bias cannot be controlled by increasing the number of observations. Rather, we simulate the choice probabilities $P(\{i_{t,n}\}|\{X_{it,n}\}; \beta, M)$ by drawing pseudo-random realizations from the underlying error process.

The most straightforward simulation method is to simulate the choice probabilities $P(\{i_{t,n}\}|\{X_{it,n}\}; \beta, M)$ by observed frequencies (Lerman and Manski 1981):

$$\tilde{\tilde{P}}(i_{tn}) = N_{tn}(i)/N_{tn}, \tag{7}$$

where N_{tn} denotes the number of draws or replications for individual n at period t and

$$N_{tn}(i) = \text{count}(u_{itn} \text{ is maximal in } \{u_{jtn} \mid j = 1, \ldots, t\}). \tag{8}$$

One then maximizes the simulated likelihood function

$$\tilde{\tilde{\mathcal{L}}}(\beta, M) = \prod_{n=1}^{N} \prod_{t=1}^{T} N_{tn}(i)/N_{tn}. \tag{9}$$

However, in order to obtain reasonably accurate estimates (7) of small choice probabilities, a very large number of draws is required. That results in unacceptably long computer runs.

We exploit instead an algorithm proposed by Geweke (1989) that was originally designed to compute random variates from a multivariate truncated normal distribution. This algorithm is very quick and depends continuously on the parameters β and M. One concern is that it fails to deliver unbiased multivariate truncated normal variates.[4] However, as Börsch-Supan and Hajivassiliou (1990) show, the algorithm can be used to derive unbiased estimates of the choice probabilities. We sketch this method in the remainder of this section.

Univariate truncated normal variates can be drawn according to a straightforward application of the integral transform theorem. Let u be a draw from a univariate standard uniform distribution, $u \in [0, 1]$. Then

$$e = G^{-1}(u) = \Phi^{-1}\{[\Phi(b) - \Phi(a)] \cdot u + \Phi(a)\} \tag{10}$$

is distributed $N(0, 1)$ s.t. $a \leq e \leq b$ since the cumulative distribution function of a univariate truncated normal distribution is

$$G(z) = \frac{\Phi(z) - \Phi(a)}{\Phi(b) - \Phi(a)}, \tag{11}$$

4. This was first pointed out by Paul Ruud.

where Φ denotes the univariate normal cumulative distribution function. Note that e is a continuously differentiable function of the truncation parameters a and b. This continuity is essential for computational efficiency.

In the multivariate case, let L be the lower diagonal Cholesky factor of the covariance matrix M of the unobserved utility differences w in (3),

$$L \cdot L' = M. \tag{12}$$

Then draw sequentially a vector of $D = (I - 1) \times T$ univariate truncated normal variates

$$e = N(0, I) \quad \text{s.t. } a \leq L \cdot e \leq \infty, \tag{13}$$

where the D-dimensional vector a is defined by equation (4):

$$a_{jt} = X_{it}\beta - X_{jt}\beta \quad \text{for } i = i_t, j \neq i_t. \tag{14}$$

Because L is triangular, the restrictions in (13) are recursive (for notational simplicity, e and a are in the sequel simply indexed by $i = 1, \ldots, D$):

$$\begin{aligned} e_1 &= N(0,1) \\ &\text{s.t. } a_1 \leq \ell_{11} \cdot e_1 \leq \infty \\ &<=> a_1/\ell_{11} \leq e_1 \leq \infty, \\ e_2 &= N(0, 1) \\ &\text{s.t. } a_2 \leq \ell_{21} \cdot e_1 + \ell_{22} \cdot e_2 \leq \infty \\ &<=> (a_2 - \ell_{21} \cdot e_1)/\ell_{22} \leq e_2 \leq \infty, \end{aligned} \tag{15}$$

etc. Hence, each e_i, $i = 1, \ldots, D$, can be drawn using the univariate formula (10). Finally, define

$$w = Le. \tag{16}$$

Then (12) implies that w has covariance matrix M and is subject to

$$a \leq Le \leq \infty <=> a \leq w \leq \infty \tag{17}$$

as required.

The probability for a choice sequence $\{i_{tn}\}$ of observation n is the probability that w falls in the interval given by (4), which is the probability that e falls in the interval given by (13), that is,

$$\begin{aligned} P(\{i_{tn}\}) = {} & \Pr(a_1/l_{11} \leq e_1 \leq \infty) \cdot \\ & \Pr[(a_2 - l_{21} \cdot e_1)/l_{22} \leq e_2 \leq \infty \mid e_1] \cdot \ldots \end{aligned} \tag{18}$$

For a draw of a D-dimensional vector of truncated normal variates $e_r = (e_{r1}, \ldots, e_{rD})$ according to (15), this probability is simulated by

$$\tilde{P}_r(\{i_{tn}\}) = [1 - \Phi(a_1/l_{11})] \cdot [1 - \Phi(a_2 - l_{21} \cdot e_{r1})/l_{22})] \cdot \ldots, \tag{19}$$

and the choice probability is approximated by the average over R replications of (19):

$$(20) \qquad \tilde{P}(\{i_{tn}\}) = \frac{1}{R}\sum_{r=1}^{R} \tilde{P}_r(\{i_{tn}\}).$$

Börsch-Supan and Hajivassiliou (1990) prove that $\tilde{P}$ is an unbiased estimator of P in spite of the failure of the Geweke algorithm to provide unbiased expected values of e and w.

Like the univariate case, both the generated draws and the resulting simulated probability of a choice sequence depend continuously and differentiably on the parameters β in the truncation vector a and the covariance matrix M. Hence, conventional numerical methods such as one of the conjugate gradient methods or quadratic hillclimbing can be used to solve the first-order conditions for maximizing the simulated likelihood function

$$(21) \qquad \tilde{\mathcal{L}}(\beta, M) = \prod_{n=1}^{N}\sum_{r=1}^{R} \tilde{P}_r(\{i_{tn}\}).$$

This differs from the frequency simulator (7), which generates a discontinuous objective function with the associated numerical problems.

Moreover, as described by Börsch-Supan and Hajivassiliou (1990), the choice probabilities are well approximated by (20), even for a small number of replications, independent of the true choice probabilities. This is in remarkable contrast to the Lerman-Manski frequency simulator that requires that the number of replications be inversely related to the true choice probabilities. The Lerman-Manski simulator thus requires a very large number of replications for small choice probabilities.

Finally, it should be noted that the computational effort in the simulation increases nearly linearly with the dimensionality of the integral in (5), $D = (I - 1) \times T$, since most computer time is involved in generating the univariate truncated normal draws.[5] For reliable results, it is crucial to compute the cumulative normal distribution function and its inverse with high accuracy. The near linearity permits applications to large choice sets with a large number of panel waves.

3.3 Data, Variable Definitions, and Basic Sample Characteristics

In this paper, we employ data from the Survey of the Elderly collected by the Hebrew Rehabilitation Center for the Aged (HRCA). This survey is part of an ongoing panel survey of the elderly in Massachusetts that began in 1982. Initially, the sample consisted of 4,040 elderly, aged 60 and above. In addition to the baseline interview in 1982, reinterviews were conducted in 1984, 1985,

5. The matrix multiplications and the Cholesky decomposition in (12) require operations that are of higher order. However, the generation of random numbers takes more computing time than these matrix operations, even for reasonably large dimensions.

1986, and 1987. The sample is stratified and consists of two populations. The first population represents about 70 percent of the sample and was drawn from a random selection of communities in Massachusetts. This first subsample is in itself highly stratified to produce an overrepresentation of the very old. The second population, which constitutes the remaining 30 percent, is drawn from elderly participants in the twenty-seven Massachusetts home health care corporations. In the second population, the older old are also overrepresented. The sample selection criteria, sampling procedures, and exposure rates are described in more detail in Morris et al. (1987) and Kotlikoff and Morris (1989).

In addition to basic demographic information collected in the baseline interview, each wave of the HRCA panel contains questions about the elderly's current marital status, living arrangements, income, and number and proximity of children. The surveys pay particular attention to health status, recording the presence and severity of diagnosed conditions and determining an array of functional (dis)abilities.

Table 3.1 presents the age distribution of the elderly at baseline in 1982. The average age is 78.5, 78 percent are age 75 or older, and 20 percent are age 85 or older. Among the U.S. noninstitutionalized population aged 60 and over, 27.9 percent are age 75 or older, while only 5.5 percent are over age 85. The overrepresentation of the oldest old in our sample is indicated by the impressive number of eight centenarians in our sample! Because the sample overrepresents the very old, it is also characterized by a very large proportion of women. In 1982, 68.7 percent of the interviewed elderly were female; by 1986, this percentage had risen to 70.7.

The lower part of table 3.1 provides information about family relationships and the isolation of some of the elderly. In 1982, 32.9 percent of the elderly in the HRCA baseline sample were married, and 55.0 percent were widowed. Four years later, 26.7 percent of the surviving elderly were married, and 61.4 percent were widowed. As of 1986, 41.4 percent of the elderly report no children, 15.2 one, 17.8 two, 12.7 three, and 12.8 percent four or more children. Because the elderly in the sample are quite old, some of their children are elderly themselves, and some children may even have died earlier than their parents. A total 47.0 percent of the elderly have siblings who are still alive, 25.5 percent of all elderly report that they have no relatives alive at all, and 39.3 percent report that they have no friends.

Average yearly income of the elderly rises between 1984 and 1986 from \$8,750 to \$10,500. This 20 percent increase is larger than the concomitant growth in average income for the general population, which was only 13.2 percent. It is interesting to note that elderly without children have a significantly lower income (\$7,500) than elderly with at least one child (\$9,500) in 1984, although in 1986 this difference becomes smaller (\$9,700 as opposed to \$10,750).

One of the major strengths of the HRCA survey is its detailed information

Table 3.1 Demographic Characteristics

A. Age Distribution at Baseline 1982

	60+	65+	70+	75+	80+	85+	90+	95+	100+
No.	212	233	231	985	826	400	150	32	8
%	6.9	7.6	7.5	32.0	26.8	13.0	4.9	1.0	.3

B. Marital Status

	1982	1984	1985	1986
Married	32.9	29.3	28.6	26.7
Widowed	55.0	58.8	59.4	61.4
Never married	8.2	8.1	8.2	8.3
Divorced/separated	3.9	3.7	3.7	3.6

C. Number of Children in 1986

	Number of Children								
	0	1	2	3	4	5	6	7	8+
No.	1,275	468	549	392	189	87	51	31	35
%	41.4	15.2	17.8	12.7	6.1	2.8	1.7	1.0	1.1

D. Isolated Elderly

Percentage of Elderly in 1986 Without:					
Children	Siblings	Children or Siblings	Any Relatives	Friends	Any Relatives or Friends
41.4	53.0	31.2	25.5	39.3	24.5

Source: HRCA Survey of the Elderly, Working Sample of 3,077 Elderly.

on the health status of the elderly. Three kinds of health measures are reported: a subjective health index, an array of diagnosed conditions, and an array of functional ability measures. The subjective health index (SUBJ) is coded "excellent" (1), "good" (2), "fair" (3), or "poor" (4). The presence and severity of seven chronic illnesses are reported: cancer, mental illness, diabetes, stroke, heart disease, hypertension, and arthritis. Each of these illnesses are scored as either "not present" (0), "present but does not cause limitation" (1), or "present and causes limitation" (2). We condense this information in a summary measure, ILLSUM, the (unweighted) sum of all seven scores. Five measures of functional ability are used: the distance an elderly person can walk or wheel, whether an elderly person can take medication, can attend to his or her own personal care, can prepare his or her own meals, and can do normal housework. The first measure is scored from 0 to 5, representing mobility from "can walk more than half mile" down to "confined to bed." The other measures can attain five values, representing "could do on own," "needs some help sometimes," "needs some help often," "needs considerable help," and "cannot do at all," with associated scores from 0 to 4. As with the chronic illnesses, we condense these indicators in a simple summary measure of functional ability, ADLSUM, the (unweighted) sum of all five scores.

Börsch-Supan, Kotlikoff, and Morris (1989) discuss more sophisticated measures, the correlation among the several measures of health status, and their relative performance in predicting living arrangements. While the subjective health rating performs poorly and is barely correlated with the measures of functional ability and diagnosed conditions, ILLSUM and ADLSUM are as good in predicting living arrangement choices as more sophisticated summary measures of health status.

Although the 1982 sample did not include institutionalized elderly, subsequent surveys have followed the elderly as they moved, including moves into and out of nursing homes. The type of institution was carefully recorded in the survey instrument. In addition, in each wave the noninstitutionalized elderly were asked who else was living in their home. This provides the opportunity to estimate a general model of living arrangement choice, including the process of institutionalization, conditional on not being institutionalized at the time of the first interview. In the longitudinal analysis, we distinguish three categories of living arrangements:

1. *Independent living arrangements:* The household does not contain any other person besides the elderly individual and his or her spouse (if the elderly individual is married and his or her spouse lives with him or her).
2. *Shared living arrangements:* The household contains at least one other adult person besides the elderly individual and his or her spouse. In most cases, the household contains only the elderly individual, his or her spouse, and the immediate family of one of his or her children, including a child-in-law. Less frequently, the household also contains other related or unrelated persons.
3. *Institutional living arrangements:* This category includes the elderly who are living on a permanent basis in a health-care facility.

The institutional living arrangements category comprises the entire spectrum ranging from hospitals and nursing homes to congregate housing and boarding houses. Living arrangements are reported as of the day of the interview—therefore, temporary nursing home stays are not recorded unless they happen to be at the time of interview. Rather, most nursing home stays in our data set represent permanent living arrangements.[6] It is important to keep this in mind when comparing the frequency and risk of institutionalization in this paper with numbers in studies that focus on short-term nursing home stays.

6. Garber and MaCurdy (1990) present evidence on the distribution of lengths of stay in a nursing home.

Table 3.2 presents the distributions of living arrangements in the five waves of the HRCA panel. The frequencies in this table are strictly cross-sectional and are based on all elderly who were living at the time of each cross section and for whom living arrangements were known.

Most remarkable is the decreasing but still very high proportion of the elderly living independently in spite of the very old age of most of the elderly in the sample. Approximately one out of every six elderly shares a household with his or her own children, whereas very few elderly share a household with distantly related or unrelated persons. The dramatic increase over time in the proportion of institutionalized living arrangements reflects two effects that must be carefully distinguished. Institutionalization increases because the sample ages and their health deteriorates, as is obvious from table 3.2. This effect is confounded by the way the sample was drawn. In 1982, the sample is noninstitutionalized by design. Only a few elderly happened to become insti-

Table 3.2 Living Arrangements of the Elderly (percentages)

	1982	1984	1985	1986
Independent living arrangements:				
Alone	56.8	51.2	50.5	46.4
With spouse	18.5	14.0	11.9	10.8
Total	75.3	65.2	62.4	57.2
Shared living arrangements:				
Alone with kids	16.6	17.4	15.7	13.7
With spouse and kids	1.4	1.7	1.8	1.8
Other relatives or nonrelatives present	5.9	5.9	5.7	5.1
Total	23.9	25.0	23.2	20.6
Institutional living arrangements:				
Convent, rectory, CCRC, congregate housing or retirement home	.0	.2	.7	.6
Foster home, community or domestic care	.0	.2	.2	.3
Nursing home (ICF)	.2	5.4	8.0	11.6
Nursing home (SNF)	.0	2.9	3.5	7.0
Rest home (level IV)	.0	.4	.7	1.3
Hotel, boarding or rooming house	.6	.3	.3	.2
Hospital	.0	.4	1.1	1.2
Total	.8	9.8	14.5	22.2
No. of Observations:	3,070	2,965	1,130	2,331

Source: HRCA Survey of the Elderly (cross-sectional subsamples of elderly with completed interviews).

tutionalized between the time of the sample design and the actual interview. Four years later, more than one-fifth of the surviving elderly live in an institution, almost all in a nursing home. As of 1986, very few elderly live in the "new" forms of elderly housing, such as congregate housing or continuing care retirement communities.

Table 3.3 examines the temporal evolution of living arrangements. It enumerates all living arrangement sequences that are observed among the 1,196 elderly whose living arrangements could be ascertained from 1982 through 1986. A little less than half (47.8 percent) of the elderly maintained the same living arrangement from 1982 through 1986. Another 21.0 percent died before 1986 without an observed living arrangement transition. This stability confirms the results by Börsch-Supan (1990) and Ellwood and Kane (1990). About 40 percent of the sampled elderly lived independently from 1982 through 1986. Another 15.6 percent remained independent until they died prior to 1986. Another 24.6 percent lived for at least some time with their children, and 21.1 percent experienced at least one stay in an institution. The most frequently observed transition is from living independently to being institutionalized. These sequences are observed for 42.4 percent of all elderly who change their living arrangement at least once. Only 13.7 percent change from living independently to living with their children. Most other sequences are very rare.

3.4 Estimation Results

For the longitudinal econometric analysis, we extract a small working sample of 314 elderly who were interviewed in all five waves, whose living arrangements could be ascertained in all five waves, and for whom we have reliable data on all covariates in all five waves. This results in a sample biased toward the more healthy elderly. While we have not done so here, the econometric model can easily be extended to accommodate sample truncation due to exogenous factors, most important, death and health-related inability to conduct an interview. Table 3.4 presents a description of the variables employed and the usual sample statistics of this subsample.

The presentation of results is organized according to four intertemporal specifications (pooled cross sections, random effects, autoregressive errors, and random effects plus autoregressive errors) and two or three specifications of correlation pattern across alternatives (the IIA assumption; correlation between random effects, if applicable; and the full MNP model). Three replications (draws) were used to simulate the choice probabilities entering the log likelihood function. Using fewer replications produces less reliable results, but increasing the number of replications up to nine, as we did for the final estimate, does not change results in any substantive way.

The goodness of fit in the various specifications is examined in table 3.5. This table reports the value of the simulated log likelihood function at esti-

Table 3.3 Living Arrangement Sequences, 1982, 1984, 1985, 1986

	Sequence								
	IIII	IIIC	IIIO	IIIN	IIID	IICI	IICC	IICN	IIOI
No.	474	17	6	40	3	1	8	2	2
%	39.63	1.42	.50	3.34	.25	.08	.67	.17	.17
	IIOO	IION	IINI	IINN	IIND	IIDD	ICII	ICIN	ICCC
No.	1	3	1	42	1	110	1	1	20
%	.08	.25	.08	3.51	.08	9.20	.08	.08	1.67
	ICCN	ICOO	ICNN	ICDD	IOII	IOIO	IOCN	IOOI	IOOO
No.	2	1	4	6	1	1	1	3	6
%	.17	.08	.33	.50	.08	.08	.08	.25	.50
	IONN	IODD	INCC	INNO	INNN	INND	INDD	IDDD	CIII
No.	2	4	1	1	47	2	26	74	3
%	.17	.33	.08	.08	3.93	.17	2.17	6.19	.25
	CIIC	CIIO	CIDD	CCII	CCCI	CCCC	CCCO	CCCN	CCCD
No.	1	1	1	6	6	87	4	18	1
%	.08	.08	.08	.50	.50	7.27	.33	1.51	.08
	CCNN	CCDD	CODD	CNII	CNNN	CNDD	CDDD	OIII	OINN
No.	8	36	1	1	12	7	11	6	1
%	.67	3.01	.08	.08	1.00	.59	.92	.50	.08
	OCCC	OCCN	OCNN	OCDD	OOIN	OOCI	OOCC	OOCO	OOCN
No.	2	1	2	1	1	2	1	11	2
%	.17	.08	.17	.08	.08	.17	.08	.92	.17
	OOOO	OOON	OONI	OONN	OODD	ONNN	ONDD	ODDD	NIII
No.	7	1	1	6	9	4	3	7	1
%	.59	.08	.08	.50	.75	.33	.25	.59	.08
	NICC	NICN	NIDD	NCNN	NNNN				
No.	1	1	1	1	4				
%	.08	.08	.08	.08	.33				

Source: HRCA Survey of the Elderly (1,196 Elderly, excludes elderly not interviewed or without ascertained living arrangement in at least one wave).

Note: Living arrangements are denoted as follows: I = lives independently; C = lives with children; O = lives with other relatives or nonrelatives; N = lives in nursing home; D = dead.

Table 3.4 Variable Definitions and Statistics in Longitudinal Subsample

A. Dependent Variable

Choice and Definition	Sample Frequency 1982	1984	1985	1986	1987
1: Independent living arrangements	.790	.742	.732	.697	.643
2: Shared living arrangements	.210	.229	.220	.236	.223
3: Institutional living arrangements	.000	.029	.048	.067	.134
No. of observations	314	314	314	314	314

B. Explanatory Variables

Variable and Definition	Sample Average 1982	1984	1985	1986	1987
AGE: Age of elderly person	78.2	80.3	81.2	82.2	83.2
FEMALE: 1 if female, 0 if male	.85	.85	.85	.85	.85
KIDS: No. of living children	2.31	2.31	2.31	2.31	2.31
MARRIED: 1 if married, 0 if widowed or not married	.178	.134	.121	.115	.105
SUBJ: Subjective health rating	2.74	2.65	2.60	2.64	2.65
ADLSUM: Score of functional disability	5.25	5.75	5.82	6.27	7.38
ILLSUM: Score of diagnosed conditions	3.47	3.40	3.70	3.98	4.12
INCOME: Real annual income (in $1,000 1987)	6.10	6.18	6.27	6.85	7.19

Note: Each explanatory variable is interacted with choice 1 (living independently) and choice 2 (living with children or others), while choice 3 (living in an institution) is the base category.

mated parameter values and the pseudo-R^2 associated with this log likelihood value.[7] The cross-sectional estimates yield a pseudo-R^2 of more than 40 percent, a satisfactory fit for this kind of data. However, introducing random effects in order to account for unobserved time-invariant characteristics dramatically increases the fit. If shocks are allowed to taper off in a first-order autoregressive process rather than to persist in the form of a random effect, the fit is even better. Finally, the combination of random effects and the AR(1) structure yields significantly better results than if either specification is employed separately.[8] Clearly, the unobserved utilities of this model include both time-invariant and time-varying components.

Correlation across alternatives is also present. The full multinomial probit specifications (the rightmost column in table 3.5, headed "MNP") fare everywhere significantly better than the models that obey the IIA assumption (the leftmost column in table 3.5, headed "IIA"). Interalternative correlation ap-

7. The pseudo-R^2 is defined as 1 − (actual likelihood)/(likelihood at zero coefficients and identity covariance matrix).

8. Significance as measured by the likelihood ratio statistic.

Table 3.5 **Estimation Results: Goodness of Fit (log likelihood values, pseudo-R^2 in parentheses)**

A. Pooled Cross Sections, $\varepsilon_{i,t} = \nu_{i,t}$

IIA		MNP
−996.46		−957.94
(.422)		(.445)

B. Random Effects Included, $\varepsilon_{i,t} = \alpha_i + \nu_{i,t}$

IIA	RE-Corr	MNP
−715.70	−711.79	−671.93
(.585)	(.587)	(.610)

C. First-Order Autoregressive Errors Included, $\varepsilon_{i,t} = \rho_i \cdot \varepsilon_{i,t-1} + \nu_{i,t}$

IIA		MNP
−673.72		−652.74
(.609)		(.622)

D. Random Effects and First-Order Autoregressive Errors Included, $\varepsilon_{i,t} = \alpha_i + \eta_{i,t}, \eta_{i,t} = \rho_i \cdot \eta_{i,t-1} + \nu_{i,t}$

IIA	RE-Corr	MNP
−648.07	−647.60	−632.45
(.624)	(.625)	(.633)

Note: Three different specifications of correlations across alternatives are employed, denoted as follows: IIA: independence of irrelevant alternatives imposed, i.e., $\sigma(\nu_i, \nu_j) = \sigma(\alpha_i, \alpha_j) = 0$; RE-Corr: random effects correlated, i.e., $\sigma(\alpha_i, \alpha_j) \neq 0$, $\sigma(\nu_i, \nu_j) = 0$; MNP: unobserved time-specific utility components correlated, i.e., $\sigma(\nu_i, \nu_j) \neq 0$, $\sigma(\alpha_i, \alpha_j) = 0$.

pears to work through the contemporary error components rather than through the random effects, as can be seen by comparing the numbers in the "RE-Corr" column with those in the "MNP" column.

Detailed estimation results follow in tables 3.6–3.9. These four tables correspond to the four intertemporal specifications (pooled cross sections, random effects, autoregressive errors, and random effects plus autoregressive errors). The two or three panels in each table pertain to the correlation pattern across alternatives: the leftmost panel relates to the IIA assumption, the rightmost to a full MNP model. In the models with random effect, the middle panel reports on the estimation with correlated random effects. For each variable, we measure (1) the relative influence on the likelihood of living alone relative to the likelihood of becoming institutionalized (e.g., AGE1), and (2) the rela-

Table 3.6 Pooled Cross-Sectional Probit Estimates

	Error Structure, $\varepsilon_{i,t} = \nu_{i,t}$			
	IIA (Spec. A)		MNP (Spec. E)	
Variable	Estimate	*t*-Stat.	Estimate	*t*-Stat.
AGE1	−.0319	−2.64	−.0234	−2.87
AGE2	−.0169	−1.39	−.0159	−1.87
FEMALE1	.4490	1.81	.3687	1.72
FEMALE2	.4163	1.56	.3102	1.38
KIDS1	.0447	.99	.0624	1.54
KIDS2	.1325	2.86	.1258	2.86
MARRIED1	.4243	1.21	.1870	.66
MARRIED2	−.3468	−.92	−.3640	−1.20
SUBJ1	.1263	1.08	.0843	.81
SUBJ2	−.0658	−.54	−.0333	−.29
ADLSUM1	−.2343	12.38	−.1769	10.08
ADLSUM2	−.1239	−6.61	−.1132	−5.22
ILLSUM1	−.0256	−.66	−.0242	−.68
ILLSUM2	−.0195	−.48	−.0139	−.36
INCOME1	.0788	2.45	.0809	2.61
INCOME2	.0922	2.86	.0905	2.92
CONSTANT1	5.5292	4.92	4.1058	5.65
CONSTANT2	2.7875	2.45	2.5686	3.26
SD (ν_1)	1.0000	(fix)	.2834	−2.36
corr (ν_1, ν_2)	.0000	(fix)	.4465	1.72
Log likelihood	−996.46		−957.88	
Log likelihood at zero	−1,724.82		−1,724.82	
Pseudo-R^2 (%)	42.23		44.46	
No. of observations	1,570		1,570	

Note: In this and the following tables, the *t*-statistics of the elements of the covariance matrix refer to the reparameterized estimated values. They are evaluated around zero for correlations and around one for standard deviations.

tive influence on the likelihood of living with others relative to the likelihood of becoming institutionalized (e.g., AGE2).

We first comment on the cross-sectional results, table 3.6. Four variables describe the influence of demographic characteristics on the living arrangement choices of the elderly person. Age per se decreases both the likelihood of living alone and the likelihood of living with others relative to the likelihood of becoming institutionalized, holding all other variables constant, particularly health. Female elderly are more likely to live alone. The number of children considerably increases the likelihood of a shared living arrangement. These results are as expected. A surprising result, however, is the insignificance of the indicator variable for being married.

Table 3.7 **Random Effects Probit Model**

	Error Structure, $\varepsilon_{i,t} = \alpha_i + \nu_{i,t}$					
	IIA (Spec. B)		RE-Corr (Spec. F1)		MNP (Spec. F2)	
Variable	Estimate	*t*-Stat.	Estimate	*t*-Stat.	Estimate	*t*-Stat.
AGE1	−.0570	−2.64	−.0604	−3.05	−.0643	−3.50
AGE2	−.0307	−1.22	−.0311	−1.40	−.0360	−1.79
FEMALE1	.5597	1.38	.4370	1.11	.7641	2.21
FEMALE2	1.0004	1.82	1.2543	2.37	.8631	2.16
KIDS1	.0329	.38	.0094	.12	.0586	.78
KIDS2	.2235	2.16	.2036	2.24	.1398	1.73
MARRIED1	.6279	1.29	.5589	1.20	.3121	.73
MARRIED2	.2165	.38	.1706	.31	−.1039	−.22
SUBJ1	.0889	.50	.1023	.60	.0521	.33
SUBJ2	−.1938	−1.00	−.2192	−1.18	−.0756	−.46
ADLSUM1	−.2985	−11.28	−.2850	−11.05	−.2472	−10.12
ADLSUM2	−.1824	−6.24	−.1716	−6.04	−.1981	−7.17
ILLSUM1	−.0905	−1.53	−.0977	−1.73	−.0900	−1.66
ILLSUM2	−.0743	−1.10	−.0741	−1.16	−.0704	−1.23
INCOME1	.1190	2.28	.1149	2.30	.0988	2.29
INCOME2	.1361	2.59	.1328	2.64	.1074	2.47
CONSTANT1	9.2564	4.71	9.3513	5.12	8.9092	5.21
CONSTANT2	3.9987	1.75	3.4848	1.68	5.2459	2.78
SD (ν_1)	1.0000	(fix)	1.0000	(fix)	.5833	−2.79
corr (ν_1, ν_2)	.0000	(fix)	.0000	(fix)	.7485	4.81
SD (α_1)	1.1305	1.03	.9650	−.29	.7386	−2.21
SD (α_2)	1.9847	7.93	1.7488	5.23	1.1366	.71
corr (α_1, α_2)	.0000	(fix)	−.5495	−3.18	.0000	(fix)
Log likelihood	−717.79		−711.79		−671.93	
Log likelihood at zero	−1,724.82		−1,724.82		−1,724.82	
Pseudo-R^2 (%)	58.38		58.73		61.04	
No. of observations	1,570		1,570		1,570	

Note: See table 3.6.

Three variables measure health. While neither the subjective health rating (SUBJ) nor the score of diagnosed conditions (ILLSUM) predicts living arrangement choices very well, the score of functional ability (ADLSUM) is by far the most significant variable. The performance of the functional ability index confirms the results of most health-oriented studies of institutionalization.[9] The poor performance of subjective health ratings in predicting living arrangement choices is perhaps not so surprising given that this variable exhibits, on aver-

9. For a survey of health-oriented studies of institutionalization, see Garber and MaCurdy (1990).

Table 3.8 **Probit Model with Autoregressive Errors**

	Error Structure, $\varepsilon_{i,t} = \rho_i \cdot \varepsilon_{i,t-1} + \nu_{i,t}$			
	IIA (Spec. C)		MNP (Spec. G)	
Variable	Estimate	t-Statistic	Estimate	t-Statistic
AGE1	−.0458	−3.23	−.0368	−2.51
AGE2	−.0237	−1.63	−.0033	−.16
FEMALE1	.2286	.91	.4414	1.79
FEMALE2	.6579	2.27	.6295	1.56
KIDS1	.0176	.34	.0541	.97
KIDS2	.1351	2.50	.1801	2.50
MARRIED1	.1352	.44	.2048	.66
MARRIED2	−.1184	−.35	−.3845	−.93
SUBJ1	−.0146	−.12	.0100	.08
SUBJ2	−.1266	−1.03	−.1055	−.72
ADLSUM1	−.1972	−11.06	−.1953	−8.15
ADLSUM2	−.1419	−7.83	−.1286	−4.92
ILLSUM1	−.0464	−1.18	−.0300	−.70
ILLSUM2	−.0511	−1.24	−.0285	−.55
INCOME1	.0635	2.06	.0910	2.36
INCOME2	.0694	2.25	.1007	2.58
CONSTANT1	7.2253	5.66	5.6732	4.08
CONSTANT2	3.6772	2.79	.8886	.45
SD (ν_1)	1.0000	(fix)	.2678	−3.27
corr (ν_1, ν_2)	.0000	(fix)	.0137	.08
ρ_1	.9278	10.40	.9065	7.53
ρ_2	.8059	15.56	.8648	19.13
Log likelihood	−673.73		−652.74	
Log likelihood at zero	−1,724.82		−1,724.82	
Pseudo-R^2 (%)	60.94		62.16	
No. of observations	1,570		1,570	

Note: See table 3.6.

age, very little change over time, in spite of distinct changes over time in average functional ability scores (see table 3.4).

The results reveal a significant income effect. The higher the income of the elderly person, the less likely he or she is to be institutionalized. The direction of the income effect is in line with most previous studies, although many studies fail to measure this income effect with much precision.[10] It is quite difficult

10. For a survey, see Börsch-Supan, Kotlikoff, and Morris (1989).

Table 3.9 Random Effects Probit Model with Autoregressive Errors

Error Structure, $\varepsilon_{i,t} = \alpha_i + \eta_{i,t}, \eta_{i,t} = \rho_i \cdot \eta_{i,t-1} + \nu_{i,t}$

	IIA (Spec. D)		RE-Corr (Spec. H1)		MNP (Spec. H2)	
Variable	Estimate	*t*-Stat.	Estimate	*t*-Stat.	Estimate	*t*-Stat.
AGE1	−.0646	−3.96	−.0644	−3.74	−.0513	−3.60
AGE2	−.0421	−2.32	−.0424	−2.25	−.0279	−1.43
FEMALE1	.6071	1.80	.6237	1.84	.5791	1.90
FEMALE2	.9769	2.41	.9257	2.24	.7492	1.62
KIDS1	.0469	.66	.0500	.71	.0465	.79
KIDS2	.1554	1.96	.1534	1.94	.1666	1.99
MARRIED1	.1969	.50	.1960	.49	.2004	.57
MARRIED2	−.1502	−.34	−.1549	−.35	−.3729	−.83
SUBJ1	.0461	.32	.0421	.29	.1059	.79
SUBJ2	−.0724	−.47	−.0683	−.44	−.0450	−.28
ADLSUM1	−.2358	−10.01	−.2356	−10.09	−.2201	−10.50
ADLSUM2	−.1811	−7.27	−.1826	−7.29	−.1612	−6.35
ILLSUM1	−.0848	−1.67	−.0843	−1.67	−.0864	−1.89
ILLSUM2	−.0694	−1.26	−.0703	−1.28	−.0718	−1.28
INCOME1	.0866	2.11	.0869	2.06	.0892	2.23
INCOME2	.0943	2.29	.0942	2.22	.0987	2.44
CONSTANT1	8.9868	6.30	8.9608	5.88	7.2120	5.59
CONSTANT2	5.2089	3.25	5.3660	3.21	3.3559	1.92
SD (ν_1)	1.0000	(fix)	1.0000	(fix)	.0278	−3.77
corr (ν_1, ν_2)	.0000	(fix)	.0000	(fix)	−.3898	−2.59
SD (α_1)	.0027	−.14	.1288	−1.98	.0022	−.16
SD (α_2)	1.0582	.34	1.0239	.13	.0054	−.16
corr (α_1, α_2)	.0000	(fix)	1.0000	.05	.0000	(fix)
ρ_1	.9499	7.87	.9571	6.87	.9865	2.75
ρ_2	.6692	7.67	.6946	7.08	.8719	20.54
Log likelihood	−648.07		−647.60		−632.45	
Log likelihood at zero	−1,724.82		−1,724.82		1,724.82	
Pseudo-R^2 (%)	62.43		62.46		63.33	
No. of observations	1,570		1,570		1,570	

Note: See table 3.6.

to construct a variable measuring the relative costs of ambulatory and institutional care for the Massachusetts communities included in our sample. Hence, there are no prices included in our estimation.

In the righthand panel of table 3.6, two contemporaneous covariance terms are estimated. The IIA assumption of the lefthand panel is clearly rejected, as can be seen by the large difference in the log likelihood values. The unobserved component in the utility of living independently exhibits significantly less variation than in the utility of the other two choices. Note that the *t*-statistics are measured around the null hypotheses $\sigma(\nu_i) = 1$, $\text{corr}(\nu_i, \nu_j) = 0$ for $i \neq j$, and relate to the following reparameterized values: the *t*-statistic of $\sigma(\nu_i)$ refers to $\exp[\sigma(\nu_i)]$, and the *t*-statistic of $\text{corr}(\nu_i, \nu_j)$ refers to $\{\exp[\text{corr}(\nu_i, \nu_j)] - 1\}/\{\exp[\text{corr}(\nu_i, \nu_j)] + 1\}$. This parameterization implicitly imposes the inequalities $\sigma(\nu_i) \geq 0$ and $|\text{corr}(\nu_i, \nu_j)| \leq 1$.

The coefficient estimates remain qualitatively unchanged when the IIA assumption is dropped in favor of a cross-sectional multinomial probit analysis. However, some coefficients change their relative numerical magnitudes. The income effect, to take just one example, is strengthened relative to the influence of the measure of functional ability.

We now put the panel structure into place. Introduction of random effects (see table 3.7) dramatically raises the pseudo-R^2 to almost 60 percent. Some of the time-invariant characteristics become less significant, while the time-varying variables come out much stronger. Such an effect might be expected because the time-varying variables have falsely captured some effects in each cross section that are now attributed to the random effects. Note that time-invariant characteristics are identified in the random effects model as opposed to a fixed effects specification.

In table 3.8, autoregressive error components, instead of random effects, link the different waves. Finally, table 3.9 reports on the full model, where the random effects are augmented by two autoregressive error components. The autocorrelation coefficients ρ_i are highly significant, and they drastically reduce the significance of the random effect terms in the combined specification, table 3.9. However, they do not replace the random effects. While they are close to one, the large *t*-statistics imply that they are significantly different from one. In addition, the likelihood ratio statistic shows a significant difference between the specification in table 3.9 and those in tables 3.7 and 3.8. We conclude that the unobserved utilities determining living arrangements of the elderly include both time-invariant and time-varying components. The panel is too short, however, to separate the two error structures precisely, as is evident by the high standard errors of the random effect terms at the bottom of table 3.9.

The demographic, health, and income variables are remarkably stable across the different specifications of the covariance matrix, in spite of their different fits in terms of achieved likelihood values and quite different numerical values of covariance elements (see table 3.10). This stability pertains both to alternative intertemporal and to interalternative correlation patterns. The likelihood of living independently decreases dramatically with age, even after correcting for the decline in health and functional ability, as measured by the variables ADLSUM and ILLSUM. The gender gap—elderly men are more likely to live in institutions; elderly women are more likely to live independently—is evident across all specifications. As opposed to other studies, elderly

Table 3.10 Covariance Matrix of Random Utility Term in Specification H

Error Structure,

$$\varepsilon_{i,t} = \alpha_i + \eta_{i,t}, \quad \eta_{i,t} = \rho_i \cdot \eta_{i,t-1} + \nu_{i,t}, \quad i = 1, \ldots, I - 1,$$

where

$$\mathrm{corr}(\nu_{i,t}, \nu_{j,s}) = \begin{cases} 0 & \text{if } t \neq s, \\ \omega_{ij} & \text{if } t = s, \end{cases}$$

and

$$\mathrm{cov}(\alpha_i, \alpha_j) = \delta_{ij}$$

which implies

$$\mathrm{cov}(\varepsilon_{i,t}, \varepsilon_{j,s}) = \delta_{ij} + \rho_i^{(t-s)} \frac{\sqrt{(1-\rho_i^2)} \cdot \sqrt{(1-\rho_j^2)}}{1 - \rho_i\rho_j} \omega_{ij}, \quad i, j = 1, \ldots, I - 1.$$

		$t = 1$			$t = 2$			$t = 3$			$t = 4$			$t = 5$		
s	j	$i = 1$	$i = 2$	$i = 3$	$i = 1$	$i = 2$	$i = 3$	$i = 1$	$i = 2$	$i = 3$	$i = 1$	$i = 2$	$i = 3$	$i = 1$	$i = 2$	$i = 3$
1	1	.03	−.08	.0	.03	−.07	.0	.03	−.06	.0	.03	−.05	.0	.03	−.04	.0
	2	−.08	4.17	.0	−.08	3.64	.0	.08	3.17	.0	−.07	2.76	.0	−.07	2.41	.0
	3	.0	.0	2.0	.0	.0	1.0	.0	.0	1.0	.0	.0	1.0	.0	.0	1.0
2	1	.03	−.08	.0	.03	−.08	.0	.03	−.07	.0	.03	−.06	.0	.03	−.05	.0
	2	−.07	3.64	.0	−.08	4.17	.0	−.08	3.64	.0	−.08	3.17	.0	−.07	2.76	.0
	3	.0	.0	1.0	.0	.0	2.0	.0	.0	1.0	.0	.0	1.0	.0	.0	1.0
3	1	.03	−.08	.0	.03	−.08	.0	.03	−.08	.0	.03	−.07	.0	.03	−.06	.0
	2	−.06	3.17	.0	−.07	3.64	.0	−.08	4.17	.0	−.08	3.64	.0	−.08	3.17	.0
	3	.0	.0	1.0	.0	.0	1.0	.0	.0	2.0	.0	.0	1.0	.0	.0	1.0
4	1	.03	−.07	.0	.03	−.08	.0	.03	−.08	.0	.03	−.08	.0	.03	−.07	.0
	2	−.05	2.76	.0	−.06	3.17	.0	−.07	3.64	.0	−.08	4.17	.0	−.08	3.64	.0
	3	.0	.0	1.0	.0	.0	1.0	.0	.0	1.0	.0	.0	2.0	.0	.0	1.0
5	1	.03	−.07	.0	.03	−.07	.0	.03	−.08	.0	.03	−.08	.0	.03	−.08	.0
	2	−.04	2.41	.0	−.05	2.76	.0	−.06	3.17	.0	−.07	3.64	.0	−.08	4.17	.0
	3	.0	.0	1.0	.0	.0	1.0	.0	.0	1.0	.0	.0	1.0	.0	.0	2.0

women are also more likely to live with their children.[11] The larger the number of living children, the more probable is living together with one of them.

Among the health variables, the simple functional ability index employed in this paper performs best. It is the most significant variable in the model. In the presence of this variable, subjective health ratings have no predictive power whatsoever. The simple index of diagnosed conditions is weakly significant, but a more detailed analysis of the illnesses included may produce better results.

Finally, economics does matter. The income effect is measured precisely and robustly across all specifications. It is slightly underestimated in cross-sectional analysis and slightly overestimated in the pure random effects model.[12] Those elderly with higher incomes choose institutions less frequently. Gauged by this willingness to spend income in order not to enter an institution, institutions appear to be an inferior living arrangement. The elderly's income may be spent on ambulatory care, thereby making living independently feasible in spite of declining functional ability. The ability to buy ambulatory services may also increase the likelihood of living with children rather than becoming institutionalized because these services substitute some of the burden that otherwise rests solely on the children. In addition, income may be spent on avoiding institutionalization by making transfer payments to children so that the children are more willing to take in their parents.[13] The results also suggest that increasing the income of the elderly does not raise their probability of living alone relative to the probability of living with their children.

3.5 Concluding Remarks

The simulated likelihood method works well and requires a very small number of replications. It easily accommodates highly complex error structures and can handle different error structures without major programming effort.

Two main conclusions follow from the estimation results. First, a careful specification of the temporal error process dramatically improves the fit. It also appears that ignoring intertemporal linkages does bias some estimation results numerically, although the different specifications produce qualitatively similar coefficients of the substantive parameters.

Second, living arrangement choices are governed predominantly by functional ability and to a lesser degree (but still statistically and numerically significantly) by age. The income effect is measured precisely and robustly. Institutions are an inferior living arrangement as measured by the willingness to

11. Börsch-Supan, Kotlikoff and Morris (1989) report the opposite for the same basic data set, but a much less selected sample.

12. These differences are not statistically significant.

13. On this "bribery" hypothesis, see Kotlikoff and Morris (1990).

spend income in order not to enter one. A somewhat surprising result is that changes in marital status do not appear to matter a great deal. The only supply factor that is included in our analysis, the number of living children, is, as can be expected, a significant factor for choosing shared living arrangements.

There are several weak points in the statistical analysis. The autoregressive specification "solves" the initial value problem by invoking a stationarity assumption. This is unsatisfactory, particularly with a short panel, such as in this application. It is possible to estimate a simple nonparametric specification of the initial value distribution, although in practice the random effects should capture a great deal of these effects.

The sample is selective because it includes only survivors. Whether this sample selection is innocent in the sense of not biasing the estimated coefficients remains to be studied. There is no problem if the choice of a living arrangement leaves mortality and morbidity probabilities unaffected. If, however, mortality and morbidity are, ceteris paribus, higher in nursing homes (e.g., because of inferior treatment), there is a serious sample selection problem.

Our panel of five waves is short. The identification difficulties apparent in table 3.9 are indicative of this short panel length. However, the dramatic differences in goodness of fit indicate that, even in a short panel, the rewards for controlling for intertemporal linkages are quite sizable.

References

Börsch-Supan, A. 1986. Household Formation, Housing Prices, and Public Policy Impacts. *Journal of Public Economics* 25:145–64.

———. 1990. A Dynamic Analysis of Household Dissolution and Living Arrangement Transitions by Elderly Americans. In *Issues in the Economics of Aging,* ed. D. A. Wise, 89–114. Chicago: University of Chicago Press.

Börsch-Supan, A., and V. Hajivassiliou. 1990. Smooth Unbiased Multivariate Probability Simulators for Limited Dependent Variable Models. Cowles Foundation Discussion Paper no. 960. New Haven, Conn.: Yale University.

Börsch-Supan, A., L. Kotlikoff, and J. Morris. 1989. The Dynamics of Living Arrangements of the Elderly: Health and Family Support. NBER Working Paper. Cambridge, Mass.: National Bureau of Economic Research.

Chamberlain, G. 1984. Panel Data. In *Handbook of Econometrics,* vol. 2, ed. Z. Griliches and M. D. Intriligator. Amsterdam: North Holland.

Daganzo, C. 1981. *Multinomial Probit.* New York: Academic.

Ellwood, D. T., and T. J. Kane. 1990. The American Way of Aging: An Event History Analysis. In *Issues in the Economics of Aging,* ed. D. A. Wise, 121–44. Chicago: University of Chicago Press.

Garber, A. M., and T. MaCurdy. 1990. Predicting Nursing Home Utilization among the High-Risk Elderly. In *Issues in the Economics of Aging,* ed. D. A. Wise, 173–200. Chicago: University of Chicago Press.

Geweke, J. 1989. Efficient Simulation from the Multivariate Normal Distribution Subject to Linear Inequality Constraints and the Evaluation of Constraint Probabilities. Working Paper. Durham, N.C.: Duke University.

Hajivassiliou, V., and D. McFadden. 1990. The Method of Simulated Scores for the Estimation of LDV Models. Cowles Foundation Discussion Paper no. 967. New Haven, Conn.: Yale University.

Kotlikoff, L. J., and J. N. Morris. 1989. How Much Care Do the Aged Receive from Their Children? A Bimodal Picture of Contact and Assistance. In *The Economics of Aging*, ed. D. A. Wise, 151–75. Chicago: University of Chicago Press.

———. 1990. Why Don't the Elderly Live with Their Children? A New Look. In *Issues in the Economics of Aging*, ed. D. A. Wise, 149–69. Chicago: University of Chicago Press.

Langdon, M. G. 1984. Methods of Determining Choice Probability in Utility Maximising Multiple Alternative Models. *Transportation Research* B 18:209–34.

Lerman, S., and C. Manski. 1981. On the Use of Simulated Frequencies to Approximate Choice Probabilities. In *Structural Analysis of Discrete Data with Econometric Applications*, ed. C. Manski and D. McFadden. Cambridge, Mass.: MIT Press.

McFadden, D. 1984. Qualitative Response Models. In *Handbook of Econometrics*, ed. Z. Griliches and M. D. Intriligator. Amsterdam: North Holland.

———. 1989. A Method of Simulated Moments for Estimation of Discrete Response Models without Numerical Integration. *Econometrica* 57:995–1026.

Morris, J. N., C. E. Gutkin, C. C. Sherwood, and E. Bernstein. 1987. Interest in Long Term Care Insurance. Final report in connection with HCFA Cooperative Agreement no. 18-C-98375/1. Washington, D.C.: HCFA, June.

Pakes, A., and D. Pollard. 1989. Simulation and the Asymptotics of Optimization Estimators. *Econometrica* 57:1027–57.

Comment Steven F. Venti

Axel Börsch-Supan, Vassilis Hajivassiliou, Laurence J. Kotlikoff, and John N. Morris have provided us with some useful results on the determinants of the living arrangements of the elderly and a valuable application of an econometric method appropriate to deal with this and similar problems. There are really two papers here. One is substantive and deals with the effects of health and income on the living arrangements of the elderly. The other, which is methodological, presents a computationally feasible econometric model for longitudinal data on discrete outcomes. The reason there are very nearly two distinct papers rather than one is that the new panel multinomial probit (PMNP) model introduced here does not reveal much more about living arrangements than a simple cross-sectional model. This is unfortunate because estimation of the PMNP is a remarkable achievement, has much to recommend its use in the present application, and should have a significant effect on future research in this area.

Briefly, the authors begin by estimating the parameters of a simple pooled

Steven F. Venti is associate professor of economics at Dartmouth College and a research associate of the National Bureau of Economic Research.

cross-sectional model of living arrangements. The results for this benchmark model support some rather well-known "facts" about elderly housing choices. The preference for living alone or in a shared arrangement (both relative to institutionalization) decreases with age, increases with income, and decreases with the number of functional limitations. The likelihood of living in a shared arrangement is higher for women and, not unexpectedly, for elderly with living children. Perhaps the one surprising finding is that the choice of living arrangements is unrelated to marital status.

These results give us a good picture of the preference ordering among living arrangements for the typical elderly family. Institutionalization is least preferred. But between the other two choices—living alone or in a shared arrangement—the distinction is less sharp. Evaluation of probabilities at the sample means reveals that living alone is preferred to a shared arrangement, but the preference advantage narrows with either an increase in income or an improvement in health. Thus, these results are broadly consistent with the conventional premise that the elderly, if able, will choose to live alone.

Caution must be exercised generalizing these results because of some peculiar features of the sample. The authors find that nursing homes are the least preferred arrangement. I have no doubt that this is true, yet given the way the sample was drawn it is hard to believe that we could detect otherwise. First, the initial sample is restricted to noninstitutionalized persons. Thus, any person with a strong propensity for this type of living arrangement is weeded out to begin with. Second, all persons who die by 1986 are also dropped from the estimation sample. Since nursing home stays often are associated with severely declining health, this restriction also systematically excludes persons most likely to display a preference for nursing homes.

There are a number of possible limitations to this simple specification that may lead to skepticism concerning the results. First, living arrangements are discrete choices, and the well known independence of irrelevant alternatives (IIA) problem arises if the unobserved correlation between attributes of the choices is ignored. The second problem has to do with the presence of unobserved family-specific components (heterogeneity). If these random effects (e.g., characteristics of children) are correlated with observed variables (e.g., income of the elderly), then the effects of observed variables on living arrangements may be estimated with bias. Finally, there is the issue of autocorrelated errors that may arise if, for instance, persons become accustomed to living arrangements they have experienced in the past. One cannot do much about these latter two problems using only cross-sectional data.

The question then is whether the basic "facts" about living arrangements are sensitive to these potential sources of bias. To find out, the authors use panel data to attack this problem head on, explicitly relaxing covariance restrictions one at a time and jointly to address each bias. This is quite a remarkable feat. If one begins with a simple independent probit model, the choice probability for an observation will involve two integrals. To relax the IIA assumption adds two covariance terms. The addition of an error structure to accommodate a very general covariance matrix for a four-period panel adds five more covariance terms and brings the number of integrals to eight. Evaluation of the likelihood for each observation is made possible by recent advances in the solution of high-dimensional integral equations.

As it turns out, implementing this model has little qualitative effect on the results. This is too bad because the potential of the model is not readily apparent from the results. Often in cases such as this, the econometric modeling is dismissed as a test of the robustness of simpler specifications. But it is much more than this because the PMNP is, as I shall argue below, consistent with a much broader range of behavioral models than alternative cross-sectional specifications and has the potential to reveal much more than in the present case.

If the paper has one weakness, it is the absence of a behavioral framework to guide model selection. I encourage the authors to devote part of their future effort to the choice problem faced by elderly households. There is a tendency, I think, for researchers not to treat the living arrangements of the elderly as a choice problem at all but rather to view living arrangements as the consequence only of constraints that may be exogenously determined. The idea here is that all elderly prefer to live at home but that some do not because they cannot afford to or are unable to take care of themselves. This overly simple approach misses much of the richness of the decision. Living options are likely to be affected by prices for institutional care and home care, private and public insurance, housing costs, the level and composition of wealth (especially in light of "spend down" rules associated with Medicaid in many states), and whether the elderly household owns a home. None of these factors are addressed directly by the authors. Perhaps they should be.

In addition, the choice decision, in particular the decision to enter into a shared living arrangement, will involve the preferences and financial status of other family members. Two of the authors have already made significant headway broadening the definition of the decision-making unit.[1] Their work and the work of others suggests that living arrangements may reflect bargaining between the elderly and their children.[2] To cite just one example, two generations may share living quarters if the parents are poor and the children are wealthy or if the children are poor and the parents are wealthy, but not perhaps if both generations are either poor or wealthy. Alternatively, the choice pro-

1. See Laurence J. Kotlikoff and John N. Morris, "Why Don't the Elderly Live with Their Children? A New Look," NBER Working Paper no. 2734 (Cambridge, Mass.: National Bureau of Economic Research, October 1988).

2. See Axel H. Börsch-Supan, "A Dynamic Analysis of Household Dissolution and Living Arrangement Transitions by Elderly Americans," in *Issues in the Economics of Aging*, ed. David A. Wise (Chicago: University of Chicago Press, 1989), 89–114; and Saul Schwartz, Sheldon Danziger, and Eugene Smolensky, "The Choice of Living Arrangements by the Elderly," in *Retirement and Economic Behavior*, ed. Henry J. Aaron and Gary Burtless (Washington, D.C.: Brookings, 1984).

cess may be characterized as a matching process where a "marriage" is observed only if both parents and their children have a preference for a joint living arrangement. These more completely specified models of family relationships may give the authors a better idea of factors that influence the choice of living arrangements.

Although such attempts may help us learn more about factors other that the health and income of the elderly, I doubt the effects of elderly health and income measured here will be much changed by their inclusion. The reason for this is that the full model (specification H) is well suited to treating many of these missing factors as unobservables. In this sense, it is likely to be broadly consistent with a number of alternative models of how living arrangement decisions are made. In particular, omitted time-invariant family-specific factors such as children's income are easily treated as random effects. Thus, the rather general error structure provides some insurance against model misspecification.

To summarize, this is an important contribution. The substantive results, although not necessarily new, tend to buttress previous findings concerning preferences for living arrangements. The econometric framework, which is new, is likely to be an important tool in future research on a number of fundamental issues related to aging. As more longitudinal data become available, there is an increasing need for econometric methods that can fully exploit the informational advantages of these data over cross-sectional data. In the past, controlling for unobserved time invariant factors and state dependence has been unmanageable in all but the shortest of panels. The authors have shown that such analyses are now practical. Thus, I expect the statistical model applied in this paper will become an important tool in future analyses of longitudinal data on discrete outcomes such as living arrangements, retirement, mobility, homeownership, and portfolio choice.

4 The Provision of Time to the Elderly by Their Children

Axel Börsch-Supan, Jagadeesh Gokhale,
Laurence J. Kotlikoff, and John N. Morris

Has support of the aged by families declined in the postwar period? While the jury is still out, there is substantial evidence pointing in that direction. Over 60 percent of the elderly (those over 60) now live alone, compared with only 25 percent in the 1940s. For the old old (those over 85), the fraction living alone has increased from 13 to 57 percent. At the same time, there has been more than a tripling of the rate of institutionalization; today almost one-quarter of the old old live in institutions, compared with only 7 percent in the 1940s (Sandefur and Tuma 1987). In addition to not living with the elderly, the children of the elderly rarely provide financial transfers to the elderly (Kotlikoff and Morris 1989), and when they do, the amounts are typically quite meager.

One defense of the children's behavior is demographic; the current number of children per elderly parent totals about half the number observed in the 1940s. Since the elderly of today had fewer children than did their parents and have, in some cases, succeeded in outliving their children, the current situation may be much of their own making. A second defense is that the relative income position of the elderly has improved, permitting them to live alone (Michael, Fuchs, and Scott 1980) and obviating the need for financial transfers from their children. A variety of studies (e.g., Boskin, Kotlikoff, and Knetter 1985; and Andrews and Hurd 1990) have demonstrated that current poverty rates of the elderly are close to, if not below, those of the nonelderly.

Axel Börsch-Supan is professor of economics at the University of Mannheim and a research associate of the National Bureau of Economic Research. Jagadeesh Gokhale is an economist at the Federal Reserve Bank of Cleveland. Laurence J. Kotlikoff is professor of economics at Boston University and a research associate of the National Bureau of Economic Research. John N. Morris is director of research of the Hebrew Rehabilitation Center for the Aged.

The authors are grateful to Konrad Stahl for his comments and suggestions. They thank the National Institute of Aging for research support and Dan Nash and Manjula Singh for research assistance.

Much of the improvement in the relative incomes of the elderly is due to increases in real Social Security benefits legislated in the 1970s. A third point to consider in assessing child support of the elderly involves payment for nursing home care. A good fraction of the elderly in nursing homes are private pay patients. Some of these payments are being made directly by children. While we are not aware of time-series data on nursing home payments by children, it seems plausible that such payments per child measured at constant dollars have increased over time.

While the elderly may need and appear to be receiving less financial help from their children, their needs for companionship and physical assistance may well have increased in the postwar period; the increased longevity of the elderly often means living for years in poor states of health. In addition, those elderly who continue to live will lose a large fraction of their old friends and even some of their children along the way. Most studies of the increasingly separate living arrangements of the elderly conclude that these arrangements reflect the preferences and improved financial means of the elderly. In contrast, Kotlikoff and Morris (1990) suggest that about half the elderly would prefer to live with their children but continue to live apart because of their children's preferences coupled with their children's financial abilities to live apart from their parents.

One reason the jury remains out on family support of the aged involves the issue of time spent by children with their elderly parents. As Morgan's (1984) research suggests, children's provision of time to their elderly parents is an important, if not the most important, form of economic transfer to the elderly by their children. This paper studies the provision of time by children to their elderly parents. We use the 1986 Hebrew Rehabilitation Center for the Aged (HRCA) follow-up survey of Massachusetts elderly and the 1986 HRC-NBER survey of the children of these Massachusetts elderly. While the child survey involved an interview of only one of the children of the elderly (the one designated by the elderly), each child was asked a set of detailed questions not only about his or her own circumstances but also about the circumstances of each of his or her siblings. The combined data are unique in their detail of demographic and economic characteristics of the elderly and each of their children.

We use these data to answer a number of questions about the provision of time by children to their parents. These questions include, How does the health status of the elderly influence the amount of time given by children? How does the health status of the children influence their provision of time to their parents? Do parents with more income and wealth receive more time from their children? How do the employment status and wage rates of children affect their provision of time? Do children free ride on their siblings' provision of time? Are home care corporations used by children as a substitute for their own time? Do the institutionalized elderly receive more or less time? Are daughters, other things being equal, more or less likely to provide time?

We take two empirical approaches in studying the data. First, we estimated

Tobits for the provision of time by children. Second, we estimate a structural model of the joint decision of children to work and to provide time to their elderly parent. Since the opportunity cost of providing time to the parent for working children is the wage, the structural model indicates how wage rates influence the allocation of time by children to the elderly. The model can account for corner solutions in the data; this is important because some children do not work, some do not provide time to their parents, and some neither work nor provide time.

Our model assumes that the child is altruistic in that he or she cares about the utility the parent receives from their time spent together. The model does not, however, consider the utility the child might derive from the consumption of the parent. Including the utility of parent's consumption in the child's utility function would require an analysis of financial transfers from children to parents. But given that only 2.6 percent of children in our sample report making financial transfers to their elderly parent(s), the extra complications of modeling financial transfers seems to outweigh the potential benefits.[1] While we ignore financial transfers, the model does consider the simultaneous decisions by siblings as to how much time each sibling should provide the parent. The model assumes that each sibling takes time provided to the parent as given; that is, the siblings play noncooperative Nash.

Another issue not considered by the model is the possibility that children are not altruistic but, in effect, sell their time (à la Bernheim, Shleifer, and Summers 1985) to their parents. The quid pro quo for this sale of time is a financial payment by parents to their children. But such transfers are also quite rare in our sample: only 0.9 percent of children report receiving financial transfers from their parents. In addition, as described below, children receiving financial transfers from their parents are no more likely to provide time to their parents than those not receiving transfers. While the possibility remains that parents pay for time transfers by leaving larger future bequests, it is not clear how one would estimate the magnitude of such contingent payments.

Section 4.1 presents our simple structural model. Section 4.2 describes the data and our sample selection. Section 4.3 presents Tobit estimates of the allocation of time by children to their parents as well as estimates of the structural model. Section 4.4 concludes the paper with a summary of our findings.

4.1 A Simple Structural Model of the Joint Labor Supply and Time Provision Decisions

4.1.1 The Model

Our model assumes that the child's utility is logarithmic and depends on his or her consumption, leisure, and the total amount of time the parent receives

1. The mean amount of transfers from children to parents, when positive, is $2,159 per year.

from him or her and his or her siblings. The utility function of sibling i, U_i, is given by

$$U_i = \alpha \log C_i + \beta \log \ell_i + \log(d_i + \sum_{j \neq i}^{N_i} d_j + m). \tag{1}$$

In (1), α, β, and m are constants. The terms C_i, ℓ_i, d_i, and d_j ($j \neq i$) stand, respectively, for consumption of child i, leisure of child i, time provided to the parent by child i, and time provided to the parent by sibling j. There are N_i siblings of child i. The displacement value m (which we set equal to one) in the logarithm of time received by the parent permits the possibility that child i provides zero time to his or her parent even if all his or her siblings also provide zero time.

The child maximizes this function subject to constraints (2), (3), and (4):

$$C_i \leq W_i(1 - \ell_i - d_i) + Y_i, \tag{2}$$

$$d_i \geq 0, \tag{3}$$

$$d_i + \ell_i \leq 1. \tag{4}$$

Equation (2) says that consumption cannot exceed labor earnings plus exogenous income, Y_i. Equation (2) says that time provided to the parent cannot be negative, and equation (3) says that the sum of leisure time plus time spent with the parent cannot exceed the endowment of time that is normalized to unity.

Since (2) will always be binding, solutions for the values of ℓ_i and d_i satisfy:

$$\left[\frac{\beta}{\ell_i} - \frac{\alpha W_i}{W_i(1 - \ell_i - d_i) + Y_i}\right](1 - d_i - \ell_i) = 0, \tag{5}$$

$$\left[\frac{1}{d_i + \sum_{j \neq i}^{N_i} d_j + m} - \frac{\beta}{\ell_i}\right] d_i = 0. \tag{6}$$

Letting $[\ ]_a$ and $[\ ]_b$ stand, respectively, for the values in the square brackets in (5) and (6), we have the following four cases:

1. $d_i + \ell_i = 1$ and $d_i = 0$ (the child is retired and provides no time) hold if $[\ ]_a > 0$ and $[\ ]_b < 0$.
2. $d_i + \ell_i = 1$ and $d_i > 0$ (the child is retired and provides time) hold if $[\ ]_a > 0$ and $[\ ]_b = 0$.
3. $d_i + \ell_i < 1$ and $d_i = 0$ (the child works and provides no time) hold if $[\ ]_a = 0$ and $[\ ]_b < 0$.
4. $d_i + \ell_i < 1$ and $d_i > 0$ (the child works and provides times) hold if $[\ ]_a = 0$ and $[\ ]_b = 0$.

4.1.2 Estimation

The condition $[\quad]_a \geq 0$ implies

$$\log[W_i(1 - \ell_i - d_i) + Y_i] - \log(W_i\ell_i) \geq \log \alpha_i - \log \beta_i,$$

and the condition $[\quad]_b \leq 0$ implies

$$\log\ell_i - \log(d_i + \Sigma_{j \neq i} d_j + m) \leq \log \beta_i.$$

In these expressions, each child has individual-specific preference parameters, that is, α and β are subscripted by i. We let $\log \alpha_i = x_i'\theta + \mu_i$ and $\log \beta_i = x_i'\psi + \upsilon_i$, where x_i' is a vector of characteristics of child i and his or her parent(s), θ and ψ are coefficient vectors, and μ_i and υ_i are mean zero independent normal errors with bivariate density $f(\mu_i, \upsilon_i)$. Define

$$H_i \equiv \log[W_i(1 - \ell_i - d_i) + Y_i] - \log(W_i\ell_i) - x_i'\theta + x_i'\psi$$

and

$$Z_i \equiv \log \ell_i - \log(d_i + \Sigma_{j \neq i} d_j + m) - x_i'\psi,$$

then $H_i \geq \mu_i - \upsilon_i$ and $Z_i \leq \upsilon_i$. The probability of observing child i working and providing time can now be expressed as

$$\Pr(H_i = \mu_i - \upsilon_i \text{ and } Z_i = \upsilon_i) = f(H_i + Z_i, Z_i), \tag{7}$$

where H_i and Z_i are evaluated at the observed values of ℓ_i and d_i.

The probability of observing child i retired and providing time is

$$\Pr(H_i > \mu_i - \upsilon_i \text{ and } Z_i = \upsilon_i) = \int_{-\infty}^{H_i+Z_i} f(\mu_i, Z_i)d\mu_i, \tag{8}$$

where H_i and Z_i are evaluated at the observed value of d_i and ℓ_i is evaluated at one minus the observed value of d_i.

The probability of observing child i retired and providing no time is

$$\Pr(H_i > \mu_i - \upsilon_i \text{ and } Z_i < \upsilon_i) = \int_{Z_i}^{\infty} \int_{-\infty}^{H_i+\upsilon_i} f(\mu_i, \upsilon_i)\, d\upsilon_i d\mu_i, \tag{9}$$

where H_i and Z_i are evaluated $d_i = 0$ and $\ell_i = 1$.

The probability of observing child i working and providing no time is

$$\Pr(H_i = \mu_i - \upsilon_i \text{ and } Z_i < \upsilon_i) = \int_{Z_i}^{\infty} f(H_i + \upsilon_i, \upsilon_i)d\upsilon_i, \tag{10}$$

where H_i and Z_i are evaluated at $d_i = 0$ and ℓ_i equals one minus the observed amount of time child i spends working.

Denote L_k as the probability of the observed labor supply and time provision of child k, then the likelihood, L, of the sample with N observations is

$$L = \prod_{k=1}^{N} L_k. \tag{11}$$

4.2 The Data, Sample Section Criteria, and Data Characteristics

4.2.1 The 1986 HRCA Elderly Survey and the 1986 HRC-NBER Child Survey

The 1986 HRCA Survey of the Elderly is part of an ongoing panel survey of Massachusetts elderly that began in 1982. In addition to the 1982 and 1986 surveys, the elderly sample was reinterviewed in 1984, 1985, 1987, and 1989. The 1986 HRC-NBER Child Survey is a survey of the children of those elderly interviewed in the 1986 HRCA Survey of the Elderly. One child of each elderly respondent was interviewed and asked a set of questions concerning his or her household, parents, and siblings.

The original 1982 stratified sample of 3,856 elderly individuals was drawn from two populations. The first population, accounting for 2,674 of the elderly in the total sample, was drawn from communities in Massachusetts. In forming the community sample, the state of Massachusetts was divided into twenty-seven home care areas. Within each home care area, communities were stratified, on the basis of population, into large, medium, and small, and communities within each of the three groups were selected at random. Next, HRCA used Massachusetts police records, which record the ages and addresses of all Massachusetts residents, to stratify the elderly by age, separating those age 75 and older from those younger than age 75. Elderly individuals within each subgroup were then randomly selected. The community and age stratifications produced an intentional overrepresentation of the old old as well as the elderly living in rural communities.

The second population, which accounts for the remaining 1,182 elderly in the 1982 survey, was drawn from elderly participants of all twenty-seven Massachusetts home health care corporations. In this sample, the elderly were again stratified by age, and the older old were oversampled. The sample's selection procedures are described in more detail in Morris et al. (1987). The 1982 sample of the elderly included only the noninstitutionalized elderly, but each subsequent survey has followed the initial sample as they changed residences, including moving into and out of nursing homes.

Each of the HRCA Surveys of the Elderly include detailed questions about living arrangements and health status. The 1986 reinterview of the elderly also contains a series of questions of the elderly about their children. These questions include the names, sexes, frequency and type of contact with children, the extent of financial aid given to and received from children, and the amount of assistance given by children to their elderly parents in performing activities of daily living. In addition, the 1986 survey contains a set of questions about the elderly respondent's income and wealth.

At the close of the HRCA elderly survey, the elderly respondent was asked for permission to contact one of his or her children and ask that child to participate in our child survey. While a random selection of the child respondents would have been preferable, it was felt that the elderly respondents would be more cooperative if they were allowed to make the selection. Because of funding limitations, we were able to sample only children of the community sample of elderly; that is, we were not able to contact children of the home care sample of elderly. As mentioned, the community sample of elderly is a stratified random sample of noninstitutionalized elderly.

Like the HRCA Surveys of the Elderly, the HRC-NBER Child Survey is a telephone interview. The Child Survey is roughly forty-five minutes in length. Interviews with the child's spouse were conducted if the child was not available. The questions in the Child Survey concerning the respondent's and spouse's characteristics include age, marital status, number of young children, work and health status, occupation, industry, education, grades in high school, income, and wealth. These questions are also asked of the respondent about his or her siblings. In addition, the child was asked to indicate (1) the frequency of contact between each sibling and each sibling's spouse and the HRCA elderly respondent parent, (2) the amount of financial assistance each sibling and his or her spouse give to or receive from the HRCA elderly respondent parent, and (3) the amount of time each sibling and his or her spouse spends with the HRCA elderly respondent per month. The child is also asked about his or her parents' and in-laws' health status as well as his or her parents' income and net wealth.

The sample size of the initial 1982 Survey of the Elderly is 3,856. In contrast, the 1986 completed sample size of elderly was 2,889, with 22.5 percent of the attrition since 1982 due to death. In the 1986 data, over 90 percent of the elderly are above age 70, over 40 percent are the old old (above age 85), and over two-thirds are female. The number of child respondents in the HRC-NBER Child Survey is 850. We have data for 1,650 children of the HRCA Elderly Survey respondents (including siblings); that is, the 850 child respondents provided information on themselves plus an additional 800 siblings.

4.2.2 Sample Section

The basic sample used in our statistical analysis contains 1,650 children of 706 elderly respondents. We excluded observations if data are missing on a child's age, sex, occupation, health, education, marital status, grades received in school, and employment status. We also excluded children with missing information on time provided their parent, children younger than 18 years of age, children whose co-residence status with the parent respondent was not reported, and children whose parent's age we do not know.

4.2.3 Data Characteristics

Of the 706 elderly parents in our sample, 24 percent are age 55–70, 48 percent are age 71–80, and 28 percent are 81 and older. The 1,650 children (including siblings of the Child Survey respondents) of these parents range in age from 18 to 84; 20 percent are under 40, 29 percent are 41–50, 33 percent are 51–60, and 18 percent are 61 and older. Most of the elderly parents (70 percent) are female, and most (72 percent) are not married. In contrast, only 54 percent of children are female, and 76 percent of children are married. On average, there are 2.42 children per elderly parent. A total of 21 percent of the elderly parents have one child, 32 percent have two children, 23 percent have three, and 24 percent have four or more.

Among elderly who report their total household income, mean income is $11,247, and median income is $6,250. (These and all subsequent dollar figures are in 1987 dollars.) The corresponding figures for child households are $34,392 and $32,500, respectively. Among elderly who report total household net worth, mean net worth is $93,396 and median net worth is $40,000. The corresponding child net worth figures are $175,019 and $125,000, respectively.

Many of the elderly in our sample are in poor health; indeed, 13 percent of the sample's elderly are in nursing homes or similar institutions, and 15 percent are enrolled in home care programs. In all, 40 percent of the elderly report their health as fair or poor (as opposed to excellent or good). In terms of ADL (activities of daily living) status, 44 percent report difficulty or inability preparing their own meals, 56 percent taking out garbage, 33 percent performing house chores, 22 percent dressing themselves, 24 percent taking a bath or shower, 10 percent getting out of a chair without assistance, 21 percent maintaining bladder control, and 28 percent walking up and down stairs without assistance.

Not all the children of the elderly are in excellent or good health. A total of 13 percent of the children report their health (or have their health reported) to be either fair or poor. In the case of the 1,255 spouses of these children, 14 percent report (or have had reported) their health to be fair or poor.

In addition to time demands imposed by the elderly parent respondent, the children in our survey may need to respond to the time demands by their other parent and their parent in-laws. The fraction of children with two parents is 30 percent. In the case of in-laws, information was obtained only for the child respondents; that is, the survey did not ask the child respondents about their siblings' in-laws. For child respondents, the percentage with one or two parent in-laws is 43 percent, and 33 percent of these in-laws are reported to be in fair or poor health.

A total of 64 percent of the 1,729 children in the sample report (or have had reported) that they are employed full time, and 12 percent report (or have had reported) that they are employed part time. The average annual wage of children employed full time for those children for whom we have information on wages is \$32,914. Unfortunately, the child survey questionnaire did not ask about the wage plus salary of the child respondent and the wage plus salary of the child respondent's spouse separately but rather asked about combined household wage and salary income. And in the case of the questions about siblings, the survey asks only about the total income of the sibling and the sibling's spouse; it does not ask about siblings' wages and salaries separately.

The wage rate of children is a potentially important explanatory variable for estimation of both our Tobit and our structural models. In the estimation of these models, we use an imputed full-time wage based on a regression of wages of child respondents or their spouses who report that they are working full time and for whom we can determine their wages plus salaries. As an example, if the respondent child is married, reports that he or she works full time, and also reports that his or her spouse does not work, we know that the wages plus salaries of the couple are those of the child respondent. In this wage regression, we use education dummies for years of education, grades in school, occupation, sex, health, and a third-order polynomial in age as explanatory variables.[2]

4.3 Model Estimation

4.3.1 Tobit Estimates

The Tobit model can be viewed as a test of a simpler version of the structural model presented above. It corresponds to the case that the amount of work the child does (which may be zero) is exogenously given and the child simply divides his or her nonwork time between leisure and time spent with his or her parent. In his simpler model, consumption is exogenously determined by the sum of exogenous nonlabor plus labor income, so the child maximizes

$$U_i = \beta \log(\lambda_i - d_i) + \log(d_i + \Sigma_{j \neq i} d_j + m) \quad \text{s.t. } d_i \geq 0,$$

2. There are 157 observations in the auxiliary wage regression. The R^2 from the wage regression is .61. The coefficients (standard errors) from this regression are as follows: intercept = −28,194.65 (71,464.92); age of child = 1,017.71 (4,700.80); age^2 = −5.97 (104.17); age^3 = 0.063 (0.751); dummy for one to eight years of education = −1,599.56 (6,424.95); dummy for nine to twelve years of education = −960.82 (2,236.20); dummy for reported health as "excellent" = 2,165.11 (11,436.56); dummy for reported health as "good" = −1,619.78 (11,388.68); dummy for reported health as "fair" = 1,174.45 (12,058.25); dummy for reported grade in school as "A" = −4,827.79 (12,185.82); dummy for reported grade as "B" = 4,269.33 (11,795.60); dummy for reported grade as "C" = 1,700.29 (11,654.26); dummy for reported grade as "D" = −7,531.44 (11,800.93); dummy for occupation code 2 = 28,664.68 (16,807.28); dummy for occupation code 3 = 1,588,959 (17,069.44); dummy for occupation code 4 = 17,508.99 (17,049.96); dummy for occupation code 5 = 13,341.80 (16,908.94); dummy for occupation code 6 = 14,808.53 (17,332.27); dummy for occupation code 7 = 13,973.28 (16,926.66); dummy for male = 19,662.50 (2,085.96).

where λ_i stands for one minus the exogenously determined supply of labor. For this model, equation (6) is modified to

$$(6') \qquad \left[\frac{1}{d_i + \sum_{j \neq i}^{N_i} d_j + m} - \frac{\beta}{\lambda_i - d_i}\right] d_i = 0.$$

The provision of time is positive if the square bracket in (6′) equals zero, and it is zero if the square bracket is negative; that is, $d_i = 0$ if $0 > [-\beta(\Sigma_{j \neq i} d_j + m) + \lambda]/(1 - \beta)$ holds, otherwise $d_i = [-\beta(\Sigma_{j \neq i} d_j + m) + \lambda]/(1 - \beta)$. Let the right-hand side of this last equality equal $x_i' \gamma + \varepsilon_i$, where x_i is a vector of characteristics of child i and his or her parent and includes the amount of time provided to the parent of his or her siblings $(\Sigma_{j \neq i} d_j)$, and where ε_i is a standard normal error. Then d_i equals zero if the indicator function $I_i = x_i'\gamma + \varepsilon_i$ is negative and equals I_i if the indicator is positive. But this is the standard Tobit model. Using data on all child respondents and their siblings and taking, for each observation, the time provided by all the other siblings as one of the x's in the Tobit regression appear to be appropriate provided that the error terms, the ε_i's, are uncorrelated across siblings.

Our actual Tobit model is a slight modification of the standard Tobit specification to take account of the 29 percent of children in our sample whose parents live with them. In these cases, it is obvious that the child spends time with the parent, but we are not sure how to assess the amount of time. To accommodate these data, we assume that the time provided by the child is positive, but the exact amount of time is unknown. The standard Tobit has two pieces of the likelihood function corresponding to the probability of no time provided and the probability of a specific amount of time provided. We add to the standard likelihood function a statement for the probability of providing positive time, which is simply one minus the probability of providing zero time.

The time question in the Child Survey that provides the dependent variable for our analysis is, “In the last month, how many hours did you (and your spouse) spend with your parents, visiting, going out together, and/or helping him/her/them?” Of the 1,179 out of 1,650 children in the Tobit sample who indicate they are not living with their respondent parent, 29 percent report (or have had reported) spending zero time per month with their elderly parent. Another 31 percent report spending one to ten hours per month, 18 percent eleven to twenty hours per month, 9 percent twenty-one to thirty hours per month, 5 percent thirty-one to forty hours per month, and 8 percent forty-one or more hours per month.

Excluding children living with their parents, the average number of hours provided per month is fifteen, and the median number is eight. Within this subsample of non-co-resident children, average and median hours provided by only children are twenty-four and sixteen, respectively; average and median hours (per child) provided by children with one sibling are sixteen and nine, respectively; and average and median hours (per child) provided by children with two or more siblings are twelve and five, respectively.

Tables 4.1–4.3 report results from Tobit regressions. The first regression includes a set of thirty-three regressors (excluding the intercept). It does not, however, include the sum of time provided by siblings as a regressor, which we include in table 4.2. Table 4.3 contains the Tobit results if one excludes observations in which children live with their parents.

Table 4.1 **Result from Tobit Regression of Time Spent by Child with Parent against Child and Parent Characteristics**

Parameter	Coefficient	SE	*t*-Statistic
Intercept	6.08	7.56	.80
MR2	.25	2.19	.11
MR3	3.68	2.99	1.23
MR4	2.52	3.01	.84
PM2	−2.22	3.39	−.65
PM3	5.64	1.52	3.71
EM2	.15	2.12	.07
EM3	−4.06	2.08	−1.95
SEMPL	.98	1.54	.64
NS	−.74	.39	−1.88
SEX	−5.47	1.33	−4.13
PSEX	−.62	1.50	−.41
H14	−13.81	5.69	−2.43
SPH4	1.62	3.16	.51
PH4	4.38	2.71	1.62
PADL	.77	.32	2.40
PLV	−17.72	2.83	−6.27
PHC	−7.45	1.74	−4.29
PWH	−2.38	2.46	−.97
AG	−2.27	4.83	−.47
PAG	15.66	6.09	2.57
MILH4	11.41	3.46	3.30
FILH4	−.83	8.75	−.09
FHLPL	8.23	3.20	2.57
PHLPL	−13.81	5.70	−2.42
PYM	−2.79	1.70	−1.65
PYV	−29.73	17.44	−1.70
KYM	−.24	4.61	−.05
KYV	−17.04	15.48	−1.10
PWLM	−1.16	1.74	−.67
PWLV	1.72	1.89	.91
KWLM	−1.68	3.64	−.46
KWLV	−1.08	1.53	−.71
WAGE	−.55	.14	−4.05
SIG2	615.26	17.23	35.72

Note: Log likelihood function = −4,342.49. No. of observations = 1,650.

Table 4.2 **Result from Regression of Time Spent by Child with Parent against Child and Parent Characteristics: Includes Time Spent by Siblings as a Regressor**

Parameter	Coefficient	SE	*t*-Statistic
Intercept	6.21	7.57	.82
MR2	.29	2.19	.13
MR3	3.62	3.01	1.20
MR4	2.52	3.02	.83
PM2	−2.40	3.41	−.70
PM3	5.57	1.53	3.65
EM2	.10	2.12	.05
EM3	−4.15	2.09	−1.99
SEMPL	1.02	1.54	.67
NS	−.63	.41	−1.55
SEX	−5.45	1.33	−4.11
PSEX	−.67	1.51	−.44
H14	−13.86	5.67	−2.44
SPH4	1.71	3.17	.54
PH4	4.54	2.71	1.68
PADL	.78	.32	2.40
PLV	−17.98	2.87	−6.27
PHC	−7.42	1.73	−4.28
PWH	−2.50	2.46	−1.01
AG	−2.14	4.84	−.44
PAG	15.74	6.10	2.58
MILH4	11.38	3.47	3.28
FILH4	−1.17	8.75	−.13
FHLPL	8.19	3.21	2.55
PHLPL	−13.67	5.73	−2.39
PYM	−2.87	1.70	−1.69
PYV	−30.34	17.47	−1.74
KYM	−.40	4.63	−.09
KYV	−17.86	15.52	−1.15
PWLM	−1.12	1.74	−.64
PWLV	1.68	1.89	.89
KWLM	−1.70	3.66	−.47
KWLV	−1.04	1.53	−.68
WAGE	−.56	.14	−4.09
SIBTM	−.01	.01	−.94
SIG2	616.63	17.33	35.59

Note: Log likelihood function = −4,342.10. No. of observations = 1,650.

In considering the results, it is important to keep in mind, first, that time spent with the parent, *d*, is a censored variable and, second, that the change in expected time spent in response to a unit change in one of the regressor variables is the change in the unconditional expectation $E[d_i]$. Rather than report the simple Tobit coefficients, the reported coefficients corresponding to the product of Tobit coefficients times the probability that time spent is posi-

Table 4.3 **Result from Tobit Regression of Time Spent by Child with Parent against Child and Parent Characteristics: Includes Only Children Not Living with Parent**

Parameter	Coefficient	SE	*t*-Statistic
Intercept	13.13	7.50	1.75
MR2	−1.15	2.19	−.52
MR3	2.82	2.98	.95
MR4	−4.71	3.56	−1.32
PM2	−5.84	3.45	−1.69
PM3	2.31	1.52	1.52
EM2	.76	2.15	−.36
EM3	−4.62	2.09	−2.21
SEMPL	1.50	1.53	.98
NS	−1.79	.41	−4.37
SEX	−5.13	1.35	−3.81
PSEX	−.93	1.51	−.62
H14	−15.40	7.10	−2.17
SPH4	1.65	3.08	.53
PH4	4.01	2.71	1.48
PADL	.06	.32	.18
PLV	−5.98	2.90	−2.06
PHC	−1.22	1.76	−.69
PWH	−.55	2.50	−.22
AG	−1.21	4.89	−.25
PAG	9.34	6.10	1.53
MILH4	10.77	3.34	3.22
FILH4	−1.03	8.25	−.13
FHLPL	9.91	3.15	3.14
PHLPL	−18.81	6.90	−2.73
PYM	−1.99	1.75	−1.13
PYV	−9.12	17.75	−.51
KYM	−1.67	4.95	−.34
KYV	−20.53	14.89	−1.38
PWLM	−.90	1.77	−.51
PWLV	1.61	1.95	.83
KWLM	−1.92	3.84	−.50
KWLV	−.02	1.45	−.01
WAGE	−.52	.14	−3.84
SIG2	686.34	21.69	31.65

Note: Log likelihood function = −4,197.25. No. of observations = 1,179.

tive. By multiplying the Tobit coefficients by this probability (which, by the way, is evaluated at the sample's mean characteristics), we are simply reporting rescaled Tobit coefficients. The standard errors reported in the tables are those of the original (unscaled) coefficients.

The first set of regressors in table 4.1 (MR2–MR4) are dummies for the child's marital status. Married child is the reference case. As would be expected, separated/divorced, widowed, and never-married children provide more time to parents. Of these, separated/divorced children provide very little additional time compared to married children. Widowed children provide the most time to parents. The coefficients on all three dummies are, however, insignificant.

The coefficients on parent's marital status indicate that, compared to married parents (the reference case), divorced/separated parents (PM2) receive less time, but the standard error here is very large. In contrast, widowed parents (PM3) receive substantially more time, and the coefficient is quite significant.

The next set of dummies (EM2 and EM3) are coded 1 when the child employment status is part time (960 hours per year) and not working. The dummy for children who have full-time (1,920 hours per year) employment status (EM1) was excluded. As can be expected, children who are working part time provide marginally more time compared to children working full time. However, contrary to expectations, those who are not working provide substantially less time to parents compared to children who are employed full time. The former coefficient is insignificant, while the latter is significant at almost the 5 percent level. The dummy for child's spouse being employed either full time or part time (SEMPL) is positive. The coefficient, however, is insignificant.

The next variable (NS) indicates the number of siblings. A larger number of siblings may be expected to reduce the amount of time provided by each child since parent dependence on any one child would be lower. Moreover, if siblings free ride on each other's time provision to the parent, a larger number of siblings would provide additional scope for such free riding behavior. The regression shows that, after controlling for other influences, the presence of additional siblings reduces the provision of time to parents by about three-quarter of an hour per month for each additional sibling. The coefficient on this variable is significant at the 10 percent level, but not the 5 percent level.

The dummy for the child's sex (SEX) was set to equal one for male children. The coefficient suggests that male children who spend time spend about 5.5 hours less per month than female children who spend time. The parent's sex dummy (PSEX), which also has a value of one for males, has a negative coefficient of -0.62 hours, but it is not significant.

As expected, the dummy for child's self-reported health being "poor" (H14) shows a large negative effect on time spent with parent, and the coefficient is significant. "Poor" health of spouse (SPH4) may be expected to curtail the amount of time spent by the child with the parent. However, the opposite result is obtained from the regression. The coefficient on SPH4 is positive, but insignificant. The variable (PH4) is a dummy for parent's self-reported health status being "poor" As expected, the time provided by children is higher for parents whose health status is "poor," but the coefficient is not significant.

The variable PADL is a sum of fourteen dummies, each having a value of one if the parent is unable to perform specific tasks and a value of zero otherwise.[3] A larger value of PADL thus represents a higher degree of parent disability. The coefficient on this variable is positive and significant. Its value is close to one, indicating that for every additional count of disability the child spends an additional hour per month with the parent.

The coefficient on the dummy indicating whether the parent is in a nursing home or similar institution (PLV) is large, negative, and quite significant. The result suggests that such parents receive substantially less time from their children. A large, negative, and significant effect on child's time also arises if the parent receives services from a home care corporation (PHC). Parents receiving "Meals on Wheels" are represented as one in the next dummy variable (PWH). The coefficient is negative, but not significant. These results suggest that children substitute for their own time by using institutions, home care corporations, etc. to care for their elderly parents.

Older children spend less time with parents, but the coefficient on child's age (AG) is not significant. Older parents receive substantially more time, and the coefficient on parent's age (PAG) is significant.

The next two dummies (MILH4 and FILH4) have a value of one if mother-in-law's or father-in-law's health, as reported by the child, is "poor," for children who have either of these parents-in-law. Surprisingly, the coefficient on the former is highly positive and quite significant.[4] The coefficient on father-in-law's health is negative and insignificant.

Do children substitute financial transfers for time transfers to parents, and do parents buy time from children? The variable FHLPL is a dummy that assumes a value of one if the child made positive financial transfers to the parent within the past year. According to the coefficient on FHLPL, children who make such transfers spend about eight hours more per month with parents than children who do not. The coefficient on this variable is significant. The dummy indicating whether the parent made a financial transfer to the child (PHLPL) has a large negative coefficient, and this too is significant. Both parts of the question posed above are thus answered in the negative.

Higher total income of the parent (PYV) when parent income is reported is associated with substantially less time devoted by the child to the parent, but the coefficient is not significant. Higher total income of the child (KYV) is also

3. The variable PADL is the sum of fourteen activity dummies. These dummies had a value of one if parent does not go out of building of residence more than once a week; parent does not prepare own meals; parent thinks he or she does not get enough to eat; parent does not take out garbage himself or herself; parent not healthy enough to do ordinary work around the house; parent has problems dressing by himself or herself; parent unable to prepare bath and dry self; parent unable to get up out of ordinary chair without help; parent has bladder accidents; parent unable to climb up or down stairs without help; parent is confined to bed; parent inclined to wander and/or get lost; parent needs constant supervision; parent uses either walker, four-pronged cane, crutches, or wheelchair at least some of the time to get around.

4. The large positive and significant coefficient on the mother-in-law health dummy does not appear to be due to outliers in the data.

associated with less time spent by the child with the parent, but again the coefficient is insignificant. The signs on both these coefficients are plausible. Parents with larger incomes can afford to buy supervisory and care services and are, therefore, less dependent on their children, and children with higher incomes would be expected to have a higher opportunity cost of time.

If expectations of bequests are important determinants of parent-child relationships, one would expect richer parents to receive more time from their children and richer children to provide less time to parents. The regression indicates that parents with higher net worth (PWLV) receive more time from children and that children with higher net worth (KWLV) spend less time with parents. The coefficients on both these variables are, however, insignificant.

Children with higher wage rates (WAGE) spend somewhat less time with their parents. The coefficient on the wage rate is quite significant. The size of the wage effect seems economically quite large; increasing the child's wage by $10.00 per hour reduces his or her time spent with the parent by 5.5 hours per month.

Table 4.2 repeats the Tobit of table 4.1 but also includes the total amount of time provided by siblings (SIBTM) as a regressor. The introduction of this extra regressor does not substantially alter the estimated coefficients and standard errors for the rest of the variables. More time provided by siblings (SIBTM) is associated with a very small reduction in the amount of time provided by the child, and the coefficient is insignificant.

Table 4.3 reports Tobit results for the subsample that excludes children who live with their parents. There are few noteworthy differences between the results of tables 4.1 and 4.3. For example, the variable for number of siblings (NS) is significant and larger in absolute value in table 4.3 compared with table 4.1. The coefficient on the dummy for parents receiving home care services is now a much smaller negative number and is insignificant. Table 4.3 shows a much smaller positive coefficient on the index for parent disability (PADL), and the coefficient is now significant. This indicates that, in the subsample of non-co-resident parents and children, children seem to spend very little additional time with parents when the degree of parent disability is higher.

4.3.2 Estimates of the Structural Model

Tables 4.4 and 4.5 present maximum likelihood regression results for the structural model presented in section 4.1. The data used for this estimation are a subsample of 415 respondent children who do not live with their parent and for whom valid data on labor and nonlabor income are available.[5] Table 4.4 presents estimates of the coefficient vectors θ and ψ used to model the parameters α and β of the utility function. For this analysis, total disposable

5. Observations were deleted if data on wage income were positive, but the child's reported employee status indicated whether he or she was working or whether data on wage income were missing.

Table 4.4 **Maximum Likelihood Estimation of the Structural Model**

	Equation 1 ($\hat{\theta}$)			Equation 2 ($\hat{\varphi}$)		
Parameter	Coefficient	SE	t-Statistic	Coefficient	SE	t-Statistic
Intercept	5.50	2.61	2.11	5.45	2.73	1.99
MR2	−.79	1.03	−.77	.21	1.06	.20
MR3	−1.28	1.29	−.99	−.26	1.02	−.26
MR4	.42	1.39	.30	.98	1.30	.75
PM2	1.25	1.76	.71	1.42	1.84	.77
PM3	−.28	.52	−.54	.02	.55	.03
SEMPL	−.64	.59	−1.09	−.33	.57	−.58
NS	−.34	.17	−1.99	−.26	.17	−1.57
SEX	.23	.46	.51	.89	.48	1.84
PSEX	.09	.49	.18	.38	.54	.71
H14	2.38	6.27	.38	.28	12.39	.02
SPH4	1.26	.83	1.52	−1.12	1.16	−.97
PH4	−.41	.96	−.43	−.10	.95	−.11
PADL	.03	.11	.26	.03	.12	.24
PLV	.33	.80	.41	−.35	1.07	−.32
PHC	.32	.64	.50	.29	.67	.43
PWH	−.28	1.01	−.28	.12	.93	.13
MILH4	.06	.65	.09	−1.05	1.07	−.98
FILH4	−.37	2.68	−.14	−.15	2.62	−.06
FHLPL	−1.29	1.22	−1.06	−.35	1.03	−.34
AG	−.03	1.77	.02	−1.65	1.87	−.88
PAG	−1.46	2.23	−.65	−1.43	2.39	−.60
PYM	.18	.58	.31	.04	.65	.05
PYV	4.38	15.12	.29	3.13	15.39	.20
KWLM	.91	3.27	.28	.92	3.87	.24
KWLV	.58	.33	1.76	.62	.39	1.56
PWLV	1.72	1.89	.91			
PWLM	.22	.64	.34	.07	.73	.10
PWLV	−.28	.60	−.46	−.27	.76	−.36

Note: Log likelihood function = −1,600.03. No. of observations = 415. The variables KNLY, SIBTM, and WAGE are part of the structural specification and have therefore been omitted from x, the vector of characteristics. Work time is endogenous, and therefore EM1 and EM2 have been omitted from vector x. This subsample has no observation with parent making a financial transfer to the child; hence, the variable PHLPL was omitted from vector x.

time available for an individual per year was taken to be 4,380 hours (assuming twelve hours of disposable time per day). The estimation procedure assumes that μ_i and υ_i ($i = 1, N$) are independently and identically distributed. The vector of child and parent characteristics, x, contains a subset of the variables used as regressors in the Tobit model.

The structural estimates are rather disappointing. With the exception of the coefficient on the number of siblings (NS) in column 1, all the coefficients of the structural estimates are insignificant. As a group, however, the coefficients seem rather reasonable with respect to their sign and magnitude. Since the

Table 4.5 **Choices of *d* and *l* Implied by Estimated Parameters**

	Time Spent with Parents		Leisure	
	New Value	Diff.	New Value	Diff.
At mean values	50	0	3,368	0
MR2 = 1	134	84	2,303	−1,065
MR3 = 1	295	245	2,152	−1,216
MR4 = 1	0	−50	2,822	−546
PM2 = 1	0	−50	3,242	−126
PM3 = 1	65	15	3,245	−123
SEMPL = 1	93	43	3,225	−143
NS = 1	17	−33	3,432	64
NS = 2	78	28	3,318	−50
NS = 3	159	109	3,190	−178
NS = 4	265	215	3,045	−323
NS = 5	402	352	2,883	−485
NS = 6	575	525	2,699	−669
NS = 7	789	739	2,495	−873
SEX = 1	3	−47	2,984	−384
PSEX = 1	28	−22	3,185	−183
H14 = 1	0	−50	4,380	1,012
SPH4 = 1	0	−50	4,380	1,012
PH4 = 1	115	65	3,030	−338
PADL = 0	66	16	3,357	−11
PADL = 3	49	−1	3,369	1
PADL = 6	32	−18	3,380	12
PADL = 9	17	−33	3,390	22
PADL = 12	3	−47	3,400	32
PLV = 1	24	−26	3,875	507
PHC = 1	5	−45	3,426	58
PWH = 1	79	29	2947	−421
MILH4 = 1	84	34	4,143	775
FILH4 = 1	117	67	3,103	−265
FHLPL = 1	313	263	2,232	−1,136
child's age = mean age + 10	66	16	3,663	295
child's age = mean age − 10	30	−20	3,028	−340
parent age = mean age + 10	115	65	3,317	−51
parent age = mean age − 10	0	−50	3,409	41
parent income = mean income + 2,000	47	−3	3,376	8
parent income = mean income − 2,000	53	3	3,361	−7
child's wealth = mean wealth + 10,000	39	−11	3,373	5
child's wealth = mean wealth − 10,000	62	12	3,363	−5
parent wealth = mean wealth + 10,000	51	1	3,368	0
parent wealth = mean wealth − 10,000	49	−1	3,369	1
WAGE = mean wage + 5	46	−4	3,311	−57

Table 4.5 (continued)

	Time Spent with Parents		Leisure	
	New Value	Diff.	New Value	Diff.
WAGE = mean wage − 5	56	6	3,464	96
SIBTM = SIBTM + 20	31	−19	3,382	14
SIBTM = SIBTM − 20	69	19	3,355	−13
KNLY = KNLY + 2,000	54	4	3,435	67
KNLY = KNLY − 2,000	46	−4	3,302	−66

Note: Standard errors in this table are proportional to those of table 5

coefficients in table 4.4 are hard to interpret, we consider how changes in the exogenous variables affect the mean amount of time spent with parents and the mean amount of leisure predicted by the structural model. To do this, we use the estimated values $\hat{\theta}$ and $\hat{\psi}$ and the mean values of the vector x to obtain an estimate (at the mean of the x's) of the preference parameters α and β.[6] The optimal choices of the time transfer to parent (d) and the amount of leisure (ℓ) can then be inferred by setting the terms within the square brackets of (5) and (6) equal to zero and simultaneously solving the two resultant equations. If the optimal choice of d turns out to be negative, a corner solution is imposed by setting d equal to zero and recomputing the optimum amount of leisure.

The first row of table 4.5 presents the choices of time spent with the parent and leisure for, again, a hypothetical child with a characteristic vector x equal to the mean of x computed over the 415 observations. Out of a total of 4,380 hours per year, a hypothetical individual with mean characteristics spends 50 hours per year with the parent, consumes 3,368 hours of leisure per year, and works for the remaining 962 hours. Subsequent rows of table 4.5 present the amount of time spent with parents and the amount of leisure of the hypothetical child that result from changing the value of one of the elements in vector x while maintaining the others at their mean values. The columns labeled "Diff." indicate the change in time spent with parents and leisure from the respective values in the first row of the table.

6. The mean values of the vector of characteristics x for the subsample of 415 observations as follows:

MR2,	.089	H14,	.007	FHLPL,	.041
MR3,	.036	SPH4,	.019	child's age,	50.424
MR4,	.046	PH4,	.063	parent age,	75.328
PM2,	.048	PADL,	2.769	parent income,	9,873.494
PM3,	.624	PLV,	.169	child's wealth,	196,710.843
SEMPL,	.634	PHC,	.178	parent income,	85,924.699
NS,	1.569	PWH,	.048	WAGE,	20.283
SEX,	.402	MILH4,	.031	SIBTM,	154.207
PSEX,	.342	FILH4,	.014	KNLY,	8,728.207

Many of the results found in the Tobit analysis carry over to the structural estimates. For example, male children spend less time; divorced, separated, or widowed children spend substantially more time; children in poor health provide less time; parents in nursing homes receive less time; parents in poor health receive more time; and older parents receive more time. Surprisingly, and in contradiction to earlier results, table 4.5 shows that the time spent by children declines, and the amount of leisure consumed increases, with increasing degree of disability (PADL) of the parent.

The negative effect of time spent by siblings on the time spent by the child reflects the structural model's assumption that siblings play noncooperative Nash in providing time to their parents and respond to increased time by their siblings by cutting back on their own time.

4.4 Conclusion

This paper uses matched data on the elderly and their children to study the provision of time by children to the elderly. It develops a Tobit model as well as a structural model to analyze the determinants of this decision. The data reveal some clear patterns of time transfers from children to their elderly parents. Children appear to use institutions and home care as a substitute for their own provision of time. Parents who reside in nursing homes or are enrolled in home care programs receive, ceteris paribus, less than half the amount of time received by those in the community. The provision of time is strongly correlated with the age of the elderly parent; other things being equal, the old old receive over twice the time of the young old.

The sex, age, and health status of children are additional important determinants of time provided to the elderly. Male children and younger children spend relatively little time with their parents. Children with poor health spend almost no time with their parents. If the spouse of the child is in poor health, the child also gives very little time, at least according to the structural model's results.

Other things being equal, those elderly who report their health to be "poor" appear to receive over twice the amount of time received by elderly with better self-reports of health. Surprisingly, the degree of elderly disability does not appear to affect the amount of time provided to those elderly not living with their children, although it is a significant determinant in the larger sample that includes elderly living with their children.

The Tobit results for the entire sample of children, including those living with their elderly parents, indicate that more time is provided by single children and more time is received by single elderly, at least those who are widowed. In the structural model, the effects of the child's and parent's marital status on time provided to the elderly are less clear, but there is strong evidence that widowed children spend substantially more time with their elderly parents.

The structural model predicts that more time provided by siblings will lead to substantially less time provided by the child in question. However, this prediction is, to a large extent, simply the implication of the form of the structural model we have adopted. In the less constrained Tobit estimation, there is no evidence that siblings free ride on each others' provision of time.

Both the Tobit and the structural estimates indicate a small effect associated with higher children's wage rates; children with higher wage rates provide somewhat less time to their elderly parents than other children. In contrast to the modest effect of higher wage rates, the effect of larger values of children's wealth is quite sizable. Wealthier children and children with higher incomes appear to provide less time than poorer children, but the standard errors around these effects are quite large.

The standard errors on the effects of parent's wealth and income are also sizable. One might summarize the findings here by saying that there is certainly no strong evidence that richer parents receive more time than poorer parents; that is, the paper provides little, if any, support for Bernheim, Shleifer, and Summers's (1986) view that richer parents, in effect, purchase more time from their children.

To summarize, the results indicate that the main determinants of the amount of time given to parents are demographic. Economic variables, such as wage rate and income levels, appear to play an insignificant role in the provision of time by children to their elderly parents.

Appendix

Key to Variables Used in Tobit Regressions

MR2 = 1 if child is separated/divorced;
MR3 = 1 if child is widowed;
MR4 = 1 if child is never married;
PM2 = 1 if parent is divorced/separated;
PM3 = 1 if parent is widowed;
EM2 = 1 if child is employed part time;
EM3 = 1 if child is not working
SEMP1 = 1 if child's spouse is employed full or part time;
NS = number of siblings;
SEX = 1 if child is male;
PSEX = 1 if parent is male;
H14 = 1 if child rates his or her health as "poor";
SPH4 = 1 if child's spouse's health is "poor";
PH4 = 1 if parent rates his or her health as "poor";
PADL = index of disability (see text);
PLV = 1 if parent lives in nursing home or similar institution;
PHC = 1 if parent receives home care services;
PWH = 1 if parent receives "Meals on Wheels";
AG = child's age divided by 50;

PAG = parent's age divided by 50;
MILH4 = 1 if mother-in-law's health is reported "poor";
FILH4 = 1 if father-in-law's health is reported "poor";
FHLPL = 1 if child made financial transfers to parent within the last year;
PHLPL = 1 if parent made financial transfers to child within the last year;
PYM = 1 if data on parent's total income are missing;
PYV = parent's total income times one minus PYM (in $100,000);
KYM = 1 if data on child's total income are missing;
KYV = child's total income times one minus KYM (in $100,000);
PWLM = 1 if data on net worth of parent are missing;
PWLV = parent's net worth times one minus PWLM (in $500,000);
KWLM = 1 if data on net worth of child are missing;
KWLV = child's net worth times one minus KWLM (in $500,000);
WAGE = child's wage rate (unit = $10.00 per hour);
SIBTM = total time provided by siblings of child;
KNLY = nonlabor income of child;
SIG2 = estimated variance coefficient.

References

Andrews, Emily, and Michael Hurd. 1990. Employee Benefits and Retirement Income Adequacy: Data, Research and Policy Issues. Stony Brook: State University of New York at Stony Brook, March. Manuscript.

Bernheim, B. Douglas, Andrei Shleifer, and Lawrence Summers. 1985. Bequests as a Means of Payment. *Journal of Political Economy* 93:1045–76.

Boskin, Michael J., Laurence J. Kotlikoff, and Michael Knetter. 1985. Changes in the Age Distribution of Income in the United States, 1968–1984. NBER Working Paper no. 1766. Cambridge, Mass.: National Bureau of Economic Research, October.

Kotlikoff, Laurence J., and John N. Morris. 1989. How Much Care Do the Aged Receive from Their Children? A Bimodal Picture of Contact and Assistance. In *The Economics of Aging,* ed. David A. Wise, 151–75. Chicago: University of Chicago Press.

———. 1990. Why Don't the Elderly Live with Their Children? A New Look. In *Issues in the Economics of Aging,* ed. David A. Wise, 149–69. Chicago: University of Chicago Press.

Michael, R. T., V. R. Fuchs, and S. R. Scott. 1980. Changes in the Propensity to Live Alone, 1950–1976. *Demography* 17:39–56.

Morgan, James N. 1984. The Role of Time in the Measurement of Transfers and Well-Being. In *Economic Transfers in the United States,* ed. Marilyn Moon. Chicago: NBER Studies in Income and Wealth, vol. 49. University of Chicago Press.

Morris, John N. Claire E. Gutkin, Clarence C. Sherwood, and Ellen Bernstein. 1987. Interest in Long Term Care Insurance. Final Report in connection with HCFA Cooperative Agreement no. 18-C-98375/1. Washington, D.C.: HCFA, June.

Sandefur, Gary D., and Nancy Brandon Tuma. 1987. Social and Economic Trends among the Aged in the United States, 1940–1985. Discussion Paper no. 849-87. Institute for Research on Poverty, February.

Comment Konrad Stahl

Recent research on transfers between the elderly and their offspring has concentrated almost exclusively on bequests.[1] By contrast, research on inter vivos intergenerational transfers has been scanty, probably largely because of lack of adequate data. Such transfers may take place in terms of income and assets or of time provided by children (and their dependents) to their parents (or grandparents), and vice versa. Axel Börsch-Supan, Jagadeesh Gokhale, Laurence J. Kotlikoff, and John N. Morris concentrate on a component of these transfers important from both a strictly economic and a social policy point of view, namely, transfers in the form of time provided by children in taking care of their parents. The 1986 HRCA Survey of the Elderly combined with the 1986 HRC-NBER Child Survey provides a unique opportunity for such an analysis within a cross-sectional framework.

The empirical analysis, which is the focus of the paper, is based on a compact cross-sectional structural model of a child's decision-making behavior with the following key features. First, the shares of time apportioned to both labor/leisure and parent care are endogenous. Second, these shares may be subject to corner solutions: the child may choose not to work or devote time to the parent. By assumption, financial transfers to the parent(s) are excluded from the child's choices, as are all choices on the parent side.

These assumptions are partially motivated by observations from the data set: the financial transfers found therein are rather small.[2] Nevertheless, truncating these choices may result in simultaneity biases of several kinds. First, any substitution between children's time transfers and monetary transfers to finance nursing home or home care services is assumed away. Second, trading, on the part of the parents, inter vivos financial transfers for the provision of time by their children is not possible. However, while these transfers are excluded in the theoretical model, they are included in all estimates, even the one based on the structural model. At any rate, a final aspect of the model specification worth emphasizing is that the simultaneity in several siblings' choice of time provided to parents is rather parsimoniously accounted for. So much for the theoretical model.

The first part of the empirical results is on Tobit estimates on the allocation

Konrad Stahl is professor of economics at the University of Mannheim, Germany.

1. The pertinent literature is competently reviewed by Michael D. Hurd, "Research on the Elderly: Economic Status, Retirement, and Consumption and Saving," *Journal of Economic Literature* 28, no. 2 (1990): 565–637.

2. It is well known, however, that inter vivo transfers are heavily misrepresented in surveys.

of children's nonwork time between leisure and time spent with the parent, with an exogenous specification of time worked. Here, the authors are confronted with the problem that in almost one-third of their sample the parents live with their children, in which case the assessment of time provided by them is difficult. They elegantly resolve this problem by adding to the standard Tobit likelihood function a statement on the probability of the child providing positive time, equaling one minus the probability of providing zero time.

The basic estimate including this subsample is presented in table 4.1. With twenty-nine independent variables (excluding the intercept and dummies controlling for missing values), that estimate is not quite parsimonious. Its interpretation is not transparent and does not sufficiently account for the (in)significance associated with the individual variables. I therefore summarize the results before commenting on them.

The set of independent variables may be organized into four groups, namely, nine variables related to parent's and child's economic status, two variables on intergenerational financial transfer decisions taken by both parent and child, ten variables reporting demographic aspects, six on health status, and finally three reporting substitutes to child's time and are consumed by the parent(s).

Of the nine economic status variables, only one, the child's opportunity cost of devoting time to the parent approximated by the wage rate, is significant with the expected negative sign. In particular, both intergenerational transfer variables are significant but with the wrong sign. Of the ten demographic variables, four are significant with the expected sign: "parent widowed" and "parent age" exercise a positive effect, and "child male" a negative effect. The negative effect of the number of siblings is also weakly significant, with only a small effect on child's time devoted to parent care.

Two out of the six health variables, "child's health status" and "parent's degree of disability," show, respectively, the significant negative and positive sign. The large difference in the magnitude of effect remains unexplained. Two of the three variables on the consumption of substitute services, "parent living in nursing home" and "parent receiving home care services," are significant with the expected negative sign, with a much stronger effect of the former variable.

In all, noneconomic, that is, demographic health and real consumption–related variables exercise a much stronger effect than economic ones, a finding not uncommon in research on aging.[3]

The current model specification contains no interactions; not even obvious ones such as those between child's sex, age, and employment status. One also

3. Compare, e.g., Börsch-Supan, Hajivassiliou, Kotlikoff, and Morris (in this volume); and Laurence J. Kotlikoff and John N. Morris, "Why Don't the Elderly Live with Their Children: A New Look," *Issues in the Economics of Aging*, ed. David A. Wise (Chicago: University of Chicago Press, 1990), 149–69.

expects a combined effect—if both parents are alive—of parents' health status; indeed, it remains unclear in this case whose health status is reported in the data.

It is furthermore puzzling that several variables referring to economic status are significant with the wrong sign. For instance, we expect a significantly increased amount of time spent with the parent if the child is not working (in particular if the child is female) or if the child made financial transfers to the parent, thus providing the financial means to purchase substitutes for personal care. We may also expect substitution away from parent's care to the care of in-laws, while the signs of these variables are conflicting. Finally, one would expect effects from important variables that are insignificant in the present estimate, such as "child widowed," "poor health of child's spouse," and the other substitute variables for child's care taking.

How do the results given by the authors relate to the sparse literature on intergenerational transfers of time? The closest paper to the present one is by Bernheim, Shleifer, and Summers.[4] These authors consider the strategic use of bequests by parents in order to extract services from their children. They show a significantly positive relation between bequeathable wealth and children's attention, especially if there are several children. On the basis of empirical observations, they also reject the use of inter vivos transfers for the same purpose. The latter result contradicts the present estimate, as this shows a strong positive effect of parent-child transfers.

However, a strategic bequest motive does not show up at all in the present estimate. Neither parent total income (as a proxy for lifetime earnings) nor parent net worth exercise the positive influence on child's time spent, as emphasized by Bernheim et al. Furthermore, while only weakly significant, the negative coefficient on the number of siblings in the present estimate indicates a negative effect on the individual child's time spent with the parent, rather than the strong positive one derived by Bernheim et al. rationalized by competition for bequests. It remains open whether the results presented here carry more the flavor of the altruistic rather than the strategic bequest motivation for intergenerational time transfers.

As the inclusion of the cases where parents live with their children is econometrically more appealing, it is not too surprising that the estimates excluding these cases perform worse. Table 4.3, corresponding to table 4.1, exhibits that a mere four out of the eleven variables significant in the first estimate remain so. One of them, "number of siblings," now turns out to have a strongly significant negative effect, while it was only weakly significant before. Several variables, such as "child not working," and transfers from and to parent, now show up significant with the wrong sign.

It is surprising and unfortunate that the results are even weaker in the theo-

4. See B. Douglas Bernheim, Andrei Shleifer, and Lawrence H. Summers, "The Strategic Bequest Motive," *Journal of Political Economy* 93, no. 6 (1985): 1045–76.

retically more satisfying second part of the estimates based on the structural model. They are presented in table 4.4. Essentially none of the independent variables remains significant. In fact, only one single parameter, "number of siblings," has the expected sign while obtaining a *t*-value above unity. Therefore, the numerical estimates on the effect of the exogenous variables on the child's choice of leisure time and time devoted to parents presented in table 4.5 lack statistical foundation and can be considered preliminary at best. Of course, the same holds for the comparisons of the estimates from the structural model with the (many) insignificant ones from the Tobit model.

It remains to speculate about the reasons for the weakness, especially of the structural estimate, despite an attractively simple specification of the underlying theoretical model. The Tobit estimate could possibly be improved by introducing interaction variables as discussed before, by adding explanatory variables such as the geographical distance between child's and parent's living quarters, or by respecifying the opportunity costs of physical contact, especially for the nonworking child, for whom at present no variable reflecting opportunity costs enters the estimation. For instance, there may be other demands on personal time transfers, in particular by the child's dependents.

Without further insight into the technicalities of the estimation beyond those given in the paper, it remains unclear why the estimate of the structural model performs so drastically worse than that of the Tobit model. It is conceptually not difficult, as usual, to suggest the endogenization of further variables. In particular, the parents' choices of substitutes to the child's time and care are rather obvious candidates, possibly including the choice of living arrangements. The results of the Tobit estimate already indicate a strong interaction. This is not the case for the monetary transfers chosen by the child. This inconclusive result may well be due to the notorious paucity of survey data in recording such transfers. Nevertheless, the choice of time versus money transfers is logically a simultaneous one. At any rate, it remains to be shown whether respecifications of the model along these lines will lead to a substantial improvement of its estimate. The quality of the data may put effective limits on the estimation for such a relatively delicate structural model.

In conclusion, I would like to emphasize again that the authors have chosen to concentrate on an important component of intergenerational transfers but that substantially more work is needed to achieve satisfactory results on the topic.

5 Wealth Depletion and Life-Cycle Consumption by the Elderly

Michael D. Hurd

Although the life-cycle hypothesis of consumption has been the most important theory for the study of saving behavior, interest in the bequest motive for saving has grown considerably.[1] This interest has been stimulated by three kinds of empirical results. (1) In simulations of lifetime earnings and consumption trajectories, "reasonable" utility function parameter values lead to savings that are considerably smaller than observed household wealth (White 1978; Darby 1979). This implies that a good deal of household wealth has been inherited. Although, when the date of death is unknown, large inheritances are not necessarily inconsistent with the life-cycle hypothesis, many people would think they indicate that at least part of the bequests are intentional. (2) Kotlikoff and Summers (1981) find from estimated earnings and consumption paths that as much as 80 percent of household wealth is inherited. (3) The elderly do not seem to dissave as they age (Danziger et al. 1982; Kotlikoff and Summers 1988). Because this contradicts a prediction of the life-cycle hypothesis, it has been taken to be particularly damaging to the hypothesis.

In this paper, I first review some evidence on how wealth changes as the elderly age. The best evidence is that the elderly do dissave as required by the life-cycle hypothesis. Then I present some findings based on consumption data in the Retirement History Survey (RHS). As measured in the RHS, consumption declines as households age, which is in accordance with the life-cycle hypothesis. If a bequest motive for saving is an important determinant

Michael D. Hurd is a professor of economics at the State University of New York, Stony Brook, and a research associate of the National Bureau of Economic Research.

Support from the National Institute on Aging is gratefully acknowledged. Many thanks to Du Wang for excellent research assistance.

1. In this paper, the life-cycle hypothesis of consumption generally allows that the date of death is unknown. No utility is derived from a bequest.

of consumption, the consumption paths of parents and nonparents should differ, but no systematic difference between their consumption paths is found. The overall conclusion is that the wealth and consumption data in the RHS are consistent with the life-cycle hypothesis; they do not support a role for a bequest motive as a determinant of consumption behavior.

5.1 Wealth Change

As originally formulated, the life-cycle hypothesis (LCH) of consumption specified that utility derives only from consumption, not from bequests, and that the length of life is known with certainty. In this formulation, a condition of lifetime utility maximization is that wealth will decline to zero by the date of death. If the date of death is uncertain but the maximum age to which anyone can live is fixed and known, wealth must decline to zero at that maximum age. In either case, a prediction of the LCH is that at some age wealth will decline with increasing age. The age at which wealth should decline is not known, however, without further specification about the form of the lifetime utility function. A specification that is often made is the following (Yaari 1965).

An individual maximizes in the consumption path $\{c_t\}$

$$\int_o^N u(c_t)e^{-\rho t}\, a_t dt$$

in which $u(\cdot)$ is the instantaneous utility function, ρ is the subjective time rate of discount, a_t is the probability of living at least until t, and N is the maximum age to which anyone can live ($a_N = 0$). Because in this formulation utility does not depend on leisure, the model is valid only after retirement. The constraints on the maximization are initial wealth and the equation of motion of wealth, w_t,

$$\frac{dw_t}{dt} = rw_t - c_t,$$

in which r, the real interest rate, is constant and known. Utility maximization implies that

$$(1) \qquad u_t = u_{t+h}\frac{a_{t+h}}{a_t}e^{h(r-\rho)} \approx u_{t+h}\, e^{h(r-\rho-m_t/a_t)}$$

over an interval $(t, t + h)$ in which $w_t > 0$. u_t is marginal utility at t. m_t/a_t is the mortality hazard rate, which increases approximately exponentially at ages over, say, 60. If $\rho > r$, marginal utility will increase with age, which implies, under the usual assumption about the concavity of $u(\cdot)$ ($u'' < 0$), that consumption will fall with age. If $\rho < r$, the age at which marginal utility will begin to rise and consumption fall is found from

$$\frac{m_t}{a_t} = r - \rho.$$

For example, if $r = 0.03$ and $\rho = 0$, consumption will begin to fall at about age 66 for males and age 74 for females. If consumption declines with age, wealth must also decline: if dw_t/dt were positive and dc_t/dt negative,

$$\frac{d^2w_t}{dt^2} = r\frac{dw_t}{dt} - \frac{dc_t}{dt} > 0,$$

which implies that dw_t/dt would remain positive for all future ages, violating the terminal condition that $w_N = 0$. Therefore, the LCH makes the strong prediction that, in the absence of a bequest motive for saving, wealth should begin to fall at some age and that it will continue to fall at all greater ages. A reasonable guess would be that the wealth of retired single men would begin to fall by their 60s or possibly earlier and of retired single women by their early 70s or earlier.

Many studies, however, have found that wealth seems to increase with age in cross section (Lydall 1955; Projector and Weiss 1966; Mirer 1979; Blinder, Gordon, and Wise 1983; Menchik and David 1983). These results have been interpreted to be particularly damaging to the LCH. For example, "Perhaps the most decisive attack on the life-cycle theory of savings came from the direct examination of the wealth-age profile itself" (Kurz 1985).

The cross-sectional findings have stimulated interest in the bequest motive for saving. A common formulation is that lifetime utility depends on consumption and on a bequest (Yaari 1965). The consumer chooses $\{c_t\}$ to maximize

$$\int_o^N u(c_t)e^{-\rho t}\, a_t dt + \int_o^N V(w_t)e^{-\rho t}\, m_t dt, \tag{2}$$

in which $V(\cdot)$ is the utility from a bequest. The first-order conditions imply

$$u_t = u_{t+h}\frac{a_{t+h}}{a_t}e^{h(r-\rho)} + \int_t^{t+h} V_s\, e^{(s-t)(r-\rho)}\frac{m_s}{a_t}\,ds, \tag{3}$$

in which V_s (> 0) is the marginal utility of a bequest. Comparison of (3) and (1) shows that for given u_{t+h}, u_t will be larger with a bequest motive for saving than without a bequest motive and that the path of marginal utility will therefore be flatter. Thus, the bequest motive will flatten the consumption path and could even cause it to rise. A flatter consumption path leads to a flatter wealth path, and, depending on the form of the bequest utility function and the initial conditions, wealth could increase with age (Hurd 1989). Of course, because the bequest motive means that wealth enters the utility function (2), it follows almost directly that more wealth will be held.

Although the observation that wealth seems to increase with age in cross section was an important motivation for interest in the bequest motive, as an empirical matter it appears that the observation was itself incorrect. Table 5.1 has cross-sectional wealth profiles from four data sets, normalized so that wealth is 1.0 at ages 55–64 (Hurd 1990). The table shows that, in cross section, wealth falls with age, as required by the LCH. Just why these results differ from previous results is not clear. One explanation is that the results in the earlier papers had too much age aggregation (Wolff 1988): combining the older age intervals into one interval 65 and older can cause wealth to seem to increase with age in some of the data sets.

However, whether wealth seems to increase in cross section is practically irrelevant for assessing the LCH because of the difficulties in recovering the wealth paths of individuals (or cohorts) from the cross-sectional age-wealth relation. (1) Because the poor die earlier than the well to do, wealth can rise in cross section even though the wealth holdings of all individuals fall as they age. (2) Each cohort has different lifetime earnings and historical saving experiences that are difficult to account for. (3) In cross section, it is difficult to establish whether individuals are retired. Apparently, these problems with cross-sectional data have empirical content. In panel data, the differences between the cross-sectional wealth paths and the individual wealth paths can be studied: in the National Longitudinal Survey (NLS) "there does not appear to be any systematic differences between cross-section and cohort age-wealth profiles which could be used to correct the cross-sectional profiles" (Jianakoplos, Menchik, and Irvine 1989).

In the RHS, I found annual rates of dissaving of retired individuals and couples of about 3 percent per year excluding housing and about 1.5 percent per year including housing (Hurd 1987). In the NLS of older men, Diamond and Hausman (1984) found rates of dissaving after retirement of about 5 percent per year. Mirer (1980) used a one-year panel from the 1963 and 1964 Federal Reserve wealth surveys to find median rates of dissaving of 1.2 percent per year. These findings are good evidence that the elderly do dissave

Table 5.1 Relative Bequeathable Wealth by Age

	Data			
Age	1962 SFCC	1979 ISDP	1983 SCF	1984 SIPP
55–64	1.00	1.00	1.00	1.00
65–69	1.09	.85	1.27	.96
70–74	.96	.81	.84	.79
75–79	.89	.62*	.69	.69[a]
80+	.67	.62*	.52	.69[a]

Sources: 1962 SFCC (Survey of Financial Characteristics of Consumers) and 1983 SCF (Survey of Consumer Finances): Wolff (1988); 1979 ISDP (Income Survey Development Program) and 1984 SIPP (Survey of Income and Program Participation): Radner (1989).

[a]75 and over.

after retirement as required by the LCH, but in view of the high and variable rate of inflation during the 1970s we need studies based on data from the 1980s before we can be confident of the empirical facts.

Dissaving by the elderly is consistent with the LCH, but it is also consistent with the LCH augmented by a bequest motive, which does not rule out dissaving. However, many have argued that, even though the elderly may dissave, the rate of dissaving is so low that a bequest motive must be important (Bernheim 1987; Modigliani 1986, 1988; Kotlikoff 1988; Kotlikoff and Summers 1988). I find it difficult to assess what the appropriate rate of dissaving should be in the LCH model with mortality risk aversion. Suppose, for example, that the instantaneous utility function is

$$u(C) = \frac{1}{1-\gamma}C^{1-\gamma}.$$

Then

$$\frac{dc_t}{dt}\frac{1}{c_t} = \frac{1}{\gamma}\left(r - \rho - \frac{m_t}{a_t}\right).$$

If the risk aversion parameter, γ, is large, consumption will be practically flat. Take that extreme case, and assume a real interest rate of 3 percent and a maximum age of 105. Then wealth at age 85 would be about 65 percent of wealth at age 65, an average rate of dissaving of about 2 percent per year. This is certainly consistent with observed rates of dissaving.[2]

Because the rate of wealth decumulation does not by itself provide any evidence about the importance of a bequest motive for saving, additional information needs to be used to identify its importance. It is reasonable to suppose that parents will have a stronger bequest motive than nonparents (V_s will be larger in [3]). Then, ceteris paribus, they will dissave at a lower rate, and the difference in the rates of dissaving will be a measure of the bequest motive.

In the RHS, the rates of dissaving of parents and nonparents are practically the same whether measured in a way that is almost free of functional form restrictions or in a way that imposes a good deal of functional form (Hurd 1987, 1989). I take this to be good evidence either that the bequest motive is weak for most people or that it is not operable.[3]

5.2 Consumption Paths

Consumption data offer a more promising way to estimate parameters associated with the LCH and to test for the presence of a bequest motive than wealth data: the rate of change of consumption depends directly on current

2. The rate of wealth decumulation increases with age. With less risk aversion than the extreme case, the rate of decumulation predicted by the LCH could be rather small at the younger ages observed in the RHS and NLS.

3. For a discussion of the difference between an operable and an inoperable bequest motive, see Abel (1987).

mortality rates and the degree of risk aversion, whereas the rate of change of wealth depends on the level of consumption, which depends on the entire time path of mortality rates. The importance of annuities (mainly Social Security) further complicates estimates based on wealth: they enter the utility maximization problem as a flow, not a stock of wealth. Because the optimal level of the consumption path depends on the entire path of annuities, the rate of change of wealth depends on the entire time path of annuities. However, the rate of change of consumption does not depend on annuities as long as a boundary condition on wealth is not binding. This greatly simplifies estimation.

Consider the utility maximization problem of (2) but with the modified equation of motion of wealth:

$$dw_t/dt = rw_t - c_t + A_t,$$

where w_t is bequeathable wealth and A_t is the flow of annuity income. Annuities are important for the elderly: in 1986, 57 percent of the elderly (age 65 and over) received more than half their money income from Social Security.

If $w_t > 0$, the solution to the utility maximization problem is given in (3); if $w_t = 0$, $c_t = A_t$. Therefore, the LCH predicts that, if $w_t > 0$, consumption will eventually decline with age. The bequest motive predicts that individuals with a strong bequest motive will have a more slowly declining consumption path than individuals with a weak bequest motive.

5.3 Consumption Data in the RHS

The RHS has direct measures of the following categories of consumption: food purchased in grocery stores, food from vendors and home delivery, food purchased away from home, nonfood items purchased in grocery stores, gifts and donations, recreation and membership fees, and gasoline and other transportation expenses (but excluding automobile purchases). I estimate that the covered categories comprise about 34 percent of total consumption by the elderly.[4] To avoid ambiguity, I will refer to the sum of the covered categories as RHS consumption.

Table 5.2 has some food consumption statistics from the six years of the RHS. These numbers are supposed to show measures of weekly food consumption in current dollars, but they are not interpretable and appear to be of no value for analysis. Case-by-case study of the household data, however, showed systematic coding errors. Detection and correction of the errors was a considerable part of the effort of this paper.

4. This estimate comes from the consumption distribution by the elderly in the 1972–73 Consumer Expenditure Survey (CES) (Boskin and Hurd 1985). The covered categories would be a larger fraction of out-of-pocket expenditures because the CES data include an imputed value of owner-occupied housing consumption, which is about 20 percent of total consumption.

Table 5.2 **Food Consumption**

Year	Mean	Median	Maximum	Minimum
1969	18.8	16	103	0
1971	1,289.6	1,200	7,500	0
1973	36.0	20	3,500	0
1975	2,722.2	2,500	50,000	0
1977	29.1	25	200	0
1979	33.5	30	400	0

Source: Author's calculations from the RHS.

Table 5.3 has some typical examples of the consumption data. Three households in the RHS (Households 1, 85, and 89) were chosen to illustrate the source of the data problems found in the food consumption data. The top panel for Household 1 has missing values in 1969–73 because the household did not retire until after 1973. The RHS has three measures of food consumption: "usual" (amount usually spent in grocery stores and on food from vendors and deliveries in a week), "general" (amount spent on food including nonfood items in general stores last week, excluding vendors and deliveries), and "foodentr" (amount actually spent on food last week including vendors and deliveries; in 1969, "foodentr" is missing for all households). I developed an algorithm for choosing among them; the algorithm aimed at selecting the measure closest to "normal" food consumption. In 1975, "usual" consumption was missing (9999998), so "general" was used with the appropriate adjustment for differences in coverage. Total consumption of Household 1 was estimated to be $4,319. In 1977, "gastran" was missing, so total consumption was missing. In 1979, "usual" was again missing; total consumption was estimated to be $90.

Obviously, there are several data problems. Data are missing in some consumption categories such as "gastran" (amount spent on gasoline and transportation not including automobile purchases) for Household 1, "donation," "memberfee," "recreation," and "gift" for Household 85 in 1973, and all 1973 data for Household 89. A more serious data problem is the extreme variation in some consumption categories and the incredible consumption levels in some years. For example, Household 1 appears to have consumed $4,319 per week in 1975 and $90 per week in 1979. Close examination of the panel data at the household level revealed that the following categories were recorded in cents, rather than in dollars, as was called for the code book:

1971: purchased from grocery stores and *general* stores last week;
food from a grocery store last week;
nonfood from a grocery store last week;
food from a *vendor* last week;
food from a *delivery* last week;

Table 5.3 Consumption by Detailed Category

A. Household 1

	Year					
	1969	1971	1973	1975	1977	1979
1. Raw data:						
usual				9999998	35	9999998
general				3,500	38	55
nonfood				0	0	5
foodentr				4,300	43	50
vendr				800	5	0
delivery				0	0	0
dinsnack				0	0	0
donation				1	0	1
memberfee				0	0	0
recreation				0	0	1
gift				10	8	16
gastran				8	9,999,995	16
consumption				4,319		90
2. Impute:						
usual				9999998	35	9999998
general				3,500	38	55
nonfood				0	0	5
foodentr				4,300	43	50
vendr				800	5	0
delivery				0	0	0
dinsnack				0	0	0
donation				1	0	1
memberfee				0	0	0
recreation				0	0	1
gift				10	8	16
gastran				8	12	16
consumption				4,319	56	90
3. Rescale and impute:						
usual				9999998	35	9999998
general				35	38	55
nonfood				0	0	5
foodentr				43	43	50
vendr				8	5	0
delivery				0	0	0
dinsnack				0	0	0
donation				1	0	1
memberfee				0	0	0
recreation				0	0	1
gift				10	8	16
gastran				8	12	16
consumption				62	56	90
4. Deflate by CPI:						
usual				9999998	21	9999998
general				24	23	28

Table 5.3 (continued)

A. Household 1

	1969	1971	1973	1975	1977	1979
nonfood				0	0	3
foodentr				29	26	25
vendr				5	3	0
delivery				0	0	0
dinsnack				0	0	0
donation				1	0	1
memberfee				0	0	0
recreation				0	0	1
gift				7	5	8
gastran				5	6	8
consumption				42	33	45
5. Deflate by detailed price index:						
usual				9999998	20	9999998
general				22	21	25
nonfood				0	0	2
foodentr				27	24	23
vendr				5	3	0
delivery				0	0	0
dinsnack				0	0	0
donation				1	0	1
memberfee				0	0	0
recreation				0	0	1
gift				7	5	8
gastran				5	6	8
consumption				40	31	43

B. Household 85

	1969	1971	1973	1975	1977	1979
1. Raw data:						
usual	0	9999998	40	7,000	9999998	9999998
general	40	3,000	35	6,000	50	25
nonfood	10	200	5	0	0	0
foodentr		4,100	35	6,700	70	25
vendr	5	1,000	5	700	20	0
delivery	4	300	0	0	0	0
dinsnack	5	3	6	7	7	3
donation	6	1		3	3	1
memberfee	0	0		0	0	0
recreation	0	0		0	0	0
gift	1	1		3	2	6
gastran	5	5	19	5	10	0
consumption	67	4,310		7,018	92	35

(continued)

Table 5.3 (continued)

B. Household 85						
	Year					
	1969	1971	1973	1975	1977	1979
2. Impute:						
usual	0	9999998	40	7,000	9999998	9999998
general	40	3,000	35	6,000	50	25
nonfood	10	200	5	0	0	0
foodentr		4,100	35	6,700	70	25
vendr	5	5	5	700	20	0
delivery	4	300	0	0	0	0
dinsnack	5	3	6	7	7	3
donation	6	1	2	3	3	1
memberfee	0	0	0	0	0	0
recreation	0	0	0	0	0	0
gift	1	1	2	3	2	6
gastran	5	5	19	5	10	0
consumption	67	3,315	75	7,018	92	35
3. Rescale and impute:						
usual	0	9999998	40	70	9999998	9999998
general	40	30	35	60	50	25
nonfood	10	2	5	0	0	0
foodentr		41	35	67	70	25
vendr	5	10	5	7	20	0
delivery	4	3	0	0	0	0
dinsnack	5	3	6	7	7	3
donation	6	1	2	3	3	1
memberfee	0	0	0	0	0	0
recreation	0	0	0	0	0	0
gift	1	1	2	3	2	6
gastran	5	5	19	5	10	0
consumption	67	53	75	88	92	35
4. Deflate by CPI:						
usual	0	9999998	33	48	9999998	9999998
general	40	27	29	41	30	13
nonfood	10	2	4	0	0	0
foodentr		37	29	46	42	13
vendr	5	9	4	5	12	0
delivery	4	3		0	0	0
dinsnack	5	2	5	5	4	2
donation	6	1	2	2	2	1
memberfee	0	0	0	0	0	0
recreation	0	0	0	0	0	0
gift	1	1	1	2	1	3
gastran	5	5	16	3	6	0
consumption	67	48	61	60	55	18
5. Deflate by detailed price index:						
usual	0	9999998	31	43	9999998	9999998
general	40	27	27	37	28	11

Table 5.3 (continued)

B. Household 85

	Year					
	1969	1971	1973	1975	1977	1979
nonfood	10	2	4	0	0	0
foodentr		38	27	42	39	11
vendr	5	9	4	4	11	0
delivery	4	3	0	0	0	0
dinsnack	5	2	5	4	4	2
donation	6	1	2	2	2	1
memberfee	0	0	0	0	0	0
recreation	0	0	0	0	0	0
gift	1	1	1	2	1	3
gastran	5	5	19	3	6	0
consumption	67	49	62	56	52	17

C. Household 89

	Year					
	1969	1971	1973	1975	1977	1979
1. Raw data:						
usual	0	14		1,400	9999998	9999998
general	10	1,200		1,200	13	14
nonfood	2	60		0	2	2
foodentr		1,140		1,200	11	12
vendr	0	0		0	0	0
delivery	0	0		0	0	0
dinsnack	0	0		92	1	1
donation	0	0		0	1	1
memberfee	0	0		0	0	0
recreation	0	0		0	0	0
gift	1	1		0	1	1
gastran	1	1		0	0	0
consumption	12	77		1,494	15	17
2. Impute:						
usual	0	14		1,400	9999998	9999998
general	10	1,200		1,200	13	14
nonfood	2	60		0	2	2
foodentr		1,140		1,200	11	12
vendr	0	0		0	0	0
delivery	0	0		0	0	0
dinsnack	0	0		92	1	1
donation	0	0		0	1	1
memberfee	0	0		0	0	0
recreation	0	0		0	0	0
gift	1	1		0	1	1
gastran	1	1		0	0	0
consumption	12	77		1,494	15	17

(continued)

Table 5.3 (continued)

B. Household 85

	Year					
	1969	1971	1973	1975	1977	1979
3. Rescale and impute:						
usual	0	14		14	9999998	9999998
general	10	12		12	13	14
nonfood	2	1		0	2	2
foodentr		11		12	11	12
vendr	0	0		0	0	0
delivery	0	0		0	0	0
dinsnack	0	0		92	1	1
donation	0	0		0	1	1
memberfee	0	0		0	0	0
recreation	0	0		0	0	0
gift	1	1		0	1	1
gastran	1	1		0	0	0
consumption	12	17		108	15	17
4. Deflate by CPI:						
usual	0	13		10	9999998	9999998
general	10	11		8	8	7
nonfood	2	1		0	1	1
foodentr		10		8	7	6
vendr	0	0		0	0	0
delivery	0	0		0	0	0
dinsnack	0	0		63	0	0
donation	0	0		0	0	0
memberfee	0	0		0	0	0
recreation	0	0		0	0	0
gift	1	1		0	1	1
gastran	1	1		0	0	0
consumption	12	15		73	9	8
5. Deflate by detailed price index:						
usual	0	13		9	9999998	9999998
general	10	11		7	7	6
nonfood	2	1		0	1	1
foodentr		10		7	6	6
vendr	0	0		0	0	0
delivery	0	0		0	0	0
dinsnack	0	0		59	0	0
donation	0	0		0	0	0
memberfee	0	0		0	0	0
recreation	0	0		0	0	0
gift	1	1		0	1	1
gastran	1	1		0	0	0
consumption	12	16		68	9	8

Source: Author's calculations from the RHS.

1975: *usually* spent on food in a week;
purchased from grocery stores and *general* stores last week;
food from a grocery store last week;
nonfood from a grocery store last week;
food from a *vendor* last week;
food from a *delivery* last week;

These coding errors were systematic, common to all households. In addition, in 1973 the food consumption data of some observations (but not all observations) were entered in cents. This is apparent from the maximum food consumption entry for 1973 (3,500) given above.

Missing values in the small categories of consumption were imputed by geometric interpolation between adjacent years or by backcasting or forecasting for end-point years. An example is the imputation of $12 for "gastran" for Household 1 in 1977. Because food consumption is about 60 percent of RHS consumption, no imputation in a particular year was made if food consumption was missing in all of its three forms in that year: RHS consumption for that household was entered as missing. The second panel shows the results of imputation and the third panel the results of both imputation and of rescaling the categories that were recorded in cents. Household 89 illustrates that no imputation is made when food consumption is missing. At this point, the data are recorded in current dollars per week.

The fourth panel has consumption measured in real dollars when the deflator is the CPI. The consumption by Household 1 is at reasonable levels but has considerable year-to-year variation due to low consumption in 1977. Examination of the individual components, however, does not reveal any that are obviously in error. Household 85 has fairly smooth consumption except for 1971 and 1979. Between 1977 and 1979, one of the spouses died, so the 1979 data will not enter any data sets based on constant household composition over two-year periods. For 1971, it is not obvious from inspection of the components which, if any, are recorded with error. Household 89 has declining consumption except in 1975. It seems probable that "dinsnack" (dinners and snacks purchased outside the home) is observed with considerable error, although it is certainly possible that in the month surveyed the household had some dinners in expensive restaurants. In any event, there is no systematic error in "dinsnack" common to all observations in 1975 that could be identified and corrected.

Some of the components of consumption were observed in the work preceding the survey, some are monthly averages (converted to weekly amounts), and some are annual averages. Prices were changing rapidly during some years of the RHS: if all the components of consumption were deflated by the CPI, considerable mismeasurement could arise simply from the timing of the measurement. Furthermore, the relative prices of some of the RHS components changed over the ten years. These considerations led to the use of monthly or annual deflators of the individual components of consumption depending on the time period over which the consumption component is defined. Table 5.4 shows the deflators and the time period of measurement. For example, "food at home" was measured for the week preceding the survey (in April), so the April food index was used as the deflator. "Gasoline" was measured on a monthly basis in 1973, so the March deflator was used. But in 1977 annual expenditure was measured, so the annual (1978) deflator was used.

These deflators can be used to define a Laspeyres price index for the consumption components of the RHS that can be compared with the CPI. Table 5.5 has the ratio of the CPI to the RHS deflator. The ratio of indices was roughly constant between 1969 and 1973, and again between 1975 and 1979, but at a different level. This was due to higher inflation rates in food and gasoline than in the other components of the CPI. For example, between 1973 and 1975, the food price index increased by 26 percent, whereas the CPI increased by just 21 percent. Between 1973 and 1979, the gasoline price index increased by 13 percent and the CPI by 61 percent. The ratio shows that deflating by the CPI could introduce mismeasurement of the changes in consumption that are systematically as large as any actual average changes. Therefore, to find the changes in real consumption of the components in the RHS, I deflated each component by the detailed price indices given in table 5.4.

Estimated consumption of Households 1, 85, and 89 are shown in the last

Table 5.4 Components of Detailed Price Index and CPI

Year	Food at Home	Date	Food away from Home	Date	Gasoline	Date	Recreation	Date	CPI	Date
1971	1.09	2	1.14	1	.96	2	1.10	3	1.10	3
1973	1.28	2	1.24	1	1.03	1	1.15	2	1.21	3
1975	1.61	2	1.57	1	1.50	2	1.40	3	1.47	3
1977	1.78	2	1.79	1	1.74	3	1.54	3	1.65	3
1979	2.18	2	2.18	1	2.44	3	1.73	3	1.98	3

Note: Date: 1 = March price index (monthly consumption was reported); 2 = April price index (weekly consumption was reported); 3 = annual average price index (annual consumption was reported).

Table 5.5 Ratio of the CPI to the Detailed Price Index

Year	Ratio
1969	1.000
1971	1.017
1973	.983
1975	.945
1977	.961
1979	.939

Source: Author's calculations from the RHS.

panel of table 5.3. Comparison of panels 4 and 5 shows that in most years the consumption levels do not depend greatly on the deflator. However, year-to-year consumption changes can be rather different: in panel 4 of Household 89, consumption fell by 2 percent between 1973 and 1975 according to CPI-deflated consumption but by 10 percent according to the RHS-index-deflated consumption measure.

The composition of RHS consumption deflated by the CPI is given in table 5.6 and deflated by the detailed price indices in table 5.7. Although the fractions in most categories are stable over time, the fractions spent on gasoline and food varied substantially regardless of which deflator was used. I imagine that this is at least partly caused by the difficulty of measuring real consumption during periods of high and varying inflation. Certainly, I would have more confidence that the variation in consumption in the RHS is a good indicator of variation in total consumption if the components of consumption in tables 5.6 and 5.7 had more stability.

The composition of consumption in tables 5.6 and 5.7 gives little guidance in choosing between the two deflators. For most of the rest of the paper, I use the detailed indices, but the basic results of the paper are unchanged if the CPI is used as the deflator.

An independent assessment of the reasonableness of the consumption mea-

Table 5.6 Composition of Consumption in Percentages: Components Deflated by CPI

Year	food	nonfood	donation	memberfee	recreation	gift	gastran	Total
1969	64	9	6	1	2	6	11	100
1971	63	8	7	1	2	6	12	100
1973	60	8	7	1	1	6	17	100
1975	66	8	8	1	2	7	7	100
1977	62	9	8	2	2	7	10	100
1979	62	9	8	1	1	8	11	100

Source: Author's calculations from the RHS.

Table 5.7 Composition of Consumption in Percentages: Components Deflated by Detailed Price Index

Year	food	nonfood	donation	memberfee	recreation	gift	gastran	Total
1969	59	8	6	1	2	6	18	100
1971	62	8	7	1	2	6	14	100
1973	64	8	8	1	2	7	10	100
1975	65	8	9	1	2	8	8	100
1977	60	9	9	2	2	7	12	100
1979	56	9	8	1	2	8	15	100

Source: Author's calculations from the RHS.

sure can be found as follows. In the 1972–73 Consumer Expenditure Survey (CES), about 17.4 percent of total expenditures were for food at home among the elderly in the relevant age range. If this percentage of income were spent by the 1978 RHS households (excluding earnings), weekly food consumption at home would have been about $29.50. This compares with the cross-sectional average (1977 and 1979) of measured food consumption at home of $31.30.

5.4 Changes in Consumption

If the measured components of consumption are normal goods, the components will fall when total consumption falls. Under that assumption, the direction of the change in total consumption can be found by studying changes in measured consumption.[5] Table 5.8 has average consumption (in 1969 dollars) by marital status for each of the initial two-year periods in the RHS. An observation is used in the calculation for a particular year if it has complete data for that year and for the second following year and if household composition remains constant over the two years. Thus, there is no control for composition: households may enter the sample at retirement, yet they may leave the sample in some other year because of missing values or change in marital status.[6] The table shows generally falling consumption each year, which indicates that, in cross section, consumption falls with age. As would be expected, consumption by couples is greater than by singles, about 77 percent greater on average. In this comparison, there is no control for economic resources that are much larger among couples.

Table 5.9 has consumption changes that hold composition constant. An observation enters one of the two-year data sets if household composition did not change during the two-year period, if the household was retired (defined to be no earnings during the remainder of the panel), and if there were no missing values.[7] Other conditions are given at the bottom of the table. The entries are

$$\frac{\Sigma(C_2 - C_0)}{\Sigma C_0},$$

which is robust against random observation error. The table shows declining consumption in each two-year period for both couples and singles. The declines are not at all constant, especially between 1973 and 1975. I imagine

5. If, in addition, the indifference curves are homothetic and relative prices are constant, the percentage change in the components of consumption gives the percentage change in total consumption. This is the implicit assumption of Hall and Mishkin (1982) and Bernanke (1984).

6. In addition, sixty-nine observations were deleted because consumption changed by more than $100 over two years. The effects of excluding these outliers will be discussed below in connection with tables 5.10 and 5.11.

7. Except for food consumption, some of the other consumption values may have been imputed.

Table 5.8 **Cross-Sectional Consumption (dollars per week)**

	Singles			Couples		
Year	Mean	SE	*N*	Mean	SE	*N*
1969	23.59	1.07	406	44.00	1.58	233
1971	23.31	.93	482	41.13	1.59	234
1973	23.55	.79	663	42.75	.88	485
1975	20.13	.39	918	35.80	.59	882
1977	20.83	.34	1,175	37.05	.50	1,180

Source: Author's calculations from the RHS.
Note: Consumption in 1969 dollars.

Table 5.9 **Consumption Change by Two-Year Periods (fraction of initial consumption)**

Years	All	Couples	Singles
1969–71	−.02	−.02	−.02
	(649)	(237)	(412)
1971–73	−.05	−.05	−.06
	(728)	(237)	(491)
1973–75	−.21	−.21	−.21
	(1,166)	(492)	(674)
1975–77	−.03	−.05	−.00
	(1,818)	(892)	(926)
1977–79	−.06	−.06	−.05
	(2,366)	(1,187)	(1,179)
All	−.38	−.39	−.35
	(6,727)	(3,045)	(3,682)

Source: Author's calculations from the RHS.
Note: Number of observations is in parentheses. In this data set there are no children in house; no human capital; no farmers; no marital status change in two adjacent years; no missing value in consumption in two adjacent years; no missing value in wealth in two adjacent years. The data set is indexed by detailed price index to 1969 dollars.

that this is due to the difficulty of measure gasoline and food consumption accurately during those years. This view is supported by the budget shares in tables 5.6 and 5.7. The last line of table 5.9 gives the estimated ten-year decline in consumption. It is just the sum of the two-year changes. The rate of decline is about 4 percent per year for couples and 3.5 percent for singles.

The finding of falling consumption in the panel data holds if the CPI is used to deflate all the components of consumption that are in RHS consumption: the total decline in consumption is estimated to be 31 percent for couples and 26 percent for singles.

Detailed examination of the data at the individual level showed a number of outliers. Table 5.10 has some examples. Households 2577 and 3394 have ex-

Table 5.10 Households with Large Changes in Consumption

A. Household 1

	Year					
	1969	1971	1973	1975	1977	1979
1. Household 2577:						
usual	35	9999998	9999998	10	34	46
general	50	37	39	31	28	41
nonfood	5	5	4	0	6	6
foodentr		34	38	33	28	41
vendr	6	2	3	2	6	6
delivery	0	0	0	0	0	0
dinsnack	0	0	6	12	4	4
donation	9	9	8	7	3	3
memberfee	0	0	0	0	0	0
recreation	17	1	3	8	0	0
gift	4	7	6	5	5	7
gastran	6	7	10	438	7	12
consumption	75	62	74	479	57	79
2. Household 3093:						
usual			9999998	9999998	9999998	11
general			19	124	11	0
nonfood			0	1	2	1
foodentr			19	11	10	0
vendr			0	0	0	0
delivery			0	0	0	0
dinsnack			0	0	0	3
donation			0	0	0	0
memberfee			0	0	0	0
recreation			0	0	0	0
gift			1	2	1	1
gastran			0	1	0	0
consumption			21	127	13	18
3. Household 3394:						
usual	24	9999998	9999998	16	11	9
general	20	23	19	9	14	14
nonfood	2	5	2	0	0	0
foodentr		18	19	9	14	14
vendr	0	0	1	0	0	0
delivery	0	0	0	0	0	0
dinsnack	0	0	0	0	0	0
donation	0	3	2	1	0	0
memberfee	0	0	0	0	0	0
recreation	0	0	0	0	0	0
gift	6	1	2	3	5	1
gastran	4	5	4	539	2	3
consumption	36	32	28	559	18	13
4. Household 3539:						
usual	0	9	9999998	16	11	9999998
general	15	7	16	12	8	14

Table 5.10 (continued)

A. Household 1

	Year					
	1969	1971	1973	1975	1977	1979
nonfood	0	0	0	1	1	2
foodentr		8	16	12	8	11
vendr	2	0	0	0	0	0
delivery	0	1	0	0	0	0
dinsnack	1	1	2	1	0	1
donation	1	1	1	1	0	0
memberfee	0	0	0	0	0	0
recreation	0	0	0	0	0	0
gift	0	1	1	1	2	2
gastran	1	123	2	0	0	0
consumption	20	135	21	19	13	17
5. Household 3835:						
usual	0	9999998	9999998	9	9999998	9999998
general	10	9	39	16	11	9
nonfood	1	2	4	1	1	0
foodentr		7	35	14	11	9
vendr	0	0	0	0	0	0
delivery	0	0	0	0	0	0
dinsnack	2	3	2	1	1	3
donation	12	9	10	10	6	10
memberfee	0	0	0	0	1	0
recreation	0	1	1	1	0	1
gift	3	9	7	5	6	8
gastran	200	2	15	0	5	5
consumption	228	33	74	29	30	35

Source: Author's calculations from the RHS.

ceptionally large gasoline expenditures in 1975. In that year, actual weekly expenditures were recorded. Those households showed no strong propensity for substantial driving during the other years of the survey; the most plausible explanation is a coding error that recorded expenditures in cents rather than in dollars.[8] Household 3093 apparently generally spent \$124 on groceries in 1975, whereas in other years it generally spent about one-tenth as much. In that all entries of "general" in 1975 have already been divided by 100 (under the assumption that they were recorded in cents rather than in dollars), the entry looks like a misplaced decimal point. Gasoline consumption of Household 3539 in 1971 and of Household 3835 in 1969 appears to have been entered in cents rather than in dollars.

8. At \$1.00 per gallon (1969 prices) and fifteen miles per gallon, household 2577 would have driven 6,570 miles in a week.

These are typical examples of thirty-one couples and thirty-eight singles whose consumption changed by more than $100 in absolute value over two adjacent years.[9] Deleting the observations with a change in consumption of more than $100 in absolute value produces the consumption changes in table 5.11. In line with the previous discussion of the large price changes near 1975, the most observations (eighteen) were deleted in the 1973–75 and 1975–77 data sets. Deleting the observations causes the estimated ten-year decline in consumption to fall from 39 to 28 percent for couples and from 35 to 18 percent for singles. The year-to-year pattern becomes more uneven, and in particular estimated consumption rose between 1971 and 1973 and between 1975 and 1977. Nonetheless, the overall conclusion is that consumption declined as the households aged, as required by the LCH.

Imputing the small categories of consumption changes somewhat the year-to-year pattern of the change in consumption but does not alter the overall conclusions of declining consumption. Consider table 5.12, which compares consumption changes calculated over all observations with changes calculated only over observations with no imputations. (Comparisons cannot be made for the years 1971–73 and 1973–75 because all observations had imputations in 1973.) About 33 percent of couples and 36 percent of singles had at least one imputed value.[10] The total decline in consumption over the years in the table is the same regardless of whether observations with imputed values are included or not, even though there is some year-to-year variation in the rate of decline.

I have been writing of consumption as measured in the RHS as if it were total consumption. The conclusion that consumption declines with age is based on the observation that the total of the components in the RHS declines with age. But if, as people age, they change the composition of their consumption, RHS consumption could decline even though total consumption was stable or even rising.[11] A way to test for taste changes associated with aging is to compare the change in consumption of households who have bequeathable wealth with households who have no bequeathable wealth. A condition of utility maximization is that consumption equals annuity income if bequeathable wealth is zero. Therefore, households who have no bequeathable wealth and constant annuity income should have constant consumption. Then, if there is no age effect on the components of consumption, the RHS measure of consumption should be constant.

Table 5.13 shows consumption by singles and couples classified according

9. One household can account for two observations on large changes. For example, household 3394 has a positive change of $531 from 1973 to 1975 and a negative change of $541 from 1975 to 1977, accounting for two of the outliers.

10. Again, food consumption is never imputed: if it is missing, the observation is dropped.

11. Of course, the allocation of consumption could change because of price and/or wealth changes. Investigation of changes associated with price and wealth changes will be the subject of future research.

Table 5.11 Consumption Change by Two-Year Periods: Outliers Excluded (fraction of initial consumption)

Years	All	Couples	Singles
1969–71	−.06	−.08	−.04
	(639)	(233)	(406)
1971–73	.04	.06	.03
	(716)	(234)	(482)
1973–75	−.19	−.21	−.17
	(1,148)	(485)	(663)
1975–77	.03	.02	.04
	(1,800)	(882)	(918)
1977–79	−.06	−.07	−.04
	(2,355)	(1,180)	(1,175)
All	−.24	−.28	−.18
	(6,658)	(3,014)	(3,644)

Source: Author's calculations from the RHS.
Note: Number of observations is in parentheses. In this data set there are no children in house; no human capital; no farmers; no marital status change in two adjacent years; no missing value in consumption in two adjacent years; no missing value in wealth in two adjacent years. The data set is indexed by detailed price index to 1969 dollar, and there is no consumption change of more than $100 per week in two years.

Table 5.12 Consumption Change by Two-Year Periods: Effects of Imputation (fraction of initial consumption)

	Couples		Singles	
Years	Not Imputed	Imputed	Imputed	Not Imputed
1969–71	−.07	−.08	−.00	−.04
	(130)	(233)	(242)	(406)
1975–77	.01	.02	.04	.04
	(603)	(882)	(605)	(918)
1977–79	−.08	−.07	−.07	−.04
	(799)	(1,180)	(762)	(1,175)
All	−.13	−.13	−.04	−.04
	(1,532)	(2,295)	(1,609)	(2,499)

Source: Author's calculations from the RHS.
Note: Number of observations is in parentheses.

to whether they had any bequeathable wealth (excluding housing wealth). Those with no wealth were further restricted to those whose only annuity is Social Security, which is taken to be constant. The change in consumption holds composition constant in that it is the average over five two-year periods in each of which composition is constant. As would be expected, those households with no bequeathable wealth consumed less than households with bequeathable wealth. Singles both with and without bequeathable wealth reduced consumption as they aged, but the average rate of reduction was about

Table 5.13 Test of Age Effects

	Singles		Couples	
	Zero Wealth	Positive Wealth	Zero Wealth	Positive Wealth
Initial consumption (C_0)	15.54	22.37	22.76	38.68
Second-period consumption (C_2)	14.86	21.55	22.87	36.36
$C_0 - C_2$	.67	.82	−.11	.232
	(.57)	(.20)	(1.77)	(.27)
No. of observations	314	3,330	43	2,971

Source: Author's calculations from the RHS.
Note: Standard errors are in parentheses.

4 percent for both. The null hypothesis that $\Delta c = 0$ cannot be rejected for singles whose bequeathable wealth is zero, but it can be for singles whose bequeathable wealth is not zero. Of course, because of the small sample size, the first test has low power, so this is very weak evidence for no age effect on tastes. Among couples, the sample size is even smaller. Couples who had no bequeathable wealth increased consumption slightly, whereas couples with bequeathable wealth decreased consumption by about 6 percent over a two-period on average. This again offers mild evidence in support of the view that taste changes associated with aging are not the cause of the fall in RHS consumption.

Tests based on the fraction of households with falling consumption produce about the same conclusion as shown by table 5.14. More households who had bequeathable wealth had a fall in consumption than households who did not have bequeathable wealth. The null hypothesis that the probability of a decline in consumption is 0.5 cannot be rejected for households with no bequeathable wealth, but it can be for households with bequeathable wealth. Again, this is mild support for no taste changes with age.[12]

The LCH with a bequest motive implies that a strong bequest motive will flatten the consumption path. Under the assumption that parents have a stronger bequest motive than nonparents, parents should have consumption paths that decline more slowly than nonparents. Table 5.15 has average consumption of singles and couples according to whether the household had children.[13] No children lived in the households. Singles both with and without

12. If the sample for this test is restricted to 1975–79 (Social Security benefits were better indexed over those years), and if the definition of "no wealth" is made either less than $500 or less than $1,000, the same general results are found.

13. Although the RHS has no information on the ages of the children, most were probably in their 30s and 40s.

Table 5.14 Fraction of Households with a Decline in Consumption

	Wealth Equals Zero	Wealth Greater Than Zero
Singles	.538	.562
	(.028)	(.009)
Couples	.512	.585
	(.076)	(.009)

Source: Author's calculations from the RHS
Note: Standard errors are in parentheses.

Table 5.15 Test of Bequest Motive

	Singles		Couples	
	No Children	Children	No Children	Children
Initial consumption (C_0)	22.72	21.35	37.89	38.58
Second-period consumption (C_2)	21.44	20.76	35.95	36.22
$C_0 - C_2$	1.28	.59	1.93	2.37
	(.34)	(.23)	(.54)	(.30)
No. of observations	1,160	2,484	563	2,451

Source: Author's calculations from the RHS.
Note: Standard errors are in parentheses.

children had declining consumption on average, but the consumption of single parents declined somewhat less. This supports a bequest motive. Couples also had declining consumption, but the parents had the greater decline, which offers no support to the bequest motive. Table 5.16 gives the difference between the consumption change of nonparents (C_{nc}) and the consumption change of parents (C_c) and summarizes this test of the bequest motive. Under the null hypothesis of no bequest motive, the differences should be zero; under the hypothesis of a bequest motive, the differences should be negative. For singles the null hypothesis cannot be rejected, and for couples the statistic has the wrong sign of rejection.

An alternative test is based on the fraction of households with declining consumption. If a bequest motive is important, a smaller fraction of parents than of nonparents should have falling consumption. As shown in the first two columns of Table 5.17, this holds among singles but not among couples. The third column has the differences in the fractions and the standard errors of the differences. Under the null hypothesis of no bequest motive, the differences in the fractions should be zero; under a bequest motive, they should be positive. Although for singles the sign of the difference supports the bequest motive,

Table 5.16 **Test of a Bequest Motive Based on the Difference in Consumption Change**

	$\Delta C_{nc} - \Delta C_c$	
	Singles	Couples
	−.69	.44
	(.41)	(.61)

Source: Author's calculations from the RHS.
Note: Standard errors are in parentheses.

Table 5.17 **Fraction of Households with Declining Consumption**

	No Children	Children	Difference
Singles	.572	.554	.018
	(.015)	(.010)	(.018)
Couples	.568	.587	−.019
	(.021)	(.010)	(.023)

Source: Author's calculations from the RHS.
Note: Standard errors are in parentheses.

the null hypothesis cannot be rejected. For couples the statistic has the wrong sign for rejection.

5.5 Conclusion

When the date of death is unknown, the LCH implies that consumption by individuals of sufficient age will decline with age. If consumption is observed to increase with age, it may simply be that the individuals are not old enough to be on the downward-sloping part of their consumption trajectories. However, it is likely that, at least by the end of the panel, the RHS cohorts were old enough to have declining consumption. If consumption is falling, bequeathable wealth should fall: if it does not, a terminal condition on wealth will be violated. In the RHS, observations on both consumption and wealth are consistent with the LCH in that both are observed to decline after retirement.

While the findings that consumption and wealth decline with age are consistent with the LCH, they are not inconsistent with a bequest motive for saving: the bequest motive (if it is operable) will change the shape and level of the consumption and wealth paths, but they will not necessarily rise. A test for the importance of the bequest motive is based on the assumption that the marginal utility of bequests of a parent is greater than the marginal utility of bequests of a nonparent. This assumption implies that, ceteris paribus, the wealth and consumption paths of a parent should decline more slowly than the wealth and consumption paths of a nonparent. In the RHS, the wealth paths decline at the same rate. The consumption paths of singles show some support for the bequest motive, but, possibly due to low power, the difference in the paths is not statistically significant. The consumption paths of couples show no support for the bequest motive: the rate of decline over a two-year period is about 6 percent for parents and 5 percent for nonparents.

The RHS data on wealth and consumption are consistent with the life-cycle hypothesis of consumption. They offer no support for a bequest motive for saving as an important determinant of consumption behavior.

References

Abel, Andrew B. 1987. Operative Gift and Bequest Motives. *American Economic Review* 77 (5):1037–47.

Bernanke, Ben. 1984. Permanent Income, Liquidity, and Expenditure on Automobiles: Evidence from Panel Data. *Quarterly Journal of Economics* 99 (3):587–614.

Bernheim, B. Douglas. 1987. Dissaving after Retirement: Testing the Pure Life Cycle Hypothesis. In *Issues in Pension Economics,* ed. Zvi Bodie, John B. Shoven, and David A. Wise, 237–74. Chicago: University of Chicago Press.

Blinder, Alan S., Roger H. Gordon, and Donald E. Wise. 1983. Social Security, Bequests and the Life Cycle Theory of Saving: Cross-SectionalTests. In *Income Distribution and Economic Inequality,* ed. Zvi Griliches. New York: Halstead.

Boskin, Michael J., and Michael D. Hurd. 1985. Indexing Social Security Benefits: A Separate Price Index for the Elderly? *Public Finance Quarterly* 13 (4):436–49.

Danziger, Sheldon, Jacques van der Gaag, Eugene Smolensky, and Michael Taussig. 1982. The Life Cycle Hypothesis and the Consumption Behavior of the Elderly. *Journal of Post Keynesian Economics* 5(2):208–27.

Darby, Michael R. 1979. *Effects of Social Security on Income and the Capital Stock.* Washington, D.C.: American Enterprise Institute.

Diamond, Peter A., and Jerry Hausman. 1984. Individual Retirement and Savings Behavior. *Journal of Public Economics* 23:81–114.

Hall, Robert E., and Frederic S. Mishkin. 1982. The Sensitivity of Consumption to Transitory Income: Estimates from Panel Data on Households. *Econometrica* 50 (March):261–81.

Hurd, Michael D. 1987. Savings of the Elderly and Desired Bequests. *American Economic Review* 77 (2):298–312.

———. 1989. Mortality Risk and Bequests. *Econometrica* 57 (4):779–813.

———. 1990. Research on the Elderly: Economic Status, Retirement, and Consumption and Saving. *Journal of Economic Literature* 28 (June):565–637.

Jianakoplos, Nancy A., Paul L. Menchik, and F. Owen Irvine. 1989. Using Panel Data to Assess the Bias in Cross-Sectional Inference of Life-Cycle Changes in the Level and Composition of Household Wealth. In *The Measurement of Saving, Investment, and Wealth,* ed. Robert E. Lipsey and Helen Stone Tice, 533–640. Chicago: University of Chicago Press.

Kotlikoff, Laurence J. 1988. Intergenerational Transfers and Savings. *Journal of Economic Perspectives* 2 (2):41–59.

Kotlikoff, Laurence J., and Lawrence Summers. 1981. The Role of Intergenerational

Transfers in Aggregate Capital Accumulation. *Journal of Political Economy* 89:706–32.
———. 1988. The Contribution of Intergenerational Transfers to Total Wealth: A Reply. In *Modeling the Accumulation and Distribution of Wealth,* ed. Denis Kessler and Andre Masson, 53–67. New York: Oxford University Press.
Kurz, Mordecai. 1985. Heterogeneity in Savings Behavior: A Comment. In *Frontiers of Economics,* ed. K. Arrow and S. Harkapohja, 307–27. Oxford: Blackwell.
Lydall, Harold. 155. The Life Cycle, Income, Saving, and Asset Ownership. *Econometrica* 23:985–1012.
Menchik, Paul L., and Martin David. 1983. Income Distribution, Lifetime Savings, and Bequests. *American Economic Review* 73 (4):672–90.
Mirer, Thad. 1979. The Wealth-Age Relation among the Aged. *American Economic Review* 69:435–43.
———. 1980. The Dissaving Behavior of the Retired Aged. *Southern Economic Journal* 46 (4):1197–1205.
Modigliani, Franco. 1986. Life Cycle, Individual Thrift, and the Wealth of Nations. *American Economic Review* 76 (3):297–313.
——— 1988. The Role of Intergenerational Transfers and Life Cycle Saving in the Accumulation of Wealth. *Journal of Economic Perspectives* 2 (2):15–40.
Projector, Dorothy, and Gertrude Weiss. 1966. *Survey of Financial Characteristics of Consumers.* Washington, D.C.: Board of Governors, Federal Reserve Board.
Radner, Daniel. 1989. The Wealth of the Aged, 1984. In *The Measurement of Saving, Investment, and Wealth,* ed. Robert E. Lipsey and Helen Stone Tice, 645–84. Chicago: University of Chicago Press.
White, Betsy Buttrill. 1978. Empirical Tests of the Life-Cycle Hypothesis. *American Economic Review* 68 (4):547–60.
Wolff, Edward N. 1988. Social Security, Pensions and the Life Cycle Accumulation of Wealth: Some Empirical Tests. *Annales D'Economie et de Statistique* 9:199–226.
Yaari, Menahem E. 1965. Uncertain Lifetime, Life Insurance and the Theory of the Consumer. *Review of Economic Studies* 32:137–50.

Comment Lee A. Lillard

Michael D. Hurd's paper is a continuation of his notable prior work on consumption and saving at the end of the life cycle. In that work, Hurd thoroughly explored the basic life-cycle model, in which an individual's lifetime utility depends on the path of consumption and on bequests.[1] Empirically, that prior research focused on assets and changes in assets at the end of the life cycle to test the predictions of this basic model using the panel data on assets from the Retirement History Survey (RHS). The primary contribution of this current research is to test the robustness of his previous results further using the consumption data, rather than the asset data, from the RHS. I will begin

Lee A. Lillard is senior economist and director of the Center for Aging Studies at the Rand Corporation.

1. See Michael D. Hurd, "Savings of the Elderly and Desired Bequests," *American Economic Review* 77, no. 3 (June 1987): 298–312, and "Mortality Risk and Bequests," *Econometrica* 57, no. 4 (1989): 779–813.

with comments on this current effort and then suggest areas for further theoretical and empirical enhancements of the model.

As Hurd suggests, the simple life-cycle model, with or without a bequest motive, has additional predictions about the rate of change of consumption that may be directly tested with time series of individual consumption values. A critical question is whether the RHS consumption data are worthy of this level of detailed examination. A substantial portion of the paper is devoted to a discussion of the measurement problems encountered in the various consumption items composing the observed consumption data. These problems include missing data in certain items for some individuals, alternative measures of items, systematic coding errors, purely random errors of measurement or reporting, and detection of extreme outliers. I think that Hurd has done a heroic job of addressing these problems, making imputations where necessary, and analyzing the resulting data. But one is ultimately left to wonder whether all the problem cases have been detected and solved, and what the implications are of all the various assumptions underlying the adjustments.

Even if the observed consumption data were error free, a potentially serious fault with the data is the fact that, as noted by Hurd, these covered consumption categories all together account for only about 34 percent total consumption. This is a rather small portion. The proportion of consumption accounted for by food, nonfood grocery items, gifts and donations, and gasoline and transportation may change systematically with age, with changes in health status, or with changes in the price of these goods relative to the prices of the unmeasured components. Biases could go either way. For example, as health deteriorates (on average) with age, total consumption may rise as medical expenditures increase, but consumption of the measured items may decline as individuals substitute away from, say, gifts and transportation, and therefore the measured components of consumption understate the change in total consumption. Alternatively, the relative prices of the measured items may have fallen, and therefore measured changes in consumption understated life-cycle changes.

Hurd has done a remarkably good job of analyzing inherently weak data. It is something that should be done because it does complement prior results, but the bottom line is that one is left with some uncertainty about the strength of the conclusions.

Let us turn to some potentially fruitful areas for further development of the theoretical and empirical models. These are not direct criticisms of Hurd's current effort but rather directions that the literature in general might take.

There are two major shortcomings of the theoretical model as it currently stands—the basic life-cycle consumption model with a bequest motive. One is the omission of health as a factor. It is widely recognized that health and medical care expenditures are important considerations of elderly individuals (not to mention government agencies), even within the age range of the RHS.

Recent evidence suggests that utility functions depend on health status.[2] So changes in health status with age may change both the level of consumption and its composition. In addition, potential changes of health status, and the resulting medical costs, pose an important source of uncertainty for elderly individuals, uncertainty that provides an additional motive for saving and thus may affect consumption even while those individuals are healthy.

A second omission of the theoretical and empirical models is consideration of how couples differ from single individuals. The life-cycle model is developed for an individual. Couples face two survival functions, one for the husband and one for the (usually younger) wife. Life-cycle consumption patterns should depend on both survivor functions and should account for both consumption by the widow(er) until death and the implied delay of any bequest. In the empirical implementation, couples are treated as if they were to follow the predictions of the life-cycle model developed for an individual. The predictions may be the same, but that is unclear. In any case, other testable predictions should emerge.

Empirically, the analysis relies on various forms of a simple difference in consumption between two time periods (surveys two years apart), the issue being whether consumption declines with age (for the age group represented in the RHS). First, this barely begins to exploit the richness of the panel data in the RHS, which includes up to six points in time (although fewer points after individuals retire from the labor force, as required by Hurd). Consumption changes for "pairs of adjacent years" are included whenever both years are eligible (e.g., no change in marital status, neither year's consumption is missing), and all eligible pairs of years are used. This might include more than one consumption change for a married couple or for a single person. These pairs of observations may not be independent, especially if they include a common consumption value (it was not clear whether this occurred). Some way of linking observations to exploit the full panel may be informative—such as dealing with measurement error explicitly and thus potentially improving the tests for declining consumption and for the bequest motive.

Additionally, the consumption change data might include an observed change for a married couple and an observed change for the surviving "single" widow(er) if either member of the couple dies. One may be able to exploit these changes in marital status, and other aspects of the panel, to study differences in the behavior of couples versus singles.

2. See W. Kip Viscusi and William N. Evans, "Utility Functions That Depend on Health Status: Estimates and Economic Implications," *American Economic Review* 80, no. 3 (June 1990): 353–74.

6 Patterns of Aging in Thailand and Côte d'Ivoire

Angus Deaton and Christina H. Paxson

This paper presents and discusses some facts about older people in two contrasting developing countries, Côte d'Ivoire and Thailand. We shall be concerned with standard questions in the aging literature, namely, demographic structure, living arrangements, urbanization, illness, labor force behavior, and economic status. In this paper, we shall not go far beyond the presentation of data from a series of household surveys from the two countries. Although recent years have seen increased attention in the demographic and sociological literatures to questions of aging in LDCs, data are still relatively scarce, particularly for Africa, and we see our current task as providing stylized facts to help focus further discussion.

There are two research issues that provide the structure for our discussion: household saving behavior and, more broadly, the economics of aging in countries with low living standards but with rapidly expanding shares of old people in the population.

Research on saving behavior in the United States, Japan, and Western Europe has been dominated by permanent income and life-cycle models since their introduction in the 1950s. There has been a good deal less work done on household saving behavior in LDCs, and much of the work that has been done has simply transferred the analytic framework from the more to the less developed context. It is not clear that this is the best way of proceeding. While it makes sense to work with the same basic ideas—that saving can smooth con-

Angus Deaton is Wilham Church Osborn Professor of Public Affairs and professor of economics and international affairs at Princeton University and a research associate of the National Bureau of Economic Research. Christina H. Paxson is assistant professor of economics and public affairs at Princeton University.

The authors are grateful to the World Bank for providing data and other support; this is part of a broader research project on household saving behavior in Thailand and Côte d'Ivoire. They also want to thank Noreen Goldman, Robert Hecht, Valerie Kozel, Anne Pebley, and Charles Westhoff for useful discussions and the Center for International Studies for its support.

sumption over time and that assets provide a measure of insurance against an uncertain future—there are important differences in environment and in mechanisms, and the same aims may therefore be achieved in very different ways. A much larger share of the population in developing countries is engaged in agriculture, where incomes are very variable, and there are many poor people living close to the subsistence level, so consumption insurance may be of the greatest importance.

Household size is typically larger in poorer countries. Extended families, or even simply large households, may play many of the roles that are performed by asset markets in more developed economies. For example, wealthy older men may acquire additional young wives as an alternative to an annuity. At the same time, the internal organization of the family and its living arrangements are intimately tied to patterns of inheritance, and therefore the means of transferring assets from one generation to the next will themselves vary with household structure. Because age composition within very large households may not vary very much over time, the main motive for saving becomes the protection of living standards from short-term covariate risk and has little to do with transferring resources between generations or between widely separated time periods. One of the issues that we examine in this paper is the extent to which there are clearly defined economic and demographic characteristics of households that vary systematically with the ages of their members, particularly characteristics that are likely to provide motives for saving.

A number of broader issues have been raised in the literature on aging in LDCs, and these also play a role in shaping our discussion. The dominant *demographic* fact for LDCs is the effect of the demographic transition on raising the fraction of old people in the population. In Thailand, where the demographic transition is largely complete, the share of people over 60 in the population, which was 6.2 and 5.7 percent in 1960 and 1985, respectively, is expected to rise to 11.9 percent in 2020 (United Nations 1986), figures that are repeated in much of South, Southeast, and East Asia as well as in Latin America. United Nations (1987) lists 3.8, 3.5, 5.1, and 4.3, respectively as the percentages of the population aged 65 and over in these four regions in 1980, whereas the estimated figures for 2000 are 4.8, 4.6, 7.8, and 5.2, rising in 2025 to 8.2, 8.3, 13.3, and 8.3. In Africa, where by contrast there has been little decline in the rate of population growth, the percentages of the population aged 65 and over are 3.1, 3.0, and 3.9 in 1980, 2000, and 2025, respectively. The two countries discussed in this paper are good examples of these two contrasting cases.

It is also important to note that life expectancy for older people in LDCs is high, and although life expectancy is not as high as in Japan or the United States, the difference is much smaller than the corresponding differences at birth. Life expectancy at birth in North America is 72.4 years for men and 80.1 years for women, and at age 60 men can expect to live for 17.8 years and women for 21.8 years. In South Asia and Africa, respectively, life expectancy at birth is 59.4 and 54.1 for men and 60.2 and 57.4 for women, and at age 60 it is 15.1 and 14.3 for men and 16.3 and 15.9 for women (for these and other figures, see Treas and Logue 1986). Since women live longer than men, higher life expectancy for all tends to exaggerate the predominance of women over men in the population, with the result that the ratio of males to females tends to decline with the level of development. In the more developed countries in 1980, there were sixty-two males per one hundred females aged 65 and over, compared with eighty-two per one hundred in Thailand and eighty per one hundred in China, and in parts of South Asia, where there is excess mortality among women, there are more men than women in the older age groups (see Martin 1988). Several West African countries also show a predominance of men over women (U.S. Agency for International Development 1982).

The growing relative importance of the elderly, particularly in Asia, has led to an increased academic and policy debate mirroring much of the earlier debate in more developed economies. Two excellent reviews are provided by Treas and Logue (1986) and, for Asia, Martin (1988). One of the dominant themes of this debate is the contrast between the status of the elderly in more and less developed countries. There are extreme idealized versions of both types of societies. To some, the extended family provides insurance for old age, unemployment, and sickness as well as an environment in which the elderly are an integrated, useful, and respected part of their families. This is seen as a stark contrast to the "Western" treatment of the old, whereby they are unproductive, isolated, and institutionalized, with social insurance providing only a poor substitute for family insurance. Cowgill (1974; 1986, chap. 8) sees the victimization of the elderly as a natural concomitant of development. Education, urbanization, and technical change become "processes that strip the old of claims to respect, power, and independence" (Treas and Logue 1986, 666). To others, the security of the extended family is a romanticized myth that appeals mostly to those who have long escaped the grinding poverty, poor health conditions, and low life expectancy with which it is typically associated. One person's isolation is someone else's individual freedom. It is perhaps not surprising that Asian policymakers, faced with the prospect of rapidly increasing absolute and relative numbers of old people, view Western systems of pensions, social security, and public geriatric care with a mixture of envy and alarm.

These "big" questions of the effect of development on the status of the elderly are not sufficiently well posed to be amenable to serious empirical evaluation. Nevertheless, good work has been done on more specific issues, particularly on the living arrangements of the elderly. Martin (1989) reviews a number of studies of Asian populations that suggest that the proportion of the elderly living with their children, although still high (typically between 70 and 80 percent), is declining over time, with a corresponding increase in the numbers living alone, a pattern that is consistent with a move toward living arrangements such as those in the United States, where only 15 percent of the elderly live with their children.

The remainder of the paper is organized as follows. Section 6.1 is concerned with *individuals* and reviews demographic characteristics and living arrangements for elderly people in Côte d'Ivoire and Thailand. It also presents data on urbanization, on health, on labor force participation and hours worked, and, as far as is possible, on levels of living. Section 6.2 is concerned with *households* and looks for "life-cycle"-type patterns in household size, income, and consumption patterns in relation to the ages of household members. Section 6.3 summarizes and concludes.

6.1 Individual Characteristics and Age

6.1.1 Sample Data and Population Characteristics

The data presented in this paper come from two series of household surveys from Côte d'Ivoire and Thailand. Côte d'Ivoire is listed by the World Bank (1989) in the lower-middle-income division of its middle-income category, with per capita GNP in 1987 of $740, which grew at an annual average per capita rate of 1.0 percent from 1965 to 1987. Its population in 1987 is estimated as 11.1 million and grew at an annual rate of 4.2 percent during both 1965–80 and 1980–87. The crude birth rate per thousand was fifty-two in 1965 and fifty-one in 1987, while life expectancy at birth in 1987 was 52 years. Thailand has a similar GNP of $850 but has experienced much faster growth, averaging 3.9 percent from 1965 to 1987. If these figures can be taken seriously, the average Thai was 280 percent richer in 1987 than in 1960, as opposed to an increase of only 30 percent for Ivorians over the same period. Whatever the precise magnitude, young Thais are now very much better off than were their parents, either in terms of lifetime resources or in terms of income at the same age, and this is much less true for young Ivorians. There were 53.6 million Thais in 1987, with a life expectancy at birth of 64 years. The population growth rate was 2.9 percent from 1965 to 1980, 2.0 percent from 1980 to 1987, and is projected to be 1.5 percent from 1987 to 2000; the crude birth rate per thousand fell from forty-one to twenty-five between 1965 and 1987.

The Ivorian surveys are the Living Standards Surveys of 1985 and 1986, collected by the Department of Statistics of Côte d'Ivoire with the technical and analytic support of the World Bank. The survey design, described in Ainsworth and Muñoz (1986), is a nontraditional one, carried out on a simple random sample of sixteen hundred households in each of the two years, with eight hundred households common to both surveys. Although the number of households is small compared with traditional designs, there are around fourteen thousand individuals in each of the two surveys. The emphasis is less on large sample size than on the collection of comprehensive data for each household so that interlinkages between different economic activities can be studied. The Thai surveys are the two Socioeconomic Surveys of the Whole Kingdom, collected by the National Statistical Office in the two years 1981 and 1986. These surveys are more like the traditional household income and expenditure surveys. They have sample sizes in excess of twelve thousand, they have no panel element, and there is less detailed information about many of the activities covered in the Living Standards Surveys. Even so, for the purposes of this paper, the two sets of surveys provide roughly equivalent information.

There are earlier household surveys for Thailand that could be used to examine the same issues over a longer time period. However, after the 1975 survey, the definition of the household was changed to exclude subunit households; thus, for example, a married son and his wife living with parents would have been included as part of the parents' household in 1975 but not in later surveys. As a result, it is not possible to make consistent comparisons about living arrangements over the two types of survey. This seemingly technical issue points to a deeper problem in the measurement of household structure in Thailand and, indeed, in developing countries in general. To quote Cowgill (1986, 70),

> In Thailand, however, the term *household* is somewhat elusive and ambiguous. The climate is semi-tropical, and a great portion of one's life is spent out-of-doors. To a very great extent, this includes cooking, eating, and visiting. Thus the physical structure of the home is little more than a bedroom situated within a compound, while the cooking, eating, bathing, visiting, and even much of the working takes place in the compound rather than in the physical structure of the home. Hence when we say that the young married couple lives with the parents of one of them, the young couple usually sleeps in a separate structure within the parental compound. This usually involves common cooking and eating facilities, but this too is flexible, especially since eating is more of an individual matter and less often a scheduled group activity. Western definitions of household membership are not easily applied in this type of society.

These issues must be constantly borne in mind when interpreting the figures given below. In particular, the "new" treatment of the household in the Thai surveys is likely to *overstate* the degree to which people live either alone or in small groups and to *understate* household size. By contrast, the Ivorian survey used a more inclusive concept of the household and tended to include subunits if they lived in the same compound. As a result, household size in the surveys is larger than household size in the 1975 Ivorian census, and the biases may be in the opposite direction from those in Thailand.

Figures 6.1 and 6.2 show the age pyramids and sex ratios for Bangkok and for rural Thailand in 1981 and 1986; figure 6.3 provides the same information for Côte d'Ivoire. For most of the paper, we shall follow this practice of show-

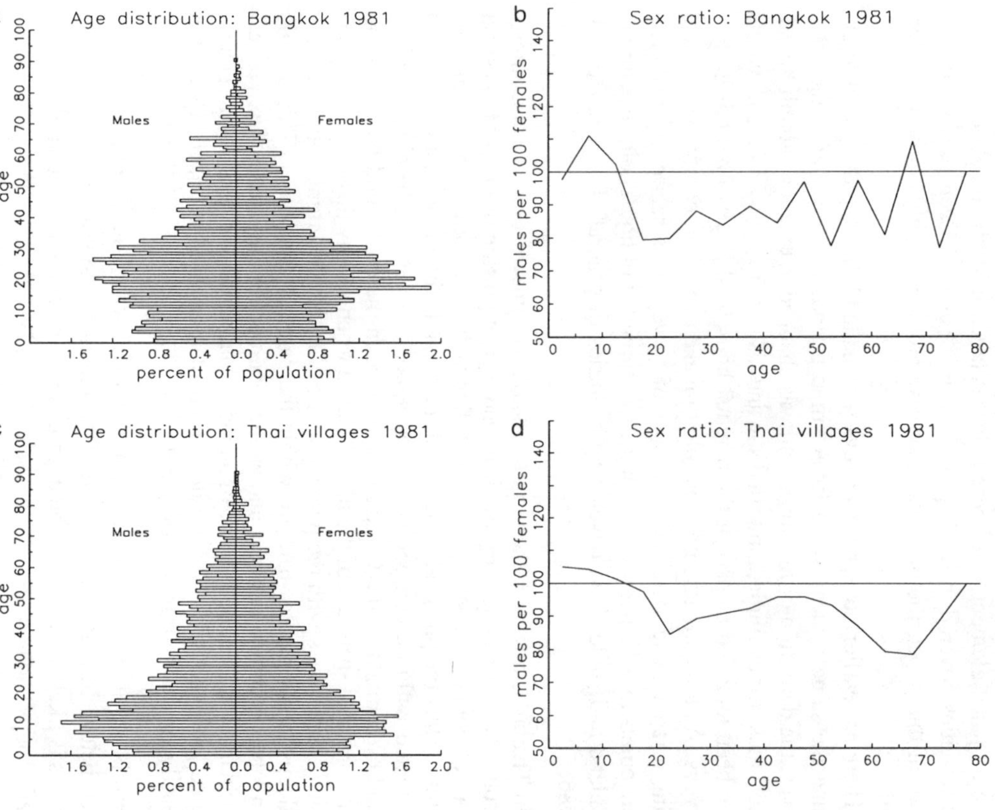
a
Age distribution: Bangkok 1981
Males
Females
age
percent of population
b
Sex ratio: Bangkok 1981
males per 100 females
age
c
Age distribution: Thai villages 1981
Males
Females
age
percent of population
d
Sex ratio: Thai villages 1981
males per 100 females
age

Fig. 6.1

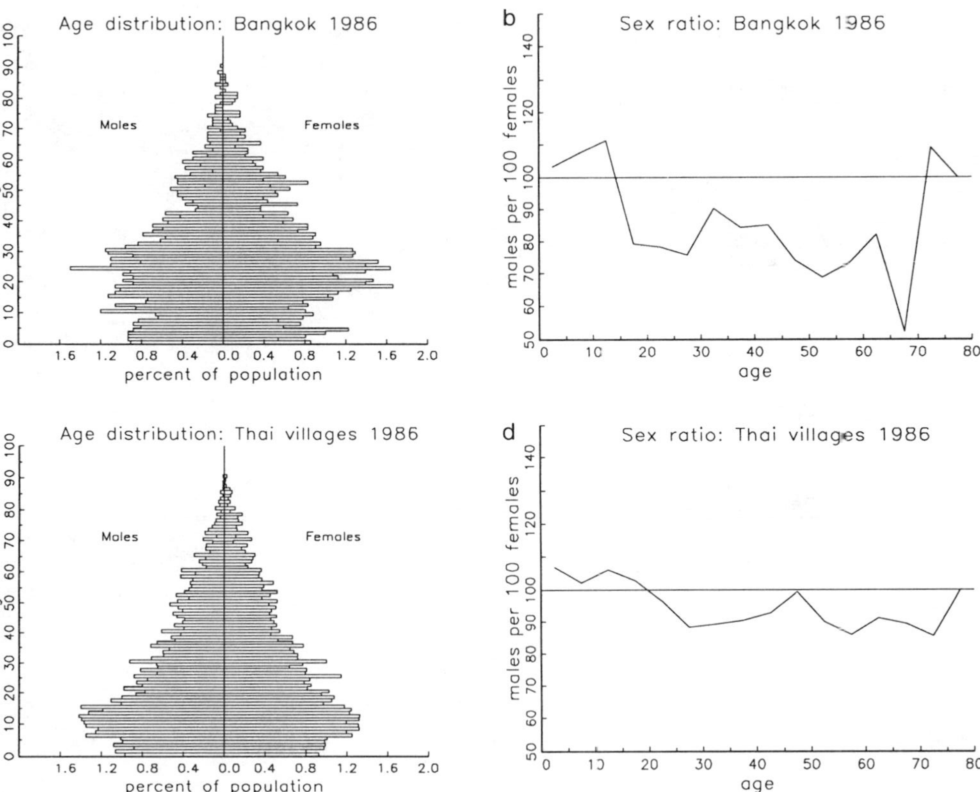
a
Age distribution: Bangkok 1986
Males
Females
age
percent of population
b
Sex ratio: Bangkok 1986
males per 100 females
age
c
Age distribution: Thai villages 1986
Males
Females
age
percent of population
d
Sex ratio: Thai villages 1986
males per 100 females
age

Fig. 6.2

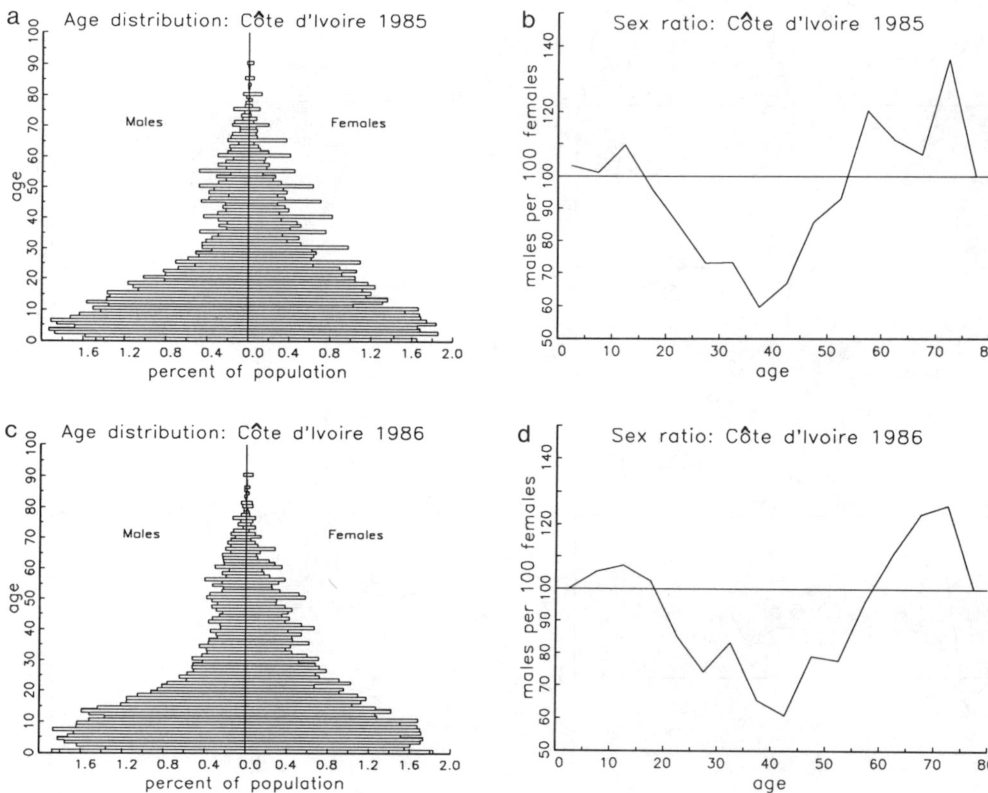
a
Age distribution: Côte d'Ivoire 1985
Males
Females
age
percent of population
b
Sex ratio: Côte d'Ivoire 1985
males per 100 females
age
c
Age distribution: Côte d'Ivoire 1986
Males
Females
age
percent of population
d
Sex ratio: Côte d'Ivoire 1986
males per 100 females
age

Fig. 6.3

ing data for Bangkok and for rural Thailand rather than for the more conventional urban-rural split. Bangkok contains nearly 70 percent of Thailand's urban population, and while the survey also collects other urban and semiurban (sanitary district) data, these seem sufficiently different from Bangkok to merit separate treatment. In order to avoid a three- or possibly four-way split for each table, we compromise with two. For the same reason, and when it is not misleading to do so, we shall normally present data from the 1986 Ivorian survey. On balance, the data from the second year are probably of somewhat higher quality.

There are a number of problems with the Ivorian data that are apparent from the figures, although none are particularly serious for older people. There is very pronounced peaking at five-year age intervals, particularly in 1985 and particularly among females. Such effects are not uncommon among uneducated populations (see, e.g., Ewbank 1981, 66–68) and are typically correlated with low education and low incomes; the 1975 Ivorian census shows similar effects (see Ahonzo, Barrere, and Kopylov 1984, 9). In 1986, interviewers placed less reliance on reported figures and acquired more supporting information, and the problem was considerably reduced. Even so, it is wise not to make much of the precise age estimates and to work instead with five- or ten-year age brackets. More serious is an apparent undercount of prime-age males; in 1986, the sex ratios (males per hundred females) in the age groups 20–24, 25–29, 30–34, 35–39, 40–44, 45–49, and 50–54 are, respectively, 85.1, 74.2, 83.2, 65.3, 60.7, 78.9, and 77.6, with between two hundred and six hundred people in each sex-age cell (see figs. 6.3b and 6.3d). Neither we nor the World Bank currently has any explanation for these results. Again, there are similar, although not identical, problems with the 1975 census and other demographic surveys as well as with census data in other African countries. Ahonzo, Barrere, and Kopylov (1984, chap. 5) find similar patterns in surveys carried out in the early 1960s as well as in the 1975 census once the predominantly young, male, non-Ivorian immigrants (22 percent of the population) are removed. Although the Living Standards Surveys include nonnationals, there are only 14 percent in the two surveys in 1985 and 1986. Since it is the same age group missing in data ten years apart, and since there is no large-scale emigration from Côte d'Ivoire, the problems must come from measurement errors, possibly in connection with the many prime-age males in the cities, where they are hard to count or survey. Respondents may also exaggerate their ages, and it is possible that men do so more often or by more than do women. The figures for the fractions of old people appear to be consistent with those from the census (again, see Ahonzo, Barrere, and Kopylov 1984; and U.S. Agency for International Development 1982); note that once again differential overreporting of age by men may account for at least part of the apparent excess of older men.

Tables 6.1A and 6.1B show the fractions of people, by sex and urbanization, who are aged over 55 in both Thailand and Côte d'Ivoire. We have cho-

Table 6.1 Age Distribution by Sex: 55 and Over

A. Thailand, 1981 and 1986

	Bangkok				Rural			
	Females		Males		Females		Males	
Age	1981	1986	1981	1986	1981	1986	1981	1986
55–59	3.2	3.5	3.5	3.0	3.3	3.8	3.0	3.4
60–64	2.3	2.3	2.1	2.2	2.5	2.6	2.1	2.5
65–69	1.6	2.1	2.0	1.3	1.8	1.9	1.5	1.8
70–74	1.1	1.0	1.0	1.3	1.4	1.7	1.3	1.5
75–79	.5	.7	.7	.5	.8	1.3	.6	.6
80+	.8	.8	.2	.8	1.0	1.0	.4	.8
> 55	9.5	10.5	9.5	9.1	10.7	12.5	9.0	10.6
Obs.	3,399	2,209	3,028	1,879	11,941	10,260	11,359	9,862

B. Côte D'Ivoire, 1985 and 1986

	Urban				Rural			
	Females		Males		Females		Males	
Age	1985	1986	1985	1986	1985	1986	1985	1986
55–59	1.5	1.8	1.9	2.0	2.7	3.0	3.6	2.9
60–64	1.1	1.3	1.5	1.5	2.1	2.7	2.3	3.1
65–69	.7	.8	.5	.6	1.7	1.7	2.2	2.5
70–74	.3	.3	.6	.5	.9	1.1	1.3	1.4
75+	.4	.5	.3	.4	1.4	1.3	1.3	1.5
> 55	3.9	4.7	4.8	5.0	8.9	9.7	10.6	11.4
Obs.	2,842	2,805	2,678	2,662	4,014	3,846	3,737	3,583

Note: Figures are percentages of the relevant group; e.g., in Thailand in 1981, 3.2 percent of all women in Bangkok were aged 55–59. "Obs." is the total number of observations for all ages in the sample; e.g., there are 2,842 females in the urban Ivorian sample in 1985. Note that the Ivorian sample is a simple random sample and that the sample numbers can therefore be used to estimate the fraction urbanized. This is not true for the Thai survey (see table 6.2 below). The Thai results exclude urban non-Bangkok and the suburban "sanitary districts" sector.

sen the young cutoff age of 55 because, particularly in a young, rapidly growing population such as that in Côte d'Ivoire, there are relatively few old people. In the 1985 Ivorian sample as a whole, there are 994 individuals aged 55 or over out of 13,271 people in all, or 7.5 percent (in 1986, 1,046 out of 12,896, or 81.8 percent). For Thailand, because the urban sector is relatively oversampled, when the appropriate weights are applied, the survey shows 9.9 percent 55 and over in 1981 (weights for the 1986 survey are not currently available). National Economic and Social Development Board (1985) gives a lower figure of 7.83 percent over 55 in 1980. This publication notes a tendency for Thai survey data to underestimate the numbers of children under the age of 10, which may explain some of the discrepancy. The two estimates for Côte d'Ivoire, which are only one year apart, provide some cross-check on reliability, although remember that half the households are common both surveys.

In rural areas of both countries, the age distributions of older men are very similar, with around 10 percent of men older than 54 in both cases. The Ivorian survey shows (absolutely) more men than women in all the age categories over 54, whereas Thailand shows the common pattern of more women than men (see figs. 6.1b, 6.1d, 6.2b, 6.2d, 6.3b, and 6.3d). In Thailand, the proportions of elderly are increasing over time (except for males in Bangkok), as is to be expected given the continuing decline in fertility. The major difference between the two halves of table 6.1 lies in the relative youth of the urban sector in Côte d'Ivoire. Only 4 percent of the urban population is aged 55 or over, as opposed to 10 percent in Thailand, and the much higher level of urbanization in Côte d'Ivoire (42 as opposed to 27 percent) is what reconciles the similarity between the rural sectors with the overall lower fraction of elderly in Côte d'Ivoire. Of course, both fractions are still much lower than those for the more developed countries of the world; in the United States, 21.3 percent of the population was aged 55 or over in 1985 (United Nations 1987), while for developed countries as a whole 15.8 percent of the population was 60 years or over in 1985.

The urbanization figures given in table 6.2 are for the elderly and for the population as a whole. In Côte d'Ivoire, the urban population grew by 8.7 percent per annum from 1965 to 1980, as opposed to 4.2 percent for the total population (World Bank 1988), and we see the picture that would be expected if it is largely the younger people who move to the cities; most old people (three-quarters) live in the countryside, as opposed to only 60 percent of the population as a whole. The towns are predominantly young; there are relatively few old people in Côte d'Ivoire in any case, and a relatively small pro-

Table 6.2 Urbanization and the Elderly, Côte d'Ivoire and Thailand

Percentages of People Living In:

	Côte d'Ivoire[a]		
	1985	1986	Thailand, 1981
Aged 55 or over:			
Urban	24.3	25.3	17.5
Semiurban			10.3
Rural	75.7	74.7	72.2
All ages:			
Urban	41.6	42.4	17.8
Semiurban			9.0
Rural	58.4	57.6	73.2

[a]In the Ivorian survey, households are categorized only as urban or rural, not as semiurban.

portion are urbanized. For Thailand, the picture is different; the distribution of elderly across rural and urban regions is virtually identical to the distribution of all people across regions. For example, in 1981, 17.5 percent of people older than 54 were urbanized, as opposed to 17.8 percent for the population as a whole. However, these numbers mask the fact that the fraction of older people urbanized exceeds the fraction of children urbanized (14.9 percent) and is less than the fraction of people aged 15–54 who are urbanized (20.9 percent). Thus, cities in Thailand have a slightly heavier concentration of younger adults than older adults. The difference between the fraction of older and younger adults who are urbanized is so small because there is relatively slow growth of urban areas in Thailand and because there are fairly high rates of migration by the elderly to urban areas other than Bangkok. The growth of the urban population in Thailand averaged 4.6 percent a year between 1965 and 1980, as opposed to a 2.6 percent annual growth rate for the population as a whole (World Bank 1988). Migrants to Bangkok tend to be young: only 2.6 percent were aged 65 or older in 1982 (National Statistical Office 1983). However, migration rates of older people to urban areas other than Bangkok have been quite high, with rates for those 65 and older exceeding rates for those aged 30–49 (World Bank 1979).

The Ivorian data also provide information on the nationality of people sampled. Côte d'Ivoire has been one of the more successful West African economies, thus attracting many migrants from its neighbors, particularly Burkina Faso, Mali, and Guinea. Of the two samples, 13.9 percent in 1985 and 13.1 percent in 1986 are non-Ivorian, divided in the ratios 4:2:1:1 among those three neighboring countries and other Africans. As one might expect if many of these migrants are young, the proportions of those 55 and over are lower—7.6 and 6.8 percent.

6.1.2 Living Arrangements

Tables 6.3A and 6.3B tabulate marital status for those aged 55 and over. For women, the modal status at ages 55–59 is married and at 70 and over widowed, with the weight shifting from one category to the other as we move from the younger to the older women. These patterns are similar in the two countries. The modal status for men is married in all these elderly age categories. In Côte d'Ivoire, where one-quarter of men have more than one wife, 83 percent of men aged 70 and over have at least one spouse. Of the 543 men in table 6.3B, 492 are household heads, and for them we have data on numbers and ages of wives. Of these, 449 have one or more wives in the household: 59 percent have one wife, 26 percent two, 11 percent three, and 4 percent four or more. The average age of these 449 men is 64, that of the first wife 51, the second wife 44, and the third wife 40. It is difficult to become a widower in Côte d'Ivoire, and even among those aged 70 or more, there are only 12 percent in this category, compared with 26 percent in rural Thailand.

For Ivorian men, there is a strong association between wealth (especially

Table 6.3 Married Status of the Elderly

	A. Thailand, 1981									
	Rural Females					Bangkok Females				
Age	Never Married	Married	Widowed	Divorced	Total	Never Married	Married	Widowed	Divorced	Total
55–59	1.8	63.9	29.6	4.8	396	2.8	73.2	15.7	8.3	108
60–64	2.0	57.6	37.3	3.1	295	3.9	39.7	48.7	7.7	78
65–69	1.8	43.6	51.8	2.7	220	1.8	49.1	43.6	5.5	55
70+	2.2	21.4	74.5	1.9	364	3.7	9.8	79.3	7.3	82
	Rural Males					Bangkok Males				
55–59	2.3	86.3	8.4	2.9	344	.0	87.6	6.7	5.7	105
60–64	.4	83.8	13.7	2.1	234	1.6	89.1	17.5	.0	63
65–69	.6	84.3	13.4	1.7	172	3.3	80.0	13.3	3.3	60
70+	.8	71.9	25.8	1.5	267	.0	60.7	36.1	3.3	61

	B. Côte d'Ivoire, 1986									
	Females					Males				
Age	Never Married	Married	Widowed	Divorced	Total	Never Married	Married	Widowed	Divorced	Total
55–59	.6	65.0	25.8	8.6	163	1.9	90.5	5.1	2.6	157
60–64	.0	54.4	39.1	6.5	138	2.0	91.5	2.0	4.6	153
65–69	.0	41.9	55.8	2.3	86	.9	85.9	11.3	1.9	106
70+	.9	15.5	81.9	1.7	116	.0	82.7	11.8	5.5	127

cash wealth), age, and number of wives. Hecht (1984) describes how, in the 1920s, which were the early years of cocoa and coffee production in Côte d'Ivoire, the cash from the new crops, which were farmed by lineages, not families, was used to provide bridewealth for the acquisition for the lineage of new wives, and thus ultimately new labor. By the 1980s, the old lineage system had largely broken down and been replaced by one of small-scale peasant farming, with alienable land and wage labor, but the surplus is still used to acquire additional wives. Indeed, the acquisition of additional young wives by wealthy Ivorians is a standard way of purchasing old age security. The occurrence of polygyny rises with age until remarkably late in life (see Ahonzo, Barrere, and Kopylov 1984, table 5.8). Only 10 percent of men aged 25–29 have more than one wife, but the proportion rises with age until it reaches nearly one-third for 65–74-year-olds. Indeed, 13 percent of men aged 70–74 have three or more wives.

The effects of polygyny on living arrangements also appear in tables 6.4A and 6.4B. Over 80 percent of Ivorian males in the table live in households with at least one spouse, as compared with only 60 percent of men aged 70 or more in Thailand. Elderly women, by contrast, are increasingly widowed and live with their children or with others. About half these "others" are brothers who take their sisters into the household; the rest are women living with a head of household who is more distantly related, perhaps a niece or nephew. Very few of the elderly, either men or women, live alone in Côte d'Ivoire; in the 1986 (1985) sample, there are only twenty-two (seventeen) people over 54 living by themselves. Indeed, there are very few couples; less than 5 percent of the elderly live in households with only two members. Households are large in Côte d'Ivoire, averaging 8.1 persons in 1986, and neither the elderly nor anyone else is likely to live in a small household; only 1 percent of the people in the survey live in households with fewer than three members.

The situation in Thailand is different, although the caveat about the definition of the Thai household must be kept in mind. Household size is smaller, with, respectively, 4.2 and 4.6 persons per household in Bangkok and rural regions in 1981 and 3.6 and 4.5 in 1986. There are correspondingly more older people who live alone or with their spouses. Among elderly women in Rural Thailand in 1981, 5.6–14 percent lived alone, and a substantial fraction among the younger elderly lived with a spouse but with no other family members. The numbers for 1986 do not reveal an increase in the tendency to live alone or with a spouse only. In fact, the fraction of rural females living alone decreased substantially between the two survey periods for all age groups. Older individuals who do not live alone or with a spouse only almost always live with adult children. The fraction of older people living with "others only" is small for all but Bangkok females. Of women who do live with "others only," the age of the household head is typically quite low, indicating that these women may live with adult grandchildren. The "Western" view of the elderly living either alone, alone with spouse, or with their children is perhaps

Table 6.4 Living Arrangements of the Elderly

A. Thailand, 1981 and 1986

	Bangkok Females							
	1981				1986			
	55–59	60–64	65–69	70+	55–59	60–64	65–69	70+
Alone	3.8	7.9	7.3	9.8	9.0	8.0	10.9	1.8
Spouse	5.7	9.2	5.5	2.4	3.9	6.0	10.9	.0
Kids	18.9	31.6	32.7	24.4	37.2	36.0	34.8	31.6
Others	8.5	11.8	9.1	22.0	6.4	16.0	13.0	14.0
Spouse + kids	49.1	22.4	25.5	4.9	33.3	26.0	21.7	5.3
Spouse + others	1.9	2.6	1.8	.0	1.3	.0	.0	5.3
Kids + others	3.8	13.2	9.1	36.6	5.1	2.0	6.5	42.1
Spouse + kids + others	8.5	1.3	9.1	.0	3.9	6.0	2.2	.0
Subtotals:								
With spouse:	65.1	35.5	41.8	7.3	42.3	38.0	34.8	10.5
With kids:	80.2	68.4	76.4	65.9	79.5	70.0	65.2	79.0
Number	106	76	55	82	78	50	46	57
	Rural Females							
Alone	5.6	13.2	12.3	13.7	3.4	5.6	9.0	7.6
Spouse	12.2	12.9	13.2	6.9	11.2	16.7	12.5	7.1
Kids	23.9	22.7	28.8	22.5	23.6	24.1	28.5	25.1
Others	5.3	3.4	9.6	14.8	3.1	3.0	4.5	11.1
Spouse + kids	42.6	38.0	23.7	7.7	49.9	41.5	29.0	10.9
Spouse + others	2.5	2.4	1.4	2.8	2.1	.4	4.0	2.1
Kids + others	3.1	4.8	7.8	28.3	2.9	5.2	7.5	29.6
Spouse + kids + others	4.8	2.7	3.2	3.3	3.9	3.7	5.0	6.4
Subtotals:								
With spouse:	62.2	55.9	41.6	20.6	67.0	62.2	50.5	26.5
With kids:	74.4	68.1	63.5	61.8	80.3	74.4	70.0	72.0
Number	394	295	219	364	385	270	200	422
	Bangkok Males							
Alone	5.7	7.9	5.0	4.9	3.5	7.3	4.2	10.2
Spouse	9.5	9.5	8.3	13.1	8.8	14.6	8.3	12.2
Kids	6.7	9.5	11.7	19.7	3.5	14.6	.0	14.3
Others	1.9	1.6	5.0	3.3	1.8	.0	4.3	6.1
Spouse + kids	61.0	55.6	55.0	36.1	66.7	48.8	75.0	30.6
Spouse + others	2.9	4.8	6.7	1.6	7.0	2.4	4.3	4.1
Kids + others	1.9	1.6	.0	16.4	1.8	.0	.0	20.4
Spouse + kids + others	10.5	9.5	8.3	4.9	7.0	12.2	4.3	2.0
Subtotals:								
With spouse:	83.8	79.4	78.3	55.7	89.5	78.1	91.7	49.0
With kids:	80.0	76.2	75.0	77.1	79.0	75.6	79.2	67.4
Number	105	63	60	61	57	41	24	49

(*continued*)

Table 6.4 (continued)

A. Thailand, 1981 and 1986

	Rural Males							
	1981				1986			
	55–59	60–64	65–69	70+	55–59	60–64	65–69	70+
Alone	5.3	5.1	2.3	4.2	2.1	2.0	3.9	3.9
Spouse	14.9	15.4	21.4	23.6	15.0	19.4	22.4	18.4
Kids	7.3	8.1	11.6	12.6	6.3	6.9	11.2	14.5
Others	2.0	3.0	1.7	2.7	1.2	2.0	1.7	3.2
Spouse + kids	61.5	58.1	52.6	35.7	64.9	59.5	48.0	39.4
Spouse + others	2.9	2.6	1.2	4.6	3.3	3.6	3.9	4.3
Kids + others	.3	2.6	2.3	10.3	.3	.4	.6	6.7
Spouse + kids + others	5.8	5.1	6.9	6.5	6.9	6.1	8.4	9.6
Subtotals:								
With spouse:	85.1	81.2	82.1	70.3	90.1	88.7	82.7	71.6
With kids:	74.9	73.9	73.4	65.0	78.4	72.9	68.2	70.2
Number	343	234	173	263	333	247	179	282

B. Côte d'Ivoire, 1986

	Females				Males			
	55–59	60–64	65–69	70+	55–59	60–64	65–69	70+
Alone	.6	.7	2.3	.0	2.5	2.6	2.8	5.5
Spouse	4.2	.7	.0	.9	1.9	4.6	1.9	3.1
Kids	2.5	2.9	.0	.9	1.3	.7	.9	.8
Others	15.3	16.7	26.7	21.6	3.8	4.6	7.5	6.3
Spouse + kids	3.7	2.2	4.7	.9	17.2	14.4	18.9	11.0
Spouse + others	20.2	23.9	16.3	5.2	3.8	11.1	6.6	10.2
Kids + others	22.1	27.5	31.4	62.1	3.8	1.3	5.7	6.2
Spouse + kids + others	31.2	25.4	18.6	8.6	65.6	60.8	55.7	56.6
Subtotals:								
With spouse	59.5	52.1	39.5	15.5	88.5	90.8	83.0	81.1
With kids	59.5	58.0	54.7	72.4	87.8	77.1	81.1	82.6
Number	163	138	86	116	157	153	106	127

Note: **Thailand:** "Alone" means living alone, "Spouse" means living with a spouse only, "Kids" means living with children only, etc. "Children" can include sons- or daughters-in-law and step-children. Only people aged 15 and over were included in household member counts, and servants were excluded. For some observations, it is not possible to determine the relationships between all people in the household. For example, an older person who is an "other relative" of the household head could potentially be the parent of another person in the household (who would also be coded as an "other relative" of the head). In this case, the older person would be coded as living with "others only." Thus, the fraction of people living with others only is likely to be overstated and the fraction living with children understated. **Côte d'Ivoire:** "Spouse" means living alone with spouse and no others, "Kids" with children and no others, and so on. Children are defined as biological children of the reference elderly person, living in the same household, so that a woman living with her spouse and the spouse's children who are not her own would be classed under "spouse and others," which is different from the treatment in Thailand.

closer to the truth in Thailand than it is in Côte d'Ivoire. The larger, more complex families in West Africa allow a wide range of living arrangements, especially for the large fraction of widows.

6.1.3 Education, Labor Supply, and Health Status

The data on education are not comparable between Thailand and Côte d'Ivoire; nevertheless, tables 6.5A and 6.5B show similar patterns across ages and sexes in the two countries. By any measure, educational standards are much higher in Thailand, and, even among rural women, over 90 percent of the 20–39 age group have had at least one year of school, whereas only 37 percent of Ivorian women in the same age group have ever been to school. Even in Thailand, however, very few individuals have ever completed elementary school (seven years of education), and, in the rural villages, fewer than 1 percent of men or women over 40 have done so. In Côte d'Ivoire, none of the sample women aged 60 or over can read a newspaper or do a simple written calculation, and only a negligible fraction of women over 50 have ever been

Table 6.5 Educational Attainment

A. By Age, Sex, and Location: Thailand, 1981

	Bangkok						Rural					
	Females			Males			Females			Males		
Age	Sch.	Elem.	Sec.	Sch.	Elem.	Sec.	Sch.	Elem.	Sec.	Sch.	Elem.	Sec.
20–39	.96	.29	.17	.99	.38	.22	.91	.02	.02	.96	.04	.03
40–49	.77	.05	.04	.89	.14	.10	.84	.00	.00	.90	.01	.01
50–59	.58	.04	.02	.67	.09	.05	.65	.01	.00	.85	.01	.01
60–69	.27	.00	.00	.40	.03	.02	.32	.00	.00	.63	.01	.01
70+	.13	.01	.01	.36	.07	.03	.06	.00	.00	.47	.00	.00

B. By Age and Sex: Côte d'Ivoire, 1986

	Females				Males			
Age	Years	Arith.	Read	Sch.?	Years	Arith.	Read	Sch.?
20–39	2.60	.35	.32	.37	5.94	.70	.66	.68
40–49	.28	.04	.03	.04	2.36	.37	.32	.32
50–59	.05	.01	.01	.01	.96	.19	.17	.18
60–69	.05	.00	.00	.01	.49	.11	.09	.09
70+	.00	.00	.00	.00	.29	.06	.05	.04

Notes: **Thailand:** "Sch." means that the respondent had completed at least one grade higher than kindergarten. "Elem." means that the respondent had completed elementary school. "Sec." means that the respondent had completed high school or a technical/vocational school. **Côte d'Ivoire:** "Years" is years of school completed. "Arith." is fraction of people who can do written calculations. "Read" is the fraction who can read a newspaper. "Sch.?" is the fraction who are attending or who have ever attended a school.

to school. But, apart from the differences in levels, the patterns are the same; men have more education than women, and young people have much more education than their elders. Conventional concerns about education separating the generations are clearly relevant in these sorts of situations. Three-quarters of Ivorian males and more than half of Ivorian females between 15 and 19 can read a newspaper, something that be accomplished by only about half their fathers, perhaps one-quarter of their mothers, and almost none of their grandparents. One might legitimately wonder if the experience and wisdom of older farmers, real though it is, may not be offset by their inability to read the label on a bag of seeds or fertilizer. Experience may be more valuable than education in a stationary environment, but much growth in LDCs has come from exploiting new crops and new growing techniques; indeed, there appear to be large gains to greater use of fertilizer and insecticide in coffee and cocoa production in Côte d'Ivoire, gains that have so far gone almost entirely unexploited (see Deaton and Benjamin 1988).

Labor force participation and hours worked show the standard life-cycle patterns in both countries. In rural areas in Thailand (table 6.6A), almost all prime-age males and females participate in (mostly agricultural) work, although substantial fractions of time are spent idle according to the dictates of the agricultural calendar. Participation rates are lower for women than for men in Bangkok and fall off very rapidly among the elderly. Among those who continue to work, hours and weeks remain high. This contrasts with behavior in the rural sector, where hours and weeks decline along with participation among the elderly, perhaps because of the physical demands of agricultural work.

Participation rates in Côte d'Ivoire are surprisingly low, especially among males in the 20–39 age group (table 6.6B). Note that these figures, although covering a broad range of activities, relate to the last seven days prior to the survey interview; thus, those farmers who did not work during that period would be counted as nonparticipants. Furthermore, the traditional allocation of tasks among many West African groups is for women to undertake food growing and trading activities, leaving men free for hunting, fishing, and fighting. Cocoa and coffee farming are, however, legitimate activities for men and are undertaken by a large fraction of Ivorian households. Participation rates among older workers remain relatively high into the late 60s, only falling off among the oldest group. Among older participants, weeks worked declines hardly at all, although both days and hours per day fall with age, which is exactly the pattern that might be expected in a predominantly agricultural economy. Note that the hours, days, and weeks figures for Côte d'Ivoire relate only to the activity defined as the main job over the last seven days. Many individuals have second jobs, and there are a large number of small family enterprises, many run by women.

Table 6.7 presents information on the health of the respondents in the Ivorian survey. These are self-reported figures, and the investigators have no means of checking the reliability of these reports. Although all respondents

Table 6.6 Labor Force Participation and Work Hours, by Age Category

A. Thailand, 1981

	Bangkok									
	Females					Males				
Age	Obs.	LFP	Weeks	Hours	Weeks Idle	Obs.	LFP	Weeks	Hours	Weeks Idle
15–19	460	.37	43.3	51.6	2.1	365	.32	48.4	45.7	6.9
20–39	1,338	.67	48.3	49.3	1.2	1,131	.85	50.2	49.4	1.8
40–54	437	.57	49.7	52.7	.0	375	.97	51.4	50.4	.7
55–59	108	.45	50.2	52.2	.0	105	.87	51.1	51.5	.0
60–64	78	.32	51.5	53.0	.0	63	.67	51.4	55.7	1.7
65–69	55	.16	51.3	62.2	.0	60	.53	49.3	53.8	.0
70–99	82	.06	52.0	58.8	.0	61	.23	52.0	53.7	1.1
	Rural									
15–19	1,304	.86	46.0	57.3	4.2	1,270	.89	47.6	58.1	5.7
20–39	3,295	.94	45.3	57.8	3.3	2,927	.99	50.6	61.4	5.0
40–54	1,569	.93	45.4	57.1	2.9	1,493	.99	50.8	61.9	4.3
55–59	396	.80	44.7	54.2	3.8	344	.96	50.9	60.0	5.4
60–64	295	.62	44.2	52.0	2.0	234	.88	49.9	55.6	4.3
65–69	220	.47	42.3	48.6	3.2	173	.77	47.2	53.9	4.2
70–99	365	.24	41.3	41.0	3.0	267	.46	46.7	49.5	4.1

B. Côte d'Ivoire, 1986

	Females					Males				
Age	Obs.	LFP	Weeks	Days	Hours	Obs.	LFP	Weeks	Days	Hours
15–19	690	.41	45.2	4.92	6.70	707	.43	44.0	5.12	7.60
20–39	1,643	.59	45.5	5.09	6.84	1,281	.66	44.7	5.43	8.02
40–54	792	.76	47.0	5.16	6.90	566	.86	47.0	5.37	8.10
55–59	163	.69	46.7	4.81	6.53	157	.73	49.4	4.90	7.56
60–64	138	.62	46.4	4.72	6.40	153	.71	45.9	5.06	7.55
65–69	86	.63	46.0	4.93	6.59	106	.63	47.2	4.72	6.61
70+	116	.22	44.5	4.52	5.72	127	.40	45.5	4.53	6.25

Note: **Thailand:** Labor force participation (LFP) was defined as spending at least one week in the last year employed, self-employed (on or off farm), or working as free family labor. Average weeks in the labor force includes weeks unemployed. Weeks unemployed ("Weeks Idle") consists mainly of weeks spent waiting for the agricultural season or "because no work was available." "Hours" is the individual's reported hours per week when working. "Obs." is the number of observations. **Côte d'Ivoire:** These relate to household members. For a person to be a nonparticipant, he or she must answer no to the following three questions: "During the past seven days, have you worked for someone who is not a member of your household, e.g., an employer, a firm, the government, or some other person outside your household?" "During the past seven days, have you worked in a field or garden belonging to yourself or your household or have you raised livestock?" "During the past seven days, have you worked in a trade, industry, business, enterprise, or profession belonging to yourself or your household, e.g., as an independent merchant or fisherman, lawyer, doctor, or other self-employed activity." "Weeks" are number of weeks during the last twelve months in main job only. "Days" is days worked in the last seven days. "Hours" is hours per day worked in the last week, again in the main job. "Obs." is the number of observations. "LPF" is labor force participation.

Table 6.7 Health and Sickness by Sex and Age, Côte d'Ivoire, 1986

	Females					Males				
Age	Ill	Days1	Days2	Con.	Med.	Ill	Days1	Days2	Con.	Med.
15–19	.16	1.5	.7	.51	.58	.12	1.0	.4	.45	.56
20–24	.21	2.0	1.0	.59	.61	.17	1.6	1.0	.51	.54
25–29	.27	2.4	1.6	.49	.60	.20	2.1	1.3	.57	.63
30–34	.27	3.3	1.6	.59	.61	.30	2.7	1.2	.52	.62
35–39	.34	4.8	2.8	.48	.55	.32	3.5	1.6	.58	.69
40–44	.36	4.7	2.1	.40	.53	.36	3.5	1.8	.50	.59
45–49	.40	5.4	2.7	.45	.50	.42	5.5	2.5	.41	.58
50–54	.36	5.2	2.2	.47	.54	.47	6.2	3.1	.43	.62
55–59	.40	6.2	2.9	.35	.45	.45	6.2	4.0	.47	.57
60–64	.41	7.2	3.7	.30	.43	.52	7.6	4.4	.41	.47
65–69	.37	5.2	3.4	.25	.38	.57	11.8	6.9	.45	.58
70–74	.50	9.8	6.0	.28	.60	.67	11.2	7.6	.26	.40
75+	.59	12.0	7.9	.10	.36	.66	13.0	9.6	.38	.48

Notes: These are self-reported figures for all household members. "Ill" is the fraction of respondents who, during the last four weeks, experienced an illness or injury, "e.g., a cough, a cold, diarrhea, an injury due to an accident, or any other illness." "Days1" is the number of days in the last four weeks during which the respondent suffered from the illness or injury, counting in zero days for those not sick. "Days2" is the number of days the illness prevented the respondent from carrying on his or her usual activities. "CON." is the fraction of persons reporting an illness who consulted "a doctor, nurse, pharmacist, healer, midwife, or other health practitioner." "Med." is the corresponding fraction of cases where the respondent bought medicine.

were weighed and measured, such measurements are of relatively little value in determining health status, except for children. Except for those under 30, more than one-quarter of all respondents in each age group report some sickness or injury in their last four weeks, with the fraction rising to well over half among the older groups. For those aged 55 or over, six to thirteen days a month are days of illness, and these illnesses are sufficiently severe to cause a suspension of normal activities for three to ten days. Women show more illness than men until about 40 years of age, after which age they show less, considerably less in some of the older age groups. Somewhat less than half of all illnesses lead to a medical consultation or the purchase of medicine, and the figures suggest that, among the elderly, a smaller fraction of illnesses in females are severe or are treated as such. Comparable data from the Thai survey are not available.

6.1.4 Levels of Living

Although much of the concern about the elderly is a concern about living standards, it is remarkably difficult to measure their consumption or income levels, even in more developed countries, and the difficulties are much greater in poor countries. In the United States, where many old people live alone or with their spouses, their household income and expenditure levels can give some idea of living standards in relation to the rest of the population. Indeed, work on the status of the low-income elderly in more developed countries (e.g., Coder, Smeeding, and Torrey 1990) effectively defines the population of interest to be this group, which is typically female, one-person families and married couples, groups that together accounted for 91 percent of the U.S. population aged 65 and over in 1982 (see Cowgill 1986, 29).

In Thailand, and even more so in Côte d'Ivoire, the vast majority of the elderly live with other people, children, spouses, and other relations; very few live alone. Household surveys collect data on household levels of living, not on those of the individuals within them. Disentangling who gets what within the household is difficult, even for "private" goods like food, and attempts to do so require costly and intrusive techniques of observation. For public goods, such as housing, entertainment, and many services, individual consumption levels are not even well defined. In contrast to consumption, many income flows can be assigned to individual members of the household, although only with great difficulty in farm households, and such assignment, even when possible, tells us only a limited amount about the distribution of welfare within the household, which is our main concern. There is a belief in much of the development literature that individuals who bring money into the household receive better treatment than those who do not, but there is little credible evidence to support this contention.

This problem of isolating the living standards of the elderly is conceptually the same as that of isolating the living standards of children, a topic on which there exists a large and venerable literature. However, as argued in Pollak and Wales (1979) and elaborated in Deaton and Muellbauer (1986), much of this literature sets out by assuming what it wants to measure, and, even after more than a century of research, no generally accepted methodology has been derived that would support the isolation of children's living standards from household-level data. One possible avenue, suggested in Deaton, Ruiz-Castillo, and Thomas (1989), is to identify a set of goods that are not consumed by adults, for example, children's goods, and, on the grounds that additional adults exert negative income effects but no substitution effects on such goods, measure the "cost" of old people versus that of younger adults by calculating their relative (negative) effects on the consumption of children's goods. However, it is difficult to isolate commodities that are consumed only by children, especially in less developed countries, where children consume little beyond food, shelter, and clothing. Moreover, (unreported) experiments with the Spanish data used in Deaton, Thomas, and Ruiz-Castillo did not lead to sensible estimates.

If these problems of measuring living standards are taken seriously, it is unclear whether it is possible to make statements about, for example, the fraction of old people living in poverty in most LDCs, let alone to address broad topics like the effect of development on the status of the old. Even so, something can be said, and we report some fragmentary but relevant evidence.

The simplest procedure is to assume that everyone in each household is treated equally and to impute to each person the per capita or per adult equivalent total expenditure or income for the household in which he or she resides. If the assumption is correct, the procedure yields the right answer. If it is false, as it almost certainly is, then the calculations are still informative. If old people live predominantly in households with low average living standards, we are more likely to be concerned about their welfare than would otherwise be the case. Of course, it may be that it is the children or younger people in such households that we should worry about, not their likely powerful elders.

Table 6.8 shows the relevant calculations for Côte d'Ivoire in 1986. In computing adult equivalents, children under 5 have been assigned a weight of 0.25 and those from 5 to 14 a weight of 0.45. These numbers are essentially arbitrary, but they are relatively low in the light of the considerations discussed in Deaton and Muellbauer (1986), and it is better to make some such assumptions than to work with either total or per capita household expenditure. As the age of the individual increases, the average number of household members with which he or she resides decreases from twelve at birth to nine at age 70, but it rises to around ten for the oldest ages. The economic measures, income, consumption, and income and consumption per equivalent, all have the same general shape, rising to their maxima for the 30–34 year age group and falling steadily thereafter. Among the oldest people, total income and expenditures in the households in which they live are little more than half the levels in the peak years, and the per equivalent measures are less than half of the peaks. If consumption per equivalent is taken as a representative measure, the average for those 55 and over is 79 percent of the average for all individuals.

Older Ivorians live in households that have less income and consumption than the national average. However, old people live mostly in rural areas, and the much better-off urban residents are typically young. Moreover, the rural-urban difference is likely overstated because no allowance is made for price differences between rural and urban areas and because urban residents typically pay rent or have rents imputed for them, something that cannot be done for rural residents. Table 6.9 repeats the information for rural areas only. Now the relation between living standards and age has essentially disappeared; while total consumption and income fall with age, at least until the late 60s, adult equivalents fall at much the same rate, and there is therefore little or no relation between age and the per equivalent measures.

Tables 6.10 and 6.11 show income and expenditure by the age of the individual for Bangkok and rural areas in 1981. Unlike Côte d'Ivoire, the number of adult equivalents per household does not vary with age. However, family income and expenditure do not vary greatly with age either. There is a small peak in income in the 50–54 age range for males in Bangkok and rural regions; in Bangkok, this peak in income is offset by a corresponding peak in the number of adult equivalents. Overall, income and expenditure, as well as

Table 6.8 **Average Household Characteristics by Age of Household Members, Côte d'Ivoire, 1986**

	NMEMS	NAE	Y	CND	YPE	CNDPE	N
0–4	11.7	7.6	1,760	1,748	267	264	2,176
5–9	12.0	7.9	1,779	1,878	248	262	2,140
10–14	11.8	7.9	1,995	2,011	278	278	1,841
15–19	12.0	8.7	2,232	2,264	294	295	1,395
20–24	11.3	8.3	2,127	2,111	296	296	1,021
25–29	10.7	7.6	2,239	2,080	366	341	763
30–34	10.1	7.0	2,262	2,143	385	387	608
35–39	10.4	7.1	1,839	1,890	313	325	528
40–44	10.4	7.2	1,610	1,661	258	252	489
45–49	10.5	7.4	1,642	1,780	239	270	423
50–54	10.2	7.4	1,356	1,407	211	220	443
55–59	9.3	6.9	1,391	1,534	224	243	320
60–64	9.4	6.8	1,815	1,468	340	220	288
65–69	8.9	6.6	1,049	1,135	169	185	190
70–74	9.8	7.2	1,262	1,378	191	246	113
75–79	10.5	7.7	1,653	1,540	227	224	64
80+	9.8	7.5	1,397	1,348	175	178	66
All	11.2	7.7	1,884	1,895	278	279	12,868
			Females Aged 55 and Over				
55–59	9.5	7.2	1,382	1,570	209	234	163
60–64	9.9	7.2	1,991	1,560	362	228	136
65–69	9.2	6.8	1,047	1,177	164	187	85
70–74	11.9	8.4	1,379	1,498	159	179	50
75–79	10.8	7.8	1,744	1,723	196	227	28
80+	10.0	7.8	1,234	1,239	159	165	38
All	11.4	7.8	1,877	1,898	273	273	6,636
			Males Aged 55 and Over				
55–59	9.1	6.6	1,400	1,497	240	252	157
60–64	8.9	6.5	1,657	1,386	322	214	152
65–69	8.7	6.3	1,050	1,100	172	183	105
70–74	8.1	6.2	1,170	1,283	216	298	63
75–79	10.3	7.5	1,583	1,398	252	221	36
80+	9.6	7.3	1,617	1,496	198	196	28
All	11.1	7.7	1,890	1,892	285	285	6,232

Note: These are calculated on an *individual* basis; i.e., each individual in the sample is assigned the number of household members, household income, or household income per equivalent, and then averages are calculated conditional on individual age. NMEMS is number of household members, NAE is number of adult equivalents, where children aged 0–4 are counted as .25, aged 5–14 as 0.45, and 15 and over as 1. Y is household income. CND is household consumption excluding purchases of durables, and YPE and CNDPE are the corresponding figures per equivalent adult. N is the number of persons over which the means are calculated. Money amounts are in thousands of CFA per year (about $3.00).

Table 6.9 **Average Household Characteristics by Age of Household Members, Rural Côte d'Ivoire, 1986**

	NMEMS	NAE	Y	CND	YPE	CNDPE	N
0–4	11.8	7.6	1,307	1,310	179	181	1,327
5–9	11.8	7.7	1,263	1,384	167	185	1,245
10–14	11.6	7.7	1,334	1,400	173	183	1,039
15–19	12.3	8.7	1,472	1,471	170	168	690
20–24	11.2	7.9	1,345	1,300	180	169	471
25–29	11.5	7.9	1,318	1,349	194	200	354
30–34	10.6	7.3	1,293	1,301	187	190	300
35–39	10.7	7.2	1,272	1,319	184	195	310
40–44	10.2	7.0	1,108	1,175	165	174	305
45–49	10.3	7.2	1,124	1,243	165	185	272
50–54	9.7	7.0	1,013	1,088	156	169	320
55–59	8.9	6.6	1,006	1,130	166	185	218
60–64	9.2	6.6	1,082	1,158	163	172	211
65–69	8.2	6.1	842	945	148	170	151
70–74	9.0	6.6	1,086	1,190	186	245	92
75–79	9.0	6.7	1,004	1,132	150	182	49
80+	9.5	7.3	1,280	1,138	165	153	55
All	11.2	7.6	1,262	1,313	173	181	7,409

Note: Y is household income. CND is household consumption excluding purchases of durables, and YPE and CNDPE are the corresponding figures per equivalent adult. N is the number of persons over which the means are calculated. Money amounts are in thousands of CFA per year (about $3.00). For other notes, see table 6.8.

income and expenditure per adult equivalent, are very flat across age groups. The average consumption per adult equivalent of those 55 and over is 100.3 percent of the average for all individuals in Bangkok and 109 percent for rural regions. On average, older Thais in both Bangkok and rural regions do not live in poorer households.

Unlike the Ivorian surveys, the Thai surveys provide a good deal of information on individual income levels and the sources of individual income. If the allocation of consumption to members within a household depends on the amount of income members bring to the household (again, this is not known to be true), then the patterns of individual income with age provide evidence on standards of living over the life cycle. Information on the distribution of income between pensions, annuities, and property income, as opposed to remittances and gifts, provides evidence on the extent to which older individuals rely on asset markets for old-age support.

It is possible to disaggregate individual income into that derived from wages, farming and self-employment (called business income), property, transfers (remittances, pensions and annuities), and other sources. The measures of profits from farming and self-employment are problematic in that they do not exclude the value of free family labor used and are usually "assigned" to the household head "or to the operator of the enterprise if he could be identified." For most family businesses, it is not clear that the profits from

Table 6.10 Average Household Characteristics by Age of Household Members, Bangkok, 1981

	NMEMS	NAE	Y	CND	YPE	CNDPE	N
0–4	5.0	3.4	7,141	5,693	2,173	1,729	565
5–9	6.0	4.3	8,031	6,600	1,949	1,615	515
10–14	6.5	4.8	7,945	6,760	1,754	1,500	629
15–19	6.2	5.5	9,044	7,540	1,678	1,423	825
20–24	5.4	4.9	9,152	7,185	1,962	1,574	816
25–29	4.7	4.1	8,518	6,260	2,229	1,680	783
30–34	4.6	3.7	8,496	6,121	2,527	1,800	546
35–39	5.1	3.9	7,947	6,240	2,208	1,752	324
40–44	5.4	4.3	8,209	6,671	2,176	1,759	317
45–49	5.7	4.9	9,057	7,159	2,059	1,574	252
50–54	5.5	5.0	9,971	8,051	2,092	1,697	243
55–59	5.1	4.8	9,467	7,135	2,111	1,591	213
60–64	4.8	4.4	9,682	6,781	2,238	1,662	141
65–69	5.3	4.6	7,659	6,354	1,778	1,518	115
70–74	5.4	4.6	8,596	7,733	1,958	1,842	69
75–79	4.6	4.3	7,026	5,872	1,929	1,596	39
80+	5.3	4.7	8,515	7,151	2,031	1,719	35
All	5.5	4.5	8,513	6,739	2,043	1,624	6,427
				Females			
55–59	4.9	4.6	8,334	6,679	1,905	1,504	108
60–64	4.6	4.2	9,196	6,195	2,220	1,655	78
65–69	5.2	4.4	7,856	6,662	1,908	1,674	55
70–74	5.4	4.6	7,757	7,587	1,795	1,784	39
75–79	4.1	3.6	5,307	4,861	1,632	1,544	17
80+	4.9	4.5	8,517	7,127	2,157	1,840	26
All	5.5	4.5	8,486	6,772	2,010	1,616	3,399
				Males			
55–59	5.3	4.9	10,633	7,604	2,324	1,680	105
60–64	5.0	4.6	10,284	7,506	2,261	1,671	63
65–69	5.3	4.8	7,478	6,072	1,660	1,376	60
70–74	5.3	4.6	9,685	7,924	2,170	1,916	30
75–79	5.1	4.8	8,355	6,653	2,159	1,637	22
80+	6.4	5.2	8,510	7,220	1,665	1,369	9
All	5.4	4.5	8,544	6,702	2,080	1,634	3,028

Note: Money amounts are baht per month. Variables are defined in tables 6.8 and 6.9 above.

the business should be assigned to any one person. In what follows, no adjustments were made for these problems.

Table 6.12 provides information on individual income and the distribution of income for males and females in Bangkok and rural regions. Unlike the household income figures discussed above, there is a clear pattern of individual income over the life cycle. For both rural and Bangkok males, income levels peak in the 50–59 age range and then decline rapidly. Female income

Table 6.11 Average Household Characteristics by Age of Household Members, Rural Thailand, 1981

	NMEMS	NAE	Y	CND	YPE	CNDPE	N
0–4	5.5	3.7	2,316	2,158	673	624	2,536
5–9	6.0	4.1	2,455	2,270	636	582	3,328
10–14	6.2	4.5	2,789	2,530	659	597	3,272
15–19	6.1	5.0	3,074	2,716	643	569	2,572
20–24	5.3	4.3	2,892	2,486	718	619	1,880
25–29	4.8	3.6	2,545	2,234	766	685	1,656
30–34	5.1	3.5	2,622	2,296	784	693	1,458
35–39	5.5	3.9	2,587	2,374	705	640	1,225
40–44	5.7	4.3	2,828	2,612	723	656	1,123
45–49	5.6	4.4	2,853	2,596	696	635	1,097
50–54	5.2	4.3	3,288	2,862	852	772	839
55–59	4.8	4.1	2,877	2,479	773	665	740
60–64	4.3	3.8	2,858	2,410	900	720	529
65–69	4.3	3.7	2,525	2,228	787	707	393
70–74	4.4	3.6	2,336	2,260	710	685	308
75–79	4.7	3.9	2,650	2,466	748	678	160
80+	4.9	4.1	2,711	2,441	724	656	164
All	5.6	4.2	2,706	2,430	703	631	23,280
				Females			
55–59	4.6	3.9	2,583	2,316	718	646	396
60–64	4.2	3.6	2,684	2,337	848	743	295
65–69	4.2	3.4	2,482	2,237	852	784	220
70–74	4.4	3.6	2,309	2,263	674	662	163
75–79	4.9	4.0	2,504	2,512	656	664	94
80+	4.9	4.2	2,834	2,472	769	677	108
All	5.5	4.1	2,699	2,435	708	640	11,935
				Males			
55–59	5.1	4.3	3,215	2,666	837	688	344
60–64	4.5	4.0	3,077	2,501	965	690	234
65–69	4.6	3.9	2,580	2,216	705	610	173
70–74	4.3	3.6	2,367	2,256	750	712	145
75–79	4.4	3.8	2,857	2,399	879	697	66
80+	4.9	4.1	2,474	2,382	639	616	56
All	5.6	4.2	2,714	2,425	697	621	11,345

Note: Money amounts are baht per month. For definitions of variables, see tables 6.8 and 6.9.

levels are flatter over the 30–60 age range but then also decline. These results are consistent with the declines in labor force participation for both males and females after the age of 60, and much of the declining income levels of older individuals can be accounted for by the increasing fraction of those who earn no income at all.

As is to be expected, the share of income from wage and business declines for older people, although the share of income from farming and self-employment remains quite high for men (49 and 79 percent, respectively, for

Table 6.12 Distribution of Income, by Age, Sex, and Location, Thailand, 1981

Age	Obs.	Mean Individual Income	%INC > 0	Share of Individual Income: Wage	Bus.	Prop.	Trans.	Other	INC/FAMINC	FREE/FAMINC
Bangkok Females										
20–29	870	1,177	.54	.75	.09	.01	.11	.04	.18	.05
30–39	468	1,733	.62	.61	.25	.01	.06	.07	.24	.05
40–49	299	1,648	.58	.39	.37	.04	.14	.07	.23	.05
50–59	245	1,764	.58	.25	.35	.03	.32	.05	.23	.04
60–69	133	1,523	.47	.05	.31	.06	.56	.03	.19	.07
70+	82	456	.26	.00	.10	.12	.74	.05	.11	.05
Bangkok Males										
20–29	729	2,141	.71	.81	.09	.00	.08	.02	.34	.05
30–39	402	4,517	.93	.73	.24	.01	.01	.02	.62	.06
40–49	268	4,899	.96	.60	.37	.00	.01	.02	.65	.05
50–59	211	5,418	.89	.48	.41	.01	.06	.04	.53	.03
60–69	123	2,719	.67	.26	.49	.07	.15	.04	.34	.07
70+	61	1,168	.41	.07	.23	.11	.58	.01	.16	.08
Rural Females										
20–29	1,893	241	.39	.67	.21	.00	.09	.03	.09	.06
30–39	1,400	394	.42	.50	.36	.02	.07	.04	.12	.04
40–49	1,134	473	.46	.35	.45	.03	.13	.04	.17	.04
50–59	830	369	.44	.23	.49	.03	.21	.05	.17	.05
60–69	515	384	.46	.10	.42	.07	.38	.03	.16	.08
70+	365	129	.38	.08	.21	.12	.55	.04	.10	.10
Rural Males										
20–29	1,643	808	.71	.55	.42	.00	.01	.01	.37	.05
30–39	1,283	1,591	.94	.27	.69	.00	.01	.02	.66	.04
40–49	1,086	2,031	.98	.18	.77	.01	.02	.02	.68	.04
50–59	749	2,278	.96	.16	.75	.01	.05	.02	.65	.04
60–69	407	1,665	.87	.06	.75	.03	.13	.03	.55	.06
70+	267	825	.63	.03	.54	.10	.29	.04	.29	.09

Note: Individual income includes wages, business income (farm plus self-employment income), property income (interest, dividends, income from roomers and boarders), transfer income (pensions and annuities, remittances from friends and relatives), other income (lotteries, insurance, sales of durable goods). Family income (FAMINC) equals the sum of all member's individual incomes plus the rental value of owner-occupied homes, home-produced goods not included in farm income, and goods received free. FREE/FAMINC is the value of goods received free as a fraction of family income. "Obs." is number of observations.

Bangkok and rural men aged 60–69). This reflects the fact that the oldest man in the household is usually the head of the household and would typically have all family business income assigned to him.

The share of income derived from transfers (including pensions, annuities, and remittances) increases dramatically with age for both men and women in

Bangkok and rural regions. Transfers account for a large share of individual income, particularly for women. These transfers consist mainly of remittances, presumably from family members or friends in other households. Although transfers cannot be divided up between remittances and pensions and annuities at the individual level, they can be disaggregated at the household level. Of all households that receive transfers, 93 percent of those in Bangkok and 97 percent of those in rural areas receive no pensions or annuities. The share of income from property (including interest, dividends, and rents) increases with age but, like pensions and annuities, is quite small, reaching only 10–12 percent for both Bangkok and rural residents in the 70 and over age group. Thus, sources of old-age income that are standard in developed countries play only a very small role in Thailand.

Table 6.13 tabulates income by source for rural males and females who live alone or with a spouse only and for those who live with at least one person who is not a spouse. Older people living with others are less likely to earn any income at all. However, the shares of income from different sources are not too dissimilar for those in different living arrangements. The fraction of total family income derived from goods received free does vary with living ar-

Table 6.13 Income Composition and Living Arrangements, Rural Thailand, 1981

Age	Obs.	Mean Individual Income	%INC > 0	Share of Individual Income: Wage	Bus.	Prop.	Trans.	Other	INC/ FAMINC	FREE/ FAMINC
				Females, Living Alone or with Spouse Only						
50–59	157	417	.64	.27	.37	.04	.27	.05	.25	.11
60–69	133	394	.69	.11	.35	.09	.43	.03	.28	.18
70+	75	292	.84	.07	.25	.13	.52	.04	.32	.30
				Females, Living with at Least One Child or Other Person						
50–59	669	359	.40	.21	.53	.03	.19	.05	.15	.04
60–69	381	382	.38	.10	.46	.06	.35	.03	.12	.05
70+	289	87	.25	.09	.19	.11	.57	.05	.05	.05
				Males, Living Alone or with Spouse Only						
50–59	144	1,984	.99	.26	.63	.03	.08	.01	.68	.07
60–69	89	1,479	.96	.09	.67	.06	.15	.04	.59	.11
70+	73	1,038	.96	.05	.47	.15	.31	.03	.50	.18
				Males, Living with at Least One Child or Other Person						
50–59	602	2,352	.95	.14	.79	.01	.04	.03	.64	.03
60–69	318	1,717	.84	.05	.77	.03	.12	.03	.54	.04
70+	190	761	.51	.01	.59	.07	.28	.05	.22	.06

Note: See table 6.12.

rangements. For example, for rural females aged 60–69, goods received free account for 18 percent of family income for those alone or with a spouse only and only 5 percent of family income for those living with others. For females living alone or with a spouse only, free goods and transfers make up a significant share of their income.

6.2 Household Life Cycles

In this section, we shift our focus away from individuals and toward households and how they change with the ages of their members. Households in LDCs are typically larger than those in more developed countries, particularly so here for Côte d'Ivoire; thus, with several generations living together, the life-cycle patterns of the household as an aggregate may be much attenuated compared with the patterns observed in the West. Households with between ten and twenty members are not uncommon in Côte d'Ivoire, and it is possible to imagine a state of affairs in which each household's demographic composition is a miniature version of that of the country as a whole and the life cycles of the individuals within that household are subsumed into a stationary structure for the household.

In fact, such is far from being the case in Côte d'Ivoire. Table 6.14B shows the breakdown of household heads by age and sex. (Table 6.14A shows the same data for Thailand.) If household composition were stationary and the oldest male always designated the household head, there would be no heads outside this category. In reality, 42 percent of household heads are under the age of 55, and only 19 percent are men over the age of 70. Only 5 percent of households contain one or more married sons of the head, and fewer than 1 percent have two or more. Similarly, it is rare for married brothers to live together; only 3 percent of male-headed households contain a married brother. These households seem to conform well to what Cowgill (1986, 62) describes as the common pattern among polygynous households: "a man, his several wives, their (unmarried) children," and possibly "some additional consanguines, such as unmarried or widowed sisters of the husband, and perhaps his aged parents." While there is a clear bias toward older heads and there are more heads in older groups than their share of the population would warrant, there are many households headed by younger men because married sons set up new households.

The economic status of the household is also clearly related to the age of its head, as shown in table 6.15. These data are presented for both years; they are probably a good deal less reliable, particularly for assets, than previous data, so one year cannot be safely taken as representative for both. The figures show that older heads preside over bigger households but that both household income and household total expenditure reach a peak among households headed by 30–34 year-olds, declining steadily thereafter. The pattern, if it is there, is a good deal less obvious in the rural areas. As was the case for patterns in the

Table 6.14 Age and Sex Composition of Household Heads

A. Thailand, 1981

	Bangkok			Rural		
	Females	Males	All	Females	Males	All
15–19	1.05	1.31	2.36	.20	.42	.62
20–24	2.16	4.52	6.69	.52	3.87	4.39
30–34	2.62	11.67	14.30	.86	9.29	10.15
35–39	2.36	12.33	14.69	.86	11.08	11.94
40–44	2.30	8.46	10.75	1.08	10.51	11.58
45–49	2.30	8.79	11.08	1.68	10.21	11.88
50–54	2.23	7.34	9.57	2.14	10.29	12.42
55–59	2.82	6.23	9.05	2.00	7.87	9.87
60–64	2.30	5.70	8.00	2.34	6.55	8.89
65–69	2.16	3.54	5.70	1.94	4.51	6.45
70–74	1.25	2.95	4.20	1.78	3.24	5.01
75–79	.66	1.25	1.90	1.24	2.52	3.75
80+	.66	1.05	1.70	1.30	1.74	3.04
All	24.85	75.15	100.00	17.91	82.09	100.00

B. Côte d'Ivoire, 1986

	Males	Females	All
20–24	1.3	.1	1.4
25–29	1.9	.1	2.1
30–34	3.5	.2	3.7
35–39	6.1	.8	6.9
40–44	8.8	.9	9.7
45–49	9.2	1.1	10.3
50–54	11.3	.9	12.1
55–59	10.6	.8	11.3
60–64	9.4	.9	10.4
65–69	10.9	1.0	11.9
70–74	10.4	.5	10.9
75–79	6.6	.6	7.3
80+	1.8	.1	1.9
All	91.9	8.1	100.0

individual data, the hump in household incomes and expenditures is exaggerated by pooling older, poorer, rural individuals with younger, richer, urban ones. Since household size and the number of equivalents increase with the age of the head, deflation by either measure produces a pattern in which household living standards decline with the age of the head, with the result that the hump is moved to the extreme left of the age distribution.

The hump-shaped pattern, in which incomes and consumption shapes are closely matched, is one with a peak that occurs much earlier in the head's age distribution than is the case in many LDCs, particularly those in Asia (for

Table 6.15 **Members, Income, Expenditure, and Assets by Head's Age, Côte d'Ivoire, 1985 and 1986**

Age	NMEMS	NAE	Y	CND	S	AGASS	BUSASS	PERASS
				1985				
20–24	3.5	2.7	926	933	−8	911	90	386
25–29	5.3	3.8	1,491	1,542	−51	560	6,148[a]	804
30–34	7.0	4.8	1,937	1,916	21	2,435	596	910
35–39	7.5	5.0	1,885	1,880	5	2,687	275	656
40–44	8.8	5.9	1,610	1,832	−222	2,632	893	716
45–49	9.7	6.6	1,857	1,749	107	3,666	636	1,108
50–54	9.2	6.5	1,271	1,408	−137	5,167	230	796
55–59	9.2	6.7	1,496	1,377	120	3,732	708	1,008
60–64	9.7	7.0	1,497	1,537	−40	5,199	737	1,314
65–69	9.6	7.0	1,470	1,415	55	4,655	752	1,251
70+	8.0	6.1	870	932	−62	6,882	155	976
				1986				
20–24	4.1	3.0	843	912	−70	1,194	27	198
25–29	5.5	4.0	1,845	1,659	186	613	211	726
30–34	6.7	4.5	2,096	2,050	46	1,055	170	780
35–39	7.9	5.3	2,132	2,119	13	1,173	398	979
40–44	8.4	5.6	1,455	1,677	−222	1,575	296	969
45–49	9.4	6.4	1,835	1,831	4	1,693	602	1,326
50–54	9.0	6.3	1,298	1,340	−41	2,187	274	658
55–59	8.7	6.4	1,381	1,481	−100	2,710	523	1,367
60–64	8.4	6.2	1,700	1,391	310	2,199	684	1,117
65–69	8.1	6.0	994	1,041	−57	3,275	287	628
70+	8.5	6.4	1,224	1,277	−53	2,568	492	786
				Rural 1986				
20–24	5.5	3.8	1,072	602	471	2,982	9	101
25–29	6.5	4.4	1,223	1,088	135	1,672	79	211
30–34	7.3	4.9	1,185	1,022	162	2,394	89	187
35–39	8.6	5.6	1,089	1,100	−11	2,334	111	263
40–44	8.6	5.5	831	1,033	−201	2,855	79	185
45–49	9.0	6.0	1,025	1,096	−71	2,042	57	264
50–54	8.7	6.0	919	963	−44	2,699	64	192
55–59	8.1	5.9	851	998	−146	3,879	33	235
60–64	7.9	5.7	1,116	1,123	−6	2,364	390	301
65–69	8.0	5.8	842	899	−57	3,572	70	319
70+	8.1	6.1	927	1,052	−124	2,938	41	176

Note: NMEMS is number of members. NAE is number of adult equivalents. Y is household income. CND is consumption excluding purchases of durable goods. S, for saving, is the difference between Y and CND. AGASS is the value of agricultural assets, including a farmer-estimated figure for the value of agricultural land. BUSASS is the value of assets used in the family business. PERASS is the value of personal assets.

[a]This figure is dominated by one outlier, a 28-year-old head near Aboisso, in the extreme southeast of the country, who reported business assets worth more than CFA 700,000 ($2.1 million).

evidence on Thailand, Korea, Indonesia, and Hong Kong, see Deaton [1990]). These cross-country patterns are important because, as pointed out by Carroll and Summers (1991), if tastes are common across countries, then the rapidly growing countries are those where young people are relatively much richer than their parents and grandparents, and age consumption profiles should therefore peak earliest in the most rapidly growing economies. But Côte d'Ivoire is a very slowly-growing economy relative to Thailand and the other Asian countries listed above, and this slow growth is accompanied by the earliest peak in household consumption. As Carroll and Summers emphasize, these results make it difficult to believe that life-cycle saving is responsible for the cross-country correlation between growth and savings that exists in the data. Instead, the obvious alternative is that consumption tracks income over the life cycle, a hypothesis that is fully consistent with the data in table 6.15.

Saving itself is as often negative as positive and shows no clear pattern with age. The measurement of income for poor, largely illiterate, self-employed farmers in LDCs is an undertaking fraught with difficulty, and little weight should be attached to the magnitude of these figures. However, analysis of the micro data from Côte d'Ivoire provides evidence that farmers undertake short-run saving to smooth their consumption relative to their noisy incomes, and this evidence is also consistent with the earlier results on farmers' saving behavior in Thailand in Paxson (1989).

The asset figures are likely to be almost as unreliable as the savings data, and there is a still unresolved question as to why the (largely self-reported) figures for agricultural assets are so much lower in 1986 than in 1985. The data in the upper panels of table 6.15 suggest that, over the country as a whole, asset levels continue to increase with the age of the household head, but some of this is an aggregation effect; in the rural panel, agricultural assets are more or less equally distributed across age groups, something that would follow from a process in which land is closely tied to household formation. Note that, at least until recent years, land has not been particularly scarce in Côte d'Ivoire (or in Thailand), and, given permission from the lineage owning the land, new cocoa and coffee farms could be established by clearing virgin forest, with ownership gradually established by use. Even today, fathers would typically assume responsibility for providing their sons with land, and if uncultivated land is no longer available within the lineage boundaries, the acquisition or use of land elsewhere will be arranged, preferably close by, but sometimes at some considerable distance. (For a description of the evolution of land markets in response to increasing scarcities, first of labor, later of land, see Hecht [1982].)

Table 6.16 presents regressions of income, consumption, and the asset variables on household demographic structure and on dummies for the five main urbanization and agroclimatic zones in the country. These results should be

Table 6.16 Regressions of Income, Consumption, and Assets on Household Composition, Côte d'Ivoire, 1986

	Income		Consumption		Agricultural Assets		Business Assets		Personal Assets	
Variable	Est.	(t)	Est.	(t)	Est.	(t)	Est.	(t)	Est.	(t)
CONSTANT	124	(.7)	259	(2.3)	−603	(1.4)	−378	(2.9)	−791	(3.7)
M0–4	−65	(.9)	−76	(1.7)	131	(.8)	40	(.8)	29	(.3)
M5–14	67	(1.4)	127	(4.3)	−44	(.4)	−29	(.8)	−22	(.4)
M15–24	214	(3.7)	173	(4.7)	417	(3.0)	195	(4.5)	401	(5.7)
M25–34	394	(4.0)	213	(3.5)	196	(.8)	64	(.9)	229	(2.0)
M35–44	257	(1.7)	219	(2.4)	167	(.5)	59	(.5)	23	(.1)
M45–54	157	(1.0)	25	(.3)	525	(1.4)	193	(1.6)	221	(1.2)
M55–64	302	(1.8)	29	(.3)	947	(2.3)	375	(3.0)	635	(3.1)
M65–74	24	(.1)	−19	(.1)	1,475	(3.0)	248	(1.6)	373	(1.5)
M75+	373	(1.2)	124	(.7)	547	(.8)	374	(1.7)	430	(1.2)
F0–4	−47	(.7)	−107	(2.4)	180	(1.1)	−30	(.6)	15	(.2)
F5–14	64	(1.3)	90	(2.9)	−40	(.4)	10	(.3)	29	(.5)
F15–24	199	(3.0)	279	(6.8)	164	(1.1)	20	(.4)	150	(1.9)
F25–34	345	(3.5)	257	(4.1)	1,033	(4.4)	75	(1.0)	291	(2.4)
F35–44	43	(.4)	89	(1.3)	713	(2.7)	26	(.3)	222	(1.7)
F45–54	−163	(1.4)	4	(.1)	144	(.5)	66	(.8)	−37	(.3)
F55–64	196	(1.4)	102	(1.2)	408	(1.3)	147	(1.5)	360	(2.2)
F65–74	−144	(.8)	−62	(.5)	−257	(.6)	38	(.3)	142	(.6)
F75+	17	(.1)	−5	(.0)	−262	(.4)	−113	(.6)	101	(.3)
ABIDJAN	1,742	(9.0)	1,673	(13.9)	−937	(2.0)	1,077	(7.6)	1,907	(8.3)
OTHER URB	909	(4.8)	739	(6.2)	−358	(.8)	405	(2.9)	1,266	(5.6)
W. FOREST	34	(.2)	36	(.3)	1,742	(3.7)	120	(.8)	38	(.2)
E. FOREST	186	(1.0)	96	(.9)	1,979	(4.7)	16	(.1)	−74	(.3)

Note: The figures are total income, consumption, and assets, undeflated by any measure of household size. M is males, F is females, and the independent variables are the number of people in the relevant age category in the household. The omitted region is the northern savannahs.

interpreted not as structural equations but as an alternative and more informative description of the relation between head's age and these economic variables. High income and consumption levels are associated with the presence of prime-age males and females—in itself evidence of consumption tracking income. The presence or absence of individuals aged 55 and over seems to contribute little to household income or consumption levels. Asset levels, however, are positively associated with the presence of older men (but not older women), particularly those aged from 55 to 64. This is certainly consistent with a steady accumulation of assets by the male head, assets passed on to sons at or before death. Women aged 25–34 also attract a very large positive coefficient in the agricultural assets equation. Since daughters would not normally inherit land, there is no obvious explanation for this result, although it could conceivably reflect the propensity of older wealthy men to marry young second or third wives. There is no evidence of an association between business assets and women, although many small businesses in Côte d'Ivoire are owned by women.

Thai households (as defined by the Socioeconomic Surveys) are much smaller than those in Côte d'Ivoire. Using 1981 data, approximately 50 percent of rural households have four members or less, and households of ten or more members are rare. Households in Thailand are also likely to have younger household heads. Sixty-three percent of rural household heads and 69 percent of urban household heads are younger than 55 (see table 6.14A). The size of households also varies with the age of the household head. The first column of table 6.17 shows that the number of household members first increases and then decreases as the household head ages. These numbers are consistent with the "Western" pattern of children marrying and setting up their own households, which grow as children are added and then shrink as children move out. Cowgill (1986, 69–70) describes the Thai system as a "residual stem family" system, in which young married couples often live with one set of parents, but only until a younger sibling marries and takes their place. The last child married, often the last daughter married, stays with the parents until they die and then inherits the land. This would explain why households with very old household heads have, on average, four members rather than one or two.

These patterns of household formation may make life-cycle models of household consumption more relevant for Thailand than Côte d'Ivoire. With smaller households, it is less likely that household members span a broad range of ages, and the age of the household head should be a good indicator of where a household is in its life cycle. Given the fairly rapid growth in Thailand, one might expect to see younger (richer) households both earning and consuming more than older households.

The results in table 6.17 indicate that income and consumption in Thailand do follow a hump-shaped pattern similar to that seen in Côte d'Ivoire, but with a much later peak in both income and consumption. Household income reaches its highest level in the 60–64 age category for Bangkok and in the 50–54 age category for rural areas. Consumption tracks income closely, and saving also appears to follow a similar pattern, with those in the highest income groups saving most, although the pattern for saving is less pronounced. These patterns are consistent with the age patterns of individual income shown in table 6.12 and are also consistent with the patterns of household size shown in table 6.17. Household heads in their 40s and 50s have the largest households, and it is likely that the children in these households are old enough to contribute substantially to household income.

Although total household income and consumption are both strongly related to the age of the head of the household, income and consumption, after adjusting for the number of adult equivalents, are not. Since family size and the number of adult equivalents follows the *same* hump-shaped pattern as in-

Table 6.17 Members, Income, and Expenditure by Head's Age, Thailand, 1981

Age	NMEMS	NAE	Y	CND	S	Y/NAE	CND/NAE	S/NAE
				Bangkok				
15–19	1.6	1.5	2,225	1,961	264	1,682	1,467	215
20–24	2.3	2.0	3,736	3,285	451	1,939	1,779	160
25–29	3.1	2.5	6,065	4,570	1,495	2,564	1,993	571
30–34	3.9	3.0	7,239	5,348	1,891	2,724	2,002	722
35–39	4.5	3.3	7,017	5,540	1,477	2,294	1,822	472
40–44	4.8	3.8	7,598	6,165	1,433	2,437	1,940	497
45–49	5.3	4.4	6,951	6,245	706	1,758	1,543	214
50–54	5.3	4.9	9,284	7,570	1,714	2,073	1,676	397
55–59	4.9	4.6	9,831	7,114	2,716	2,289	1,670	619
60–64	4.3	4.0	10,033	6,806	3,227	2,449	1,765	684
65–69	4.8	4.3	6,933	5,941	991	1,832	1,588	244
70+	4.0	3.6	6,293	6,053	240	2,128	1,991	137
				Rural				
15–19	2.3	2.0	1,459	1,295	164	810	760	49
20–24	3.0	2.3	1,845	1,652	193	923	800	123
25–29	3.7	2.6	1,969	1,749	220	875	781	94
30–34	4.5	3.0	2,381	2,090	291	838	735	103
35–39	5.2	3.5	2,302	2,196	106	714	658	56
40–44	5.5	4.0	2,852	2,593	259	805	713	92
45–49	5.6	4.3	2,762	2,439	323	701	624	76
50–54	5.1	4.1	3,137	2,825	312	861	801	60
55–59	4.8	4.1	2,883	2,461	422	797	678	119
60–64	4.1	3.5	2,826	2,310	517	983	750	233
65–69	4.0	3.4	2,483	2,172	311	843	751	92
70+	3.7	3.1	2,095	2,010	86	756	711	44

Note: For variable definitions for the first six columns, see table 6.15. The last three columns are income, nondurable consumption expenditures, and saving divided by numbers of adult equivalents.

come and consumption, adjustment for family size results in extremely flat income and consumption profiles that appear to have no relation to the age of the household head.

The absence of any difference in income and consumption per equivalent adult between young and old households is puzzling, especially in a rapidly growing country such as Thailand. One possible explanation is that households in Thailand may be much more complex than the data suggest. As discussed earlier, a small "household" may actually be part of a larger group of several related households in a single compound, and there may be significant transfers between such households. The fact that older people "living alone" receive a large fraction of their incomes in the form of free goods (mostly food) suggests that this might be so. If each household, as measured by the survey data, is actually part of a network of closely linked households containing people in different generations, then it becomes quite unclear whether one ought to expect individual households to operate in ways predicted by life-cycle models. One can imagine a situation in which household formation is itself the mechanism that is used to smooth consumption (and income) across individuals in different generations: individuals may be "allocated" across households so as to maintain roughly equal consumption levels across all family members within a group of households. Much more detailed data on links between households would have to be collected to determine whether this is so.

6.3 Conclusions

We have presented a considerable mass of evidence, most of it not well structured by any theoretical concerns. This is perhaps inevitable given the current state of the subject; aging in developing countries is an issue that looks like it might be important, but concern is still not focused on any particular set of economic research questions or even outstanding policy issues. There are many large and attractively wooly creatures at loose in the forest: the role of development and the status of the aged; the relation between marriage patterns, polygamy, living arrangements, and the treatment of the elderly; and what policy steps, if any, should be considered by those Asian countries that are facing rapidly rising shares of elderly inhabitants. But we are very far, not only from answers, but even from a well-defined set of topics that economists could usefully think about.

Even so, we feel that we have learned something by looking at these data and by writing this paper, and it is perhaps useful to conclude by summarizing some of what is known and what might usefully be learned.

1. Questions regarding the economic status of the old in LDCs cannot be answered and must be rethought. In more developed countries, where perhaps nine-tenths of the elderly live by themselves or with elderly spouses, household surveys can tell us a great deal about their living standards. In LDCs, to a greater or lesser degree, older people do not live by themselves, and until a method can be found for measuring intrahousehold allocations, we have no method of assigning welfare levels to them or indeed to other members of the households in which they live.

2. More work needs to be done on the question of whether the source of income (i.e., who earns it) affects what individual members of the household receive. This cannot be done directly, but if the earnings of the elderly are spent differently than other household income, we should be able to detect that fact from consumption data. Data such as those from Thailand show considerable variation in source of income with age, although the patterns are quite different from those in the United States or Western Europe.

3. In the United States and other developed countries, where many elderly people live alone, there has been concern about the possible abandonment of

the old. However, such cases seem to be rare; most old people live alone because they want to, and frequency of contact with children is generally high (for a review, see Mancini and Blieszner 1989). In Côte d'Ivoire, under current living conditions, abandonment does not seem common because very few old people live alone. There are perhaps more grounds for concern in Thailand, but the population at risk is still small and is probably overstated by the survey results quoted here. However, there is evidence from elsewhere that suggests that these results should not be generalized to all poor countries. In many areas of India, living arrangements for newlyweds are strictly patrilocal, with the result that, after marriage, women are effectively cut off from their parents' family. In turn, they will be looked after in old age by their sons, their daughters having themselves moved to their husbands' families. In consequence, women who fail to produce sons, or fail to produce surviving sons, are likely to fall into destitution as widows. Drèze (1988) provides evidence on this problem and highlights it as an outstanding issue for social security and poverty policy in India.

4. The living arrangements of the elderly will vary from place to place according to marriage arrangements, agroclimatic conditions, and the availability of labor and land. The position of Indian widows has already been cited. In Côte d'Ivoire, living patterns have been changing in response to the increasing scarcity of land since sons, who were previously guaranteed land nearby, are now often required to set up households at considerable distances. The shortage of land itself reflects a great deal of immigration to the cocoa and coffee areas, an immigration that responded originally to *labor* shortage and that contributed to the destruction of the original lineage system of cocoa and coffee production. One may also wonder whether the pattern of inheritance in northern Thailand—whereby, as a result of the residual stem family system, the youngest daughter typically inherits the land—will continue unmodified into an era where land is increasingly scarce.

5. Individual participation and earnings patterns show the standard life-cycle hump shapes in Côte d'Ivoire and Thailand and presumably do so more widely. However, households act so as to make average living standards within households much less variable over the life cycle than are the individual patterns. The degree to which this happens in the data is different between the two countries and depends on how household size is measured. Even so, sharing resources between household members is presumably one of the main economic functions of the household. What needs a great deal more research is the extent to which household size and composition adapt to facilitate sharing and to guarantee the best possible living standards to household members. In both Thailand and Côte d'Ivoire, there is a great deal of migration both seasonal and nonseasonal. In Thailand, the process of household formation is explicitly tied to the pressure on resources within the compound; the departure of a previously married child on the marriage of a younger sibling is therefore as much a matter of economics as of immutable custom. In the panel house-

holds in Côte d'Ivoire, there are major differences in membership between 1985 and 1986, and while there is undoubtedly some measurement error, careful attempts were made to link household members from one year to the next. Certainly, there is a great deal of movement. Fosterage of children, often children not closely related, is a widespread phenomenon in West Africa (see Ainsworth 1989) and provides a mechanism, not only for education, training, and apprenticeship, but also for sharing economic burdens between members of the same lineage. There has been a good deal of emphasis on the role of risk sharing in determining patterns of marriage and migration (see, e.g., Rosenzweig 1988). But there is scope for more modeling here, particularly for a simple unifying theory that explains how potential household members decide how to form household groups given the economic opportunities available to them.

6. There are a number of interactions between urbanization and age distributions. Migration tends to lead to young cities and an older countryside, as is the case in Côte d'Ivoire, but much urban growth in LDCs comes from reproductive behavior as well as from migration. The fall in fertility in the demographic transition often begins in the cities, with the result that cities are likely to age more rapidly than more rural areas. The balances between these forces will produce different age distributions in different countries, for example, younger cities in Africa and older cities in Asia, and these have a number of repercussions for policy, for example, in the provision of services as well as in the likely effectiveness of older people as a political force.

7. Many LDCs are in a state of transition, not only demographic, but also educational. In both countries examined here, there are very large differences between the educational attainments of the different generations. The *consequences* of these differences are much less clear, and we do not wish to subscribe to the view that they always and everywhere undermine the status of the old. Nevertheless, models that provide a theoretical framework for the role of the elderly would do well to bear these facts in mind.

8. The life-cycle model of saving and capital accumulation, which has brought so many insights in developed countries, cannot be applied without modification to economies where the functions of households are different. Asset accumulation for old age, with a large share of the capital stock being accounted for (or not accounted for) by life-cycle saving, is not likely to be a very useful model for savings in LDCs. Households can and do provide old-age insurance without an obvious need to accumulate and decumulate assets. Our data do not suggest any run down of assets with the age of the household head. Of course, as in more developed economies, heads have a range of other motives for keeping control of assets for as long as possible.

9. As in developed countries, there is a pronounced household life cycle, with a hump-shaped income, peaking much earlier in Côte d'Ivoire than in Thailand. However, we doubt that there is much long-term consumption smoothing associated with these humps, and we tend to attach more impor-

tance to saving as a means of smoothing consumption over short-term fluctuations in income that are typically associated with agricultural activities. Indeed, it is possible that variations in household structure contribute more to long-term smoothing than do variations in assets.

References

Ahonzo, Etienne, Bernard Barrere, and Pierre Kopylov. 1984. *Population de la Côte d'Ivoire: Analyse des donnés démographiques disponibles*. Abidjan, Côte d'Ivoire: Direction de la Statistique, Ministere de l'Economie et des Finances, République de Côte d'Ivoire.

Ainsworth, Martha. 1989. Economic Aspects of Child Fostering in Côte d'Ivoire. Washington, D.C.: World Bank, September. Manuscript.

Ainsworth, Martha, and Juan Muñoz. 1986. The Côte d'Ivoire Living Standards Survey. Living Standards Measurement Study Working Paper no. 26. Washington, D.C.: World Bank.

Carroll, Christopher D., and Lawrence H. Summers. 1991. Consumption Growth Parallels Income Growth: Some New Evidence. In *National Saving and Economic Performance,* ed. B. Douglas Bernheim and John B. Shoven. Chicago: University of Chicago Press.

Coder, John, Timothy M. Smeeding, and Barbara Boyle Torrey. 1990. The Change in the Economic Status of the Low-Income Elderly in Three Industrial Countries: Circa 1979–1986. Washington, D.C.: Bureau of the Census. Manuscript.

Cowgill, Donald O. 1974. Aging and Modernization: A Revision of the Theory. In *Aging and Modernization,* ed. D. O. Cowgill and L. D. Holmes. New York: Appleton-Century-Crofts.

———. 1986. *Aging around the World*. Belmont, Calif.: Wadsworth.

Deaton, Angus. 1990. Saving in Developing Countries: Theory and Review. In *Proceedings of the World Bank Annual Conference on Development Economics 1989. World Bank Economic Review* (suppl.), 61–96.

Deaton, Angus, and Dwayne Benjamin. 1988. Coffee and Cocoa in the Côte d'Ivoire. Living Standards Measurement Study Working Paper no. 44. Washington, D.C.: World Bank.

Deaton, Angus, and John Muellbauer. 1986. On Measuring Child Costs in Poor Countries. *Journal of Political Economy* 94:720–44.

Deaton, Angus, Javier Ruiz-Castillo, and Duncan Thomas. 1989. The Influence of Household Composition on Household Expenditure Patterns: Theory and Spanish Evidence. *Journal of Political Economy* 97:179–200.

Drèze, Jean P. 1988. Social Insecurity in India: A Case Study. London: London School of Economics. Manuscript.

Ewbank, Douglas C. 1981. *Age Misreporting and Age-Selective Undernumeration: Sources, Patterns and Consequences for Demographic Analysis*. Washington, D.C.: National Academy Press.

Hecht, Robert. 1984. The Transformation of Lineage Production in Southern Ivory Coast, 1920–1980. *Ethnology* 23:261–77.

Mancini, Jay A., and Rosemary Blieszner. 1989. Aging Parents and Adult Children: Research Themes in Intergenerational Relations. *Journal of Marriage and the Family* 51:275–90.

Martin, Linda G. 1988. The Aging of Asia. *Journal of Gerontology: Social Sciences* 43:S99–S113.
———. 1989. Living Arrangements of the Elderly in Fiji, Korea, Malaysia, and the Philippines. *Demography* 26:627–43.
National Economic and Social Development Board. 1985. *Population Projections for Thailand, 1980–2015*. Bangkok: National Economic and Social Development Board.
National Statistical Office. 1983. *The Survey of Migration in Bangkok Metropolis, Nonthaburi, Pathun Thani and Sanut Prakai*. Bangkok: National Statistical Office.
Paxson, Christina H. 1989. Savings in Thailand: Responses to Income Shocks. Princeton, N.J.: Princeton University, Research Program in Development Studies. Manuscript.
Pollak, Robert A., and Terence J. Wales. 1979. Welfare Comparisons and Equivalent Scales. *American Economic Review* 69:216–21.
Rosenzweig, Mark R. 1988. Risk, Implicit Contracts and the Family in Rural Areas of Low Income Countries. *Economic Journal* 98:1148–70.
Treas, Judith, and Barbara Logue. 1986. Economic Development and the Older Population. *Population and Development Review* 12:645–73.
United Nations. 1986. *World Population Prospects: Estimates and Projections as Assessed in 1984*. New York: United Nations.
———. 1987. *Demographic Yearbook 1985*. New York: United Nations.
U.S. Agency for International Development. 1982. *Selected Statistical Data by Sex*, pt. 13, *Ivory Coast*. Washington, D.C.: USAID.
World Bank. 1979. The Population of Thailand: Its Growth and Welfare. World Bank Staff Working Paper no. 337. Washington, D.C.: World Bank, June. Manuscript.
———. 1988. *World Development Report 1988*. Washington, D.C.: World Bank.
———. 1989. *World Development Report 1989*. Washington, D.C.: World Bank.

Comment Fumio Hayashi

Angus Deaton and Christina H. Paxson have written a very useful paper. The first stage of any serious empirical research is to bury yourself in the data set and create a number of cross-tabulations, a sometimes painful and time-consuming task that requires a lot of attention to details. The second stage, which is the more enjoyable part of the empirical research, is to look at the cross-tabulations and try to figure out what sort of consistent stories one can tell from the data. I view Deaton and Paxson's paper as summarizing the first stage of their empirical research. I am happy to serve as a discussant of their paper because they have set me up for carrying out the second stage, analyzing the interesting data set they assembled.

Models of Saving Behavior

Although the models of saving behavior the authors seem to have in mind—the dynasty, the life-cycle, and consumption-tracks-income models—are the

Fumio Hayashi is professor of economics at the University of Pennsylvania and a research associate of the National Bureau of Economic Research.

three reference models often relied on when one tries to interpret savings data, it is useful to note that they are particular combinations of the following three elements: altruism, risk sharing, and consumption smoothing over time. The standard life-cycle model combines no altruism, no risk sharing, and consumption smoothing. The consumption-tracks-income model has no altruism, no risk sharing, and no consumption smoothing. The standard dynasty model has all three elements, although one can imagine a dynasty model in which individuals and households in the same dynasty (family) are altruistically linked (hence there is risk sharing between them) but in which the dynasty has no access to loan markets to smooth total dynasty consumption over time. I find it a good strategy for interpreting savings data to check and see if each of the three elements is in the data.

If one has cross-sectional data for two countries with different secular productivity growth rates, one can test altruism by comparing the cross-sectional age profile of consumption for the two countries and testing whether the cohort effect is present. If different age cohorts are altruistically linked, then the shape of the age profile should not be affected by the growth rate of the economy.[1] Another type of test of altruism is possible if data on households belonging to the same dynasty are available. Under altruism, the distribution of consumption by individuals or households within the dynasty should not be affected by the distribution of income within the dynasty.[2]

Within the set of households that enter into a risk-sharing arrangement to pool income shocks, there should be no cross-sectional correlation between consumption growth (more precisely, the growth rate of the marginal utility) and contemporaneous income growth. This test, of course, requires panel data on consumption and income. A less formal test, which can be conducted using cross-sectional data, is to identify households apparently being subject to some adverse shock and see how their consumption is financed.

Testing consumption smoothing, or lack thereof, in cross-sectional data is less straightforward. If the level of consumption is highly correlated with income in cross section, then it can be a sign of households unable to smooth consumption over time. But it also admits other interpretations. The well-known example is the life-cycle model with income that is a random walk. Another possibility is that income includes insurance payments under the guise of transfer income. Under complete income insurance, consumption is insensitive to income shocks, but the level of consumption can differ across households because households have different endowments (lifetime resources). If transfers are timed exactly to finance consumption for households experiencing adverse income shocks, then in cross section there should be

1. C. Carroll and L. Summers ("Consumption Growth Parallels Income Growth: Some New Evidence," NBER Working Paper no. 3090 [Cambridge, Mass.: National Bureau of Economic Research, 1989]) conducted this type of test of altruism.

2. This test of altruism was carried out by J. Altonji, F. Hayashi, and L. Kotlikoff ("Is the Extended Family Altruistically Linked? Direct Tests Using Micro Data," NBER Working Paper no. 3046 [Cambridge, Mass.: National Bureau of Economic Research, August 1989]).

perfect correlation between the level of consumption and income (inclusive of transfers). Conversely, even if consumption and income appear unrelated in cross section at the household level, the dynasty as a whole can be liquidity constrained. Thus, simply documenting a lack of correlation between consumption and income is not enough to assert that there is a well-functioning economy-wide capital market.

With all these preliminaries in mind, I turn now to the data for Thailand and Côte d'Ivoire. I will argue that the standard dynasty model (the model of saving that combines altruism—and hence risk sharing—and consumption smoothing) goes a long way toward explaining the data for the two countries.

Thailand

Take Thailand first. As emphasized in the paper, the family size as defined in the survey is relatively small. This means that consumption by the age of the household head should be a good approximation to consumption by age cohort. As shown in the paper (see tables 6.10, 6.11, and 6.17), there is no cohort effect in the cross-sectional age profile of consumption, which is consistent with the existence of altruism for a quickly growing country like Thailand.

Altruism implies risk sharing, so if there is altruism, we should find evidence for risk sharing in the data. In tables 6.12 and 6.13, we find that more than half of income for those 70 years or over—those experiencing an adverse longevity shock—is transfer income. This certainly is consistent with risk sharing.

Regarding consumption smoothing, the data are not informative. There is fairly strong correlation between consumption and income across households, but, as I argued above, that can be consistent with models with consumption smoothing.

Côte d'Ivoire

The family in the Côte d'Ivoire survey is much larger in size. This makes it difficult to infer the consumption profile by *age cohort*. My favorite example is the following. Suppose the *cross-sectional* (not longitudinal) age profile of earnings is flat, with the old earning on average as much as the young at any given point in time. If a typical household in the survey contains both the young and the old, which is the case for Côte d'Ivoire, and if the head of the household is the main income earner, then half the households in the sample are headed by the young and the other half by the old. If one simply draws the cross-sectional profile of consumption by the age of the household head, it will be completely flat because household consumption is the sum of consumption by the young and old. The cohort effect (under the assumption of no altruism) is that the size of consumption by the young relative to that by the old depends on secular productivity growth, but it just does not show up in the age profile of household consumption by the age of the head if households include both the young and the old.[3]

It is not clear, therefore, what one can learn from table 6.15, where consumption and income profiles *by the age of the head* are displayed. The authors note that the observed similarity between the consumption profile and the income profile is consistent with the consumption-tracks-income model, but it is also consistent with the standard dynasty model. We know (from table 6.4B) that the vast majority of households contain both parents and their children (which may or may not include the eldest son) in the same household. Take a young age bracket, say, the 25–29 age bracket for 1985 in table 6.15. Most of the household in that age bracket must contain a 25–29-year-old son who is already making more money than his father living in the same household. If earning capacity is positively correlated over generations, then having an able son surpassing his father in earnings is good news for the family because the son's children are also likely to have a high earning capacity. For such families, consumption should be high, thus explaining the correlation between consumption and income.

If the altruistic link is much stronger within the family than between families, the large family size in the data can be an advantage because we can think of family consumption as the sum of consumptions by individuals that are altruistically linked. In this context, table 6.16 has a very interesting interpretation that the authors do not seem to be aware of. The family income regression should not be controversial; it just uncovers the age profile of income by regressing family income on the number of people in the relevant age brackets. The consumption regression is much more interesting. If family members are not altruistically linked, then the consumption regression has the same interpretation as the income regression: the coefficients recover the age profile of consumption. Under this interpretation of the coefficients, the estimated age profile indicates puzzlingly low consumption for the old.

An alternative interpretation is possible if family members are altruistically linked. Take two hypothetical families, A and B, the only difference between them being the presence of old people. The difference between family A's consumption, which includes consumption by old people, and family B's consumption, which does not, is made up of two effects. The first effect, which is positive, is simply that family A has more bodies to feed. The second effect is negative and less obvious: the wealth depletion by old people producing nothing has to be financed partly by a reduction of consumption by young people (and partly by future generations of the dynasty). If family members are not altruistically linked, then the second effect is absent, and the regression coef-

3. In this paragraph about the cohort effect, we are temporarily assuming no altruism. The situation about the age profile of consumption by the age of the head for extended families will get more complicated if the two generations are altruistically linked. See the next paragraph.

ficients can indeed be interpreted as the age profile of consumption. However, if there is altruism, then the second effect must be taken into account. Even if the age profile of consumption within the family is flat, because of the second negative effect, the coefficient on old people can be smaller than that on young people in the same household. This explains the low coefficient on old people in the consumption regression in table 6.16.

A similar line of argument can be applied to explain the asset regression. Suppose for a moment that all parents live with their children and that no child has a parent maintaining a separate household. Thus, if there is a family without old people, that family has already received bequests from deceased parents. Compare family A with old people and family B without old people. On average, family A should have *lower* assets because of the asset depletion by the old. Thus, the coefficient of the number of old people should be *negative* in the family asset regression on a sample consisting of those two types of families. Now recognize the fact that some children (especially the eldest son) live separately from their parents. The sample therefore contains two additional types of families: young families whose surviving parents live separately from them and parents maintaining an independent household. If the family asset regression were run on just these last two types of households, then obviously the coefficient for the old should be *positive* and large if intergenerational transfers are in the form of bequests because family assets are still in the hands of independent parents. The actual data for Côte d'Ivoire contain all four types of families, so the coefficient on old people can be either positive or negative. If bequests are passed on to children on the death of the father without passing through the hands of his widow(s), then the assets will never reside in the fourth type of family, headed by an old mother (if there is one). This explains why the coefficient is negative for old females and positive for old males.

Conclusion

Deaton and Paxson have created a large set of informative and interesting tables. I could not find a single piece of evidence that is inconsistent with the simple dynasty model of saving.

7 Changing the Japanese Social Security System from Pay as You Go to Actuarially Fair

Tatsuo Hatta and Noriyoshi Oguchi

The current Japanese public pension system is essentially pay as you go; hence, its rate of return is not actuarially fair for each participant. This is the root of the three problems that the Japanese public pension system faces.

First, the system transfers income intergenerationally. In particular, the generation following the baby boomers is expected to make a large transfer to the baby boomer generation. By the year 2025, the average Japanese worker will have to support twice as many retirees as in 1990. This period, which is characterized by a higher percentage of retirees, will be referred to in this paper as the high-average-age period (HAAP). The arrival of the HAAP will increase the required social security contributions to maintain the promised benefits resulting in significant income redistributions among different generations. It may even make the very existence of the public pension system uncertain.

Second, the system also transfers income within each generation in a way that is difficult to justify. For example, the nonworking wife of a corporate president typically gets a much higher rate of return on her pension benefits than a worker of that company who never marries.

Third, since the social security contribution is not directly linked to the future benefit payments, the current system distorts the labor supply.

Had the system been actuarially fair from the beginning, these problems would not have arisen. Once a pay-as-you-go system is in place, however,

Tatsuo Hatta is professor of economics at Osaka University. Noriyoshi Oguchi is associate professor of economics at Tsukuba University.

The authors are grateful to Charles Horioka, Edward Lazear, and Fumio Otake for their useful comments and to Laurence Kotlikoff for bringing Boskin, Kotlikoff, and Shoven (1985) to our attention. Research assistance by Paula DeMasi, Takashi Oyama, and Maye Chen is gratefully acknowledged. The paper was written while Hatta was visiting the Economics Department of Harvard University. He would like to thank Dale Jorgenson and the department for their hospitality.

making it actuarially fair may create new problems. The principal aim of the present paper is to evaluate the economic effects of various reform plans that would eventually make the system actuarially fair.

Specifically, we examine the following three plans.[1]

1. *Switch to the Fully Funded System.* This quickly increases the government budget surplus to the level of social security wealth before the arrival of the HAAP.
2. *Switch to the Actuarially Fair System.* This switches the system over to an actuarially fair one before the HAAP. People in the baby boomer and subsequent generations will contribute the amount that exactly matches benefits received. The cumulative budget surplus never reaches the level of the social security wealth; the system never becomes fully funded.
3. *Gradual Shift to the Fully Funded System.* After an actuarially fair system is established as in plan 2, several generations pay taxes at levels greater than the actuarially fair amount until the system is eventually made fully funded. The burdens of building up the fund are shared by several generations.

Note that plan 3 contains the other two plans as special cases: plan 3 degenerates into plan 1 if it takes only one generation to build up the full fund and into plan 2 if it takes an infinite number of generations. For discussion purposes, we will consider as plan 3 the reform whereby five generations after the baby boomers equally share the burden of building up the full fund. We will study the economic effects of these reform plans on intergenerational income transfers, national saving, and government surplus using the simplest possible overlapping generation model that incorporates the HAAP.

Auerbach and Kotlikoff's (1984, 1985, 1987) pioneering work studies various economic effects of reforming a social security system in the face of demographic changes. Their empirical simulation model incorporates production function and realistic demographic changes. Honma, Atoda, and Otake (1988) and Otake (1989) also develop such models for the Japanese economy. Noguchi (1987a, 1987b) presents a model that is more abstract in production than these others but one that still assumes substitution between factors. We, on the other hand, employ a simulation model that abstracts from reality to an extreme degree. For example, per capita output level is fixed, the interest is

1. Auerbach and Kotlikoff (1984, 1985, 1987) examine the economic effects of plan 1 for the U.S. economy. Plan 2 is similar to Boskin, Kotlikoff, and Shoven's (1985) reform proposal for the United States. It is also similar to Tsukahara's (1989) "modified pay-as-you-go plan" and Honma, Atoda, and Otake's (1988) and Otake's (1989) "switch to the fully funded." Tsukahara's plan, which essentially preserves the features of the pay-as-you-go system, does not solve the problems of intragenerational distribution and labor disincentives. But his plan and our plan 2 yield identical economic effects on intergenerational distribution, national saving, and budget deficit. Honma, Atoda, and Otake (1988) and Otake (1988) assume that the pension participants do not realize the link between the social security tax and the benefit; hence, even intergenerational distributional effects are quite different from our plan 2. Hatta (1988) and Hatta and Oguchi (1989a, 1989b) propose plan 3.

given by the foreign country, and consumers have Cobb-Douglas utility functions. There are three purposes for this abstraction.

First, our model isolates the effects of the arrival of the HAAP under various public pension plans. Thus, it brings to the surface the common patterns of interactions between the HAAP and public pension plans underlying the various models constructed for both the Japanese and the U.S. economies. Also, it produces qualitative results associated with pension systems thus far found only through complicated models, such as Auerbach et al.'s (1989) observations that a pay-as-you-go system creates a positive saving after the HAAP.

Second, our model brings out sharply the qualitative differences in the economic effects between immediately building up the social security fund and merely making the system an actuarially fair but unfunded one.

Third, our model enables us readily to analyze the net government transfer to the private sector created by different public pension systems. In particular, we will give an institutional framework where the government net transfer to the private sector is represented by an increase in the balance of a government bond. It will be shown that the government could attain exactly the same economic effects as our reform plans 2 and 3 by taking the following steps: (*a*) issuing a government bond, to be called the "liquidation bond," that pays off the pension benefits of the retired at the time of reform; (*b*) immediately establishing the pension funds for subsequent generations; and (*c*) possibly redeeming the bond by increasing tax rates on subsequent generations.

After a brief review in section 7.1 of the policy issues associated with the Japanese social security system, we present the model and compare the economic effects of adapting a pay-as-you-go and a fully funded system in section 7.2. Section 7.3 discusses the effects of reforming the social security system. Section 7.4 in turn examines the effects of the reform plans on the cumulative government transfer to the private sector, and section 7.5 explores the public pension fund as an accounting concept. Concluding remarks are given in section 7.6.

7.1 Issues in the Japanese Public Pension System

In this section, we describe the public pension system in Japan and the policy issues associated with it.

7.1.1 The Public Pension System of Japan

Japan has three major public pension systems:

a) the private-sector-employee pension system;
b) the government-employee pension system; and
c) people's pension system.

The first two systems share similar structures in that both have two benefit components: the basic pension benefits and the earnings-related pension benefits. The former component yields benefits solely on the basis of years of participation; it does not reflect the participant's earnings.

Anyone who is not covered by the first two pension systems is required to join the people's pension system. This provides benefits identical to those of the basic pension component of the first two systems. The required contribution for the people's pension system is ¥8,400 ($60) per month per person. In the employee pension systems, all the benefit payments including the basic pension benefit are financed by the earnings-related social security taxes as well as by the government subsidies. In March 1990, the social security tax rate for the private-sector-employee pension system was 14.3 percent of the "standard monthly earnings" for men and 13.8 percent for women.

The basic pension benefit for a participant of forty years is ¥55,500 ($400) per month, and benefit payments start at age 65. Payments for the private-sector-employee pension systems start at age 60 for men and 58 for women. The three pension systems are subsidized by the General Account of the government budget, which is financed by non–social security taxes. All three systems can be considered virtually pay-as-you-go systems. Indeed, Ueda, Iwai, and Hashimoto (1987) estimate that, for a household headed by a 60-year-old in 1985, the percentage of a government transfer in pension benefits is 87 percent for the private-sector system and 85 percent for the people's pension.

The postwar Japanese public pension systems were established in 1954, overhauling the then existing systems. The new systems were essentially fully funded at the beginning. As time passed, however, benefits were raised more than contributions, and they became less and less fully funded. This tendency toward a pay-as-you-go system became entrenched by the reform in 1973, which introduced indexation and set the replacement ratio to be 60 percent for an average earner. It was carried out under the extreme optimism of a pre-OPEC high-growth period.

7.1.2 Intergenerational Redistribution

When a more modest growth rate is expected, maintaining a replacement ratio of 60 percent will cause a rapid depletion of the accumulated fund. Since a sharp demographic change is expected in Japan, this will entail a heavy burden on the working-age generation as the percentage of the retired population increases.

As figure 7.1 shows, the ratio of those people 65 years of age or older to the total population stayed constant until the mid-1950s but has risen sharply since then. This ratio is expected to rise until approximately 2025. In fact, it is predicted that it will double in only twenty-six years in Japan, whereas it took 115 years in France, eighty-five years in Sweden and forty-five years in the United Kingdom and West Germany for this ratio to increase from 7 to 14 percent. This steep increase in the proportion of aged people reflects a significant decline in the mortality rate during the postwar period and a sharp rise in the birth rate immediately after the war.

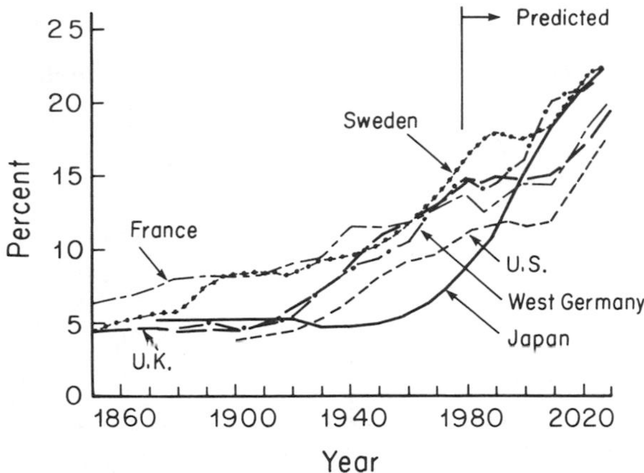

Fig. 7.1 The percentage of those 65 years old or older to the total population
Source: Institute of Demographic Studies, Ministry of Welfare, *Demographic Statistics* (1986).

Figure 7.2 shows the age-based demographic composition of Japan in 1985. We see a relatively high concentration of the population between the ages of 35 and 60, including a bulge at ages 35–40 that reflects the postwar baby boom. Under a pay-as-you-go system, this demographic structure will cause large income transfers from the post–baby boomers to the baby boomers.

7.1.3 Intragenerational Redistribution

The Japanese pension systems redistribute income not only among different generations but also within each generation. Although a certain limited equalization of income within a generation occurs, income is also redistributed in directions that are difficult to justify:

1. *From the wives of the self-employed to the nonworking wives of the employed.* The wife of a self-employed person has to join the people's pension and make social security contributions in order to receive basic pension benefits in the future. The nonworking wife of the employed person can receive the same benefits without any additional contributions made either by herself or by her husband.
2. *From unmarried employees to nonworking wives of employees.* A nonworking wife of an employee receives the following from her husband's employee pension system: (*a*) survivors' benefits if the husband dies; and (*b*) basic pension benefits. Despite these additional benefits given to the wife, her husband's social security contribution stays the same regardless of his marital status. The rate of return on public pension that a nonworking wife of a company president receives is much higher than that of a worker of the same company who stays single for her entire life.

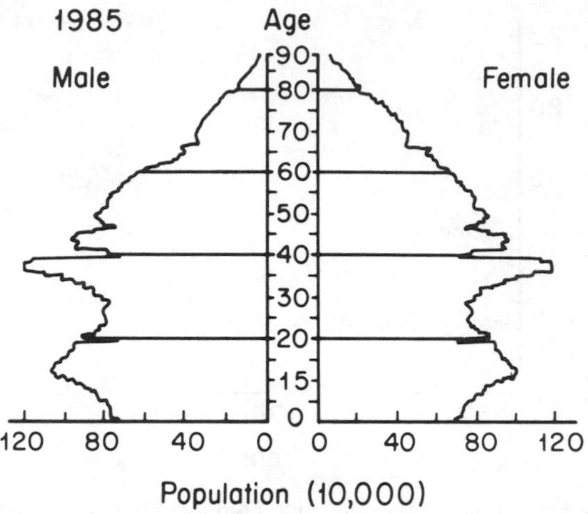

Fig. 7.2 Japan's demographic composition by age
Source: Ministry of Welfare, *Nihon no Jinkou—Nihon no Shakai* (Demography of Japan—Society of Japan) Tokyo: Toyo Keizai Shinposha Press, 1988, 104.

3. *From the working wives of employees to the nonworking wives of employees.* When the husband of a working wife dies, she has to choose between receiving benefits from her own employee pension or survivors' benefits from her husband's pension. She cannot receive both. If she chooses the former, she cannot enjoy the benefits that all nonworking wives receive. If she chooses the latter, she wastes the contributions she has made to her own pension program.

The rate of return on the current pension system is not linked to the market rate of return. Because of this, it is hard for an individual to estimate how much net benefit or loss he or she receives from the public pension system. This creates a situation where political forces tend to dominate the direction of redistribution. This seems to be the reason why the Japanese pension system has erratic income transfers.

7.1.4 Policy Issues

To sum up the arguments so far, the Japanese social security system is essentially pay as you go rather than actuarially fair, and this fact is the source of the dual problems of inter- and intragenerational redistribution the system has. This fact also creates two other well-known problems.

First, the pay-as-you-go system distorts labor supply. The participant in this system perceives the social security contribution as a tax since there is no clear-cut link between future benefits and the amount of the contribution he makes now. The Japanese system especially discourages housewives' participation in full-time employment. On the other hand, an actuarially fair social security system does not distort labor supply. An actuarially fair system gives the same rate of return as the market return. Thus, a contributor will perceive the contribution as his own saving and hence as a part of his own income.

Second, the pay-as-you-go system reduces the cumulative saving of an economy since people will reduce their saving for retirement when the benefits are guaranteed in the future. If the government has increased its saving by the amount that individuals have reduced private saving, then national saving will not be affected. Under the pay-as-you-go system, however, the social security contribution will be used up for the benefit payments to the current recipients, and the government will maintain, not increase, its saving. The pay-as-you-go system, therefore, reduces national saving.

These problems would not have arisen had the system been actuarially fair.[2]

7.2 Basic Pension Systems

In this section, we formally analyze the effects of introducing a pay-as-you-go public pension system and compare them with these of introducing a fully funded system. We will focus particularly on the effects on intergenerational redistribution, national saving, and budget surplus.

7.2.1 The Model

The Japanese social security system is characterized by the relatively recent implementation of a pay-as-you-go system and a rapidly increasing proportion of aged people. In this section, we present the simplest possible model that captures these characteristics.

Consider a two-period life-cycle model, where the working period and the retirement period are of equal length. There are an infinite number of generations, but we focus on ten, which we refer to as 0–IX. Among them, generation III is the baby boom generation; we assume that its population consists of two people, while all other generations contain one person. In each period, the generation in its working age and another in its retirement live concurrently. Figure 7.3 depicts the population size of each generation in each period. The horizontal axis measures the period and the vertical axis the generations. The white boxes show the size of the working-age population and the shaded boxes the size of the population in retirement.

In interpreting this model in the context of the Japanese economy, we regard the working ages to be 40–59 and the retirement ages to be 60–79. The former may be partially justified because the wage profile rises steeply in the Japanese seniority system. In view of figure 7.2, it is possible to regard generation I as

2. The U.S. Social Security system shares many of these problems, as pointed out by Kotlikoff 1987). An important difference between the Japanese and the U.S. systems is that there is little penalty for working in the Japanese system.

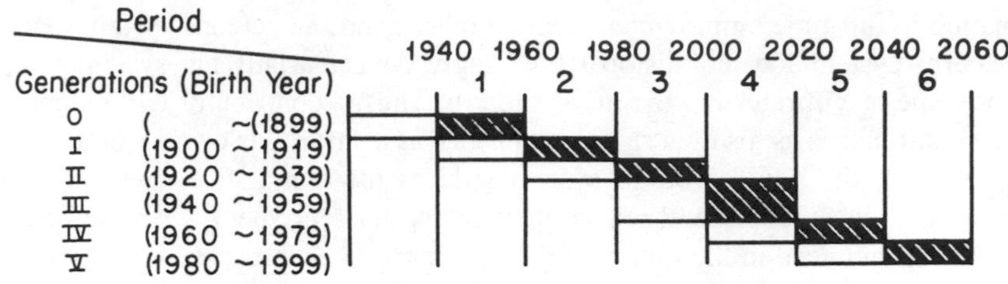

Fig. 7.3 Demographic composition

born between 1900 and 1919, generation II between 1920 and 1939, generation III between 1940 and 1959, and generation IV between 1960 and 1979.

We assume that one worker produces ten units of output when he is young but does not work in old age. Accordingly, we have

(1) $$Y_t = 10N_t,$$

where Y_t is the output level of the economy and N_t the population size of the working generation in period t.

We further assume that an individual saves half his expected lifetime disposable income when he is young and dissaves it when he retires. (This amounts to assuming a Cobb-Douglas utility function.) The interest rate is assumed to be zero. The government has no expenditures other than pensions, and there are no taxes other than the social security tax. Taxes are imposed only on the working generation of the period. There are no inheritances or bequests. Thus, the aggregate budget equation for the working generation in period t is written as

(2) $$C^y_t = C^r_{t+1} = (Y_t + B_{t+1} - T_t)/2,$$

where C^y_t is the aggregate consumption level of the working generation in period t, C^r_{t+1} is that of the retired generation in period $t + 1$, B_{t+1} is the public pension benefit that the retired generation in period $t + 1$ receives, and T_t is the tax that the working generation pays in period t.

When no public pension system exists, a person in any generation consumes five units during his working years and another five units during his retirement years. The consumption of any person in any period is equal. Define national saving, S_t, by

(3) $$S_t = Y_t - C^y_t - C^r_t.$$

There is no investment in this economy, and the macro saving gap is adjusted by the balance of trade. Positive national saving implies a surplus in the balance of payments, while positive cumulative national saving implies a positive net foreign asset position.

Once N_t, B_{t+1}, and T_t are given, equation (1) determines the output level, (2) the consumption levels, and (3) the national saving.

7.2.2 Intergenerational Redistribution

Let b_t be the social security benefit one retiree receives in period t and τ_t the social security tax that a working person pays. Then by definition we obtain

$$T_t = \tau_t N_t \tag{4}$$

and

$$B_t = b_t N_{t-1}. \tag{5}$$

The *net benefit* or *net transfer* that a working person in period t receives during his lifetime, $g[t]$, is given by

$$g[t] = b_{t+1} - \tau_t.$$

Throughout the paper we assume that $b_t = b$ holds if the pension benefit is paid in period t. Thus, we have

$$g[t] = b - \tau_t.$$

A Fully Funded System

Now suppose that in period 2 an actuarially fair public pension system is introduced. By definition we have

$$B_{t+1} = T_t, \quad t > 1, \tag{6}$$

and, hence,

$$b = \tau_t, \quad t > 1.$$

This pension will not affect the consumption pattern of any generation and, hence, will not redistribute income among generations.

When a pension system is actuarially fair from the beginning of its establishment, the system has a cumulative budget surplus equal to the social security wealth, as we will see in section 7.2.4 below. Hence, we will call this system *fully funded.*

A Pay-as-You-Go System

Now suppose that the pay-as-you-go system is implemented in period 2. By definition, the benefits are financed by the social security taxes paid by the currently working generation. Thus,

$$B_t = T_t, \quad t > 1. \tag{7}$$

This yields

$$\tau_1 = 0$$

and

$$bN_{t-1} = \tau_t N_t, \quad t > 1.$$

Thus, the net benefit of each generation can be written as

$$g[1] = b$$

and

$$g[t] = b(1 - N_{t-1}/N_t), \quad t > 1.$$

After the system is introduced, therefore, the net benefit of the working generation in a given period is positive if and only if the population of the retired generation in the same period is smaller than its own.

Figure 7.4 depicts per capita pension benefits received, contributions, and net benefits of each generation under the assumption that $b = 4$. (We will make this assumption in all subsequent figures.) The benefits are shown as a positive number and contributions as a negative number; if the net benefit line is above (below) the horizontal axis for a generation, it receives a net benefit (loss).

The figure reveals two features of a pay-as-you-go system. First, the introduction of the system increases the sum of consumption of all generations. Figure 7.4 shows that the net benefit of generation III is equal to the net loss of generation IV since the population size of the former is twice the latter. Hence, the economy as a whole gains by the net benefit of generation I, that is, by four. Thus, the introduction of a pay-as-you-go system creates a net increase in the consumption for the economy as a whole.

Second, an introduction of the pay-as-you-go system creates income inequity among generations, as observed earlier. Generation I, which is in retirement when the pension system is introduced, receives the most net benefits from the system. The baby boomers receive net benefits to some extent because the tax rate they face when young is low. Generation IV, which comes immediately after the baby boom generation, receives negative net benefits because it has to support the retired baby boomers.

7.2.3 National Saving

Public pension systems affect national saving. We now turn to study this relation in the face of demographic changes.

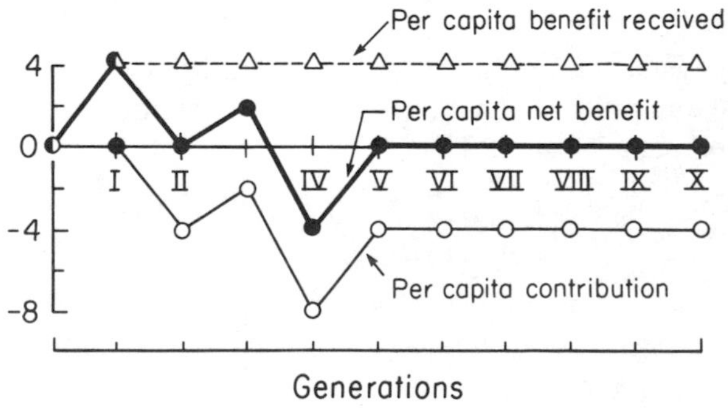

Fig. 7.4 Net benefits under the pay-as-you-go system

Even in the absence of a public pension system, fluctuations in demographic composition can cause national saving to vary each period in our model, where the per capita saving of each generation is kept constant. Indeed, from (1), (3), (5), and (6), we have

$$\begin{aligned} S_t &= Y_t - \frac{1}{2}Y_t - \frac{1}{2}Y_{t-1} \\ &= 5(N_t - N_{t-1}). \end{aligned}$$

The national saving is therefore positive (negative) if the population size of the working generation is greater (less) than that of the retired generation.

The thick line of figure 7.5a shows the fluctuations of national saving when a public pension system is unavailable. The level of national saving reaches its peak in period 3, when the baby boomers are of working age, while it reaches its bottom in period 4, when a large number of baby boomers are dissaving.[3]

The thick line in figure 7.5b shows the cumulative balance of national saving when a public pension system is unavailable. The balance is positive when the baby boomers are of working age; it reaches zero when they are retired and remains zero afterward.

A Fully Funded System

As previously observed, the introduction of an actuarially fair pension system does not affect the consumption patterns of any generation and, hence, does not affect national saving in any period.

A Pay-as-You-Go System

The introduction of a pay-as-you-go public pension system in period 2, however, does affect consumption patterns and therefore national saving.

The retired in period 2 will consume all the unexpected benefit in this period, which yields

$$C_2^r = \frac{1}{2}Y_1 + B_2.$$

Also, from (2) and (3) we have

$$C_t^y = C_{t+1}^r = (Y_t + B_{t+1} - B_t)/2, \quad t > 1. \tag{8}$$

In view of (3), (1), and (5), therefore, we have the following:

3. As fig. 7.5a shows, the post-HAAP dissaving occurs regardless of the pension system. Horioka (1989), using a saving function based on international cross-sectional data of demographic compositions and saving ratios, predicts that Japanese private saving will become negative after 2012, when the ratio of retirees to working-aged people becomes high. Fukao and Doi (1985), Noguchi (1987a), and Auerbach et al. (1989) also obtain similar predictions.

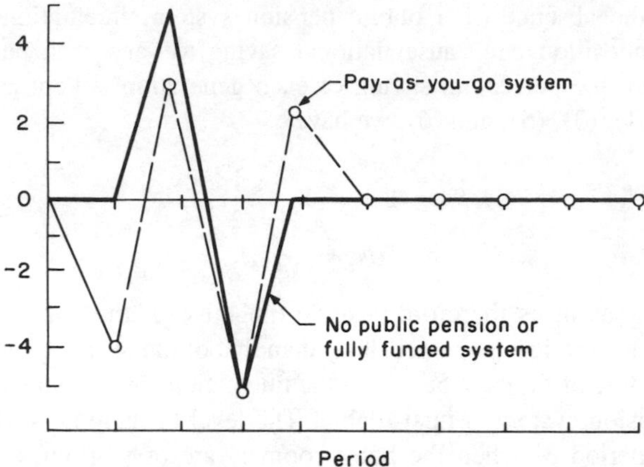

Fig. 7.5a **National saving**

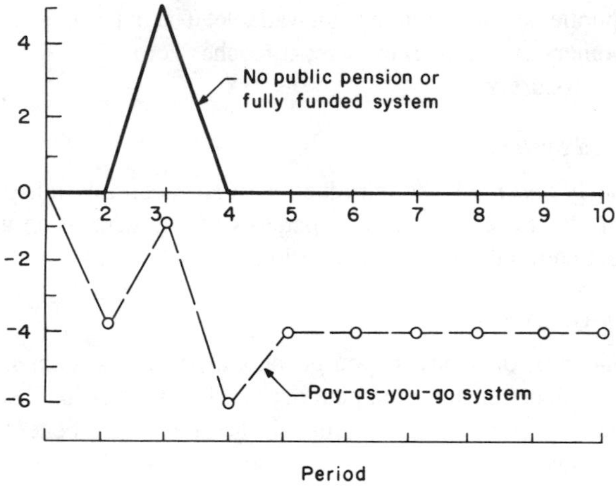

Fig. 7.5b **Cumulative balance of national saving**

$$S_2 = 5(N_2 - N_1) - \frac{b}{2}(N_2 + N_1),$$

$$S_t = 5(N_t - N_{t-1}) - \frac{b}{2}(N_t - N_{t-2}), \quad t > 2.$$

Thus, national saving in a given period is influenced by the population size of the current and possibly two preceding generations.

The thin line in figure 7.5a indicates the fluctuations of national saving under the pay-as-you-go public pension system. The graph has two troughs and two peaks. The first peak in period 3, which immediately precedes the HAAP, is lower than under the fully funded system. The positive saving in the second peak in period 5, which is immediately after the HAAP, did not exist under the fully funded system. Two factors explain these features.

The first relates to the consumption surge by generation I in period 2, which receives the unexpected free-ride benefits from the newly started social security system. This creates a negative saving balance in the second period. If the population size did not change thereafter, national saving in each period after period 2 would remain zero permanently.

The second relates to the existence of the baby boomers, or generation III. In period 3, the baby boomers, who are then in their working years, consume more under the pay-as-you-go system than under the fully funded system because they receive positive net benefits during their lifetime. This is the reason why national saving is smaller under the pay-as-you-go system than under the fully funded system. Moreover, national saving in period 5, which is immediately after the HAAP, is positive because the post–baby boomer generation, with reduced per capita lifetime disposable income, is dissaving in this period at a lower rate than under the fully funded system. This was called the "overshooting" of saving by Auerbach et al. (1989).

The thin line in figure 7.5b indicates that the negative cumulative balance of savings in period 2 is created by generation I, as we have already discussed. The balance fluctuates during periods 3 and 4, when baby boomers work and retire. In period 5, when the baby boomers have disappeared, the savings balance returns to its original level and remains constant. Even if the baby boomer generation did not exist and the population remained constant, the negative cumulative balance of savings created in period 2 would remain permanently. Thus, the influence of the baby boomers on the cumulative balance of savings is transitory; the cumulative balance returns to the pre–baby boom level when the economy returns to the steady state.

In sum, the introduction of a pay-as-you-go public pension system immediately creates a negative national saving balance, which is carried forward permanently. On the other hand, the saving fluctuations caused by the baby boomers eventually die out and, therefore, have no long run effect.

We pointed out in section 7.2.2 that the introduction of the pay-as-you-go system increases the sum of the consumption of all generations by the amount of the net benefits received by the first generation. The introduction of the pay-as-you-go system also creates the negative cumulative balance of savings to be carried forward to future generations by the amount that is exactly equal to the net benefits to the first generation. In other words, the "consumption increase" caused by the pay-as-you-go system is made possible by a reduction in the cumulative saving; the apparent welfare improvement is a result of a Ponzi game. A correct evaluation of the welfare increase must be based on a combined consideration of the utility increase and the change in the cumulative saving, which embodies the potential utility.

7.2.4 Budget Surplus

The government budget surplus and deficit created by a public pension system rightly or wrongly have attracted public attention.[4]

Define the government *budget surplus*, S_t^g, by

$$S_t^g = T_t - B_t. \tag{9}$$

Assuming that there was no public pension system until $t = 0$, we can write the *cumulative budget surplus*, Z_t^g, as

$$Z_t^g = \Sigma_0^t S_j^g. \tag{10}$$

When there is no public pension system, $T_t = B_t = 0$ holds; hence, the yearly and cumulative budget surpluses are zero in any period.

A Fully Funded System

A social security system may be called actuarially fair in period t if it satisfies (6) for a given t. It may be called *fully funded* in period t if the cumulative budget surplus is equal to the social security wealth, that is, if it satisfies

$$Z_t^g = B_{t+1} \tag{11}$$

for a given t. Note that, in general, a system satisfying (6) in period t does not necessarily satisfy (11) for the same t if

$$S_j^g \neq 0 \quad \text{for some } j < t.$$

Thus, a system that happens to be actuarially fair in a given period is not necessarily fully funded in the same period.

Suppose that an actuarially fair pension system is introduced in period 2 in the same manner as before. Then (6) holds for all $t > 1$. This and (9) yield

$$\begin{aligned} S_t^g &= B_{t+1} - B_t \\ &= b(N_t - N_{t-1}) \end{aligned} \tag{12}$$

for all $t > 1$. Thus, the relative population size of the working and retired generations determines the budget surplus.

The thin line in figure 7.6a shows the budget surplus under this system. It indicates that government saving is positive in period 2, when the system is introduced, since no benefits are paid out in that period. It is also positive in period 3, when the baby boomers are in their working ages, because their contributions exceed the amount of benefits being paid out. Government saving turns negative in period 4, however, since the retirees outnumber the young. It remains zero thereafter.

Equations (10) and (12) imply that

4. The definition of budget surplus in the presence of a public pension system is arbitrary, as Kotlikoff (1986, 1988, 1989) has emphasized.

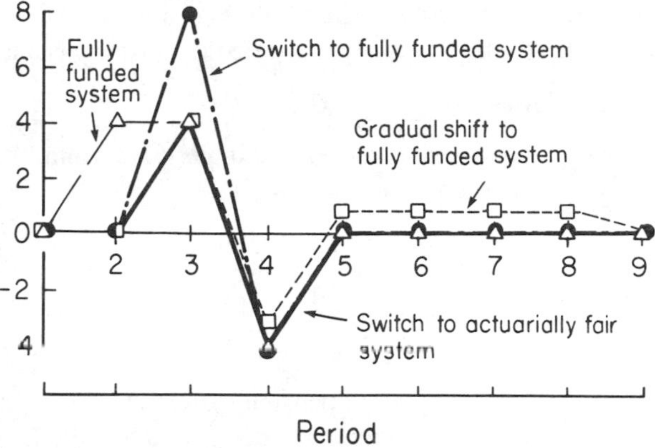

Fig. 7.6a Budget surplus after reforms

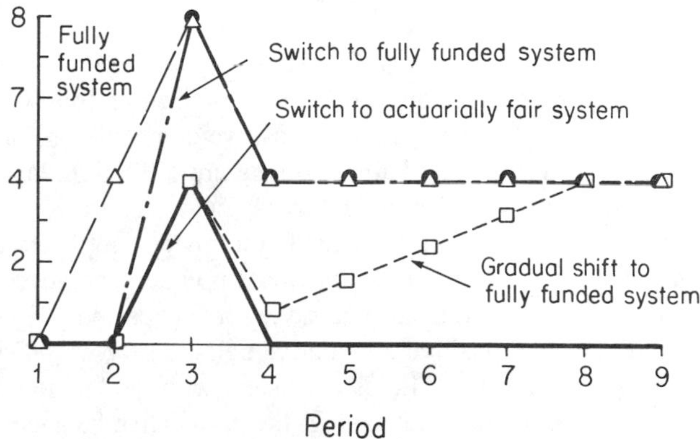

Fig. 7.6b Cumulative budget surplus after reforms.

$$\begin{aligned} Z_t^g &= \Sigma_2^t(B_{j+1} - B_j) \\ &= B_{t+1} - B_2 \end{aligned}$$

for all $t > 1$. Noting that $B_2 = 0$, we have (11) for all $t > 1$. If a social security system is actuarially fair in every period of its existence, therefore, it is also fully funded in each of these periods.

The thin line in figure 7.6b indicates the cumulative balance of the budget surplus under the fully funded system. It reaches its peak in period 3, when the baby boomers are in their working years, and returns to a steady-state level of four in period 4, when they retire. Under the fully funded system, therefore, the government will never have to borrow.

Despite the cumulative budget surplus it creates, the introduction of an actuarially fair pension system has no influence on the saving of the economy as a whole, as we have seen earlier. The positive government saving created by this system is exactly offset by the reduced saving by the consumers.

A Pay-as-You-Go System

If the pay-as-you-go system is introduced in period 2, from (9) and (3), the budget surplus is always zero, and we have

(13) $$S_t^g = 0, \quad t > 1.$$

This and (10) yield

(14) $$Z_t^g = 0, \quad t > 1.$$

The introduction of a pay-as-you-go pension system in an economy where no public pension system existed, therefore, does not affect the level of the cumulative budget surplus. This contrasts with our earlier observation that it affects the cumulative balance of national saving.

7.2.5 Summary

The observations in this section may be summarized as follows. First, in the absence of a public pension system, a positive cumulative balance of national saving is created when the baby boomers are of working age. But the cumulative balance returns to zero in the HAAP and afterward.

Second, an introduction of a fully funded system does not affect consumption patterns of any generation. Hence, it causes no intergenerational transfer of income. Nor does it affect the national saving in any periods. However, the introduction does create a positive cumulative balance of government budget surplus, or government saving. This is consistent with the fact that the introduction does not affect the national saving; the cumulative balance of private saving is reduced exactly to offset the budget surplus of the government.

Third, an introduction of a pay-as-you-go system creates a negative cumulative balance of national saving, which is permanently carried forward. Also, it creates income inequity among generations: it benefits the first and the baby boomer generations, while a net burden is borne by the generation that comes immediately after the baby boomers. Moreover, the introduction increases the sum of the present value of consumption of all generations while reducing the cumulative balance of saving at the steady state by exactly the same amount.

Thus, an introduction of a pay-as-you-go system creates income inequality among generations, but it does not create efficiency gain or loss within this model. If the model is expanded to incorporate elastic labor supply, then the price distortions created by the pay-as-you-go system will cause inefficiency on top of the income inequality that this model shows.

7.3 Evaluation of the Reform Plans

7.3.1 Overview

As we have seen in the previous two sections, if an actuarially fair system had been implemented from the beginning, it would not have caused such microeconomic problems associated with a pay-as-you-go system as inter- and intragenerational redistribution and labor supply disincentives.

Let us now assume that a pay-as-you-go system was introduced in period 2 and that the system is reformed in period 3 in order to attain an actuarial fairness eventually. Specifically, we will consider the effects of the three reform plans outlined above on intergenerational distribution, national saving, and government budget surplus.

7.3.2 Economic Effects

Switch to the Fully Funded

Let us first consider the reform that makes the system fully funded in period 3 and afterward, which we will call a *switch to the fully funded.* The reform will be attained by (*a*) raising the tax rate on generation III so as to finance not only the current benefit payment for generation II but also the future benefit payment for generation III and (*b*) imposing taxes on generation IV and subsequent generations by the amount equal to the benefits received. Thus, the taxes and benefits satisfy the following:[5]

(15)
$$T_3 = B_3 + B_4,$$
$$T_t = B_{t+1}, \quad t > 3.$$

Equations (15) imply that the per capita tax rates after the reform are

(16)
$$\tau_3 = b + b/2,$$
$$\tau_t = b, \quad t > 3.$$

The chain line in figure 7.7 depicts the net benefits of each generation after the switch to the fully funded. Generation IV and all subsequent generations receive zero net benefits. But the switch turns the net benefit of generation III from positive to negative.

The switch to the fully funded gives a rattle to the macroeconomic balance of period 3. The chain line in figure 7.8a shows this.[6] When the system is switched in period 3, national saving reaches a peak of seven, exceeding the

5. Since the system is made fully funded, (11) holds for all $t > 2$. In particular, $Z_3^g = B_4$. Since $Z_2^g = 0$, we have $S_t^g = B_4$. On the other hand, equations (9) and (10) yield $T_3 = B_4 + B_3$.

6. From (8), we have $C_3^r = 5$. From (1), (2), and (15), we attain $C_3^y = C_4^r = (20 - 4)/2 = 8$ and $C_t^y = C_{t+1}^r = (10 - 0)/2 = 5$ for $3 < t$. Thus, from (3), we obtain $S_3 = 20 - 13 = 7$, $S_4 = 10 - 13 = -3$, and $S_t = 0$ for $4 < t$.

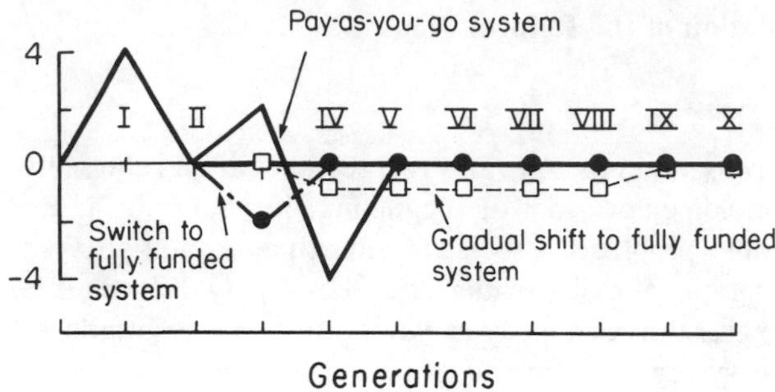

Fig. 7.7 Net benefits after reforms

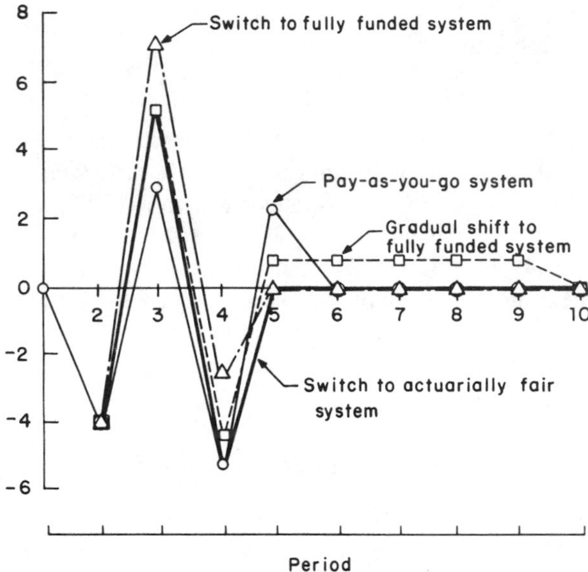

Fig. 7.8a National saving after reforms

level under the fully funded system. This is because the baby boomers now have to save more than they need for their own retirement. As the chain line in figure 7.8b depicts, the cumulative balance of national saving is no longer negative in period 4 and afterward.

The chain line in figure 7.6b shows that in period 3 the cumulative budget surplus becomes equal to the size of the social security wealth. The switch gives a wild fluctuation in government budget, as illustrated by the chain line in figure 7.6a.[7] It soars to eight in period 3, plummets to minus four in period 4, and then returns to zero after that period.

7. From (15) and (9), we have $S_3^g = (B_4 + 4) - B_3 = 8$, $S_4^g = B_5 - B_4 = -4$, and $S_t^g = B_{t+1} - B_t = 0$ for $t > 4$.

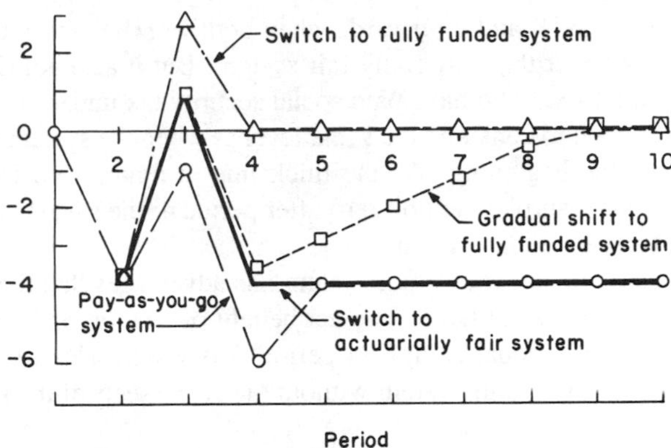

Fig. 7.8b Cumulative national savings after reforms

Even though the problems of the Japanese public pension system pointed out earlier will disappear in the HAAP and afterward, this reform is politically difficult to accomplish. First, it puts a large burden on the baby boom generation—the working and the decision-making generation when the switch is made. Second, it will have the destabilizing macro effect in the HAAP.

Switch to the Actuarially Fair System

The system can be made actuarially fair without being accompanied by the shortcomings that the switch to the fully funded causes.

Let us assume that the pay-as-you-go system is switched to an actuarially fair one in period 3. This reform will be attained by making the tax rate on generation III and subsequent generations exactly equal to the present value of the benefit each of them receives. Thus, we have (6) for all $t - 2$; hence,

(17) $$t_t = B_{t+1}, \quad t \geq 3.$$

This implies that the per capita tax rates after the reform are

$$\tau_t = b, \quad t \geq 2.$$

We will call this reform a *switch to an actuarially fair system.* Generation III faces a higher tax rate after the reform under this system than under the pay-as-you-go system.

The horizontal axis in figure 7.7 depicts the net benefits of each generation after this reform. Generation III and all subsequent generations receive zero net benefit. Thus, intergenerational income inequity is eliminated after the reform.

In period 3 and afterward, national saving is equal to the level that would be attained if the system were actuarially fair from the beginning, as the thick line in figure 7.8a depicts. (Compare this and the thick line in fig. 7.5a.) This is natural for period 4 and afterward, when both working and retired generations live only under the actuarially fair system. But it also holds in period 3 since the then retired, who have paid social security tax under the pay-as-you-go system, happen to consume the same level as when the system was actuarially fair from the beginning. As the thick line in figure 7.6b indicates, the cumulative budget surplus will be zero after period 4; the system will never be made fully funded by this reform.

The switch to an actuarially fair system has advantages that the switch to a fully funded one does not have. The net benefit of generation III is no longer negative, and the national saving in period 3 is lower. This reform has the merits of an actuarially fair system without the side effects of the switch to the fully funded.

Gradual Shift to the Fully Funded System

From the macroeconomic viewpoint, there is a difference between the fully funded system and the merely actuarially fair system discussed above; the cumulative balance of national saving is zero in the former when the steady state is reached, while it remains negative in the latter. In some situations, because of the macroeconomic considerations it may be necessary to make the system fully funded eventually. The following gradual reform would do this without causing the turbulence associated with the switch to the fully funded:

a) First, switch the system to actuarially fair in period 3.

b) Then impose taxes on several generations subsequent to the baby boomers at rates higher than the actuarially fair level of the expected social security benefits in order to build up the cumulative budget surplus. This process would continue until the system is made fully funded. We will call that portion of taxes paid by a generation in excess of the actuarially fair level of the expected benefit the *pension surtax* of the generation.[8] Thus the several generations after the baby boom generation pay actuarially fair taxes plus pension surtaxes.

c) After the system becomes fully funded, the pension surtaxes are eliminated, and the system returns to actuarially fair.

To make the proposal concrete, we assume that a pension surtax of 0.8 is imposed on each person in generations IV–VIII so as to make the cumulative budget surplus in period 9 exactly equal to social security wealth. Thus, taxes after the reform may be written as

$$
\begin{aligned}
T_3 &= B_4, \\
T_t &= B_{t+1} + .8N_t, \quad 3 < t < 9, \\
T_t &= B_{t+1}, \quad 8 < t.
\end{aligned}
\tag{18}
$$

8. In the context of this reform, there are no unexpected benefits, and the pension surtax is equal to the difference between the tax payments and the total benefit receipts of the generation concerned. Thus, the pension surtax is equal to the negative of the net pension benefit received by the generation in this case.

The corresponding per capita tax rates are

$$\begin{aligned} \tau_3 &= b, \\ \tau_t &= b + .8, \quad 3 < t < 9, \qquad (19) \\ \tau_t &= b, \quad 8 < t. \end{aligned}$$

We will call this reform *gradual shift to fully funded.*

Intergenerational Redistribution. The dashed line in figure 7.7 depicts the net benefits of each generation under the gradual shift. Generations I and II are not affected by this shift. On the other hand, each member of generation III now receives zero net benefits. Since generation IV and subsequent generations pay a pension surtax of 0.8 in addition to the four units of the actuarially fair contribution to the pension fund, each member of these generations pays 4.8 in total per capita tax while receiving four units of benefit. The figure clearly shows that the shift mitigates the inequity of income distribution among generations.

Macro Balance. The dashed line in figure 7.8a shows that, when the system is reformed in period 3, national saving reaches five, equaling the level under the fully funded system.[9] This level is higher than under the pay-as-you-go system but lower than under the switch to the fully funded. The reform reduces the national dissaving in HAAP (period 4) to 4.6 from the level of five under the pay-as-you-go system. This is because the reform reduces the consumption of the baby boomer generation in this period more than it increases the consumption of the post–baby boomer generation. The reform makes national saving in period 5 lower than under the pay-as-you-go system. This is because the post–baby boom generation now consumes more; it no longer has to support the baby boomers, who now finance their retirement consumption by the pension fund that they themselves have accumulated during their working years.

During periods 4–9, saving under this regime is higher than under the pay-as-you-go system. The reason is that generations IV–IX reduce their consumption to pay the pension surtax. We have seen that the negative cumulative balance of saving remains permanently under the pay-as-you-go system as indicated by the thick line in figure 7.8b. On the other hand, the dashed line in that figure shows that the level of national debt is gradually reduced after the reform and reaches zero in period 9 under the gradual shift. This reduction essentially pays off the consumption increase enjoyed by generation I at the time the pay-as-you-go system was created.

Thus, the gradual shift reduces the fluctuations of national saving and the

9. We have $C_3^r = 5$ from (8) and $C_3^y = C_4^r = 10$ and $C_t^y = C_{t+1}^r = 4.6$ for $3 < t\ 9$ from (19) and (2). Thus, we obtain $S_3 = 20 - 15 = 5$, $S_4 = 10 - 14.6 = -4.6$, $S_t = 10 - 9.2 = .8$ for $4 < t < 9$, $S_9 = 10 - 9.6 = .4$, and $S_t = 0$ for $9 < t$.

trade balance associated with the arrival of the HAAP but gives macro repercussions for a longer period than the reforms considered earlier.

Budget Surplus. The dashed line in figure 7.6a shows the budget surplus.[10] It takes a positive value in period 3, when the baby boomer generation is paying the pension tax. In period 4, when the baby boomers retire, the high level of benefit payments leads to negative government saving. But the size of the deficit is not quite as big as in the case of pay-as-you-go because generation IV and subsequent generations are paying the pension surtax. The government surplus remains positive from period 5 through period 8 for the same reason. Figure 7.6b shows the process of accumulating the cumulative balance of the budget surplus to the steady-state level of the pension fund.

7.3.3 Evaluation of Reform Plans

Switching the pension system to fully funded before the arrival of the HAAP places an unusually high burden on the baby boom generation, creating new inequity among generations. At the time of reform, it also creates a large national saving that even exceeds the amount that would take place if the system were fully funded from the beginning. Thus, this reform causes instability both in distribution and in macro balance during the transition phase.

We have examined two other reform plans that make the system actuarially fair eventually. Both will reduce intergenerational distributional inequity and labor disincentive problems associated with the current system, but neither creates the transitional problems. The switch to the actuarially fair system never builds up a cumulative government budget surplus to the level of social security wealth, while the gradual shift eventually builds up a cumulative budget surplus to that level. The choice between the two reforms should be made on the basis of macroeconomic considerations.

In fact, the final target of the cumulative government surplus need not be limited to the level of either zero or the social security wealth. Any amount in between the two levels or even an amount above the social security wealth level will do. Gradually building up the cumulative budget surplus toward any such amount after first making the system actuarially fair will be more desirable than continuing the pay-as-you-go system or the switch to the fully funded, so long as such a surplus is built up through a fair allocation of the pension surtax rates among different generations.

So far we have assumed that the interest rate is zero. In the economy where the international interest rate is positive, switching the system to actuarially fair is critically different from the gradual shift to the fully funded in that the latter reduces the interest payment to foreign countries to zero when the re-

10. The government budget surpluses are obtained from (18) and (9): $S_3^g = B_4 - B_3 = 4$, $S_4^g = (B_5 + .8) - B_4 = 4.8 - 8 = -3.2$, $S_t^g = .8$ for $4 < t < 9$, and $S_t^g = 0$ for $8 < t$.

form is completed, whereas the former does not. Even then, however, the present value of the total income from foreign investments exactly matches the present value of the sum of the pension surtaxes collected to build up the budget surplus. Under both these reform plans, postreform generations are contributing at least an actuarially fair amount for their pension systems. The question here is how much surtax should be imposed on these generations to pay off the national debt caused by the prereform generations, in particular the first generation. This is not a problem specific to the pension reform, but it should be viewed as a type of the general optimal saving problem.

7.4 Government Saving in the Agency View

7.4.1 The Principal View versus the Agency View

In the previous section, we defined the government budget surplus by (9). Budget surplus (or deficit), however, is "an inherently arbitrary accounting construct," as Kotlikoff (1986, 53) eloquently argues. Budget surplus or government saving is more generally defined as follows:

(20) $$\text{Government saving} = \text{Government revenue} - \text{Government expenditures}.$$

What should be called government revenue or government expenditures is not unique. For example, depending on whether the social security contributions are treated as a tax or as private saving, the amount of government revenue changes.

The Principal View

We have so far regarded social security contributions as government tax revenue and benefit payments as government expenditures. Government saving was equal to the difference between the social security contributions and benefits. Thus, the government was regarded as the saving principal rather than as an agent who simply manages the saving of the private sector. We will call this the *principal view* of government saving. When we refer to *government saving* or *budget surplus* later without qualifications, the concept will be in the principal view.

The Agency View

Alternatively, we may regard the social security system as a pension system that a government operates in lieu of private pension funds. We will call this the *agency view* of government saving since the government is viewed as an agent who manages the saving of the private sector.

In the agency view, the portion of the social security contribution that matches the expected future benefits is regarded as a premium for the pension, and hence private saving, but not as a tax. Thus, only the pension surtax (the portion of social security contribution that exceeds the actuarially fair present value of the expected benefits) is regarded as the tax paid by the working generation of the given period. Similarly, the expected portion of the social security benefits may be regarded as the dissaving of the retirees in the program rather than as their income and government expenditure. Only the unexpected benefits paid in the given period may be regarded as the income of the retirees and a government expenditure in that period. The government saving in the agency view in a given period is, therefore, equal to the pension surtax paid by the working generation minus the unexpected benefits paid to the retirees of the period.

This view regards the government as managing an imaginary public pension fund, from which the retiree withdraws benefits and to which the working generation makes actuarially fair contributions. We will call this imaginary pension fund the Pension Fund, which is essentially an accounting concept.

In the agency view, therefore, the government's involvement with the public pension is twofold: (i) receiving (or making) a transfer from (to) each generation and (ii) managing an actuarially fair Pension Fund. We will discuss the transfer between the government and the private sector in the rest of this section and the Pension Fund in section 7.5.

7.4.2 The Budget Surplus in the Agency View and Income Transfers

We can regard the income transfers between a person and the government through a pension system to be generated either at the time of his retirement or at the time he realizes that he can expect to receive benefits in the future. We will call the former the *postpaid version* and the latter the *prepaid version* of the agency view.

If a pension system already exists, working-age people will expect to receive benefits in their retirement. They plan their lifetime consumption in their youth after taking into account their total lifetime income, including the net income transfer. Thus, it is natural to consider that the net income transfer to members of this generation is already generated when they are in their working years. In this paper, therefore, we adopt the prepaid version of the agency view. When we say simply the "agency view" without qualifications, we mean the prepaid version.

Let us now decompose the benefit B_t into the expected component B_t^e and the unexpected component B_t^u. Thus, we have

$$B_t = B_t^e + B_t^u.$$

In the agency view, B_t^e is the income of the currently retired generation in the previous period and B_t^u the income of the same generation in this period.

In the agency view, the government receives the tax revenue of T_t from the working generation in period t, while it pays this generation the transfer of B_{t+1}^e and the retired generation the transfer of B_t^u in the same period. Letting $\bar{S}_t^g$ denote the government saving in the agency view, therefore, we have

$$(21) \qquad \bar{S}^g_t = T_t - B^e_{t+1} - B^u_t$$

from (20). This represents the income transfer from the generations living in period t to the government that takes place in period t. Thus, $\bar{S}^g_t$ is a better measure of income transfer in period t than S^g_t in that it measures the effect of the government pension activities in this period on the lifetime utility level of the generations living in this period, unlike the latter.

Now assume that the public pension system is introduced in period 0 for the first time, by which we mean that none of the following happens before period 0: (i) the working generation pays pension tax; (ii) future pension benefits of the currently working generation are announced; and (iii) the retired generation receives unexpected benefit payments. Then we can define the cumulative balance of the government surplus in the agency view as

$$(22) \qquad \bar{Z}^g_t = \Sigma^t_0 \bar{S}^g_j.$$

Equations (21) and (22) yield the following:

$$(23) \qquad \bar{Z}^g_t = [-B_0 + \Sigma^{t-1}_0 (T_j - B_{j+1})] + (T_t - B^e_{t+1}).$$

The term B_0 on the right-hand side represents the unexpected benefits by the retired generation in period 0. (This can of course be zero.) This equation states that the cumulative government saving in the agency view equals the sum of (*a*) the cumulative income transfer to the government from all the generations older than the current working generation and (*b*) the pension surtax paid by the currently working generation. In this sense, the cumulative budget surplus in the agency view may be regarded as the cumulative transfer from the past and current generations to the future generations.

Equation (23) can be rewritten to yield yet another interpretation of $\bar{Z}^g_t$:

$$(24) \qquad \bar{Z}^g_t = \Sigma^t_0 (T_j - B_j) - B^e_{t+1} = Z^g_t - B^e_{t+1}.$$

Thus, the cumulative budget surplus in the agency view is the cumulative budget surplus in the principal view minus the expected benefit payment to the working generation in the given period. This difference is caused by the fact that the expected benefit payment is treated as the government expenditure of this period in the agency view but as that of the next period in the principal view.

Note that, if the retired generation in period $t + 1$ receives only expected benefits, equations (21), (23), and (24) become

$$(21') \qquad \bar{S}^g_t = T_t - B_{t+1},$$

$$(23') \qquad \bar{Z}^g_t = \Sigma^t_0 (T_j - B_{j+1}) - B_0,$$

$$(24') \qquad \bar{Z}^g_t = Z^g_t - B_{t+1},$$

respectively.

If a system is actuarially fair in period t, for example, equations (21′) and (6) yield

$$\bar{S}^g_t = 0. \tag{25}$$

This is only natural since the government receives no transfers from the private sector in period t under the actuarially fair system. If the system is fully funded in period t, (24′) and (11) yield

$$\bar{Z}^g_t = 0, \tag{26}$$

implying that the government receives zero cumulative transfers from the private sector.

If a pay-as-you-go system is introduced in period 2, the budget surpluses in both flow and the cumulative balances are zero from (13) and (14). Thus, (24′) implies

$$\bar{Z}^g_t = -B_{t+1}. \tag{27}$$

This indicates that, under the pay-as-you-go system, the cumulative budget surplus in the agency view in a given period is equal to the social security wealth in that period. The variables $\bar{S}^g_t$ and $\bar{Z}^g_t$ are depicted for the case of pay-as-you-go in figures 7.9a and 7.9b, based on (21′) and (27), respectively.

7.4.3 Effects of Reforms on Transfers between the Government and the Private Sector

Under a pay-as-you-go system, therefore, the cumulative transfer from the government (i.e., the future generations) to the current and past generations is equal to the social security wealth of the current period. Thus, the cumulative transfer fluctuates as the economy passes through the HAAP. Our three reform plans may be viewed as different methods of managing this transfer and stabilizing its movements.

To examine how our three plans affect $\bar{S}^g_t$ and $\bar{Z}^g_t$, the following proposition is useful.

PROPOSITION 1. *Suppose that a pay-as-you-go public pension system is reformed in period 3. Assume that under the reformed system all the pension benefits are announced prior to the payments and that taxes are still paid only by the working generations. Then the following holds:*

$$\bar{Z}^g_t = -B_3 + \Sigma^t_3(T_t - B_{j+1}), \quad t \geq 3. \tag{28}$$

Proof. Equation (23′) implies

$$\bar{Z}^g_t = \Sigma^2_0(T_j - B_j) - B_3 + \Sigma^t_3(T_j - B_{j+1}).$$

Since the system satisfies $B_j = T_j$ for $0 \leq j \leq 2$, this yields the proposition. Q.E.D.

Thus, $\bar{Z}^g_t$ is equal to the cumulative sum of the pension surtaxes paid by the

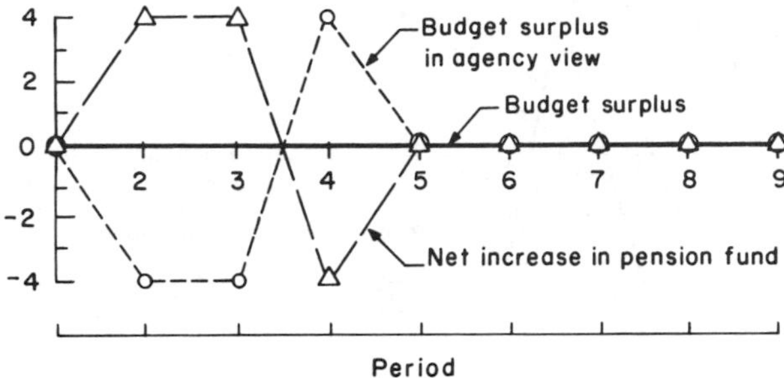

Fig. 7.9a Budget surplus under the pay-as-you-go system

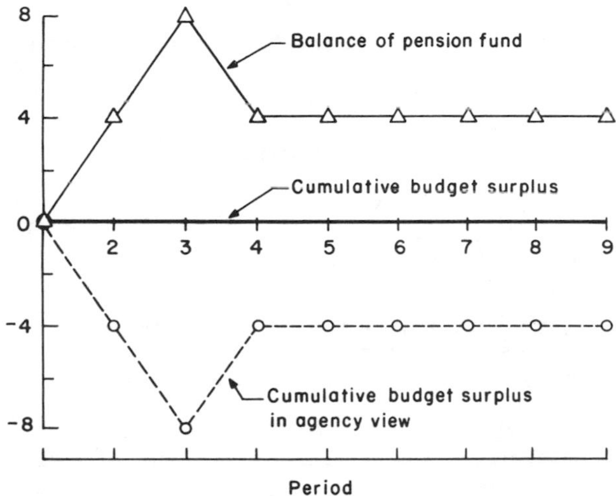

Fig. 7.9b Cumulative budget surplus under the pay-as-you-go system

working generations during periods 3 through t minus the benefits received by the retired in period 3. Note that this formula holds only if the prereform pension system is pay as you go. An interpretation of this equation is straightforward. Since the economy is under the pay-as-you-go system in period 2, the term $-B_3$ on the right-hand side of (28) is equal to the cumulative balance of the government saving in the agency view in period 3 from (27). In view of (21′), this balance is increased in each period by the amount of the pension surtax. Thus, (28) indicates that the cumulative balance of government saving in the agency view in period t is equal to the balance in period 2 plus the increase in the balance that took place after the reform.

Switch to Fully Funded

Suppose that the system is switched to fully funded in period 3. Then from (15) and proposition 1 we have $\bar{Z}^g_t = 0$ for $t \geq 3$. Thus, the cumulative bud-

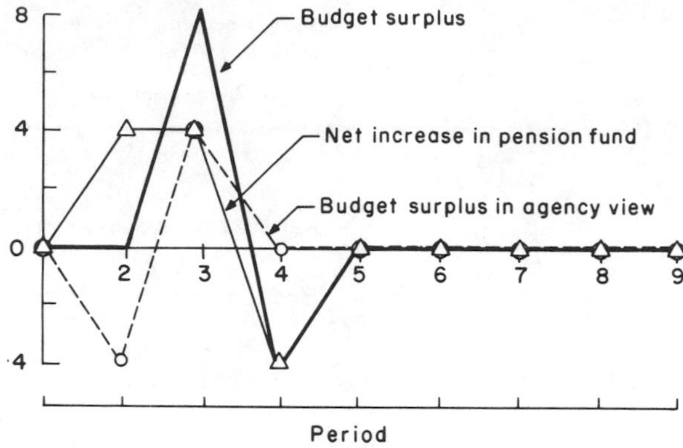

Fig. 7.10a **Budget surplus after the switch to the fully funded system**

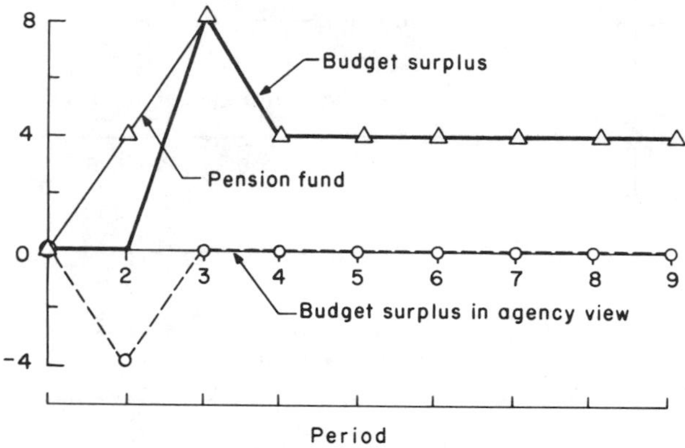

Fig. 7.10b **Cumulative budget surplus after the switch to the fully funded system**

get surplus in the agency view disappears immediately. The dashed line in figure 7.10b shows this. Also, from (15) and (21′) we have $\bar{S}^g_3 = B_3$ and $\bar{S}^g_t = 0$ for $t \geq 4$. The dashed lines in figure 7.10a shows that a positive transfer to the government takes place in period 3.

Switch to Actuarially Fair

When the system is switched to actuarially fair in period 3, proposition 1 and (17) imply $\bar{Z}^g_t = -B_3$ for $t \geq 3$. Thus, the cumulative budget deficit in the agency view remains fixed at the level of the pension payment in period 3. The dashed line in figures 7.11b shows this. Also, from (17) and (21′) we have $\bar{S}^g_t = 0$ for $t \geq 3$. The dashed lines in figures 7.11a shows this.

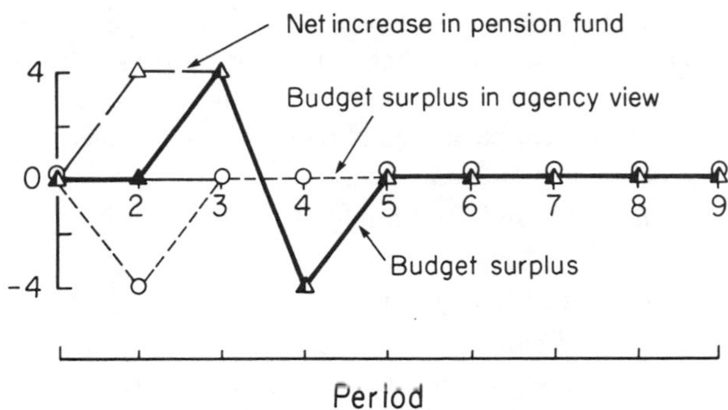

Fig. 7.11a Budget surplus after the switch to the actuarially fair system

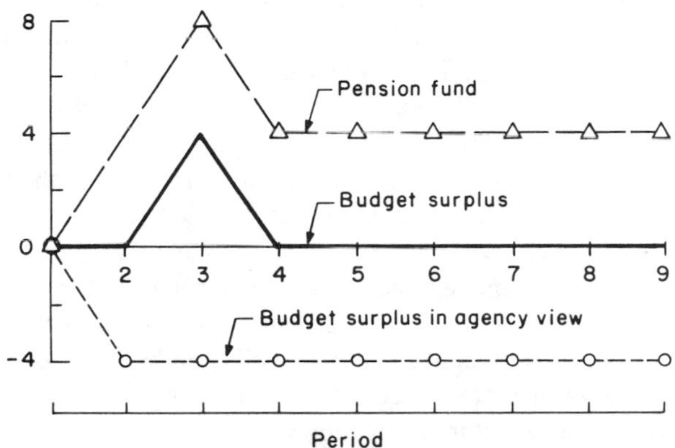

Fig. 7.11b Cumulative budget surplus after the switch to the actuarially fair system

A comparison of figures 7.10a and 7.11a shows that the budget surpluses in the agency view between the two reform plans are different only in period 3.

Gradual Shift to Fully Funded

When the system is gradually shifted to fully funded starting in period 3, (18) and proposition 1 imply

$$\bar{Z}_3^g = -B_3,$$
$$\bar{Z}_t^g = -B_3 + .8\ \Sigma_3^t N_t, \quad 3 < t \leq 8, \tag{29}$$
$$\bar{Z}_t^g = 0, \quad 8 \leq t.$$

The dashed line in figure 7.12b depicts the fluctuation $\bar{Z}^g_t$. The cumulative budget surplus in the agency view, that is, the cumulative government transfer to the private sector, gradually diminishes until it reaches zero in period 8. The pension surtax spreads the burden of reducing the cumulative government transfer evenly among generations.

On the other hand, (18) and (21′) imply $\bar{S}^g_3 = 0$, $\bar{S}^g_t = .8N_t$ for $3 < t < 9$, and $\bar{S}^g_t = 0$ for $9 \leq t$. The budget surplus in the agency view during periods 4–8 reflects the pension surtax paid by the working generations of these periods. The dashed line in figure 7.12a depicts the fluctuation of $\bar{S}^g_t$.

We may sum up our observations here as follows. Under the pay-as-you-go system, the cumulative government transfer to the private sector (i.e., cumulative government saving in the agency view) in a given period is equal to the promised pension benefit payments to the working generation of that period. The switch to the fully funded eliminates this cumulative government transfer immediately. The switch to the actuarially fair keeps the cumulative balance fixed at the level of period 2. The gradual shift to the fully funded reduces the balance over time until it is eliminated.

Each of the three reform plans smooths the fluctuations of the cumulative government transfer after the reform. Not all the plans smooth the fluctuations of the government flow transfer after the reform, however. The switch to the fully funded requires a heavy transfer to the government in period 3. The other two reforms smooth the movement of the transfer in each period like that of the cumulative transfer. In planning a gradual building up of the cumulative budget surplus as in the gradual shift to the fully funded, the government can allocate the burden fairly among generations by using the concept of the cumulative government deficit in the agency view.

7.5 Pension Fund

7.5.1 The Pension Fund and Pension Wealth

Earlier, we saw that, in the agency view, the government's involvement with the public pension is twofold: receiving transfers from the private sector and managing the actuarially fair Pension Fund. We turn now to the Pension Fund.

The growth of the Pension Fund may be described as follows. In period t, the young generation contributes to the Fund by B^e_{t+1}, which is $T_t - (T_t - B^e_{t+1})$,[11] while the retired generation receives the benefit of B^e_t from the Fund. Thus, the net increase of the Fund in this period, denoted ΔF_t, is

$$\Delta F_t = B^e_{t+1} - B^e_t. \tag{30}$$

11. The social security tax T_t minus the pension surtax $T_t - B^e_{t+1}$ may be equivalently expressed as the sum of the social security tax T_t and the transfer income that the young generation receives in this period, i.e., $B^e_{t+1} - T_t$.

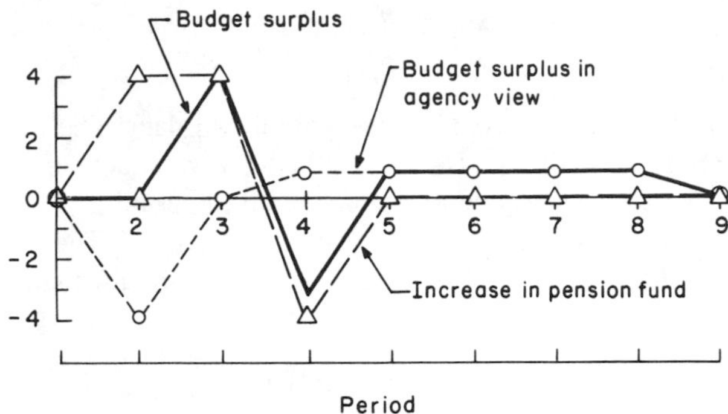

Fig. 7.12a Budget surplus under the gradual shift to the fully funded system

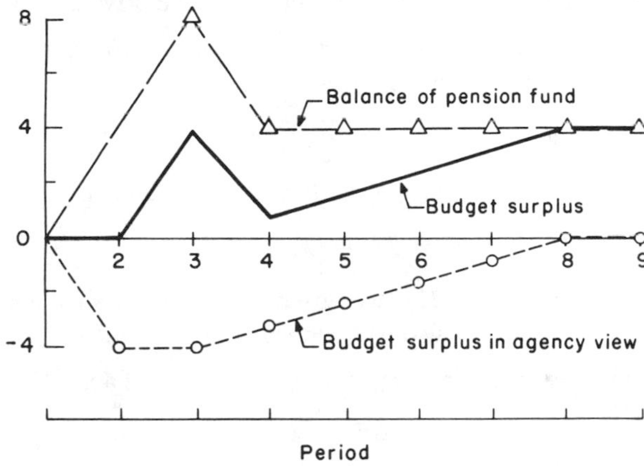

Fig. 7.12b Cumulative budget surplus under the gradual shift to the fully funded system

Define the cumulative balance of the Pension Fund by

(31) $$F_t = \Sigma_0^t \Delta F_j,$$

where it is assumed that the public pension system is introduced for the first time in period 0. From (30) and (31) and the fact that $B_0^e = 0$, we have

(32) $$F_t = B_{t+1}^e, \quad t \geq 0.$$

Thus, the balance of the Pension Fund is always equal to the pension wealth B_{t+1}^e. This holds whether the social security system is fully funded, pay as you go, or somewhere in between.

Note that, if the retired generation in period $t + 1$ receives no unexpected benefits, equations (30) and (32) collapse to

(30′) $$\Delta F_t = B_{t+1} - B_t,$$

(32′) $$F_t = B_{t+1}.$$

These can easily be computed from the population data. The identical thin lines in figures 7.9a, 7.10a, 7.11a, and 7.12a depict the fluctuation of ΔF_t if a per capita social security payment of b is started in period 2. These lines are the same no matter how the benefits are actually financed. The identical thin lines in figures 7.9b, 7.10b, 7.11b, and 7.12b depict the fluctuation of F_t for the same case.

7.5.2 The Pension Fund and Government Saving

How can the imaginary Pension Fund be funded? According to the following proposition, the growth (cumulative balance) of the Pension Fund can be financed by the budget surplus (cumulative budget surplus) and the government transfer (cumulative government transfer) to the private sector.

PROPOSITION 2. *The increase in the Pension Fund has the following relation with saving in the principal and agency views:*

(33) $$\Delta F_t = S_t^g - \bar{S}_t^g \quad t > 1.$$

The cumulative balances of each variable satisfy the following:

(34) $$F_t = Z_t^g - \bar{Z}_t^g, \quad t > 1.$$

Proof. From (9), (30), and (21), we observe (33). Thus, (10) and (31) yield (34). Alternatively, (34) can also be obtained from (24) and (32). Q.E.D.

If a system is actuarially fair in period *t*, proposition 2 and (25) imply

(35) $$\Delta F_t = S_t^g.$$

Since the increase in the Pension Fund is equal to the budget surplus in this case, the lines for the increase in the Pension Fund in figures 7.9a, 7.10a, 7.11a, and 7.12a are drawn identically to the line for the budget surplus for the fully funded system in figure 7.6a. If the system is fully funded in period *t*, (26) and proposition 2 immediately yield

(36) $$F_t = Z_t^g.$$

In this case, therefore, the balance of the Pension Fund is equal to the cumulative budget surplus in the same period. Thus, the lines for the Pension Fund in figures 7.9b, 7.10b, 7.11b, and 7.12b are identical to the lines for the cumulative budget saving for the fully funded system in figures 7.6a and 7.6b. As we observed earlier, an actuarially fair system in period *t* may not be fully funded in the same period. Thus, (35) does not necessarily imply (36).

If a pay-as-you-go system is introduced in period 2, proposition 2 and (13) imply

(37) $$\Delta F_t = -\bar{S}_t^g;$$

hence,

$$F_t = -\bar{Z}^g_t, \tag{38}$$

for all $t > 1$. Under a pay-as-you-go system, therefore, the increase in the Pension Fund in any given period is the mirror image of the government transfer to the private sector. Also, the balance of the Pension Fund is equal to the cumulative government transfer to the private sector under this system. Proposition 2 is illustrated for this case in figures 7.9a and 7.9b.

Figure 7.10b shows that the cumulative budget surplus and the Pension Fund coincide when the cumulative government transfer disappears in period 3. Figures 7.10a–7.12b illustrate proposition 2 for each tax reform plan.

7.5.3 The Institutional Pension Fund

The Pension Bond

We have seen that, if the system is fully funded in period t, the Pension Fund is equal to the cumulative government surplus. Now suppose that the system is not fully funded in period t; hence,

$$F_t \neq Z^g_t.$$

Must the Pension Fund necessarily be imaginary in this case? The answer is no. The government can institutionally establish a Pension Fund that has a balance equal to the pension wealth, F_t, as long as it issues a government bond to finance the difference between F_t and Z^g_t. We will call this bond the *pension bond* and denote its balance by D_t. By definition, we have

$$D_t \equiv F_t - Z^g_t. \tag{39}$$

In order to maintain the institutional Pension Fund after its establishment, the government has to adjust the outstanding balance of the pension bond in response to the gap between the Pension Fund and the cumulative saving increases. If the gap increases, additional pension bonds must be issued; if it decreases, some of the pension bonds must be redeemed.

If the system is kept actuarially fair while the institutional Pension Fund is being maintained, the outstanding balance of the pension bond will stay constant from (35) and (39). No new bond is issued and no outstanding bond redeemed. In this case, the cumulative balance of the budget surplus will fluctuate in parallel response to the balance of the Pension Fund.

Even under the pay-as-you-go system the government can institutionally establish a Pension Fund by issuing a pension bond to finance it. Since there is no cumulative budget surplus in this case from (39), we have $D_t \equiv F_t$; hence, the balance of the pension bond must be at the level of the Pension Fund itself. This and (20) yield

$$D_t = B_{t+1}. \tag{40}$$

Suppose that the government institutionally establishes a Pension Fund by issuing the pension bond in period 2 while the system is still pay as you go. Then the switch to the fully funded system in period 3 would eliminate the outstanding balance of the pension bonds since the switch would make the cumulative balance of the budget surplus exactly equal to the balance of the Fund. On the other hand, the switch to the actuarially fair system would not affect the outstanding balance of the pension bond at all since the switch keeps constant the difference between the cumulative balance of the budget surplus and the balance of the Fund at the level of period 2. Finally, the gradual shift to the fully funded would not affect the outstanding balance of the pension bond in period 3 but would gradually reduce it as the cumulative balance of the budget surplus is built up to the level of the Pension Fund.

Note that issuing the pension bond does not affect the government budget surplus or deficit at all. The budget deficit created by this bond exactly cancels out the increase in the budget surplus brought about by the establishment of the Fund.

The Pension Bond and Government Saving in the Agency View

The definition of D_t and (34) yield the following interpretation of the pension bond.

PROPOSITION 3. *When the Pension Fund is institutionally maintained in period t, the balance of the outstanding pension bond is equal to the cumulative government budget deficit in the agency view, that is,*

$$D_t = -\bar{Z}_t^g. \tag{41}$$

Thus, the pension bond is nothing but the cumulative government deficit in the agency view. Issuing the pension bond at the time the institutional Pension Fund is created, therefore, simply exposes the cumulative government deficit that already existed in the agency view at the time of issuing; it does not create a new government deficit even in the agency view. Proposition 3 can also be viewed as giving an institutional interpretation to the government deficit in the agency view.

Suppose that a pay-as-you-go pension system for which the Pension Fund has been institutionally established is reformed in period 3. Then from propositions 1 and 3 the balance of the pension bond in period t is expressed as:

$$D_t = B_3 - \sum_{j=3}^{t}(T_j - B_{j+1}), \quad t \geq 3. \tag{42}$$

Since the economy is under the pay-as-you-go system in period 2, B_3 on the right-hand side of (42) is the balance of the pension bond in period 2 from (40). In view of (41) and (21′), the bond is redeemed in each period by the amount of the pension surtax. Thus, (42) indicates that the outstanding balance of the pension bond in period t is the outstanding balance in period 2 minus the cumulative redemption of the bond after the reform. Equation (42) gives an alternative explanation for the fluctuations of D_t under various reform plans discussed earlier.[12]

Kotlikoff (1986, 57) called the social security wealth the "social security bond." Equation (40) shows that, under a pay-as-you-go pension system, the pension bond is equal to the social security wealth in that period. As equation (39) shows, however, this equality does not generally hold under other pension systems.[13]

Modified Pension Reform Plans

We now consider issuing a bond for a purpose different from that of the pension bond. Suppose that a pay-as-you-go system is reformed in period 3 in the following manner.

First, the government issues bonds in period 3 to finance the benefits of the retirees of this period. Second, the Pension Fund is institutionally established in period 3 and is maintained afterward. No less than actuarially fair taxes are imposed on generation III and subsequent generations to finance the Pension Fund. Third, the pension surtax, if positive, is used to redeem the bond. Since the tax revenue can be decomposed as $T_t = B_{j+1} + (T_j - B_{j+1})$, the government can contribute B_{j+1} to the Pension Fund and use the pension surtax $T_j - B_{j+1}$ to redeem the pension bond. (Note that $T_j - B_{j+1} \geq 0$ by assumption.)

The purpose of issuing the pension bond was to supplement the cumulative budget surplus in establishing and maintaining the Pension Fund institutionally, and it could be issued in any period. On the other hand, the purpose of issuing a bond in the present reform proposal is to pay off the benefit of the last contributor to the pay-as-you-go system through the revenue raised by the bond, thereby liquidating the pay-as-you-go system. Hence, we will call the bond the *liquidation bond.* Issuing this bond enables the government to establish the Pension Fund from scratch by financing it with the tax revenues from the postreform generations. We will call such a pension reform a *reform plan through liquidation bond.*

Each of our three reform plans has its counterpart among the reform plans through liquidation bond. Suppose that the government issues liquidation bonds in period 3 to finance the benefits of the retirees of this period and then imposes taxes on generation III and subsequent generations at the same rates as each of the three reform plans does. Since none of the three modified reform plans imposes a negative pension surtax, the tax revenue can institution-

12. If the system is switched to actuarially fair, e.g., (42) implies that $D_t = B_3$ holds for all $t \geq 3$; the pension bond is maintained constant at the level of B_3. If the system is gradually shifted to fully funded, $D_t = B_3 - .8\,\Sigma_3^t N_t$ holds for $3 < t \leq 8$ and $D_t = 0$ for $8 \leq t$, eventually eliminating the pension bond.

13. Note that Kotlikoff's concept of social security wealth is the postpaid notion, while ours is the prepaid notion. But (24) can also be established for the postpaid notions of $\bar{Z}_t^g$ and B_{t+1}^e.

ally finance the Pension Fund in each case. The pension surtaxes, if positive, are used to redeem the liquidation bond. We thus obtain reform plans through liquidation bond that are counterparts to our three reform plans. Since the tax and benefit structures of each of our pension reform plans and their counterparts in the reform through liquidation bond are identical, their real effects on the economy are identical.

Moreover, the outstanding balance of the liquidation bond in a given period would be identical to the outstanding balance of the pension bond had it been issued instead. The amount of the liquidation bond issued in period 3 is B_3, while the total amount of redemption is represented by the summation of the pension surtaxes paid by the postreform generations, $\sum_{j=3}^{t}(T_j - B_{j+1})$. By construction, therefore, we can write the outstanding balance of the liquidation bond in period t as

$$(44) \qquad L_t = B_3 - \sum_{j=3}^{t}(T_j - B_{j+1}), \quad t \geq 3.$$

This and (28) immediately show that

$$(45) \qquad L_t = \bar{Z}_t^g \quad t \geq 3.$$

Thus, the liquidation bond may be viewed as yet another interpretation of the government saving in the agency view. Equations (44) and (42) also show that

$$L_t = D_t, \quad t \geq 3.$$

Thus, the liquidation bond may also be viewed as an interpretation of the pension bond.

Incidentally, the amount of the liquidation bond issued in period 3 is equal to the amount of the benefits received by generation I since generations I and II receive the same net benefits from the pay-as-you-go system in our numerical setting. Thus, the implicit government deficit that the liquidation bond brings out is the one created by the free-ride benefit that generation I received at the time the pay-as-you-go system was implemented in period 1.

Finally, note that our interpretation of the cumulative government saving in the agency view in terms of pension bond and liquidation bond given by proposition 3 and (45) depends crucially on the particular definition of government saving we adopted here: the prepaid version of the agency view. If we had adopted the postpaid version, proposition 3 and (45) would not hold unless the definition of the Pension Fund were similarly adjusted.

7.5.4 Summary

In this section, we have observed the following. First, an actuarially fair pension system in a given period can be interpreted as the one where the government transfer to the private sector in the agency view is zero in that period, while a fully funded system in the given period can be interpreted as the one where the cumulative government transfer in the agency view to the private sector is zero.

Second, all three reform plans we discussed inherit the cumulative government transfer to the private sector from the pay-as-you-go system. The switch to an actuarially fair system carries it over forever to the future. The gradual shift to the fully funded system reduces this cumulative government transfer in the long run. The switch to the fully funded system immediately eliminates this cumulative transfer in the period of reform.

Third, according to proposition 2, the net increase in the Pension Fund is financed by the budget surplus and the government transfer to the private sector. The Pension Fund is an accounting concept, but it can be institutionally established by issuing the pension bond.

Fourth, according to proposition 3, the outstanding amount of the pension bond is equal to the cumulative balance of the transfer from the private sector to the government by that period. Hence, the net increase in the Pension Fund may be viewed as being financed by budget surplus and by the new issue of pension bonds.

Fifth, Kotlikoff's "social security bond" is the equivalent of our pension bond under a pay-as-you-go system, but that is not generally the case under different pension systems.

Sixth, the gradual shift to the fully funded may be carried out by issuing a liquidation bond. The amount of this bond issued in the first period of the reform is exactly equal to the cumulative balance of the government transfer to the private sector that was implicit under the pay-as-you-go system in the period immediately before the reform.

Seventh, the concept of the cumulative government transfer to the private sector is useful in planning the tax policy to distribute the burden of institutional building up the Pension Fund among generations fairly.

7.6 Concluding Remarks

In the present paper, we have observed the following. First, the fact that the Japanese social security system is pay as you go creates problems with respect to both distribution and efficiency. In particular, it places a heavy burden on the post–baby boom generation by transferring income from it to the baby boom generation.

Second, switching the system to the fully funded one in one generation shifts the heavy burden to the baby boom generation. Also, it will make the national saving in the switching period even larger than what would be attained if the system were fully funded from the beginning.

Third, a switch to an actuarially fair but unfunded system eliminates microeconomic problems of the Japanese social security system without causing instability in the transition phase.

Fourth, if the accumulation of cumulative budget surplus is necessary to make the system fully funded from a macroeconomic point of view, it can be done by first changing the system into an actuarially fair but unfunded one and then gradually building up the fund by taxing several generations. Economic effects of such a gradual shift were analyzed.

Fifth, a few different interpretations of the cumulative balance of government deficit in the agency view were given. It was interpreted as the transfer from future generations to the present and past generations. It was also interpreted as the pension bond necessary to supplement the cumulative budget surplus in establishing the Pension Fund institutionally. The outstanding balance of this bond is zero when the system is fully funded, while it is equal to the social security wealth when the system is pay as you go. A systematic reduction of the outstanding amount of this bond enables the government to spread the burden of building up the fund evenly among several generations. Moreover, the cumulative balance of government deficit in the agency view was shown to be equal to the outstanding balance of the liquidation bond if the pension reform is carried out by issuing the liquidation bond.

Although the merits of the fully funded system are well known, economists are usually apprehensive about switching an existing pay-as-you-go system to the fully funded one because it creates instability in both distribution and macro balance in the transition phase. It is not necessary, however, to accumulate the budget surplus for the purpose of eliminating the distributional and efficiency problems associated with the pay-as-you-go system like the current Japanese social security system. A switch to an actuarially fair but unfunded system attains this objective.

References

Auerbach, Alan, and Laurence J. Kotlikoff. 1983. An Examination of Empirical Tests of Social Security and Savings. In *Social Policy Evaluation: An Economic Perspective,* ed. Elhanan Helpman et al. New York: Academic.

———. 1984. Social Security and the Economics of the Demographic Transition. In *Retirement and Economic Behavior,* ed. H. Aaron and G. Burtless. Washington, D.C.: Brookings.

———. 1985. Simulating Alternative Social Security Responses to the Demographic Transition. *National Tax Journal* 85 (2):153–68.

———. 1987. *Dynamic Fiscal Policy.* London: Cambridge University Press.

Auerbach, Alan, Laurence J. Kotlikoff, Robert Hagemann, and Giuseppe Nicoletti. 1989. The Dynamics of an Aging Population: The Case of Four OECD Countries. NBER Working Paper no. 2797. Cambridge, Mass.: National Bureau of Economic Research.

Boskin, Michael, Laurence J. Kotlikoff, and John Shoven. 1985. Personal Security Accounts: A Proposal for Fundamental Social Security reform. CEPR Publication no. 63.

Fukao, Mitsuhiro, and Kazuaki Doi. 1985. Aging and Saving Ratio (in Japanese). *Keizai Semina* (Economics seminar). 369:63–69.

Gravelle, Jane, and Laurence J. Kotlikoff. 1989. Corporate Taxation and the Efficiency Gains of the 1986 Tax Reform Act. NBER Working Paper no. 3142. Cambridge, Mass.: National Bureau of Economic Research.

Hatta, Tatsuo. 1988. *Chokusetu Zei Kaikaku* (Reforming direct taxes). Tokyo: Nihon Keizai Shimbun Press.

Hatta, Tatsuo, and Noriyoshi Oguchi. 1989a. Effects on Government Budget of Switching from a Pay-as-You-Go Social Security System to a Fully Funded One (in Japanese). *Kikan Shakai Hosho Kenkyuu* (Quarterly journal of social security research) 25:166–75.

———. 1989b. Switching from a Pay-as-You-Go Social Security System to a Fully Funded One (in Japanese). *Kikan Shakai Hosho Kenkyuu* (Quarterly journal of social security research) 25:66–75.

Honma, Masaaki, Naozumi Atoda, and Fumio Otake. 1988. The High-Average-Age Society and Financing Methods of the Public Pension System (in Japanese). *Fainansharu Rebyu* (Financial review) 7:50–64.

Horioka, Charles. 1899. Why Is Japan's Private Saving Rate So High? In *Record Developments in Japanese Economics,* ed. Ryuzo Sato and Takashi Negishi, 145–78. Tokyo: Harcourt Bruce Jovanovich.

Kotlikoff, Laurence J. 1986. Deficit Delusion. *Public Interest* 84:53–65.

———. 1987. Justifying Public Provision of Social Security. *Journal of Policy Analysis and Management* 6 (4):674–89.

———. 1988. From Deficit Delusion to the Fiscal Balance Rule: Looking for an Economically Meaningful Way to Assess Fiscal Policy. Boston: Boston University. Manuscript.

———. 1989. The Social Security "Surpluses"—New Clothes for the Emperor? Washington, D.C.: American Enterprise Institute. Conference paper.

Noguchi, Yukio. 1987a. The Future of the Public Pension System: International Performers List of the Japanese Economy (in Japanese). *Fainansharu Rebyu* (Financial review) 5:8–19.

———. 1987b. Intergenerational Transfers Due to Public Policy (in Japanese). *Kikan Shakai Hosho Kenkyuu* (Quarterly journal of social security research) 23:276–83.

Otake, Fumio. 1989. *Sozei, Shakai Hosho Seido no Keizai Bunseki* (Economic analysis of taxation and social security system). Osaka: Economics Department, Osaka Prefectural University.

Tsukahara, Yasuhiro. 1989. A Modified Pay-as-You-Go Pension Plan as a Substitute for the Hatta-Oguchi Plan. *Kikan Shakai Hosho Kenkyuu* (Quarterly journal of social security research) 25:255–77.

Ueda, Kazuo, Mutsuo Iwai, and Motohide Hashimoto. 1987. Public Pension and Intergenerational Transfers (in Japanese). *Fainansharu Rebyu* (Financial review) 6:44–57.

Comment Edward P. Lazear

This was an excellent paper. I was impressed by the clarity of thought and exposition, and I learned a great deal by reading it. I recommend it to you. It is a very nice model for tracing out the effects of various funding schemes on savings, government deficits, and trade balances.

Edward P. Lazear is the Isidore Brown and Gladys J. Brown Professor of Urban and Labor Economics at the University of Chicago, a senior fellow at the Hoover Institution, and a research associate of the National Bureau of Economic Research.

I must confess to having a real soft spot for simplicity. The words "simple model" are overused. Almost every author calls his model simple. This one really is, but it gets to the essence of what the authors want to discuss. In particular, it does an excellent job of exposing what is real and what is illusory, that is, what is truly of economic significance and what is merely accounting.

I view it as a starting point for thinking about these problems. In order to start, it is important to know the effects of the different funding patterns on the key driving variables. Thus, knowing the effect on the driving variables of changing from a pay-as-you-go funding system to a fully funded one is essential before we can ask some bigger questions. What I would like to do is address some of the big questions that I believe are not yet covered in this paper. I see these as extensions of the current work, but I believe that some are very important extensions that should be undertaken so that we can understand the significance of the effects that Tatsuo Hatta and Noriyoshi Oguchi are tracing out.

The main shortcoming of the paper to my mind is that it focuses a bit too heavily on accounting and ignores economic behavior. To put it most generally, there is no way in the current model to evaluate which scheme is best. While the model does an excellent job of tracing out the savings and consumption patterns of the different generations under the two scenarios, the authors do not attempt to analyze which is better. In fact, they cannot perform that analysis in the current model because savings plays no role in a macroeconomic sense. Let me be a bit more specific.

In the model, there is no effect of current consumption and therefore savings on future income. The investment side of the problem is not modeled. I will return to this point later, but the main idea here is that intergenerational savings does not perform a useful function as it does in the traditional overlapping generation models or as it does in the newer increasing-returns-based growth models. Specifically, a fully funded pension scheme does not result in a different flow of total income over time from the pay-as-you-go system. But pay as you go yields a different pattern of savings than a fully funded system. In a closed economy, one might expect this to make a difference to the income path because it affects capital accumulation, and the differences might carry over to an open economy as well.

One obvious possibility is that changes in savings over time may have very different efficiency effects because the different tax rates and structures may imply different distortions. Any distortionary effects of the tax changes are ignored in the current model.

Even ignoring issues of capital accumulation, the pay-as-you-go scheme implies a different distribution of income and consumption than does the fully funded one. There is no way to evaluate the two different approaches, however. Because the analysis is not embedded in a maximizing framework, one cannot tell whether fully funded is preferable to pay as you go. Similarly, while the switch from pay as you go to fully funded seems to work in this context, there is no way to make any welfare judgment about the switch. In the pay-as-you-go scheme, the post–baby boom generation gets hit badly, and a switch to fully funded evens this out. But depending on the nature of intergenerational transfers and altruism, this could have either beneficial, detrimental, or no effects on utility.

Investment is not modeled in the current discussion. This leaves us begging for more because investment may have a life of its own. While this will not be true in a closed economy, the discussion in this paper is explicit in thinking of Japan as an open economy. Reference to trade surpluses and deficits are found throughout.

Others have looked at the relation of savings to investment. Feldstein in particular has argued that savings and investment are not as independent as they should be in a perfect capital market open economy. But this does not mean that they are the same.

The point is best seen by comparing the United States and Japan. The United States is currently running a trade deficit. Hatta and Oguchi say that a high savings rate and large trade surplus are inevitable when the baby boom generation is in its working years. This does not fit the United States. While we are not aging as quickly as Japan, the difference results from relatively high levels of investment in the United States that are financed by foreign savings. And we have a negative trade balance. In the open economy context, the difference between savings and investment is an important one, which might be discussed in the current paper.

To make another general point, the government is modeled in two ways in this paper, what the authors call the principal view and the agency view. These analyses were informative, but they could be extended. In particular, there is no discussion of other sources of government revenue and other areas of expenditure. This may be a useful approximation, but I think that it is problematic. There is evidence for the United States, compiled by John Cogan, that reveals that the trend has been to raise trust fund revenues against general fund revenues.[1] Cogan finds that during the postwar period there is a dollar-for-dollar substitution of trust fund for general fund revenue relative to GNP. This suggests that, if Japan changes the structure of social security funding, we may expect a corresponding change in other aspects of the tax structure. If this kind of substitution occurs, a change in the funding structure may not alter government receipts the way the model predicts.

A related question arises. Even if there is no corresponding cutback in other sources of government revenues, will social security funding be dedicated to expenditures on social security payments, or will it generate an expansion in

1. See John F. Cogan, "The Federal Deficit in the 1990s: A Tale of Two Budgets," in *Thinking about America: The United States in the 1990s,* ed. Annelise Anderson and Dennis L. Bark (Stanford, Calif.: Hoover Institution Press, 1988), 277–87.

other kinds of government expenditure so that the post–baby boom generation is left in almost the same shape as it would have been had the switch in funding not occurred?

To make one final point, there is no discussion of the effects of government savings on private savings. Assumptions about the displacement of private savings by government savings should be made explicit because this is an important part of the controversy over any funding plan.

In sum, this is an excellent paper that allows us to begin to think about some of the related big questions. It is a first step, and without it we would have had no hope of thinking about the other issues that I have discussed in any systematic way.

8 Payment Source and Episodes of Institutionalization

Alan M. Garber and Thomas E. MaCurdy

In this paper, we explore the relation between the duration of nursing home admissions and the source of payment for nursing home care. This subject has assumed critical importance as a growing number of private insurers begin to offer long-term care insurance, millions of middle-aged and elderly Americans plan for future long-term care needs, and policymakers debate the role that government should play in financing, delivering, and regulating long-term care.

Both private and public initiatives for financing long-term care need accurate projections of utilization, but few studies have examined the effects of insurance on utilization. The size of the insurance subsidy effect on utilization, or moral hazard, is not readily inferred from observed price variation. It is notoriously difficult to gauge the price of nursing home care faced by consumers of this service, in part because price variation reflects differences in the characteristics of nursing homes (e.g., the quality of nursing services, meals, and housing amenities). In the absence of comprehensive, reliable price data or of direct measures of the effects of alternate financing mechanisms on long-term care utilization, studies of the relation between payment source and utilization provide important clues to the likely consequences of changing long-term care insurance benefits.

Alan M. Garber is assistant professor of medicine at Stanford University, staff physician at the Palo Alto Veterans Administration Medical Center, and a research associate of the National Bureau of Economic Research. Thomas E. MaCurdy is professor of economics at Stanford University, senior fellow at the Hoover Institution, and a research associate of the National Bureau of Economic Research.

This research was supported in part by grant AG07651 from the National Institution on Aging, by grant 12761 from the Robert Wood Johnson Foundation, and by the Far West Health Services Research and Development Field Program of the Department of Veterans Affairs, Alan Garber is a Henry J. Kaiser Family Foundation Faculty Scholar in General Internal Medicine. The authors are grateful to Andrew Dick for his expert assistance.

The measure of utilization that we examine is the length of each nursing home admission. While information about the duration of spells is a key component, additional information is needed to complete any comprehensive picture of nursing home utilization. Comprehensive measures of utilization (or cumulative duration) also require information about both the likelihood that a spell will occur at all and the frequency of readmission. In the long-term care literature, recidivism is recognized as a frequent event (Lewis, Cretin, and Kane 1985). The length of an individual spell has an entirely different interpretation if it is only one of a series of admissions rather than a unique occurrence.

Nursing home utilization also depends on the mode of exit, which in most duration analyses is of little concern. In other medical contexts, the nature of exit may have minimal significance because there is only one way a spell (of an illness, e.g.) may terminate (in death); in economic contexts, even if there is more than one way to end a spell (of unemployment, e.g.), the nature of the exit may be of secondary interest. The type of exit from nursing homes, in contrast, has substantive economic and welfare implications. Nursing home admissions terminate in return to the community, transfer to a hospital, or death. Although the type of discharge clearly matters to the patient, it also affects future long-term care utilization and overall health expenditures. Transfer to a hospital, for example, is often a costly interruption in a lengthy nursing home stay, while discharge to the community may signal resumption of independent living. The length of a nursing home spell, if it terminates in hospital admission, may be short in relation to overall utilization. To accommodate these phenomena, we complement the analysis of duration distributions with an investigation of the association between the probabilities of alternate modes of exit and several other factors, including personal characteristics, payment source, and length of the nursing home admission.

We investigate these issues by analyzing data on a sample of frail, disabled, and otherwise vulnerable elderly men and women who were believed to be likely to enter a nursing home. They were enrolled in the National Long-Term Care (Channeling) Demonstration, a randomized controlled trial of case management as a deterrent to institutionalization. While this sample is not representative of elderly Americans generally, it represents a group of particular interest: persons who are expected to consume a disproportionate share of long-term care and who are likely to be excluded from the purchase of private long-term care insurance. If associations between payment source and duration patterns are significant in this sample, the relation in the general population might be stronger, particularly if the demand for nursing home care among Channeling participants is inelastic.

In the following section, we describe the current environment for financing nursing home care. After discussing the challenges facing the development of private long-term care insurance, we review salient characteristics of government programs that pay for long-term care. The second section of the paper describes the data used in the empirical analysis. The third section describes the empirical model used to analyze the duration of nursing home spells and how it accommodates the duration dependence that some forms of health insurance promote. Results of the empirical analysis of nursing home duration and exit type are presented in the fourth section. We conclude with a discussion of the implications of this analysis for the design of long-term care insurance.

8.1 How Nursing Home Care Is Financed

Three payment sources accounted for nearly all nursing home expenditures in 1986: Medicaid (41.4 percent), Medicare (1.6 percent), and direct private payment (51.0 percent). Private health insurance paid for 0.8 percent, and miscellaneous government sources were responsible for the remainder (U.S. Department of Health and Human Services 1988, 161). Much of the current interest in long-term care policies is a response to perceived shortcomings of existing financing arrangements.

Perhaps the most notable feature of long-term care financing in the United States is the minor role played by private long-term care insurance. In contrast to the ubiquitous presence of both privately and publicly funded insurance for other forms of health care, long-term care insurance has paid for a small proportion of total long-term care expenditures in this country. The failure to develop a thriving market for private insurance reflects, in part, insurers' vulnerability to adverse selection and moral hazard. Insurers fear that adverse selection is likely because potential purchasers of insurance are better able to know whether they have an unusually high risk of needing long-term care than the insurer. Although there are several ways to deter adverse selection—such as restrictive benefits or a premium structure that encourages enrollment years before the need for long-term care is likely to arise—adverse selection is less problematic for government insurers than for private firms.

Like private insurers, government programs are also subject to moral hazard. In routine health insurance, moral hazard refers to the "overuse" of covered services. The effective subsidy for covered services can be so large that the price facing the patient or consumer is negligible. Even though moderate copayments may not be sufficient to curtail the demand for covered services, at least one important characteristic of conventional health services limits their utilization: utility derives not from the consumption of the service itself but from the improvement in health that it produces. The marginal benefit of most health interventions eventually becomes negative; the prospect of minimal or no health benefit from uncomfortable medical procedures deters gross overuse.

In contrast, long-term care includes housing, food services, and personal services as well as specialized nursing care. Because these services are potentially valuable to any elderly person, not only to the severely disabled or mentally impaired persons who are the intended recipients, long-term care is particularly likely to be subject to moral hazard. Insurers often implicitly ration care by setting medical criteria for reimbursement. However, if they hope to limit the effect of moral hazard by requiring interviews and physical examinations as a condition for reimbursement, they may be stymied by the primitive state of measurement of the "need" for long-term care. These measurements consist of functional and health status indicators, along with characterizations of the availability of social supports. The need for long-term care is determined in large part by self-reported disabilities or reports of family members, who may have an incentive to misrepresent the severity of the impairment when seeking to obtain coverage for desired services. In the absence of reliable objective indicators of disability, it is not surprising that measures of the need for long-term care are rarely as reproducible and credible as the laboratory tests and physical signs of illness that are used to evaluate the need for acute medical services. Consequently, non-price rationing is not a fully satisfactory response to moral hazard.

Although they usually lack private long-term care insurance, nearly all older Americans participate in Medicare. If they are admitted to nursing homes and meet several criteria, Medicare will reimburse part of the cost. The Medicare Catastrophic Act, which was repealed before its full implementation, would have extended the duration of benefits and eased reimbursement requirements but would not have altered the Medicare nursing home benefit substantially. Medicare contributes to the payments for a stay in a nursing home only if the nursing home is a certified skilled nursing facility. This eliminates most custodial care, which does not require the high level of skilled nursing care and rehabilitation services that characterize certified skilled nursing facilities. In addition, five conditions must be met before a patient's stay in a skilled nursing facility could generate any reimbursement: (1) a patient must have been in a hospital at least three consecutive days prior to transfer to the skilled nursing facility; (2) admission to the skilled nursing facility must occur within thirty days after hospital discharge; (3) admission to the skilled nursing facility must be for the treatment of the same condition as was treated in the hospital; (4) the admission must be certified by a physician; and (5) the stay must not be disapproved by a utilization review committee. If all five conditions are met, Medicare will contribute for up to one hundred days of care in each benefit period. Medicare pays the full charges for covered services during the first twenty days in a skilled nursing facility. However, the copayments during the twenty-first through hundredth days are substantial; in 1986, Medicare paid for all but $61.50 each day of the covered charges for days 21–100.

Thus, despite near universal participation, Medicare pays for relatively little nursing home care because its coverage rules are so restrictive. Eligibility for Medicaid is much more limited, yet Medicaid pays for a substantial fraction of U.S. nursing home care. To be eligible for Medicaid benefits, an individual must meet income and asset tests or have health expenses that are large in relation to income. Because Medicaid is a combined federal and state program, eligibility criteria and benefit structure vary from one state to another (U.S. Department of Health and Human Services 1985). In most states, Medicaid does not limit the duration of benefit, nor are nursing home benefits restricted to stays in skilled nursing facilities.

Although Medicaid typically requires no copayments, its reimbursement levels can be well below private pay charges for nursing home care. Consequently, there are usually delays before a Medicaid patient can be admitted to a nursing home. Furthermore, Medicaid patients who are transferred to hospitals risk losing their place in the nursing home if the hospital stay is not brief.

There would be narrower interest in Medicaid if it covered only the nursing home stays of impoverished older persons. However, Medicaid often serves as a long-term care insurer for middle-class elderly. This is a consequence of the "medically needy" category of Medicaid eligibility.

Besides standard income-based criteria for Medicaid enrollment, most states have a provision that enables individuals who "spend down" to qualify for Medicaid, even if they do not meet other Medicaid eligibility requirements. Persons can obtain Medicaid benefits if their health expenses are so large that their remaining income is only one-third higher than the poverty level. Institutionalization is the most common reason for such large expenditures, at least in part because the average monthly charges for nursing homes in 1985 were $1,456. This figure includes "no-charge" residents along with paying residents (U.S. Department of Health and Human Services 1988, 163). The specific rules for each state are described elsewhere (U.S. Department of Health and Human Services 1985). Although Medicaid rules are stringent, loopholes and uneven enforcement enable many elderly Medicaid recipients to conserve assets (Kidwell 1988).

Private pay patients would ordinarily pay full charges for nursing home care, but as they approach "medically indigent" health expenditures they may face a complex price schedule. For persons expecting to "spend down" to Medicaid eligibility, the price of a day in a nursing home will eventually fall to zero. The implicit deductible is a function of the patient's assets and income and varies across states. The "spend-down" is important only for long stays, but it is so frequent that it explains much of Medicaid's large expenditures for nursing home care. In 1986, the 14.0 percent of Medicaid recipients aged 65 and over accounted for 36.9 percent of Medicaid payments (U.S. Department of Health and Human Services 1988, 177); 36.3 percent of Medicaid's total expenditures were for nursing home care (U.S. Department of Health and Human Services 1988, 174).

If only because nursing home patients face different price schedules under each arrangement, the duration of nursing home admissions may differ according to payment source. The price the patient pays for nursing home care increases at twenty and one hundred days if covered by Medicare. Consequently, there may be jumps in the discharge rates near days 20 and 100. Patients covered by Medicaid pay nothing, but because the nursing home receives less money for Medicaid patients than for private pay patients, the providers may influence discharge rates. The time pattern of discharge rates would be less clear, but because Medicare patients are primarily admitted for posthospital care, and because Medicaid patients are not paying for their nursing home care, we would expect Medicaid admissions to be longer. For other payers, the patient usually bears the full cost until approaching "spend-down." The private pay patients may be a very heterogeneous group. They may include some people who are extremely disabled and would be expected to stay in a nursing home for a long time but whose financial resources exceed the Medicaid levels. They may also include individuals who are expected to have short stays in a nursing home but whose admissions do not qualify for Medicare reimbursement. The duration of nursing home stays for this group would seem likely to be intermediate between Medicare and Medicaid stays.

Because Medicare finances posthospitalization nursing home care, we would expect frequent hospital readmissions, particularly after the implementation of Medicare's Prospective Payment System. Prospective payment for hospital care gave hospitals an incentive to discharge patients early, and there have been widespread complaints that Medicare patients were being discharged "quicker and sicker." In addition, the Prospective Payment System encouraged substitution of outpatient services for inpatient care. Thus, the average Medicare patient admitted to a hospital after implementation of the new system was sicker than before since healthy Medicare recipients received more of their care as outpatients. Although these changes imply that more Medicare patients would be discharged from hospitals to nursing homes than before, there was not a surge in total Medicare nursing home expenditures. Inasmuch as Medicare inpatients were sicker and discharged earlier, we expect patients transferred from the hospital to nursing homes to be readmitted to hospitals at a high rate.

8.2 Data for the Analysis of Nursing Home Spells

Our data were obtained as part of the Channeling Demonstration, a large-scale randomized controlled trial that was organized in 1980 by the Department of Health and Human Services in order to test an intervention called "case management." This intervention gave professional personnel the responsibility for arranging and coordinating services for impaired elderly "clients." According to its advocates, case management would decrease nursing home utilization and improve the long-term care of the elderly. The Channeling Demonstration tested this hypothesis by enrolling high-risk elderly participants at ten sites around the country. The intervention did not significantly reduce nursing home utilization or improve functional status or objective measures of health, so our analyses do not incorporate estimates of the effect of case management. We have described the data elsewhere (Garber and MaCurdy 1990); the entire April 1988 issue of *Health Services Research* is devoted to the evaluation of the Channeling Demonstration.

To participate in the study, an individual had to be at least 65 years old, suffer limitations in several basic activities of daily living or instrumental activities of daily living, and have unmet needs, meaning that because of functional impairments he or she required help with at least two categories of service for six months. Because this was primarily a study of disabled elderly people living in the community, persons who were in nursing homes at the time of enrollment were included only if discharge was likely within three months. The sample meeting these criteria was relatively old (mean age 80), poorly educated, poor, and disabled.

Extensive baseline data were collected from 5,626 individuals between September 1982 and July 1983. Follow-up interviews were conducted at six, twelve, and eighteen months following the enrollment period.

Severe disability and the presence of multiple chronic illnesses were reflected in very high mortality rates. In the first year of study, 26 percent of all Channeling participants died, and about 16 percent entered nursing homes. Hospitalization was frequent and sometimes prolonged. In the first six months of the study, hospital use averaged thirteen days, and approximately 45 percent of the participants were admitted to a hospital at least once (Wooldridge and Schore 1988, 119). Monthly health care costs varied among sites and between intervention and control groups, ranging from about $1,330 to $1,879.

A large percentage of participants were admitted to nursing homes, often for repeated stays. Nearly a thousand participants had at least one admission, 292 had at least two spells, ninety-three had at least three, and twenty had four or more admissions. Medicare paid for at least part of the costs for 43 percent of the first spells, Medicaid paid for 26 percent, and other (private) payers were responsible for 31 percent. The proportion covered by Medicare or others fell steadily with admission number; Medicaid was the payer for 50 percent of third and 60 percent of fourth admissions.

A subset of the many personal characteristics recorded as part of the Channeling study appears as the explanatory variables in our analyses. We described the association between several characteristics and cumulative utilization in a previous paper (Garber and MaCurdy 1990); we found that the presence of a severe impairment in an activity of daily living (ADL) and Medicaid coverage were closely associated with increased risk of entering a nursing home. Medicaid patients who were admitted to nursing homes were less likely to terminate an admission by death. Gender was also important; men were much more likely than women to end a nursing home admission by dying. These previous estimates were based only on data on cumulative nursing home utilization and did not provide direct information about spell length.

The estimates we report here are based on additional data that include the dates of admission to and discharge from nursing homes, allowing a richer empirical specification and a more precise characterization of the roles of payer source and duration effects. The explanatory variables we use include the payment source at entry to the nursing home, the source of the admission (hospital or community), gender, age, and the presence of severe impairment in at least one ADL. Summary statistics for key variables, for the entire sample of nursing home admissions and by payer type, appear in table 8.1. The variables include ENTRY, which takes the value of zero if an individual enters a nursing home from the community and a value of one if the subject

Table 8.1 Summary Statistics

Variable	Mean	SD
Entire sample of spells ($N = 1,396$)		
ENTRY	.706	.46
AGE	80.594	7.54
AGE^2	6,552.200	1,213.80
SEX	.250	.43
SVADL	.760	.43
MEDICARE	.389	
MEDICAID	.306	
OTHER	.305	
SPELL LENGTH (days)	99.225	107.85
RIGHT CENSORED SPELLS	.220	.41
Medicare subsample ($N = 543$)		
ENTRY	.924	.29
AGE	80.039	7.50
AGE^2	6,462.500	1,203.70
SEX	.267	.44
SVADL	.759	.43
SPELL LENGTH (days)	55.692	74.23
RIGHT CENSORED SPELLS	.908	.29
Medicaid subsample of spells ($N = 427$)		
ENTRY	.639	.49
AGE	80.958	7.59
AGE^2	6,611.800	1,228.90
SEX	.194	.40
SVADL	.785	.41
SPELL LENGTH (days)	133.620	127.13
RIGHT CENSORED SPELLS	.611	.49
Other payment source ($N = 426$)		
ENTRY	.493	.50
AGE	80.937	7.49
AGE^2	6,606.800	1,204.70
SEX	.284	.45
SVADL	.737	.44
SPELL LENGTH (days)	120.230	104.18
RIGHT CENSORED SPELLS	.786	.41

enters from a hospital; AGE and AGE^2 the age and square of age at admission; SEX, which is set to one for men and zero for women; and SVADL, which equals one if a severe ADL limitation is present and zero otherwise.

8.3 An Empirical Framework

To address the issues raised in the introduction, we propose two sets of empirical specifications: one that describes how the length of stay in nursing homes varies by payment source and a second that describes the link between financing sources and the mode of exit from nursing home stays. In the subsequent formulations, we envision a person as residing in any one of four states at a given time: community residence (state c); hospitalization (state h); nursing home occupancy (state n); and death (state d). The number of days composing a spell in state n represents the length of a nursing home stay. On termination of a spell, an individual exits to state c, h, or d. Thus, our empirical requirements translate into introducing specifications that capture the relation between payment source and spell length in state n and the connection between payment source and the probability of moving to state c, h, or d when an exit from state n occurs.

8.3.1 Duration Distributions, Survivor Functions, and Hazard Rates

A duration distribution characterizes the likelihood that an individual experiences a given number of days of continuous residence in a nursing home given admission into the institution. A formulation for such a distribution is given by

$$f(\tau) = S(\tau - 1)\,[1 - P(X, \tau)], \tag{1}$$

with

$$S(\tau - 1) = \prod_{t=1}^{\tau-1} P(X, t), \tag{2}$$

where $P(X, t)$ represents a probability that conditions on the variables X and t. The function $f(\tau)$ specifies the probability that duration in a status will last exactly τ days for individuals falling into a category characterized by attributes X who are known to have entered the status at some time. The quantity $S(\tau - 1)$, the survivor function, represents the probability that individuals in this category will experience at least $\tau - 1$ days in the status. For the problem of concern in this analysis, τ corresponds to the duration of a nursing home spell, and the covariates X include factors influencing the length of spells, such as financing sources.

In the specification of the probabilities $P(X, t)$, the variables X are set at the time of entry into the status, and the variable t represents the level of duration accumulated up to the point of evaluation. The literature terms the influence of t on P "duration dependence." If $P(X, t)$ increases (decreases) as a function of t, then positive (negative) duration dependence is said to exist.

Proposing a specification for f and S requires the acquisition of some basic information concerning the appropriate functional form of the probabilities $P(X, t)$. Two aspects of this functional form are critical to specification. The first involves the nature of duration dependence applicable for the data under investigation, which primarily determines how P varies with t. The second concerns the possibility that central features of duration dependence change as the values of X change. To account for this possibility, the specification of P must allow interaction between X and t to capture the underlying nature of the relation.

Plotting hazard rates is a popular mode for presenting information about the character of duration dependence. A hazard rate is defined as follows:

$$H(\tau) = \frac{f(\tau)}{S(\tau - 1)} = 1 - P(X, \tau). \tag{3}$$

Formally, the hazard rate $H(\tau)$ represents the probability that a spell terminates on day τ given that this spell has already lasted $\tau - 1$ days. Consequently, it shows the fraction of the institutional population who, having been in the nursing home for $\tau - 1$ days will leave on the τth day of their spell. Plotting $H(\tau)$ against τ indicates how $P(X, \tau)$ varies as a function of τ.

8.3.2 An Empirical Specification for Spell Lengths in Nursing Homes

Graphs of hazard rates reveal that empirical specifications of the probabilities $P(X, t)$ must admit nonmonotonic duration dependence and allow the form of this dependence to vary according to the attributes X. Accounting for such features rules out "proportional hazards," one of the most popular choices in the duration literature, as a specification for P. We require a formulation for P that admits flexibility both in the functional form for duration dependence and in the way in which this dependence varies for different values of the covariates X.

The following specification for the probability $P(X, t)$ has these properties:

$$P(X, t) = \frac{1}{1 + e^{X_1\beta + g(t, X_2, \alpha)}}, \tag{4}$$

where X_1 and X_2 are vectors of variables made up of the covariates X, β is a parameter vector,

$$g(t, X_2, \alpha) = \sum_{j=1}^{K} [\Phi_j(t) - \Phi_{j-1}(t)][\alpha_{0j}X_2 + t \cdot \alpha_{1j} + t^2\alpha_{2j}], \tag{5}$$

$\Phi_j(t)$ denotes the cumulative distribution function of a normal random variable possessing mean μ_j and variance σ_j^2, and the α_{ij}'s in (5) represent parameter vectors. Specification (4) models P as a logit function.

The function $g(t, X_2, \alpha)$ determines the duration properties of nursing home admissions. The presence of X_2 in g allows duration dependence to vary according to all the attributes included in X_2. To describe the characteristics of g, suppose for the moment that X_2 consists only of an intercept, j, so

$$\alpha_{0j}X_2 + t\alpha_{1j} + t^2\alpha_{2j} = \alpha_{0j} + \alpha_{1j}t + \alpha_{2j}t^2.$$

The presence of the cumulative density functions in (5) permits us to incorporate spline features in g so that the quadratic polynomial $\alpha_{0j} + \alpha_{1j}t + \alpha_{2j}t^2$ represents g over only a prespecified range of t. In particular, suppose that we wish to set $g = \alpha_{01} + \alpha_{11}t + \alpha_{21}t^2$ for values of t between zero and t^* and to set $g = \alpha_{02} + \alpha_{12}t + \alpha_{22}t^2$ for values of t between t^* and some upper bound $\bar{t}$. To create a specification of g that satisfies the property, assign $K = 2$ in (5); fix the three means determining the cumulative density functions as $\mu_0 = 0$, $\mu_1 = t^*$, $\mu_2 = \bar{t}$; and pick very small values for the three standard deviations σ_0, σ_1, and σ_2. These choices for the μ's and the σ's imply that the quantity $\Phi_1(t) - \Phi_0(t)$ equals one over the range $(0, t^*)$ and zero elsewhere and that the quantity $\Phi_2(t) - \Phi_1(t)$ equals one over the range $(t^*, \bar{t})$ and zero elsewhere. Accordingly, g possesses the desired property. Further, $g(t, X_2, \alpha)$ is differentiable in t. With the values of the μ_i and the σ_i set in advance of estimation, $g(t, X_2, \alpha)$ is strictly linear in the parameters α and in known functions of t and X_2. One can control where each spline or polynomial begins and ends by adjusting the values of the μ's. Also, one can control how quickly each spline cuts in and out by adjusting the values of the σ's, with higher values providing for a more gradual and smoother transition from one polynomial to the next.

In the subsequent estimation dealing with nursing home spells, we pick a specification of $g(t, X_2, \alpha)$ by setting $K = 3$ in (5), with $\mu_0 = -1.0$, $\sigma_0 = .5$, $\mu_i = 15$, $\sigma_1 = 5$, $\mu_2 = 50$, $\sigma_2 = 5$, and μ_3 equal to a numerical value that exceeds the highest spell length. Thus, the polynomial $\alpha_{01}X_2 + t\alpha_{11} + t^2\alpha_{21}$ determines g from zero to about fifteen days. After fifteen days, g switches to the polynomial $\alpha_{02}X_2 + t\alpha_{12} + t^2\alpha_{22}$, which determines its value until about fifty days. Over the interval from day 40 to day 60, g again switches to become the polynomial $\alpha_{03}X_2 + t\alpha_{13} + t^2\alpha_{23}$, where it remains for the highest values of duration. The empirical analysis estimates the α coefficients. The following empirical analysis considers several specifications of the explanatory variables incorporated in X_1 and X_2.

8.3.3 Empirical Specifications for Exit Probabilities

A second aspect of our empirical analysis characterizes the routes by which individuals exit from nursing home spells. We seek to identify the connection between payment sources and the likelihood of following various exit alternatives. On the termination of a spell in a nursing home or, equivalently, in state n, an individual either dies, enters the community, or transfers to a hospital, which we designate as states d, c, and h, respectively. Define the probabilities

$$\text{(6)} \qquad \Pr(n \rightarrow i) \equiv \Pr(n \rightarrow i \mid \tau, X), \quad i = c, h, d,$$

for the probability of exit from state n to state i after experiencing a spell of τ days in state n. Formally, the quantity $\Pr(n \rightarrow i)$ represents the probability that an individual moves from state n to residency in state i conditional on ending a spell of τ days in state n and on the covariates X. By incorporating indicators of payment sources in X, one can relate the circumstances under which a nursing home stay ends to the financing sources used to fund this stay.

We parameterize these probabilities using a multinomial logit specification. Subsequent empirical formulations take the form

$$\text{(7)} \qquad \Pr(n \rightarrow i) = \frac{e^{Z\beta_i}}{\sum_{j=c,h,d} e^{Z\beta_j}}, \quad i = c, h, d.$$

The vector Z contains polynomials and interactions involving the duration variable τ and the elements of the covariates X.

8.4 Empirical Results

In this section, we describe the empirical relation linking the length of nursing home stays, the circumstances under which spells end, and the financing sources used to (partially) fund the spells. The analysis initially describes the estimation of duration distributions $f(\tau)$, with covariates incorporated to control for demographic characteristics and health conditions. After discussing the implications of the empirical findings for spell lengths, we consider the mode of exit from institutions.

8.4.1 Estimation Results for Duration Distributions

To estimate the distribution $f(\tau)$, we apply conventional maximum likelihood methods of the sort found in duration analysis to compute values for the coefficients β and α appearing in specification (4). Our sample consists of observations on nursing home spell lengths. Our procedure accounts for right censoring when spells are interrupted.

We estimate distinct models for three types of payment sources: (1) spells financed by Medicare at admission; (2) spells financed by Medicaid at admission; and (3) spells financed by private funds at admission. If Medicare paid any part of the nursing home costs, it was considered to be the payer. If Medicaid, but not Medicare, paid any of the costs of the admission at the time of entry, Medicaid was considered the payer. "Other payer" was considered to be the payment source if neither Medicare nor Medicaid contributed to the nursing home payments at the time of admission. An individual who "spent down" to Medicaid eligibility *during* a nursing home admission would not be considered a Medicaid patient during that admission since Medicaid was not the payer at the outset.

Table 8.2 presents coefficient estimates and standard errors for $f(\tau)$ associated with the three payment sources. The results reported correspond to a specification of $P(X, t)$ given by (4) in which $X_2 = 1$ and X_1 includes ENTRY, SEX, AGE, AGE², and SVADL. Before reaching this specification, we explored a number of formulations. Likelihood ratio tests at conventional levels of significance indicate acceptance of the restriction that the variables ENTRY, SEX, and SVADL can be excluded individually and jointly as components of X_2. From our examination of a variety of candidates for inclusion in X_2, no other variables appear to alter the form of duration dependence after accounting for payment source.

For Medicare spells, none of the coefficients of the covariates in X_1 reaches conventional levels of statistical significance. For Medicaid spells, AGE is statistically significant, and SEX is of borderline significance. For payment from other sources, SEX is statistically significant, and SVADL is of borderline sig-

Table 8.2 **Parameter Estimates from Duration Analyses (standard errors in parentheses)**

Variable	MEDICARE	MEDICAID	OTHER
ENTRY	.17083	.06436	.03396
	(.17971)	(.13300)	(.11121)
AGE	.07680	−.11256	.01195
	(.10991)	(.01600)	(.15604)
AGE^2	−.00058	.00070	−.00004
	(.00069)	(.00013)	(.00098)
SEX	.08427	.28961	.36174
	(.10677)	(.15471)	(.13246)
SVADL	.08176	.07688	.19968
	(.10631)	(.16030)	(.12979)
α_{01}	−7.02882	−.94959	−6.82207
	(4.35469)	(.55863)	(6.1759)
α_{11}	.12874	.01401	.21060
	(.09200)	(.05454)	(.20456)
α_{21}	−.00678	.00000	−.00606
	(.00607)	(.00048)	(.01180)
α_{02}	−5.66112	.00000	−5.71846
	(4.34942)	(.04839)	(6.23813)
α_{12}	−.02220	−.01990	−.00784
	(.01354)	(.01720)	(.01995)
α_{22}	.00000	.00000	.00000
	(.00000)	(.00000)	(.00000)
α_{03}	−6.65183	−.77403	−6.11224
	(4.35140)	(.57684)	(6.18819)
α_{13}	−.00379	−.00280	.00049
	(.00131)	(.00091)	(.00080)

nificance. More of the information pertinent to the duration of the spell appears to be embedded in payment source than in these covariates.

8.4.2 Implications of the Findings for Duration

To summarize the influence of various explanatory variables on the duration of nursing home admissions, tables 8.3A–8.3C report percentiles associated with the survivor functions for alternate values of the five basic characteristics used as covariates in the model, by payment source. In each of these specifications, payment source is fully interacted with the covariates. Listed in the first row of each set of results, the baseline case is a man, age 75, who has no severe impairment in basic activities of daily living and who was transferred from a hospital to the nursing home. Subsequent rows of each table show the

Table 8.3 Quantiles of Nursing Home Duration

A. Days in Nursing Home, for Admissions Covered Initially by Medicare

Specification	Percentile				
	10th	25th	50th	75th	90th
Baseline[a]	7	15	32	79	167
Entry source = hospital	6	13	27	62	129
Age = 85	8	17	38	101	220
Gender = female	7	16	35	89	191
Severe ADL limitation = present	6	14	30	70	147

B. Days in Nursing Home, for Admissions Covered Initially by Medicaid

Specification	Percentile				
	10th	25th	50th	75th	90th
Baseline[a]	16	38	114	298	> 549
Entry source = hospital	15	36	105	270	> 549
Age = 85	16	39	116	305	> 549
Gender = female	20	55	166	514	> 549
Severe ADL limitation = present	15	35	103	264	> 549

C. Days in Nursing Home, for Admissions Covered Initially by Other Payment Sources

Specification	Percentile				
	10th	25th	50th	75th	90th
Baseline[a]	12	33	97	203	336
Entry source = hospital	12	32	94	196	325
Age = 85	12	31	92	193	320
Gender = female	16	53	144	291	471
Severe ADL limitation = present	11	26	77	166	277

[a]Baseline characteristics are as follows: entered nursing home from community; age 75; male; no severe impairment in activities of daily living.

predicted quantiles associated with a change in the value of one covariate at a time. To compare the baseline cases for the three forms of financing, figure 8.1 presents plots of the survivor functions associated with the three cases. The results in table 8.3 and figure 8.1 demonstrate that there are striking differences in duration by payer source, with Medicaid admissions having the greatest length and Medicare the shortest. Table 8.3 indicates that women have longer nursing home stays than men, especially if Medicaid or "other source" initially finances the stay. Age is associated with an increased length of stay for Medicare admissions, but not for the other payment sources.

Just as the parameter estimates indicate that the presence of a severe ADL impairment and the source of admission could be excluded from the model, table 8.3 shows that the predicted duration varies little with changes in these variables. Severe ADL impairment was of borderline significance in the duration analyses for other payment source, and table 8.3C shows that duration is shorter for persons with a severe ADL impairment than for the baseline case, if payment comes from "other source." The overall lack of explanatory power for ADL impairment may be somewhat surprising, but is consistent with our earlier finding that severe ADL impairment was a statistically significant predictor of mortality and of the probability of admission to a nursing home but not of the probability of discharge from a nursing home (Garber and MaCurdy 1990). As we will see in the next section, the current analysis confirms that, while the presence of a severe ADL impairment has little effect on duration, it is associated with the probability that a spell will terminate in death.

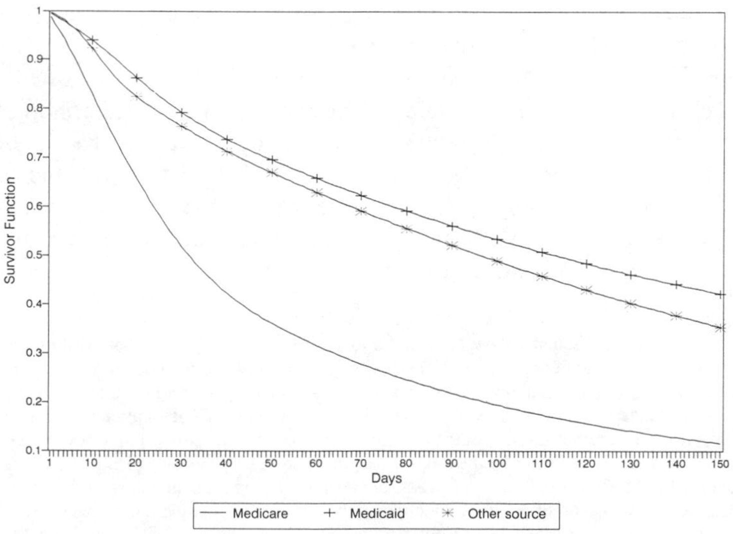

Fig. 8.1 Survivor functions by payment source

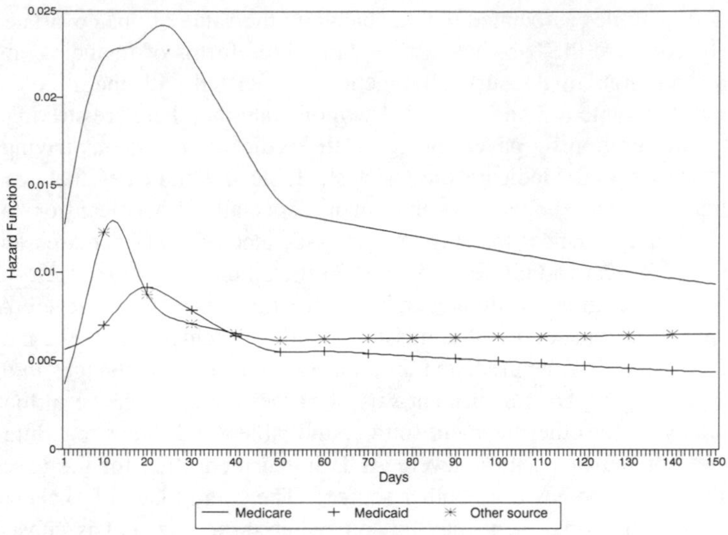

Fig. 8.2 Hazard functions by payment source

The hazard functions for each payer type, plotted in figure 8.2, demonstrate the nature of duration dependence. Medicare nursing home spells, but not the others, would be expected to show fluctuations in the value of the hazard because of the changes in the effective price induced by the Medicare rules. Private pay patients would not be expected to experience changes in price during a nursing home admission unless they were approaching the spend-down to Medicaid eligibility. Medicaid patients face zero price, so rapid changes in hazard rates are not expected.[1]

Although the hazard functions are qualitatively similar for persons with different characteristics, the magnitude of the rate is variable. Furthermore, there are striking differences in hazards according to payer type. At baseline characteristics there is a broad peak in the hazard rate between days 10 and 40. As table 8.3 reveals, this early peak in the hazard corresponds to a relatively short length of stay. Half the Medicare admissions have ended by thirty-two days, and three-fourths have ended by seventy-nine days.

1. Particularly for Medicaid patients, transfer to a hospital or discharge to the community is not simply a demand phenomenon, so other factors may be responsible for fluctuations in the hazard rate. Nursing homes can influence discharges and may have special incentives for doing so when Medicaid is the payer. Gertler (1989) has argued that, while private pay patients can be charged more than Medicaid reimburses, Medicaid patients are admitted because regulations prevent nursing homes from discriminating on the basis of payment source. There is typically excess demand for Medicaid-financed beds. One implication of Gertler's argument is that nursing homes have an incentive to discharge or transfer Medicaid patients whenever there is an increase in demand among private payers or when health deterioration increases the cost of caring for a Medicaid patient.

Medicaid hazard rates are lower than Medicare hazards, corresponding to the much longer average length of stay for a Medicaid admission. Medicaid hazards have an attenuated peak at about twenty days (possibly reflecting dual coverage). As the Medicaid survivor function shows, the probability of remaining in the nursing home declines slowly and smoothly with time. Even after a hundred days, more than half the Medicaid admissions remain in the nursing home; the seventy-fifth percentile for Medicaid is 298 days at baseline characteristics and exceeds a year for women.

Hazard rates for admissions reimbursed by private funds exhibit an early peak, at about two weeks, but the peak is not nearly as high as for the Medicare admissions. At later times, the hazard rate remains higher than for Medicaid patients (but lower than for Medicare). For example, at the baseline values of the variables, the hazard rate under "other insurance" is .0065 at one hundred days, but only .005 for Medicaid. The Medicare hazard rate, in contrast, is about .012 at one hundred days.

Despite the somewhat higher hazard rates, spells paid by "other payer" are only slightly shorter than Medicaid spells, as the survivor functions (fig. 8.2) suggest.

8.4.3 Estimation Results for Exit Probabilities

To estimate the probabilities $\Pr(n \rightarrow i)$ defined by (5), we apply standard maximum likelihood procedures in a multinomial logit framework to compute values for the parameters β appearing in specification (7). Our sample consists of observations on the residency status of an individual immediately following the termination of a nursing home spell. The values of the variables Z are fixed at the time of entry into the spell. As an arbitrary normalization, the coefficients in the transition to death are set equal to zero, so reported coefficient estimates measure $\Pr(n \rightarrow h)$ and $\Pr(n \rightarrow c)$ relative to $\Pr(n \rightarrow d)$.

Table 8.4 presents parameter estimates and standard errors associated with the exit probabilities. The variables incorporated in Z include polynomials in the spell-length quantity τ and many of the same variables introduced in the duration analysis presented above. The intercepts and the polynomial terms τ, τ^2, and τ^3 are fully interacted with the three dummy variables MEDICAID, MEDICARE, and OTHER, which identify payment source at the time of admission into the institution. Such a parameterization allows patterns for the relation between spell lengths and exit probabilities to vary by payment source. Interactions between SVADL and the three financing dummies also permit separate influences for severe ADL limitations. The inclusion of the variables AGE, AGE^2, and SEX control for demographic characteristics. Likelihood ratio tests at conventional levels of significance imply acceptance of the restriction that the associations of demographic characteristics with exit probabilities do not vary by payment source. Additional hypothesis tests indicate that the ENTRY variable, which describes residency status prior to institutionalization, is not a statistically significant determinant of exit outcomes.

Table 8.4 Parameter Estimates of the Exit Probabilities (standard errors in parentheses)

Variable	$\Pr(n\to c)/\Pr(n\to d)$	$\Pr(n\to h)/\Pr(n\to d)$
CONSTANT × MEDICARE	.516020	−1.445786
	(9.643600)	(9.659844)
SPELL LENGTH × MEDICARE	.032360	.009396
	(.010600)	(.011443)
SPELL LENGTH^2 × MEDICARE	−.000242	−.000059
	(.000085)	(.000100)
SPELL LENGTH^3 × MEDICARE	.000000	.000000
	(.000000)	(.000000)
CONSTANT × MEDICAID	.316500	−.711479
	(9.655840)	(9.676097)
SPELL LENGTH × MEDICAID	.009850	.009584
	(.019530)	(.018069)
SPELL LENGTH^2 × MEDICAID	−.000127	−.000120
	(.000162)	(.000152)
SPELL LENGTH^3 × MEDICAID	.000000	.000000
	(.000000)	(.000000)
CONSTANT × OTHER	1.487810	−1.469308
	(9.805370)	(9.821161)
SPELL LENGTH × OTHER	.019757	.028884
	(.030393)	(.030842)
SPELL LENGTH^2 × OTHER	−.000097	−.000168
	(.000291)	(.000293)
SPELL LENGTH^3 × OTHER	.000000	.000000
	(.000001)	(.000001)
SVADL × MEDICARE	−.640180	−.238538
	(.334980)	(.347173)
SVADL × MEDICAID	.049353	.513870
	(.524721)	(.473625)
SVADL × OTHER	.342004	.629457
	(.621751)	(.651149)
AGE	.033890	.068363
	(.241234)	(.241742)
AGE^2	−.000356	−.000516
	(.001493)	(.001497)
SEX	−.592309	−.402908
	(.219186)	(.221017)

8.4.4 Implications of the Findings for Exits

To develop the implications of the empirical results given above for the relation between financing sources and the circumstances under which a nursing home spell ends, table 8.5 reports predictions for the exit probabilities for different values of the covariates. The results in table 8.5 imply that, for 75-year-old men, the presence of severe impairment in at least one activity of daily living raises the probability that a Medicare-paid nursing home admission will terminate in death. The association between severe impairment and death is not present when Medicaid or other sources finance the admission.

Table 8.5 Exit Probabilities, by Duration, Characteristics, and Payment Source

A. From Hospital, Age 75, Male, No Severe ADL Impairment

SPELL	MEDICARE			MEDICAID			OTHER SOURCE		
LENGTH	COMMUNITY	HOSPITAL	DEATH	COMMUNITY	HOSPITAL	DEATH	COMMUNITY	HOSPITAL	DEATH
5	.4239	.3482	.2279	.2461	.5736	.1802	.6369	.2256	.1375
10	.4530	.3362	.2108	.2480	.5775	.1745	.6387	.2355	.1258
15	.4798	.3246	.1956	.2495	.5808	.1697	.6397	.2448	.1155
25	.5265	.3033	.1702	.2517	.5857	.1625	.6403	.2613	.0984
50	.6038	.2656	.1306	.2530	.5906	.1564	.6386	.2907	.0707
75	.6348	.2505	.1147	.2499	.5872	.1630	.6395	.3047	.0559
100	.6315	.2542	.1143	.2437	.5769	.1794	.6457	.3061	.0482

B. From Hospital, Age 85, Male, No Severe ADL Impairment

SPELL	MEDICARE			MEDICAID			OTHER SOURCE		
LENGTH	COMMUNITY	HOSPITAL	DEATH	COMMUNITY	HOSPITAL	DEATH	COMMUNITY	HOSPITAL	DEATH
5	.3885	.3487	.2628	.2238	.5700	.2063	.6029	.2333	.1638
10	.4172	.3384	.2444	.2257	.5744	.1999	.6057	.2441	.1502
15	.4440	.3282	.2278	.2273	.5782	.1945	.6077	.2542	.1381
25	.4911	.3091	.1998	.2296	.5838	.1866	.6099	.2720	.1180
50	.5705	.2742	.1553	.2310	.5893	.1797	.6110	.3039	.0851
75	.6029	.2600	.1371	.2278	.5851	.1871	.6132	.3193	.0675
100	.5996	.2637	.1366	.2215	.5732	.2053	.6203	.3213	.0583

C. From Hospital, Age 75, Female, No Severe ADL Impairment

SPELL	MEDICARE			MEDICAID			OTHER SOURCE		
LENGTH	COMMUNITY	HOSPITAL	DEATH	COMMUNITY	HOSPITAL	DEATH	COMMUNITY	HOSPITAL	DEATH
5	.5058	.3438	.1504	.3000	.5785	.1215	.7080	.2075	.0845
10	.5343	.3281	.1375	.3016	.5811	.1173	.7072	.2158	.0770
15	.5602	.3135	.1263	.3029	.5833	.1139	.7060	.2235	.0705
25	.6041	.2879	.1080	.3046	.5866	.1088	.7029	.2374	.0598
50	.6741	.2453	.0806	.3055	.5901	.1044	.6955	.2620	.0426
75	.7010	.2289	.0700	.3025	.5883	.1091	.6932	.2733	.0335
100	.6978	.2324	.0699	.2971	.5820	.1210	.6976	.2736	.0288

D. From Hospital, Age 75, Male, With Severe ADL Impairment

SPELL	MEDICARE			MEDICAID			OTHER SOURCE		
LENGTH	COMMUNITY	HOSPITAL	DEATH	COMMUNITY	HOSPITAL	DEATH	COMMUNITY	HOSPITAL	DEATH
5	.3080	.3780	.3140	.2480	.5792	.1729	.6152	.2904	.0943
10	.3343	.3707	.2951	.2498	.5829	.1673	.6129	.3013	.0857
15	.3592	.3631	.2777	.2513	.5861	.1626	.6104	.3114	.0783
25	.4042	.3479	.2478	.2534	.5909	.1557	.6049	.3291	.0661
50	.4837	.3179	.1984	.2546	.5956	.1498	.5933	.3600	.0466
75	.5175	.3052	.1773	.2515	.5923	.1562	.5892	.3742	.0366
100	.5142	.3092	.1766	.2455	.5824	.1721	.5935	.3750	.0315

However, for people whose nursing home stays are not financed by either government program, the presence of a severe impairment in an activity of daily living is associated with a decreased likelihood of return to the community.

As the parameter estimates imply, gender differences in exits are significant. Table 8.5C presents results for a woman identical to the baseline case in every way except gender. Although the probability of hospital transfer does not appear to differ by gender, death is much less likely for a woman than for a man, and the probability of discharge to the community is somewhat greater.

The well-described heterogeneity of nursing home admissions (Keeler, Kane, and Solomon 1981) suggests that the probability of each type of exit would not be fixed over time. Nursing home residents who have severe chronic disabilities and cannot live independently in the community are likely to terminate nursing home spells either by death or by transfer to a hospital. Such individuals predominate among the long-stayers. Discharges that occur early in a nursing home admission represent mixtures of people admitted for terminal care or for convalescence; one would expect few hospital transfers among early discharges. Whether death would be more likely for early discharges than for long-stayers depends in large part on the mix of terminal patients and convalescent patients among short-term nursing home stays.

Although there is no relation between duration of the spell and exit probabilities for Medicaid patients, exit probabilities change with time for Medicare and "other source." For Medicare patients, the probability of community discharge increases with duration, while the probability of hospital transfer and death both fall with duration. For admissions paid by other sources, the probability of discharge to the community does not vary with duration of the admission, but the probability of death declines, and the probability of hospital admission rises. Without knowing the subsequent pattern of utilization or the outcomes of hospitalization, it is difficult to ascertain the significance of the time trend of exit probabilities for "other source," but it appears likely that a relatively high percentage of Medicare admissions for terminal care end early.

Even for admissions of the same duration, predicted exit probabilities demonstrate striking variation with payer type. Return to the community is most likely if other sources pay for the nursing home admission. Death is most likely for Medicare patients, although Medicaid patients are also more likely to terminate a nursing home spell in death than are patients whose admissions are financed by other sources. Medicaid patients are the least likely to return to the community. These results and the duration findings together imply that Medicaid patients are likely to enter nursing homes for very long periods that terminate in either death or transfer to a hospital; our analyses do not enable us to say whether the hospital transfers ended in death, transfer back to a nursing home, or return to the community. These results make it seem unlikely that subsequent long-term care utilization by Medicare or "other" patients will be nearly as great as for Medicaid patients.

8.5 Conclusions

As planning for and financing long-term care have achieved new prominence in policy circles, there is an urgent need for reliable estimates of the effect of insurance on long-term care utilization. We have attempted to take a step toward understanding the effect of insurance by measuring the association between payer type and utilization within a high-risk population of older Americans. One might argue that the absence of an association between type of coverage and utilization suggests that the demand for nursing home care is inelastic, an assumption implicit in much of the policy discussion regarding long-term care insurance. Many advocates of broader long-term care insurance coverage believe that widespread adoption of long-term care insurance would not increase the utilization of nursing homes.

Our analysis finds that the distribution of the length of nursing home stays differs substantially among payer types, in ways that may not simply reflect selection. These differences are apparent even in a population of frail elderly individuals who lack social supports and are felt to have "unmet needs." The differences also persist despite the control of the additional covariates incorporated into our model. Although our study was not designed to assess whether the differences in nursing home duration by payer are causal relations, the persistence of strong relations between payer type and duration of nursing home admission despite the selection of the population and the control for additional covariates suggests that the incentive effects of the subsidy of nursing home care may play an important role in nursing home utilization.

The results of the duration analyses reported here suggest that the payment source is strongly associated with the length of nursing home admissions. The covariates have a weak independent association with duration, at least within this population and in the time period studied, but some of them, such as the presence of a severe ADL impairment, are associated with the type of exit. Medicare-financed admissions are much shorter than admissions funded by either Medicaid or "other" payment source, and there is a striking early peak in the hazard rate for Medicare admissions.

The type of exit from the nursing home is also highly associated with the payment source. Exit probabilities reflect the "success" of a nursing home admission, and they also give clues to future utilization of long-term care. Nursing home spells financed by "other," primarily private, payers last nearly as long as Medicaid admissions but are much more likely to end with return to the community. The length of admission and payment source interact, at least for Medicare spells; the longer a Medicare patient is in a nursing home, the more likely is discharge to home. Even long Medicare admissions seem short in comparison to Medicaid admissions and are much more likely to end in return to the community. For the Medicaid admissions, the high rate of discharge to hospitals and the high rate of death are discouraging signs for return to independent living. A study that traced paths of nursing home patients found that 14 percent of the patients discharged to a hospital died within forty-eight hours. Of the remaining hospital transfers, 11 percent died in the hospital, and about 80 percent returned to a nursing home (Lewis, Cretin, and Kane 1985).

Although the results of this study may be interpreted to imply that the demand for nursing home care is responsive to price, such a broad interpretation is premature. First, the population studied does not readily generalize to all elderly Americans. Channeling participants were selected because they were at high risk of entering a nursing home. The selection rule makes it difficult to generalize to all America's elderly population, particularly since the criteria for "unmet needs" were not explicit. On the other hand, this population is inherently interesting. The Channeling population used nursing homes heavily. Many of them would have been unable to purchase private long-term care insurance because they could not afford the premiums. In addition, many would have been ineligible because of preexisting chronic diseases or because their conditions would not be covered by many nursing home care policies. This is the group that is most likely to benefit from a federal program for long-term care insurance and would account for a disproportionate share of program costs.

Furthermore, while the Channeling population is special, the basic phenomena we describe may occur in similar fashion in the general population. There is some evidence that the outcomes of nursing home spells were *more* favorable in the Channeling population than among all nursing home spells. An analysis of the 1977 National Nursing Home Survey found that 49.7 percent of Medicare admissions ended in discharge to the community, slightly *less* than predicted in our analyses, at the mean duration of fifty-six days. Similarly, "other" payment source and Medicaid admissions had a lower rate of discharge to the community in the 1977 National Nursing Home Survey than predicted in our analysis of Channeling. The analysis did not present the percentage who died, subsequent outcomes, or variation in discharge status with length of stay (Weissert and Scanlon 1985).

A second difficulty arises from the endogeneity of payer source. Medicaid patients are likely to have been chronically debilitated, and they may have been enrolled for substantial periods before entering the Channeling study. Other admissions must meet several requirements before they qualify for Medicare reimbursement. Inasmuch as there is a need for recent hospitalization, a relatively high death rate for Medicare admissions has little to do with causal effects of the payment system and much to do with the selection rules. Nearly all Medicare patients would have had either an acute illness or an acute exacerbation of a chronic illness; the same phenomenon need not have been true for the other payers.

Our results to date should be viewed as suggestive findings, not as definitive answers about insurance effects. As such, they make it clear that a complete understanding of nursing home utilization must be based on an adequate characterization of paths leading to and from nursing homes and that it must account for multiple admissions.

References

Garber, A. M., and T. E. MaCurdy. 1990. Predicting Nursing Home Utilization among the High-Risk Elderly. In *Issues in the Economics of Aging*, ed. D. A. Wise. Chicago: University of Chicago Press.

Gertler, P. J. 1989. Medicaid and the Cost of Improving Access to Nursing Home Care. NBER Working Paper no. 2851. Cambridge, Mass.: National Bureau of Economic Research.

Keeler, E. B., R. L. Kane, and D. H. Solomon. 1981. Short- and Long-Term Residents of Nursing Homes. *Medical Care* 19:363–69.

Kidwell, K. D. 1988. *Medicaid Estate Recoveries*. Washington, D.C.: Office of Analysis and Inspections, Office of the Inspector General, U.S. Department of Health and Human Services.

Lewis, M. A., S. Cretin, and R. L. Kane. 1985. The Natural History of Nursing Home Patients. *Gerontologist* 25:382–88.

U.S. Department of Health and Human Services. Office of the Actuary. Health Care Financing Administration. 1985. *Health Care Financing Program Statistics: Analysis of State Medicaid Program Characteristics, 1984*. Baltimore, Md.: Health Care Financing Administration.

U.S. Department of Health and Human Services. 1989. *Health United States 1988*. DHHS Publication no. (PHS) 89-1232. Hyattsville, Md.: Public Health Service, Centers for Disease Control, National Center for Health Statistics.

Weissert, W. G., and W. J. Scanlon. 1985. Determinants of Nursing Home Discharge Status. *Medical Care* 23:333–43.

Wooldridge, J., and J. Schore. 1988. The Effect of Channeling on the Use of Nursing Homes, Hospitals, and Other Medical Services. *Health Services Research* 23:119–27.

Comment Paul J. Gertler

How to finance long-term care is being intensely debated at all levels of government. At issue is whether to promote private insurance alternatives or expand current entitlement programs. Further, there is substantial controversy over how to structure benefits under any alternative. Answers to these questions clearly depend on the properties of the demand for long-term care. Alan M. Garber and Thomas MaCurdy make an important contribution to understanding the determinants of the use of long-term care. In particular, they investigate the likely moral hazard properties of private long-term care insur-

Paul J. Gertler is Senior Economist at the Rand Corporation.

ance. The authors argue that one possible argument as to why a private long-term care insurance market does not exist is moral hazard.

Garber and MaCurdy also move the empirical modeling of health care demand out of a static framework into dynamic models. While theoretical work has recognized dynamics, few empirical studies have attempted dynamic models. In addition, the empirical work is careful, and the authors go to great lengths to maintain maximum flexibility in their econometric specifications.

The authors' model the duration of a nursing home stay (conditional on the entry decision) and mode of exit (home, hospital, or death). The first stage estimates hazard models separately by payment source (Medicare, Medicaid, and private pay). The major empirical issue is identification of price effects. Nursing home patients can be categorized into three groups based on method of payment: private pay, Medicaid, and Medicare. The biggest source of price variation faced by patients is in the private pay market. However, Garber and MaCurdy argue that one cannot accurately estimate the true prices faced by private pay patients because of hard-to-measure quality differences across nursing homes. For the remaining patients, there is limited cross-sectional price variation. Medicaid patients face zero prices, and all Medicare patients face the same copayments. However, the Medicare copayment changes over time, so Medicare patients face an increase in copayments during their nursing home stay. It is this variation that Garber and MaCurdy exploit to identify price effects.

While Garber and MaCurdy have made an important contribution to identifying price effects, there is some question as to how useful their estimates are. Medicare accounts for a very small percentage of nursing home patient days and expenditures. The question boils down to whether Medicare price effects are representative of the price elasticity of demand by the majority of patients (Medicaid and private pay). Indeed, the three types of patients are very different.

Consider the differences between Medicare and non-Medicare patients. Almost all Medicare patients have entered the nursing home after a hospitalization for some acute morbid event. Their nursing home stay is directly related to their illness, and their reason for being in a nursing home is typically rehabilitative. Therefore, unless these patients die quickly, one would expect them to get better and return to the community. Medicare patients are short-stayers. Medicaid and private pay patients typically enter nursing homes because of a long-term chronic problem that has so incapacitated them that they require help in their activities of daily living. Their purpose for being in a nursing home is typically life-style maintenance, and they are long-stayers. Indeed, the data reported by Garber and MaCurdy support these differences. The majority of Medicare patients enter nursing homes from hospitals, and their average length of stay is only fifty-five days (9 percent of the observations are right censored). On the other hand, the majority of Medicaid and private pay patients do not enter from a hospital, and their average length of stay is about 125 days (70 percent of the observations are right censored).

Now consider the differences between Medicaid and private pay patients. One must be financially indigent to be eligible for Medicaid. Private pay patients tend to be wealthier and healthier than Medicaid patients. Medicaid status is commonly used as a measure of overall poor health in many studies in medical literature. Thus, one would expect Medicaid patients' health to deteriorate much more quickly. Therefore, their stays are shorter, and they are more likely to exit via hospitalization or death. This is borne out in the data. Medicaid patients exit nursing homes faster than private pay patients: 75 percent of Medicaid patients exit via death or hospitalization, whereas 35 percent of private patients exit via these methods. This is either because the initial state of health is poorer for Medicaid patients or because nursing homes quality discriminate.

What these differences suggest is that there is substantial underlying patient heterogeneity across patients in the three groups. If price elasticities depend on health status, wealth, and other demographic factors, then Garber and MaCurdy's price elasticity estimates have limited usefulness. However, this is not the authors' fault. It is a limitation of the available price variation in nursing home data. Indeed, Garber and MaCurdy should be commended for finding a way to exploit the limited variation to obtain any estimates at all.

A more fundamental problem concerns the extent to which Garber and MaCurdy have estimated complete price elasticities. The paper attempts to measure the effects of financial incentives on the demand for nursing home care by investigating length of stay conditional on the decision to enter a nursing home. While modeling the duration of stay captures an important component of demand, other elements need to be considered to obtain a complete alternative. Most obvious is the decision to enter a nursing home at all. Financial incentives are likely to have a big effect on the initial entry decision. Not incorporating entry is somewhat surprising given Garber and MaCurdy's previous work on entry decisions using the same data. Second, quality as measured by the services nursing homes provide has been shown to respond dramatically to the incentive structure of Medicaid reimbursement rules and the level of private pay demand. Indeed, some nursing homes may respond to alternative financial incentive structures by adjusting quality instead of quantity (length of stay). A complete picture of the demand for nursing home care needs to incorporate the entry decision and quality.

A more complete model is important for examining the policy implications of the price effects. For example, the Rand health insurance experiment demonstrated that hospital entry and length of stay have very different price elasticities. If this is the case for nursing homes, then moral hazard estimates depend crucially on the entry decision. Given their data, they can follow individuals through the complete course of medical treatment, not just beginning with nursing home entry. By looking only at nursing homes, they have a selected sample and therefore cannot examine how policies that affect hospitalization (diagnostic related groups, or DRGs) affect nursing home demand. Moreover, they cannot investigate how policies affect total medical care expenditures. In the end, we are more interested in the total medical care expenditures than in just the nursing home component.

A next step for Garber and MaCurdy would be to use the information on entire episodes of illness (hospitalization, who does not enter a home, and what happens to patients pre– and post–nursing home stay). The could easily expand their dynamic framework to include hospitalization and other forms of care so as to get complete resource use model. In addition, resource use is modeled as an input into a health production function whose dependent variable is length of life. This more complete framework is easier to interpret from a welfare perspective. It would have individuals moving in and out of four states: home, hospital, nursing home, death (absorbing state). Indeed, one could expand this to include living arrangements and get at the question of substitutability of formal and informal care.

Let me turn now to the exit model. A discrete choice model conditional on length of stay is specified. The possible modes of exit are community (get better), hospitalization (health deteriorates), and death (health deteriorates further). This suggests that length of stay is an input into the production of health. However, it seems to matter only for Medicare patients. It does not affect the other types of patients getting better.

How should length of stay be interpreted in the exit model? Are short stops good or bad? The moral hazard story implies that short stays are good if patients return home because fewer resources are used. Alternatively, long stays may be good if nursing home care substitutes for hospital care. If patients exit to death, then long stays (ignoring quality of life) are better. What this again suggests is that the authors need a more complete theoretical model to guide the empirical specification. Initial health conditions are determined by whether and when to enter a nursing home. It would be easier to interpret results if they follow changes in health status over time.

In summary, Garber and MaCurdy have made an important contribution to the understanding of the demand for nursing home care as well as moving the demand for medical care literature into dynamic models. I hope that they continue to expand their work into more complete dynamic models.

9 Incentive Regulation of Nursing Homes

Specification Tests of the Markov Model

Edward C. Norton

In Norton (1990), I presented evidence that changing the reimbursement system to nursing homes to account for performance had a positive effect both on quality and on controlling costs. The analysis used a simple Markov model to estimate transition probabilities between states of health in the nursing home. A comparison of the probabilities for the control group (no incentives) and the experimental group (positive incentives) found them to be different. People in the experimental group stayed for a shorter time and had better outcomes.

The simple Markov model maintains several strong assumptions. For example, it assumes that the transition probabilities are constant over time, independent of past states, and the same for all people. If any of these assumptions are false, the conclusions of the previous paper may be ill founded. This paper extends the analysis to more general models and in doing so subjects the simple Markov model to a series of rigorous specification tests. Most of the specification tests are done on data from the control group nursing homes only so as not to mix effects of the experiment with those of the assumptions. Each section of the paper tests one of the assumptions listed below:

1. *First order.* The probability of being in state *j* next period depends only on the current state, not on past states.
2. *Homogeneity.* The probabilities are independent of personal characteristics, such as age, sex, race, and marital status.
3. *Stationarity.* The probabilities are constant over time.

Edward C. Norton is a postdoctoral fellow in the Project on the Economics of Aging at the National Bureau of Economic Research and the Bradley Fellow at Harvard University Medical School, Department of Health Care Policy.

The author wishes to thank Rebecca Demsetz, Jerry Hausman, Paul Joskow, Daniel McFadden, Carolyn H. Norton, Mitchell Petersen, James Poterba, Sherwin Rosen, Douglas Staiger, members of the Public Finance lunch, and the NBER Conference on the Economics of Aging for helpful comments. Grant support from the National Science Foundation and the Bradley Foundation is gratefully acknowledged.

4. *Duration dependence*. The probabilities are independent of how long a person has been in the nursing home.
5. *Learning effect*. Nursing homes in the experimental group instantly switched to optimize under the new reimbursement system with no learning period.
6. *Markov assumption*. $P(T) = P(1)^T$.
7. *Measurement error.* Reporting errors by nurses have no effect on the estimated transition probabilities.

This paper contains a summary of the experiment done by the National Center for Health Services Research (NCHSR) and the data used in the analysis. Then there is a brief review of the results in Norton (1990). The remainder of the paper is a rigorous extension of the previous analysis.

9.1 Study and Data

This section contains a brief summary of the methodology of the NCHSR experiment and a description of the data collected. For a more complete discussion, see Weissert et al. (1983).

Thirty-six proprietary, Medi-Cal certified, skilled nursing facilities in San Diego participated in the study. All these nursing homes had at least thirty beds. Only four eligible nursing homes in San Diego declined to participate. NCHSR hired Applied Management Sciences Inc. of Silver Spring, Maryland, to collect the data and to supervise the team of registered nurses that did the fieldwork. After a six-month baseline data-gathering period, the nursing homes were split from a matched sample into two groups of eighteen. The experimental group received *all three* incentive payments, while the control group was paid only a nominal amount to cover the additional cost of bookkeeping. A total of 11,389 residents were tracked during the two-and-a-half-year study. Out of these residents, 58 percent were covered by Medicaid, and the incentives applied only to these people. Table 9.1 shows a time line of how the study was conducted, and table 9.2 gives summary statistics about the data.

9.1.1 Resident Classification System

The hired registered nurses visited each resident periodically to assess their health and to determine whether they achieved certain goals. New residents were assessed within two weeks of admission, and most reassessments were made at three-month intervals. When a person left a nursing home, the date and reason were recorded. Nurses classified residents as being in one of five states of health. Classification depended primarily on how much help was needed in activities of daily living (ADL). These objective measures have been used widely as the best measure of health status of the elderly (see Katz and Akpom 1976; and Börsch-Supan, Kotlikoff, and Morris 1988). There are six ADLs: bathing, dressing, eating, using the toilet, transferring, and walk-

Table 9.1 **Time Line**

November 1980 to April 1981	Collected baseline data, no incentives
30 April 1981	Homes randomly assigned to experimental or control groups
May 1981 to April 1982	New admissions eligible for admission incentives for one year
30 April 1982	End of study if admitted prior to May 1981
May 1982 to April 1983	Reassessed if admitted after 1 May 1981

Table 9.2 **NCHSR Nursing Home Data**

Subgroup	Average Age	% Women	% White	% Married
Admitted before study:				
Control ($N = 718$)	80	70	90	15
Experiment ($N = 637$)	79	73	91	16
Admitted during study:				
Control ($N = 1{,}417$)	80	72	91	16
Experiment ($N = 1{,}080$)	80	74	89	17

Table 9.3 **Classification of the Five States of Health**

Type	Dischargeable within 90 days?	ADL Index	% of Sample at Admission
A	Yes	Usually ADL ≤ 2	23
B	No	$1 \leq$ ADL ≤ 4	22
C	No	ADL $= 5$	31
D	No	ADL $= 6$	18
E	No	ADL ≥ 4 and required special nursing services	5

ing. A person who needs assistance in four of these categories has an ADL index of four. Classification also depended on how soon someone was likely to be discharged and whether special nursing care was needed. Type A people are the "healthiest" and type E the "sickest." Table 9.3 summarizes the classification scheme.

9.1.2 Incentive Payments

Admission

Medicaid reimbursement in California was a flat prospective rate ($36 in 1981), with the result that nursing homes were reluctant to admit people who required more than average care. Nursing homes in the experimental group received a per diem bonus when they admitted type D and E residents. The size of the bonuses reflected wages needed to pay for increased nursing care coverage. The per diem bonuses for types A, B, C, and D were 0, −2.5, 0, and 5, respectively. The rate for E ranged from 3 to 28, depending on the amount of special care needed.

Outcome

Some residents needed special rehabilitation to improve their functional or health status. This requires a large fixed cost to the nursing home that is not reimbursed under flat rate reimbursement and is therefore discouraged. Experimental group nursing homes received a lump sum bonus if selected residents improved their health status (corresponding to E → D, C → B or D → B, and B → A). These goals were designed to reduce ADL dependence and eliminate the need for special nursing services. Nursing homes were paid only if the goal was met within ninety days. It is important to remember that, in order to be eligible for a goal, a resident first had to be nominated by his or her nursing home. Nursing homes nominated residents whom they felt would benefit from costly rehabilitation services, and the hired NCHSR nurses had to approve each nomination. In the experimental group nursing homes, 150 nominations were approved. The hired nurses nominated residents in the control group nursing homes. Nursing homes received an amount equal to the estimated wages needed to pay for extra nursing help, ranging from $126 to $370.

Discharge

People well enough to be discharged are also the least expensive to care for. Nursing homes prefer to keep these people, although they cannot legally prevent anyone from leaving. To encourage appropriate discharges, nursing homes received a lump sum bonus if certain residents were discharged from the nursing home promptly *and* the resident stayed out of the nursing home for ninety days. Payment was designed to offset the cost of a vacant bed and the administrative costs of discharge. Type A residents were not eligible for discharge bonuses since they were expected to be discharged soon anyway. Payment ranged from $230 down to $60, with more paid for a timelier discharge. Like outcome incentives, experimental group nursing homes had to nominate residents and have their choices approved (113 were approved).

9.2 Markov Model

An implicit assumption in the NCHSR experiment is that the way nursing homes are paid affects their effort, which in turn affects residents' health. This section briefly describes a model of how reimbursement affects health. A first-order Markov model is described completely by a set of probabilities (see Amemiya 1985, chap. 11). Let P_{ij} be the probability that a person goes from state i to state j in one period. There are nine states in the model, five states of health within in the nursing home and four states to go to outside the nursing home. State of health is based on an objective index of a person's ability to perform basic tasks of living, known as the Activities of Daily Living Index.[1] When residents leave a nursing home, their state of health determines where they go next: home, intermediate care facility, hospital, or death. Although health is a random variable, it does not depend solely on biology but depends also on the nursing home's effort, e, which in turn is a function of the reimbursement system, I. Let $P_{ij} = P[e(I)]_{ij}$. Presumably, larger incentives trigger greater effort and better health.

A simple test of the plan's effectiveness is to estimate P for both the control and the experimental groups and to compare the transition matrices. One would expect that, if the program is effective, the probability of improving one's health will be greater in the experimental group nursing homes. Also, using the Markov model allows one to compare estimates of the length and cost per spell in the nursing home. If the results show no differences between the groups, it could be because the incentives were too small to induce much more effort. It could also be that increased effort from the current level would not change a resident's fortunes, and it would therefore not be worthwhile to increase effort.

The P matrices were estimated by maximum likelihood. Estimation controlled for censored observations and the fact that the time between observations was not constant. The transition probabilities were estimated for a two-week time period.

The results can be summarized as follows. Incentive regulation of nursing homes had beneficial effects on both quality and cost of care. People in experimental group nursing homes were more likely to go home or to a lower-level nursing home and less likely to be hospitalized or to die than people in control group nursing homes. The admission incentives induced nursing homes to admit more people with severe disabilities. The most striking difference between the experimental and the control groups is that both the mean and the median length of stay are much shorter in the experimental group. The incentives do seem to cause the nursing homes to discharge residents more quickly. Were this program implemented, the cost savings would not come directly from shorter stays since high occupancy rates mean a nearly constant Medicaid population in nursing homes. Instead, the more rapid turnover rate would transfer patients out of hospitals and save hospital costs. The administrative and incentive costs of the NCHSR program are negligible compared to the potential savings.

1. There are five categories in this study based on the six ADLs (eating, bathing, transferring into and out of bed, using the toilet, walking, and dressing). ADLs are good determinants of ability to function alone (see Katz and Akpom 1976). The five categories are described in section 9.3.

9.3 First Order versus Second Order

The assumption that the Markov model is first order means that the transition probabilities depend only on current health. Any information from the past should not help predict the future. A more general model would incorporate information about whether a person has been improving, has been getting worse, or has remained stable. The first-order assumption can be tested against the alternative that the model is *second order.* If the model is second order, then the probabilities depend on both health now and health last period.

A second-order model can be written as a first-order model with many more initial states. Specifically for the nursing home data, the first-order model has five possible states of health and the second-order model thirty. More precisely, let P_{ijk} be the probability that a person will be type k next period, given that he or she is type j now and was type i last period. The index j ranges over the five categories A–E. The indices i and k range over those five and also the state of being out of the nursing home. If the model is first order, then the following probabilities in the second-order model should be the same:

$$P_{Ajk} = P_{Bjk} = P_{Cjk} = P_{Djk} = P_{Ejk} = P_{Ojk} \; \forall \, j, k.$$

Anderson and Goodman (1957) give a test for the null hypothesis that a model is first order against the alternative that it is second order. The test uses probability estimates from the expanded second-order matrix. Stationarity and homogeneity are maintained hypotheses. Anderson and Goodman show that the likelihood ratio criterion for testing the null hypothesis for a current state j is

$$\chi_j^2 = \sum_{i,k} n_{ij}\left(\hat{P}_{ijk} - \hat{P}_{jk}\right)^2/\hat{P}_{jk},$$

where $n_{ij} = \sum_k n_{ijk}$, n_{ijk} = the number of observed transitions $i \rightarrow j \rightarrow k$, $\hat{P}_{ijk} = n_{ijk}/n_{ij}$, and $\hat{P}_{jk} = \sum_i n_{ijk}/\sum_{i,k} n_{ijk}$.

The tests use data from the control group nursing homes for all people admitted during either the study or the baseline periods. The four absorbing states outside the nursing home were combined into a single state, GONE. This is different than having not yet entered the nursing home. The rows marked "O" in table 9.4 indicate out of nursing home prior to admission. These are the people who are currently in the nursing home but who had not yet been admitted last period. Only people who were observed at least twice were included.[2]

For this test, the model assumes that the time between observations is always three months. In fact, 87 percent of all observations occurred three

2. Leaving the nursing home (GONE) counted as being observed, but being right censored did not.

Table 9.4 **Test of First Order versus Second Order**

		Future State						
Previous	Current	A	B	C	D	E	GONE	*N*
A	A	*38*	28	2	0	0	32	133
B	A	17	*45*	1	0	0	36	69
C	A	11	28	0	0	0	61	18
D	A	67	0	0	0	0	33	3
E	A	0	50	0	0	0	50	4
O	A	22	15	7	1	1	*53*	374
Average		25	22	5	1	1	47	
A	B	*16*	50	9	1	0	25	122
B	B	8	*59*	8	1	0	24	567
C	B	5	42	*37*	1	0	14	201
D	B	11	47	11	0	0	32	19
E	B	0	57	0	0	0	43	7
O	B	7	44	18	3	1	*27*	383
Average		8	51	16	1	0	24	
A	C	*4*	26	56	4	4	7	27
B	C	3	*26*	48	4	1	18	172
C	C	0	11	*62*	7	0	19	627
D	C	0	7	53	*17*	1	22	101
E	C	0	19	31	0	6	44	16
O	C	2	18	46	5	1	*27*	546
Average		1	15	54	7	1	22	
A	D	0	0	20	40	40	0	5
B	D	0	0	24	59	0	18	17
C	D	0	0	*28*	33	0	40	83
D	D	0	0	13	*54*	4	28	230
E	D	0	0	20	40	0	40	5
O	D	1	6	19	34	3	37	314
Average		0	3	18	42	3	34	
A	E	0	0	75	0	25	0	4
B	E	100	0	0	0	0	0	1
C	E	0	0	23	8	8	62	13
D	E	0	0	6	*18*	24	53	17
E	E	0	5	7	0	*44*	44	41
O	E	3	6	8	2	24	*57*	90
Average		2	4	10	4	28	52	

Note: Numbers are probabilities. The elements on the main diagonal that are the largest in their column (if the number of observations in the row ≥ 20) are set in italic.

months after the previous observations. Furthermore, 89 percent of all first assessments were taken within three months of admission. Finally, most people who left a nursing home did so within three months of their last assessment. The few observations that did not fit were left in the analysis. I decided that it was better to include observations with timing problems than to use only a partial history for some people. The results are robust against leaving these observations out of the sample.

Surprisingly, going from a first- to a second-order model simplifies the issue of timing. A large fraction of observations are over a short time interval because they are of transitions between admission and first assessment. The second-order model conditions first on the current state, then on the past state. The exact time between admission and the first assessment is not important, as long as it is less than three months. In contrast, the first-order model conditions only on the current state. Parameter estimates would be biased if either observations from admission to a first assessment were left out or if it were assumed that the time interval was exactly three months.

The results of the chi-squared tests are shown in table 9.5A both by group and overall. The null hypothesis is soundly rejected, not only overall, but also group by group. Therefore, a person's recent history affects the transition probabilities. It is possible that the model is of a higher order than second, but there are not enough data to test this.

We can learn more by looking at the estimated second-order transition matrix in table 9.4 An interesting pattern can be seen in the blocks of $\hat{P}_{ijk}$. The elements on each block's main diagonal are particularly large relative to the other numbers in their column (when $n_{ij} \geq 20$, with one exception). If the first-order assumption were true, then the probabilities in each column (for a given block) would all be about the same. In other words, a person who is

Table 9.5 Test of First Order versus Second Order

A. Test of Null Hypothesis That Model Is First Order	
A	χ^2 = 66.08 rejects null at .000014 level
B	χ^2 = 137.40 rejects null at .000000 level
C	χ^2 = 109.10 rejects null at .000000 level
D	χ^2 = 68.81 rejects null at .000006 level
E	χ^2 = 77.64 rejects null at .000000 level
Total	χ^2 = 459.03 rejects null at .000000 level

B. Renormalized Test of Null Hypothesis That Model Is First Order	
A	χ^2 = 29.59 rejects null at .24 level
B	χ^2 = 39.78 rejects null at .031 level
C	χ^2 = 48.92 rejects null at .0029 level
D	χ^2 = 37.21 rejects null at .055 level
E	χ^2 = 60.96 rejects null at .000077 level
Total	χ^2 = 216.46 rejects null at .000000 level

now type j would be type k next period with a probability that is independent of last period's state. However, the pattern in this table shows that, if a person is type j now, the probability that she will become type k next period increases if we also know that she was type k last period. Of course, people are still most likely to stay in the state they are in, and if they change states, they are most likely to go the adjacent state. This pattern can also be expressed as

$$\Pr(k \text{ future} \mid j \text{ now}) < \Pr(k \text{ future} \mid j \text{ now}, k \text{ before}).$$

The chi-squared test can be taken one step further to see whether it still rejects when controlling for the effect outlined above. To do this, renormalize the numbers in table 9.4 so that the $k \to j \to k$ pattern is eliminated but all other features of the data are preserved. If the test on renormalized data does not reject, then this is the only interesting pattern to be found. The matrix in table 9.6 is a renormalized version of table 9.4, and each block has the following properties:

1. The weighted average of any column equals the element on the main diagonal.
2. Each row sum is one.
3. By construction, the main diagonal terms contribute nothing to the likelihood ratio test.

Nonetheless, the results of the renormalized chi-squared test indicate that more than half the variation in the original test is due to the fact that people tend to return to their previous state (see table 9.5B). Although three of the group tests still reject, it is clear that the $k \to j \to k$ pattern is the primary reason that the original first-order test rejected.

The test of first order against the alternative of second order was thoroughly rejected, which implies that past information is important for predicting the future health of nursing home residents. In addition, investigating the numbers highlighted the surprising fact that people who get worse in one period do not continue to decline but instead tend to rebound to their former state. A second-order model has the advantage of being more general but the disadvantage of being large to the point of being unwieldy. Furthermore, the rebounding effect has been noticed in other studies of longitudinal data and found to be an artifact of measurement error (see Poterba and Summers 1986). This possibility is explored below.

9.4 Homogeneity

Although nursing homes admit people from widely varying backgrounds, the simple Markov model does not control for heterogeneity. As a first cut, it is far simpler to assume that transition probabilities are constant. However, preliminary work showed that Markov matrices for subgroups chosen by age, sex, and marital status differ significantly. This section tests for heterogeneity

Table 9.6 Test of First Order versus Second Order

		Future State						
Previous	Current	A	B	C	D	E	GONE	*N*
A	A	25	34	2	0	0	39	133
B	A	24	22	1	0	0	52	69
C	A	10	26	6	0	0	57	18
D	A	67	0	0	1	0	33	3
E	A	0	50	0	0	1	50	4
O	A	26	18	8	1	1	45	374
Average		25	22	6	1	1	45	
A	B	8	54	10	1	0	27	122
B	B	10	51	10	1	0	29	567
C	B	7	59	13	1	0	20	201
D	B	11	46	11	2	0	31	19
E	B	0	57	0	0	0	43	7
O	B	7	44	18	3	1	27	383
Average		8	51	13	2	0	27	
A	C	1	27	57	4	4	7	27
B	C	4	13	56	5	1	21	172
C	C	0	13	56	8	0	22	627
D	C	0	8	59	7	1	25	101
E	C	0	20	33	0	0	47	16
O	C	2	19	50	5	1	22	546
Average		1	13	56	7	0	22	
A	D	0	0	20	40	40	0	5
B	D	0	3	23	57	0	17	17
C	D	0	0	19	37	0	45	83
D	D	0	0	19	35	6	40	230
E	D	0	0	19	38	4	38	5
O	D	1	6	18	33	3	39	314
Average		0	3	19	35	4	39	
A	E	2	0	73	0	24	0	4
B	E	95	5	0	0	0	0	1
C	E	0	0	10	9	9	72	13
D	E	0	0	7	2	28	63	17
E	E	0	7	10	0	23	61	41
O	E	3	6	8	2	24	58	90
Average		2	5	10	2	23	58	

Note: Numbers are probabilities.

in two different ways, both of which control for the three characteristics outlined above and also for race. The first method adds terms to each cell of the Markov matrix, and the second is an ordered logit model.

The obvious correction for heterogeneity is to add parameters to each cell in the transition matrix. The transition probabilities then depend on a constant and on personal characteristics (X includes age, sex, race, marital status):

$$\begin{aligned}\hat{P}_{ij} &= \exp(\beta_{ij} + X\gamma) \\ &= \exp(\beta_{ij} + \gamma_1\text{AGE} + \gamma_2\text{SEX} + \gamma_3\text{RACE} + \gamma_4\text{MARRIED}) \\ &= \exp(\beta_{ij})\exp(\gamma_1\text{AGE})\exp(\gamma_2\text{SEX})\exp(\gamma_3\text{RACE})\exp(\gamma_4\text{MARRIED}).\end{aligned}$$

Notice that the effects are assumed to be multiplicative, not additive. If a characteristic has no effect, then its corresponding γ_i should be zero; thus, $\exp(\gamma_i X) = 1$. AGE is defined to be true age minus eighty, divided by ten.[3] The other characteristics are dummy variables: SEX equals one if male, RACE equals one if nonwhite, and MARRIED (marital status) equals one if currently married.

Unfortunately, there are too few observations in most cells to be able to parameterizc fully. Instead, the matrix was reduced to five rows by five columns by combining states. Also, some parameters were constrained to be equal across cells. Table 9.7 depicts how this was done. A Greek letter (except β) denotes a four-element vector of parameters. There were only four parameters per characteristic, far fewer than one per cell. Note that the main diagonal equals one minus the row sum, and two cells have only constants.

The results are shown in tables 9.8 and 9.9. Only AGE and SEX have significant coefficients, so it appears that heterogeneity is quite weak. Looking at probability matrices for different types of people, we see a few interesting patterns. Older people are less likely to go home, as are women. Nonwhites are the least likely to die or go to a hospital, while married people are the most likely.

Another way to check for heterogeneity is to run an ordered logit model.[4] This has the advantage of controlling for many individual characteristics, but it does not have the special timing structure of the Markov model. One ordered logit was run for each of the five states of health in the nursing home. The dependent variable was the set of possible outcomes (collapsed from nine states into only five; see table 9.10). The outcomes were ranked; worse outcomes, like death, had a higher number.

The α's reported in table 9.11 are the cutoff values for the different categories. They are strictly monotonic, with higher thresholds for worse states of health. Thus, people who are type A have the highest α's and are the least likely to go to a bad state. This is consistent with the results of the Markov model.

3. Eighty was chosen because it is the average age of a nursing home resident.

4. For an explanation of ordered logit models, see Maddala (1983).

Table 9.7 **Parameterization for Test for Homogeneity**

	Home & ICF	Hosp. & Death	A	B, C	D, E
Home & ICF	1	0	0	0	0
Hosp. & Death	0	1	0	0	0
A	$\exp(\beta_{11}+X\mu)$	$\exp(\beta_{12}+X\gamma)$	(1 − row sum)	$\exp(\beta_{13}+X\theta)$	$\exp(\beta_{14})$
B, C	$\exp(\beta_{21}+X\mu)$	$\exp(\beta_{22}+X\gamma)$	$\exp(\beta_{23}+X\delta)$	(1 − row sum)	$\exp(\beta_{24}+X\theta)$
D, E	$\exp(\beta_{31}+X\mu)$	$\exp(\beta_{32}+X\gamma)$	$\exp(\beta_{33})$	$\exp(\beta_{34}+X\delta)$	(1 − row sum)

Note: ICF = intermediate care facility. Hosp. = hospitalization.

Table 9.8 **Test of Homogeneity: Maximum Likelihood Estimation of Parameters for Three-Month Matrix with Heterogeneity Correction**

Parameter	From	To	Coefficient	SD
β_{11}	A	Home, ICF	−2.46	.19
β_{12}	A	Hosp., Death	−2.87	.23
β_{13}	A	B, C	−1.16	.11
β_{14}	A	D, E	−3.90	.46
β_{21}	B, C	Home, ICF	−4.22	.18
β_{22}	B, C	Hosp., Death	−3.09	.11
β_{23}	B, C	A	−3.26	.13
β_{24}	B, C	D, E	−3.11	.12
β_{31}	D, E	Home, ICF	−4.32	.35
β_{32}	D, E	Hosp., Death	−2.29	.13
β_{33}	D, W	A	−5.14	.63
β_{34}	D, E	B, C	−1.43	.10
μ_1 AGE	A–E	Home, ICF	−.332	.067
γ_1 AGE	A–E	Hosp., Death	−.003	.069
δ_1 AGE	B–E	Better in NH	−.048	.074
θ_1 AGE	A–D	Worse in NH	.137	.072
μ_2 SEX	A–E	Home, ICF	.52	.23
γ_2 SEX	A–E	Hosp., Death	.34	.17
δ_2 SEX	B–E	Better in NH	.04	.19
θ_2 SEX	A–D	Worse in NH	.08	.19
μ_3 RACE	A–E	Home, ICF	.16	.35
γ_3 RACE	A–E	Hosp., Death	−.41	.28
δ_3 RACE	B–E	Better in NH	−.19	.27
θ_3 RACE	A–D	Worse in NH	−.09	.32
μ_4 MARRIED	A–E	Home, ICF	.13	.31
γ_4 MARRIED	A–E	Hosp., Death	.37	.20
δ_4 MARRIED	B–E	Better in NH	−.03	.23
θ_4 MARRIED	A–D	Worse in NH	.14	.29

No. of transitions = 2,512
−Log (likelihood) = 1,983.05

Note: Sample is all people in control group nursing homes admitted after 1 May 1981. AGE = (true age − 80)/10. SEX = 1 if male, 0 else. RACE = 1 if nonwhite, 0 else. MARRIRED 1 if married now, 0 else. Hosp. = hospitalization. ICF = intermediate care facility. NH = nursing home.

Table 9.9 **Test of Homogeneity: Estimated Three-Month Markov Transition Matrix**

This Period	Next Period				
	Home, ICF	Hosp., Death	A	B, C	D, E
	Base case: 80-Year-Old Single White Woman				
A	8.5	5.7	52.3	31.5	2.0
B, C	1.5	4.6	3.8	85.6	4.5
D, E	1.3	10.2	.6	23.8	64.1
	AGE: 90-Year-Old Single White Woman				
A	6.1	5.7	56.2	30.0	2.0
B, C	1.1	4.5	3.7	85.6	5.1
D, E	0.9	10.1	.6	27.4	41.0
	SEX: 80-Year-Old Single White Man				
A	14.3	8.0	42.9	32.8	2.0
B, C	2.5	6.4	4.0	82.3	4.8
D, E	2.2	14.3	.6	25.7	57.2
	RACE: 80-Year-Old Single Nonwhite Woman				
A	10.0	3.8	58.2	26.0	2.0
B, C	1.7	3.0	3.2	88.0	4.1
D, E	1.6	6.8	.6	21.7	69.3
	MARRIED: 80-Year-Old Married White Woman				
A	9.7	8.2	49.4	30.7	2.0
B, C	1.7	6.6	3.7	82.9	5.1
D, E	1.5	14.8	.6	27.4	55.7

Note: ICF = intermediate care facility. Hosp. = hospitalization.

Table 9.10 **Ordered Logit Test for Homogeneity**

States
Go home, or go to ICF
Get better, but stay in NH[a]
Stay the same
Get worse but stay in NH[b]
Go to hospital or die

Note: ICF = intermediate care facility. NH = nursing home.

[a]Does not apply to state A.

[b]Does not apply to state E.

Table 9.11 **Test of Homogeneity: Results of Ordered Logit Models**

Variable	A	B	C	D	E
α_1[a]	2.72	−1.33	−4.46	−7.60	−9.4
	(.57)	(.40)	(.38)	(.64)	(1.1)
α_2[a]	4.14	−.69	−2.64	−4.80	−6.7
	(.59)	(.40)	(.39)	(.61)	(1.2)
α_3[a]	5.75	1.72	−.01	−2.62	−4.2
	(.58)	(.41)	(.40)	(.60)	(1.2)
α_4[a]		2.82	.49	−2.38	
		(.40)	(.39)	(.60)	
TIME (days)	.435	−.051	−.543	−.834	−1.42
	(.048)	(.028)	(.029)	(.038)	(.17)
TIME^2	−.0145	.0067	.0294	.0422	.076
	(.0021)	(.0011)	(.0012)	(.0013)	(.011)
NH type (treatment = 1)	−.35	−.305	−.029	.14	.24
	(.16)	(.100)	(.089)	(.13)	(.23)
AGE (true age)	.0230	.0117	.0111	−.0045	−.0009
	(.0067)	(.0048)	(.0042)	(.0066)	(.012)
SEX (male = 1)	−.01	−.01	.08	.05	−.82
	(.17)	(.11)	(.11)	(.17)	(.28)
RACE (nonwhite = 1)	−.31	.01	−.38	−.11	.50
	(.28)	(.18)	(.14)	(.21)	(.40)
MARRIED (married = 1)	.23	.40	.21	.33	−.07
	(.24)	(.15)	(.12)	(.19)	(.32)
−Log (likelihood)	972.91	2,284.69	2,662.65	1,103.85	334.57
% predicted correctly	53	53	60	60	64
N	779	1,737	2,241	996	370

Note: Standard deviations are in parentheses. NH = nursing home.
[a]Dummy cutoff variables.

The coefficients for personal characteristics vary greatly in their effect. For example, a positive coefficient on AGE[5] means that older people are more likely to be less healthy at their next assessment. SEX and RACE seem to have no effect. AGE and MARRIED have significant and positive coefficients in three models. However, by far the most significant coefficients are those for TIME (since admission) and TIME^2. Although it would be nice to be able to control for age and marital status in the Markov model, the coefficients for TIME since admission (and TIME^2) suggest that duration should be an essential part of any model of transitions in and out of nursing homes.

The conclusion seems to be that personal characteristics have only weak effects on the transition probabilities, particularly race. Including extra parameters slows down the computation substantially. The benefits of control-

5. In this test, AGE equals true age.

ling for heterogeneity in a Markov model do not outweigh this cost. Other aspects of these data are more important to model.

9.5 Stationarity

The simple Markov model assumes that the probabilities are constant over time. Time can be measured on both a "relative" and an "absolute" scale, and the simple model requires that the probabilities are constant for both. Here, the relative scale measures time since admission. Stationarity on a relative scale refers to the assumption that the transition probabilities are independent of the length of time a person has been in the nursing home. The absolute scale refers to calendar time. In this case, stationarity means that there is no general trend over time. For example, all nursing homes are assumed to have adjusted instantly to the new system at the start of the experiment.

Since the stationarity assumption could fail in two different ways, it is tested in two different ways. The tests of stationarity, implications of failure, and corrections to the model are different for each method. The following section tests for duration dependence in a parametric duration model, and the one following tests whether the transition matrices for the experimental group change over the study period.

9.6 Duration Dependence

The simple Markov model assumes that transition probabilities are independent of how long a person has been in a nursing home. There are two reasons why this assumption may be false. Cumulative time spent living in a nursing home may affect probabilities directly. For instance, the initial move into a nursing home may be an unpleasant shock that fades as a person makes new friends and grows accustomed to the new surroundings. The second reason is that unobserved (or uncontrolled for) heterogeneity will cause duration dependence. Heckman and Singer (1984, p. 78) give the following explanation: "Intuitively, more mobility prone persons are the first to leave the population leaving the less mobile behind and hence creating the illusion of stronger negative duration dependence than actually exists."

Heckman and Singer go on to explain that ignoring heterogeneity will cause bias toward more negative duration dependence. It would therefore be incorrect to test for duration dependence without trying to control for heterogeneity. The two tests in this section control for the four observed characteristics: age, sex, race, and marital status. If the test rejects the hypothesis of no duration dependence, it could be due either to real duration dependence or to unobservable characteristics.

The first test treats time in the nursing home like another personal characteristic. A variable for time since admission is added to each cell. As before, a five by five matrix is used to estimate the three-month transition probabilities. In addition to time, both age and sex were used as explanatory variables (race and marital status were shown to be less important by the heterogeneity tests in sec. 9.1). The null hypothesis is rejected if the parameters for time are significantly different than zero.

The effects of time in this model are insignificant, as shown in table 9.12. Not one parameter differed significantly from zero. Not surprisingly, the parameters for age and sex were very close to values estimated in the section on heterogeneity. Thus, it does not seem necessary to control for duration dependence in this model.

The second test for duration dependence is a standard parametric duration model, the Weibull model, which measures both duration dependence and

Table 9.12 Test of Duration Dependence: Maximum Likelihood Estimation of Parameters for Three-Month Matrix with Time Heterogeneity Correction

Parameter	From	To	Coefficient	SD
β_{11}	A	Home, ICF	−2.38	.29
β_{12}	A	Hosp., Death	−2.88	.28
β_{13}	A	B, C	−1.17	.20
β_{14}	A	D, E	−3.89	.46
β_{21}	B, C	Home, ICF	−4.11	.35
β_{22}	B, C	Hosp., Death	−3.02	.22
β_{23}	B, C	A	−3.29	.23
β_{24}	B, C	D, E	−3.10	.23
β_{31}	D, E	Home, ICF	−4.38	.48
β_{32}	D, E	Hosp., Death	−2.23	.22
β_{33}	D, E	A	−5.15	.64
β_{34}	D, E	B, C	−1.49	.19
μ_1 AGE	A–E	Home, ICF	−.345	.069
γ_1 AGE	A–E	Hosp., Death	−.023	.067
δ_1 AGE	B–E	Better in NH	−.052	.068
θ_1 AGE	A–D	Worse in NH	.127	.071
μ_2 SEX	A–E	Home, ICF	.55	.24
γ_2 SEX	A–E	Hosp., Death	.41	.16
δ_2 SEX	B–E	Better in NH	−.02	.18
θ_2 SEX	A–D	Worse in NH	.05	.19
μ_3 TIME	A–E	Home, ICF	−.049	.060
γ_3 TIME	A–E	Hosp., Death	−.011	.042
δ_3 TIME	B–E	Better in NH	−.022	.044
θ_3 TIME	A–D	Worse in NH	−.012	.047

No. of transition = 2,512
−Log (likelihood) = 1,986.57

Note: Sample is all people in control group nursing homes admitted after 1 May 1981. AGE = (true age − 80)/10. SEX = 1 if male, 0 else. TIME = time since admission. ICF = intermediate care facility. Hosp. = hospitalization. NH = nursing home.

Table 9.13 Test of Duration Dependence: Weibull Model

Control/ Experiment	Type at Admission	Duration Parameter (α)	CONSTANT (β_0)	AGE (β_1)	MALE (β_2)	NONWHITE (β_3)	MARRIED (β_4)
Control	A	.628	−3.43	−.161	.27	.09	.31
		(.025)	(.15)	(.037)	(.11)	(.16)	(.15)
Control	B	.677	−4.12	−.336	.03	−.49	.34
		(.033)	(.21)	(.058)	(.16)	(.22)	(.18)
Control	C	.683	−4.34	−.076	.42	.30	.40
		(.028)	(.18)	(.047)	(.11)	(.17)	(.13)
Control	D	.577	−3.09	.049	.24	.09	.12
		(.024)	(.15)	(.056)	(.12)	(.17)	(.15)
Control	E	.701	−3.54	.056	.50	.26	.04
		(.052)	(.31)	(.088)	(.23)	(.32)	(.26)
Experiment	A	.719	−3.46	−.131	.06	.12	−.31
		(.042)	(.24)	(.076)	(.20)	(.30)	(.25)
Experiment	B	.764	−4.45	−.137	.26	−.31	−.31
		(.054)	(.34)	(.072)	(.19)	(.32)	(.30)
Experiment	C	.814	−4.90	−.006	.44	−.06	.17
		(.044)	(.27)	(.066)	(.16)	(.19)	(.17)
Experiment	D	.695	−3.86	−.037	.48	−.28	.02
		(.039)	(.24)	(.067)	(.17)	(.22)	(.18)
Experiment	E	.658	−3.51	.22	−.19	.02	.48
		(.052)	(.32)	(.11)	(.25)	(.27)	(.24)

Note: Standard deviations are in parentheses. AGE = (true age − 80)/10. SEX = 1 if male, else 0. RACE = 1 if nonwhite, else 0. MARRIED = 1 if married now, else 0. TIME = days.

heterogeneity. This test sacrifices many aspects of the Markov model, but it has the advantage of being easy to compute. The Weibull model has only two states: a person is either in or out of a nursing home. Because duration depends on a person's health, and because health usually remains constant, all residents were grouped according to their health at admission (types A–E). Also, because the model was estimated on both the control and experimental samples, this provides confirmation that the average length of stay was shorter in the experimental group.

The hazard function for the Weibull model depends on time-invariant characteristics X and a duration parameter α:

$$h(t|X) = \alpha t^{\alpha - 1}\exp(X\beta)$$

X includes a constant term and variables for age, sex, race, and marital status, as defined before. The parameter α distinguishes the Weibull model from the exponential model, which has a constant hazard. If α is greater (less) than one, the model has positive (negative) duration dependence.

The results from the Weibull model tests are shown in table 9.13. The most striking result is that the estimated duration parameter, $\hat{\alpha}$, is significantly less than one in all cases. The models have *negative* duration dependence, which means that the probability of leaving the nursing home declines over time. Note that, for all types except E, $\hat{\alpha}$ is greater in the experimental group than in the control, so duration dependence is less pronounced in experimental group nursing homes. However, the constant term for experimental group nursing homes is the same or more negative. This implies that, at admission, the hazard rate is no larger in the experimental group, but over time the hazard rate declines more slowly. This partially explains the shorter length of stay found in Norton (1990).

Once again, the results on heterogeneity are mixed. Age and sex are significant in about half the cases. Surprisingly, older people have lower hazard rates than younger, and men have higher hazard rates than women. Only race is clearly insignificant.

The results from the Markov and Weibull tests are quite different. When time terms were added to the Markov model, the results were insignificant. However, the Weibull model showed strong results that there is strong negative duration dependence. It is not clear why time should be so much more significant in one model than the other.

9.7 Learning Effect

Whenever a new program is put into effect, it takes time for the participants to adjust to the new system. Too often, though, economists assume that people adjust instantly and perfectly at the start of a new program. The NCHSR nursing home experiment was a complicated system of incentives and assessments. Although the nursing homes did have a six-month period in which to learn about the new reimbursement system, they did not know whether they would be in the control or the experimental group until the day before the reimbursement system went into effect. This was good for experimental design in some ways, but it meant that nursing homes in the experimental group needed time to adjust.

In a previous paper (Norton 1990), I found that the distribution of types of health at admission changed slowly from the beginning to the conclusion of the study. The nursing homes did not adjust immediately to the new admission incentives. If they also did not adjust promptly to the outcome and discharge incentives, then the test in the previous paper may be biased toward no effect. Suppose that the experimental group took a while to hire new nurses and set new operational procedures. Then the effects of the experiment would not appear in the Markov transition matrix until after several months had passed.

To test whether there was a learning period, the data for the experimental group were split into two parts: those admitted during the first six months of the study and those admitted thereafter.[6] Two-week transition matrices were

6. The background period lasted from 1 November 1980 to 30 April 1981. All thirty-six nursing homes were then divided randomly into one of two groups. Anyone admitted to an experimental

estimated using the continuous time model for people admitted during each period.

The results for the two groups are clearly different, as can be seen in tables 9.14 and 9.15. The second group has a much shorter average length of stay and better outcomes in general. In particular, the probability of dying decreased, and the probability of going home increased, for almost all types. Therefore there is strong evidence that it took the nursing homes in the experimental group time to adjust, and the results in the previous paper may be underestimated.

9.8 Markov Assumption

The key step in correcting the problem that the times between observations varied widely is to use the identity from Markov processes that

$$P(T) = P(1)^T,$$

where $P(T)$ is the matrix of transition probabilities over T time periods. I call this the *Markov assumption*. This allows parameters from the transition matrix of any time interval to be expressed in terms of the parameters of the shortest time interval. This assumption is false if the probabilities depend on anything other than a constant. If the model is not first order *and* homogeneous *and* stationary (in both senses), it will fail this test. Testing the Markov assumption is therefore a good summary test of specification error.

On the other hand, the test is not valid if there is selection bias on the basis of time interval. Here, selection bias means that certain types of transitions are oversampled (or undersampled) at particular frequencies because of the way in which the data were collected. For example, if all transitions within the nursing home are observed at three-month intervals but people leave at random times, then there is selection bias. The estimated matrix for any time other than three months will have positive probabilities only for leaving. A test of the Markov assumption on this data would fail simply because of the selection bias. The nursing home data have this problem since almost all observations over a short time period are of people entering or leaving a nursing home. Therefore, the test includes only transitions in the nursing home.

The test of the Markov assumption compares transition matrices of different time periods ($\hat{P}(T)$ for different T). Since the data for each matrix have the same time interval, estimation is easy. The continuous time correction is not needed, so an element $\hat{P}_{ij} = n_{ij}/\sum_j n_{ij}$. The test uses control group nursing home data for periods of two, three, and four months.

group nursing home during the following year was eligible for three types of incentives. Although residents were reassessed after 1 May 1982 and could earn bonuses for the nursing home, anyone admitted after that time was not eligible to earn bonuses.

Table 9.14 Test of Learning Effect: Early Part of Study

	Next Period								
	Home	ICF	Hosp.	Death	A	B	C	D	E
A	4.6	2.5	2.1	.6	83.5	6.1	.4	.2	.0
B	.7	1.7	1.2	.5	.9	91.6	3.2	.2	.0
C	.3	.2	1.0	.9	.1	2.9	92.6	1.8	.2
D	.1	.1	2.0	3.2	.1	.2	4.6	88.8	.9
E	.0	.5	1.8	4.5	.0	.6	1.6	.7	90.3

	Length of Stay	
	Mean	Median
A	16.6	8
B	25.6	17
C	30.0	22
D	23.3	15
E	18.5	11

	Probability That Person Starting in State Leaves Nursing Home in State			
	Home	ICF	Hosp.	Death
A	35	27	26	13
B	17	30	31	21
C	13	17	36	34
D	7	10	36	48
E	4	11	29	57

Note: ICF = intermediate care facility. Hosp. = hospitalization.

The estimated matrices show that the Markov assumption does not hold in the nursing home data (see table 9.16). The left-hand column has one-period matrices, which are not comparable. The right-hand column has these matrices raised to the sixth, fourth, and third powers; they are therefore comparable since the time interval is forty-eight weeks (almost one year). As a general misspecification test, this confirms the results in the previous sections that the simple Markov model was misspecified.

9.9 Measurement Error

Poterba and Summers (1986) showed that even a small probability of reporting error can lead to large errors in duration estimates when using a Markov model. They adjusted labor market transition probabilities using reporting errors in the Census Population Survey. Reporting errors distort the true

Table 9.15 Test of Learning Effect: Late Part of Study

This Period	Next Period								
	Home	ICF	Hosp.	Death	A	B	C	D	E
A	4.6	2.7	1.8	1.2	85.0	3.7	1.0	.0	.0
B	.8	1.0	1.5	.7	3.2	88.7	3.3	.0	.8
C	.3	.4	2.0	1.1	2.8	.8	92.4	.0	.2
D	.2	2.5	2.5	3.1	.0	.0	1.1	90.4	.2
E	.0	.0	3.9	2.9	.0	.0	1.5	3.4	88.3

	Length of Stay (3 months)	
	Mean	Median
A	12.8	8
B	19.5	14
C	20.3	15
D	13.1	9
E	14.9	10

	Probability That Person Starting in State Leaves Nursing Home in State			
	Home	ICF	Hosp.	Death
A	38	24	23	14
B	24	21	35	20
C	21	17	40	23
D	5	28	32	36
E	4	10	48	38

Note: ICF = intermediate care facility. Hosp. = hospitalization.

probabilities by overestimating the frequency of transitions between different states. A person who is unemployed for a long time and who misreports being employed makes it seem as if he has much shorter spells of unemployment. After adjusting for error rates of only 5 percent, Poterba and Summers found that true spells of unemployment were as much as 80 percent longer than conventional measures.

The nursing home data may be subject to a similar problem. Nurses assessed each resident's health periodically according to somewhat subjective criteria. The decision was based primarily on a person's activity of daily living (ADL) index. Although the ADL index was designed to be an objective measure of disability in performing basic functions, in practice there is some subjectivity in assessing whether another person can do something satisfactorily. It is especially difficult to judge whether a person is type A, which includes people expected to be sent home within ninety days, regardless of current

Table 9.16 Test of Markov Assumption

	2 Months					→	1 Year (48 weeks)				
	A	B	C	D	E		A	B	C	D	E
A	60	25	15	0	0		11	46	36	7	0
B	5	75	18	2	0		8	47	38	8	0
C	2	23	69	6	0		7	43	40	10	0
D	2	2	31	65	0		6	36	43	15	0
E	0	0	25	0	75		4	29	42	7	18
	3 Months					→	1 Year (48 weeks)				
	A	B	C	D	E		A	B	C	D	E
A	52	36	9	1	1		17	44	31	6	2
B	11	67	20	2	0		13	43	36	7	2
C	2	20	70	8	1		8	34	44	12	2
D	1	4	29	61	5		6	24	44	22	5
E	7	13	25	5	50		10	32	39	10	8
	4 Months					→	1 Year (48 weeks)				
	A	B	C	D	E		A	B	C	D	E
A	27	60	6	3	3		12	46	32	8	3
B	13	57	26	3	0		10	44	37	7	2
C	2	26	66	4	3		7	36	45	8	4
D	0	10	29	54	7		4	25	41	24	7
E	0	0	14	43	43		2	16	36	34	13

ADL level. Less than half were actually discharged on time, so there was considerable error for this category.

The NCHSR study tried to minimize the problems of measurement error (see Applied Management Sciences 1986, apps. 8–10). Nurses were trained during a six-month baseline period before the study began. There were four types of tests used throughout the study to check reliability. In two of the tests, nurses assessed residents in pairs, either concurrently or successively. Also, thirty-three residents were videotaped while being assessed. These tapes were reviewed periodically to check agreement between nurses. These reliability studies give some idea of the magnitude of the reporting error problem.

This section adjusts the observed transition probabilities, given knowledge of the measurement errors, to estimate the true transition probabilities P^*. Following Poterba and Summers, we will estimate flows of people, F, then convert the flows back to probabilities. Let f^*_{ij} and f_{ij} be the true and the observed numbers of people to go from state i to state j in a single period. Define Q to be the matrix of error rates, where q_{ij} = Pr(observed state = j | true state = i). The estimated flows, F, depend on Q and F^* as follows:

$$f_{ij} = \sum_{k,l} q_{ki} f^*_{kl} q_{lj}.$$

In matrix notation,

$$F = Q'F^*Q.$$

This can be rewritten to solve for F^* and then converted to P^* by dividing by the row sum:[7]

$$F^* = (Q^{-1})'F(Q^{-1}).$$

The reliability tests did not estimate the matrix Q explicitly, so we must use limited information to construct a plausible Q. First, note that the measurement error is a problem only when classifying residents in the nursing home. A misreport of where someone went after discharge is more likely to be a clerical than a judgment error. Classification within the nursing home depends on three judgments: need for special care, ADL level, and whether dischargeable within ninety days. Only the last two are subject to much discretion since it should be clear whether someone is comatose, requires tube feeding, or receives decubitus ulcer care. Therefore, type E is always assumed to be correctly classified. The reliability tests found that trained nurses agreed 90 percent of the time on residents' ADL level. It is plausible to assume that each nurse reports the truth 95 percent of the time and that errors are uncorrelated. Then a person who is truly type B, C, or D (where classification depends on ADL level) would be misclassified 5 percent of the time (types B and D reported as C, type C reported as either B or D). The most important test distinguishing types A and B is the Mental Status Questionnaire (see Applied Management Sciences 1986, app. 8A, p. 7). Since this also had an agreement of 90 percent, assume that 5 percent of As and Bs each were misclassified as the other type. A plausible Q is then

$$Q = \begin{bmatrix} .95 & .05 & 0 & 0 & 0 \\ .05 & .90 & .05 & 0 & 0 \\ 0 & .025 & .95 & .025 & 0 \\ 0 & 0 & .05 & .95 & 0 \\ 0 & 0 & .10 & 0 & 1 \end{bmatrix}.$$

The matrix F was constructed from a three-month probability matrix, not directly from data on flows. It would be wrong to use the estimated two-week matrix for P since the average time between observations is three months, and this would imply misreporting at two-week intervals. Therefore, we use $P = P(2\text{ week})^6$, estimated in Norton (1990). To convert from probabilities

7. The reader may wonder why Q was not defined in the obvious way to avoid taking inverses. Meyer (1988) compares these two methods and concludes that the second depends on a subtle but implausible assumption.

to flows, each column of the probability matrix was multiplied by a weighting vector of the probability distribution over the five types at admission.

Unlike in Poterba and Summers, reporting errors seem to have little effect, as shown in table 9.17 compared to the corrected values in table 9.18. The matrices P^* and P differ by a few percentage points in many cells, and in general the off-diagonal terms are smaller in P^*. There is almost no difference, though, in the length of stay and in the probability of ending in each of the absorbing states. The differences are much smaller than between the control and the experimental groups. Even when the errors estimated in Q were increased dramatically, these basic results were unchanged.

There are several conclusions that can be drawn from these findings. Poterba and Summers probably found larger effects because all their states were liable to be misclassified, while only four of the nine nursing home states were. Furthermore, the major results, such as average length of stay and probability of ending in each absorbing state, are not very sensitive to measure-

Table 9.17 **Test of Measurement Error: Uncorrected Three-Month Markov Transition Matrix**

	Next Period								
	Home	ICF	Hosp.	Death	A	B	C	D	E
A	17.3	10.4	12.0	2.5	31.0	21.0	4.5	.8	.5
B	2.8	3.0	7.1	2.6	5.4	61.7	15.8	1.3	.2
C	1.4	.9	7.5	5.1	.9	13.7	64.4	5.5	.6
D	.9	.4	11.0	11.3	.4	2.1	17.2	54.6	2.2
E	3.2	.3	18.0	23.3	1.6	4.3	10.9	3.2	35.2

	Length of Stay	
	Mean	Median
A	3.7	2
B	5.7	4
C	5.9	4
D	4.9	3
E	3.2	2

	Probability That Person Starting in State Leaves Nursing Home in State			
	Home	ICF	Hosp.	Death
A	31	20	35	13
B	17	15	45	22
C	13	10	47	30
D	8	6	46	39
E	9	4	42	45

Note: ICF = intermediate care facility. Hosp. = hospitalization.

Table 9.18 Test of Measurement Error: Corrected Three-Month Markov Transiton Matrix

This Period	Next Period								
	Home	ICF	Hosp.	Death	A	B	C	D	E
A	17.3	10.4	12.0	2.5	33.9	19.3	3.3	.8	.5
B	2.8	3.0	7.1	2.6	.4	71.7	11.2	.9	.2
C	1.4	.9	7.5	5.1	.2	11.4	70.5	2.4	.6
D	.9	.4	11.0	11.3	.3	1.5	12.6	59.8	2.3
E	3.2	.3	18.0	23.3	1.5	4.3	11.0	3.0	35.2

	Length of Stay	
	Mean	Median
A	3.7	2
B	6.2	5
C	6.3	5
D	4.9	3
E	3.4	2

	Probability That Person Starting in State Leaves Nursing Home in State			
	Home	ICF	Hosp.	Death
A	31	21	35	13
B	15	15	46	23
C	12	9	48	30
D	7	5	47	41
E	9	4	42	45

Note: ICF = intermediate care facility. Hosp. = hospitalization.

ment error within the nursing home. This would be different if nurses could not tell reliably whether a person had gone home or died. These results also put the conclusions of section 9.1 in perspective. A quick calculation from table 9.7 shows that shifting 10 percent of the sample would eliminate the effect that people return to their past state. Thus, about half the rebound effect found in the first-order section is probably due to measurement error.

9.10 Conclusion

This paper tested the assumptions of the simple Markov model on nursing home data and found that several tests failed. The model is not first order but second order. In particular, people tend to rebound to the state they were in last period more than a first-order model would predict. The Weibull model shows that there is strong negative duration dependence. Dividing the data into two parts shows that the nursing homes in the experimental group took time to adjust to the reimbursement system. Finally, a test of the Markov assumption, as a general specification test, failed.

Some tests supported the use of the simple model. In a variety of tests, heterogeneity seemed to have weak effects. Thus, the increase in complexity by controlling for heterogeneity overshadows any gains in information. Correcting for measurement error has almost no effect on the average length of stay or on the probability of ending in the absorbing states, only small effects on transitions within the nursing home. In light of this, controlling for second-order effects does not seem worthwhile, especially since about half the rebound effect was due to measurement error. Also, the duration dependence that is so strong in Weibull models was not detected in a Markov model. Finally, the fact that the nursing homes in the experimental group did not adjust instantly means that the results of the previous paper are underestimated.

The Markov model should be viewed as a reasonable but imperfect model of transitions in nursing homes. Research in this area could benefit from trying other kinds of duration models, such as competing hazard and semiparametric. These models may have advantages in speed of computation, a more flexible form, and an emphasis on duration and outcome that are important for public policy.

References

Amemiya, Takeshi. 1985. *Advanced Econometrics*. Cambridge, Mass.: Harvard University Press.

Anderson, T. W., and Leo A. Goodman. 1957. Statistical Inference about Markov Chains. *Annals of Mathematical Statistics* 28:89–110.

Applied Management Sciences Inc. 1986. Controlled Experiment to Evaluate the Impacts of Incentive Payments on Nursing Home Admissions, Discharges, Case Mix, Care, Outcomes, and Costs: Documentation Report. Prepared for the National Center for Health Services Research and Health Care Technology Assessment. Rockville, Md.: National Technical Information Services, February. Manuscript.

Börsch-Supan, Axel, Laurence J. Kotlikoff, and John N. Morris. 1988. The Dynamics of Living Arrangements by the Elderly. NBER Working Paper no. 2787. Cambridge, Mass.: National Bureau of Economic Research.

Heckman, James J., and Burton Singer. 1984. Economic Duration Analysis. *Journal of Econometrics* 24 (1/2):63–132.

Katz, Sidney, and C. A. Akpom. 1976. Index of ADL. *Medical Care* 14 (5):116–18.

Maddala, G. S. 1983. *Limited-Dependent and Qualitative Variables in Econometrics*. New York: Cambridge University Press.

Meyer, Bruce D. 1988. Classification-Error Models and Labor-Market Dynamics. *Journal of Business and Economic Statistics* 6 (3):385–90.

Norton, Edward C. 1990. Incentive Regulation of Nursing Homes. Cambridge, Mass.: Massachusetts Institute of Technology, March. Manuscript.

Poterba, James M., and Lawrence H. Summers. 1986. Reporting Errors and Labor Market Dynamics. *Econometrica* 54 (6):1319–38.

Weissert, William G., William J. Scanlon, Thomas T. H. Wan, and Douglas E. Skinner. 1983. Care for the Chronically Ill: Nursing Home Incentive Payment Experiment. *Health Care Financing Review* 5 (2):41–49.

Comment Sherwin Rosen

This is a promising empirical analysis of whether monetary incentives affect the selection and length of stay of nursing home residents. Using data from a Medicaid experiment in San Diego, Edward C. Norton finds that incentives apparently caused shorter lengths of stay and more frequent admissions of patients in poorer health. These results are interesting but, like all experiments, must be reenforced by replication in independent samples.

The data description is somewhat confusing or incomplete. We know that Medicaid finances nearly half of nursing home patients, but those reimbursements do not nearly cover average costs. To achieve financial viability, nursing homes with larger fractions of Medicaid patients must either offer a lower quality of service to Medicaid patients or cross-subsidize them by charging non-Medicaid patients more. The experiment subsidized admissions of Medicaid patients in worse states of health and rewarded favorable outcomes in selected cases, but we are not told what proportions of *all patients* were covered by the schemes or indeed the relative frequency of outcome and discharge bonus used in the experiment. A reader wants to know how important these subsidies were to the overall operations of experimental units and whether the payments were large enough or frequent enough to have a plausible effect. Knowledge of the proportions of Medicaid and non-Medicaid patients in the sample nursing homes might also be useful in assessing the general quality of care in the sample. Quality of care is known to vary among nursing homes, but the monetary incentives in the experiment were not conditioned on nursing home characteristics. If lower-quality units were more eager to participate in the experiment, the results might be biased toward the null hypothesis.

In assessing the results, it should also be borne in mind that the experimental design did not satisfy some commonly accepted rules. In particular, there were no double-blind safeguards in assigning patients to categories and in assessing outcomes. The same skilled nursing staff was employed for both. Complete double-blind safeguards are obviously impossible in experiments of this kind, but independent assessments of initial classifications and final outcomes would have made for a better experiment. And since many of these

Sherwin Rosen is the Edwin A. and Betty L. Bergman Professor of Economics and chairman of the Department of Economics, University of Chicago, and a research associate of the National Bureau of Economic Research.

assignments and assessments were done jointly by both the house staff and the experimental skilled nursing staff, there is potential bias if the classification criteria vary according to unobserved quality of care. Were the data available, it would be very interesting to examine the experience of non-Medicaid patients in both experimental and control group nursing homes. Using "within"–nursing home differences in patient types as well as "between"–experimental and control group nursing home differences in Medicare patients might help control for differences in nursing home quality and possible differential assignment of cases among them.

Studies of labor market and geographic mobility have found that identifying some agents as "stayers" and others as "movers" is necessary to fit the data. So many incomplete spell lengths make these distinctions more difficult to test in these data. Still, it must be noted that Norton's estimates of mean and median length of stay by category are based on manipulations of the estimated transition matrix, not on direct observation, because many spells are still in progress at the end of the experiment. This is a limitation of the experiment, certainly not of Norton's methodology, but it must in some sense increase the standard error of estimated experiment effects. If in addition some of the stayer-mover logic is applicable to nursing home residents, a resident's initial state is not a sufficient statistic for probable future states. How persons arrive at that state affects the unconditional duration estimates, and those numbers (computed in tables 9.2 and 9.4) may not be accurate. One wonders why the observed assessment intervals of residents vary so much and whether they are behaviorally related to the mover-stayer (or permanent-temporary) assessment of a resident's condition at the starting times.

It can be argued that Medicare patients in nursing homes are a more homogeneous group in the above sense because they are likely to have "spent down" any other insurance or private resources in earlier hospitalization or nursing home stays. Then these residents are more likely to be "stayers" (or permanent residents), and the strict stationary, homogeneous Markov model may be a reasonable approximation. Knowledge of residents' previous history would be very useful in assessing the importance of this point. But assuming it is true, by what mechanism do these financial incentives work to reduce turnover and length of stay? Except for the patients initially assessed in state A, there are no substantial differences in the sum of ultimate hospitalization and death probabilities between treatment and controls in tables 9.2 and 9.4. The main effects on spell length occur for persons in the better initial states. Perhaps this is as it should be. We should not be subsidizing something that cannot occur. Yet insofar as these subsidies focus greater care and attention on the temporary residents, they promote a kind of adverse selection against the most difficult and costly ("permanent") residents who may be in greatest need of care. We must assess these schemes not only in terms of the monetary costs to the Medicare system but also with regard to the values of service among various classes of patients, including those for whom improvement and rehabilitation is very unlikely.

In using a flat fee reimbursement system independent of patient condition, the existing system promotes adverse selection of the easier and less costly cases. The system investigated in the experiment does not factor in the costs of classifying or the potential abuses and moral hazard problems arising if the entire system were converted to the experimental reimbursement mechanism. The hothouse environment of the experiment does not produce any data whatsoever on these latter costs, which may be substantial in any feasible system. These costs must be weighed against any efficiency gains in levels of care and lengths of stay that these financial incentives provide.

Contributors

Axel Börsch-Supan
Universität Mannheim
Postfach 10 34 62
Gebäude A5, 6
6800 Mannheim 1, Germany

Angus Deaton
221 Bendheim Hall
Center for International Studies
Princeton University
Princeton, NJ 08544–1022

Alan M. Garber
National Bureau of Economic Research
204 Junipero Serra Boulevard
Stanford, CA 94305

Paul J. Gertler
Rand Corporation
1700 Main Street
P.O. Box 2138
Santa Monica, CA 90406–2138

Jagadeesh Gokhale
Federal Reserve Bank of Cleveland
Research Department, 9th floor
1455 East 6th Street
Cleveland, OH 44101

Vassilis Hajivassiliou
Cowles Foundation for Research in Economics
Department of Economics
Box 2125 Yale Station
Yale University
New Haven, CT 06520

Tatsuo Hatta
Institute of Social and Economic Research
Osaka University
Ibaraki, Osaka 567, Japan

Fumio Hayashi
Department of Economics
McNeil Building
University of Pennsylvania
3718 Locust Walk
Philadelphia, PA 19104–6297

Michael D. Hurd
Department of Economics
SUNY, Stony Brook
Stony Brook, NY 11794

Laurence J. Kotlikoff
Department of Economics
Boston University
270 Bay State Road
Boston, MA 02215

Edward P. Lazear
Graduate School of Business
University of Chicago
1101 East 58th Street
Chicago, IL 60637

Lee A. Lillard
Rand Corporation
1700 Main Street
P.O. Box 2138
Santa Monica, CA 90406–2138

Robin L. Lumsdaine
Department of Economics
Princeton University
Princeton, NJ 08544

Thomas E. MaCurdy
Department of Economics
Encina Hall
Stanford University
Stanford, CA 94305–6072

John N. Morris
Hebrew Rehabilitation Center for the Aged
1200 Centre Street
Boston, MA 02131

Edward C. Norton
National Bureau of Economic Research
1050 Massachusetts Avenue
Cambridge, MA 02138–5398

Noriyoshi Oguchi
Department of Social Engineering
Tsukuba University
Tsukuba, Ibaragi, Japan

Christina H. Paxson
219 Bendheim Hall
Center for International Studies
Princeton University
Princeton, NJ 08544–1022

Sherwin Rosen
Department of Economics
University of Chicago
1126 East 59th Street
Chicago, IL 60637

Sylvester J. Schieber
Wyatt Company
601 13th Street NW, Suite 1000
Washington, DC 20005

John B. Shoven
Department of Economics
Encina Hall
Stanford University
Stanford, CA 94305–6072

Jonathan S. Skinner
Department of Economics
Rouss Hall
University of Virginia
Charlottesville, VA 22901

Konrad Stahl
Department of Economics
Universität Mannheim
Postfach 10 34 62
Gebäude A5, 6
6800 Mannheim 1, Germany

James H. Stock
John F. Kennedy School of Government
Harvard University
79 John F. Kennedy Street
Cambridge, MA 02138

Steven F. Venti
Department of Economics
Rockefeller Center
Dartmouth College
Hanover, NH 03755

David A. Wise
National Bureau of Economic Research
1050 Massachusetts Avenue
Cambridge, MA 02138–5398

Author Index

Subject Index